Afrocubanas

Creolizing the Canon

Series Editors: Jane Anna Gordon, Associate Professor of Political Science and Africana Studies, University of Connecticut, and Neil Roberts, Associate Professor of Africana Studies and Faculty Affiliate in Political Science, Williams College

This series, published in partnership with the Caribbean Philosophical Association, revisits canonical theorists in the humanities and social sciences through the lens of creolization. It offers fresh readings of familiar figures and presents the case for the study of formerly excluded ones.

Creolizing Rousseau
Edited by Jane Anna Gordon and Neil Roberts

Hegel, Freud and Fanon
Stefan Bird-Pollan

Theorizing Glissant
Edited by John E. Drabinski and Marisa Parham

Journeys in Caribbean Thought: The Paget Henry Reader
Edited by Jane Anna Gordon, Lewis R. Gordon, Aaron Kamugisha, and Neil Roberts, with Paget Henry

The Philosophical Treatise of William H. Ferris: Selected Readings from The African Abroad or, His Evolution in Western Civilization
Tommy J. Curry

Creolizing Hegel
Edited by Michael Monahan

Frantz Fanon, Psychiatry and Politics
Nigel C. Gibson and Roberto Beneduce

Melancholia Africana: The Indispensable Overcoming of the Black Condition
Nathalie Etoke
Translated by Bill Hamlett

Afrocubanas: History, Thought, and Cultural Practices
Edited by Devyn Spence Benson
Translated by Karina Alma
Edited by Daisy Rubiera Castillo and Inés María Martiatu Terry

Afrocubanas

History, Thought, and Cultural Practices

Edited by
Devyn Spence Benson

Translated by
Karina Alma

Edited by
Daisy Rubiera Castillo and
Inés María Martiatu Terry

ROWMAN &
LITTLEFIELD
INTERNATIONAL

London • New York

Published by Rowman & Littlefield International Ltd.
6 Tinworth Street, London, SE11 5AL, UK
www.rowmaninternational.com

Rowman & Littlefield International Ltd. is an affiliate of Rowman & Littlefield
4501 Forbes Boulevard, Suite 200, Lanham, Maryland 20706, USA
With additional offices in Boulder, New York, Toronto (Canada), and Plymouth (UK)
www.rowman.com

Copyright © Devyn Spence Benson, 2020
Translation copyright © Karina Alma, 2020

All rights reserved. No part of this book may be reproduced in any form or by any electronic or mechanical means, including information storage and retrieval systems, without written permission from the publisher, except by a reviewer who may quote passages in a review.

British Library Cataloguing in Publication Data
A catalogue record for this book is available from the British Library

ISBN: HB 978-1-78661-481-0

Library of Congress Cataloging-in-Publication Data

Library of Congress Control Number: 2020933724

ISBN: 978-1-78661-481-0 (cloth)
ISBN: 978-1-5381-4822-8 (pbk)
ISBN: 978-1-78661-482-7 (electronic)

To African women, and their Afro-Cuban descendants, for their arduous struggle for freedom, justice, and equality. Women who since time immemorial transmitted to us, in diverse ways, their suffering, needs, achievements, everything that was given to us and has served as a source of light.

To the Afro-descended women of today who maintain this flag up high in order to light the way for the generations to come.

To all women, independent of the color of their skin.

Contents

Acknowledgments	xi
Editor's Acknowledgments	xiii
Editor's Introduction	xvii
Translator's Note	xxix
Prologue	xxxiii
Introduction	1

PART ONE: HISTORY — 5

1. Lawsuits by Slave Women in Nineteenth-Century Cuba — 7
   Digna Castañeda Fuertes

2. Reconstructing Ex-Slave Belén Álvarez's Story — 19
   Oilda Hevia Lanier

3. Women "of Color" in Santiaguera Colonial Society: A Commentary — 39
   María Cristina Hierrezuelo

PART TWO: THOUGHT — 57

4. Women of *Minerva* — 59
   María del Carmen Barcia Zequeira

5. Gratitude: To My Friends and Colleagues of the Journal *Minerva* — 73
   Úrsula Coimbra de Valverde

6	Black Voices in Favor of the Independent Party of Color *Carmen Piedra*	75
7	Our Ethnic Values *Consuelo Serra*	77
8	What We Are *Inocencía Silveira*	79
9	The Black Cuban Woman *Gerardo del Valle*	81
10	The Black Cuban Women and Culture *Catalina Pozo Gato*	85
11	Black Intelligence *Arabella Oña Gómez*	89
12	Women in Santeria or Regla Ocha: Gender, Myths, and Reality *Daisy Rubiera Castillo*	91
13	Gender and Raciality: An Obligatory Reflection in Contemporary Cuba *Yulexis Almeida Junco*	113
14	On Afrocubana Stereotypes: Construction and Deconstruction of Myths *María Ileana Faguaga Iglesias*	127
15	Proposing an Inclusive and Nonsexist Gaze: *Mulata* Women, a Profane Invention? *Onelia Chaveco Chaveco*	139
16	Hairs *Carmen González Chacón*	145
17	Passing for a White Woman *Sandra del Valle Casals*	161
18	The Revolution Made Blacks into People *Yusimí Rodríguez López*	173
19	Human Race? Ah . . . It Had to Be! *Yohamna Depestre Corcho*	177
20	A Room of Our Own for Black Cuban Women *Yesenia Selier Crespo*	181

PART THREE: CULTURAL PRACTICES — 187

21 Oriki for Elder Black Women of the Past — 189
Georgina Herrera Cárdenas

22 The Black Female Imaginary in Cuba — 195
Aymée Rivera Pérez

23 Contradictory Binaries in Nancy Morejón's *Octubre Imprescindible* and *Cuaderno de Granada* — 219
Lourdes Martínez Echazábal

24 In Memory of Excilia — 227
Coralia de las Mercedes Hernández Herrera

25 The Thick Skin of Teresa Cárdenas — 239
Leandro Estupiñán Zaldívar

26 *El Negrito* and the *Mulata* in the Vortex of Nationality — 241
Inés María Martiatu Terry

27 Popular Theater and Collective Resistance — 265
Fátima de la Caridad Patterson

28 Catalina Berroa, the Audacious Trinidadian: First Female Composer of "Cultured" Music in the Nineteenth Century — 269
Isabel González Sauto

29 The Marathon Exists for Both Men and Women — 275
Edelvis López Zaldívar

30 Making One's Dreams Come True Is Not the Same as Dreaming — 283
María Elena Mendiola

31 The Contributions of Sara Gómez — 289
Sandra Álvarez Ramírez

32 Belkis Ayón Manso, Between Heterogeneous Sensibilities — 297
Lázara Menéndez Vásquez

33 Black Women in Sports — 309
Irene Esther Ruiz Narváez

34 A Lexical Semantical Analysis on the Discourse of Women in Cuban Rap — 323
Yanelys Abreu Babi and Anette Jiménez Marata

Index	333
About the Editor and Translator	347
About the Authors	349

Acknowledgments

Through the following selections in this book, we want to thank especially African women and their Afrocubana descendants for their fight against racism and racial discrimination.

To all the women who contributed their work, who weaved a network of trust and support for us to initiate with this work, a path to banishing forgetting.

To all those who are not in this book, who have guided us well with their good-doing and better way of thinking. To Zuleica for trusting us.

Our gratitude extends not only to women but also to Tomás Fernández Robaina (Tomasito) for facilitating our access to documents that he had saved for future work. We also thank Alberto Abreu and Roberto Zurbano for their support, for listening to us, for their reading of our work, suggestions, and, finally, for their affection and their capacity to encourage us.

To everyone we did not mention, we thank you.

Editor's Acknowledgments

On January 16, 2012, Daisy Rubiera handed me the copy of *Afrocubanas: Historia, pensamiento, y practices culturales* that she had saved for me from the book's release in 2011. In the inscription inside she identified us as colleagues and sisters in the "dreams and battles for racial equality." I immediately went back to my apartment in Havana and began to devour the volume's many essays about the history and lived experiences of black women in Cuba. As soon as I read the introduction, I knew that this was a book that was desperately needed in English. My colleagues, students, and family in the United States needed the opportunity to learn about black feminisms in Cuba from black Cuban women *themselves*. Nearly a decade later, the dream of an English translation of this groundbreaking collection has become a reality thanks to the dedication and hard work of many people and organizations.

I was fortunate to build relationships with the editors and many of the contributors of *Afrocubanas* in the late 2000s during my residency in Havana for the fieldwork for my first book. I am indebted to Daisy Rubiera, Inés María Martiatu Terry (Lalita), Georgina Herrera, Sandra Álvarez, and Irene Ester Ruiz Narváez for their intellectual brilliance, persistent commitment to black feminism, and willingness to share their work with me when I was a young graduate student from the United States. Since those early years, we have collaborated on a variety of projects, and I am honored to be able to call such amazing black women my mentors and friends.

This book would not have been possible without the organizational support of the Creolizing the Canon series editors, Jane Anna Gordon and Neil Roberts. I am so grateful to Neil Roberts for initiating this project with a simple email asking if I knew any good books in Spanish that should be translated into English. From that moment forward, it has been rewarding to work with Jane and Neil on this volume. Frankie Mace and Rebecca Anastasi are the best editors at Rowman & Littlefield International, mostly because they accommodated my many extension requests, constant away messages, and because they too believed in the importance of bringing black Cuban women's voices to an English-speaking audience. I am also thankful to the volume's reviewers and cheerleaders who supported this translation from its earliest stages, Odette Casamayor-Cisneros, Alejandro de la Fuente, Tanya Saunders, and Agustín Lao-Montes.

Translating nearly four hundred pages is no easy task. Yet Karina Alma was not only up to the challenge but also brought a grace and eloquence to this project that made her a joy to work with. Her deep commitment and enthusiasm for Afrocubana history comes across in every page and note and I am grateful to this project for bringing us together. I also must thank the many Cubans and Cubanists who I called upon to help translate the Cubanisms that I wasn't familiar with either because of time period (Guadalupe García should be everyone's go to for colonial history), geographic region (Alexandra Gelbard is my Santiago guide), or theme (Henry Heredia translates little-known Regla de Ocha terms like you wouldn't believe). We made a great transnational team and the English volume is better because of each of you.

Of course, publishing a book requires time, funding, and administrative support. To that end, I am grateful to the National Endowment for the Humanities faculty fellowship, which provided me the time, via a research sabbatical, in the 2019–2020 academic year to complete this and other projects. We all owe Daniel Weiner of Global Affairs at the University of Connecticut a huge thank you for providing the funds to translate this book. I am also appreciative of the library support and funding I received from the Davidson Faculty "Jump-Start" Award from the Resilient Networks for Inclusive Digital Humanities Initiative. Thank you to Jane and Lewis Gordon, the Philosophy Department at the University of Connecticut, the Caribbean Philosophical Association, and Davidson College for their generous support toward obtaining permissions for this collection. I am also indebted to Davidson College for not only cosponsoring my sabbatical but for also supporting my interest in Afrocubana history from the moment I arrived on campus. Department chairs Tracey Hucks (Africana Studies) and Matt Sampson (Latin American Studies); departmental coordinators Elizabeth White, Rebecca Barrow, and Meg Sawicki; and student research assistants Itziri Gonzalez-Bárcenas and Isabel Ballester all facilitated visits by prominent Afrocubanas including Daisy Rubiera, Gloria Rolando, and Odaymara Cuesta and Olivia Prendes (Las Krudas) to campus. The departments of Africana Studies and Latin American Studies, the Innovation and Entrepreneurship Initiative, the Dean Rusk Center for International Studies, and students in the Organization of Latin American Studies funded these public events that provided the entire Davidson community with the opportunity to learn more about black feminism in

Cuba. In particular, I want to thank students in both the spring and fall 2017 sections of my AFR/LAS/GSS 300: Afrocubana Feminisms course for engaging with our Cuban guests and translating their public lectures.

I would not be able to do the work that I love or travel to the places that I do without the support of my friends and family. I might as well be related to Reena Goldthree and Henry Heredia for the number of times I text them when I am in a bind—thank you for always being there for me. Mom, Dad, Dionne, Jevon, Aunt Gail, and Uncle Jay—thank you for your unconditional love and support. Each of you provided childcare when I was out of town and I am so grateful that you are a part of my village. Camoren Keodouangsy, it is a privilege to be one of your parents and to watch you grow into such an amazing young adult. The year 2020 is both this book's release date and your high school graduation year—I am so proud of you! Tracey, you are my soulmate, best friend, and inspiration to always fight for what is right no matter the cost. Thank you for supporting me in making this and so many of my other dreams a reality.

Finally, to all the Afrocubanas who I met while working on this project from Havana to Santiago, from New York to Germany, thank you for your courage and willingness to speak up and share out. I am honored to learn from you.

Editor's Introduction

Black and *mulata* women have all too frequently been erased from studies of Cuban history, politics, culture, and economics despite being central to the Cuban plantation system during the colonial era, fighting for Cuban independence from 1868 to 1898, forging the republic in the first half of the twentieth century, and participating in the revolution of the 1960s. The largely male-dominated national narrative that has made Ernesto "Che" Guevara's "New Man" famous since 1959 frequently overshadows black women's contributions. Even today, when commentators talk about normalizing US relations with Cuba or going to visit the island for the first time, they are imagining visiting the Cuba of José Martí, Fidel Castro, and Ernest Hemingway. This superb edited collection by Cuban historian Daisy Rubiera Castillo and Cuban playwright and theater critic Inés María Martiatu Terry challenges this erasure. Originally published in Spanish in Havana by Editorial Ciencias Sociales in 2011, *Afrocubanas: History, Thought, and Cultural Practices* has become a canonical work of black feminism in Latin America. This translation provides a necessary entry point for English speakers interested in transnational black feminisms.

Afrocubanas places the experiences of black and *mulata* women at the center of Cuban society. Featuring essays from both well-known and newly published Cuban authors, this landmark volume examines the lives of Afro-Cuban women from the late nineteenth century to the present. In the following pages, you will learn about former enslaved women who became property owners in Santiago in the 1800s, black women who participated in Cuba's only black political party, the Independent Party of Color, in the 1900s, and black women rappers in Cuba's twenty-first-century hip-hop movement. You will also find poetry and essays about Yoruba and other African-derived religious traditions like Regla de Ocha (or Santeria), black women's struggles to embrace their hair, and testimonies about their experiences with racial discrimination. Divided into three parts—"History," "Thought," and "Cultural Practices"—the book is revolutionary both in its island-wide geographic scope and its naming of black women as being worthy of study in Cuba.

Significantly, this is the first book published in Cuba to use the term "Afrocubanas" in its title. A somewhat controversial term on the island, Afro-Cuban has long been associated with folklore or cultural tradition instead of a racial identity.[1] Many Cubans of African descent would not identify as "Afro-Cuban" and instead see it as a racially divisive word stemming from the hyphenated term "African-American"—an identity marker that conflicts both implicitly and explicitly with Cuba's unifying slogan of "not white, not blacks, only Cuban" promoted by revolutionary nationalists since the late nineteenth century.[2] For the authors of the collection, however, "Afrocubana" (Afro-Cuban women) signifies much more than its previous designations. It is a term that highlights the intersectional nature of black and *mulata* women's experiences—namely how to examine these experiences using an approach that analyzes race, gender, class, sexual orientation, ability, religion, and geographic location together. As Martiatu explains in the prologue, one of the goals of their work is to "feminize negritude and to blacken feminism." Rubiera argues that the term "Afrocubana" also connects their project to other *afrodescendiente* movements fighting against racism and discrimination in the Americas.[3] In doing so, this provocatively titled collection introduces and normalizes a new racialized and gendered language in contemporary Cuba.

One of the unique qualities of *Afrocubanas* is that the volume is the product of a grassroots, community-based working group in Havana called the Afrocubanas Project.[4] In the mid-2000s, a group of black and *mulata* women began meeting in each other's homes to strategize about how to tackle the economic difficulties and racial discrimination that emerged during Cuba's economic crisis of the 1990s. Following the collapse of Cuba's chief trading partner, the Soviet Union, in 1991, the island's financial transactions came to a near standstill as the United States tightened its trade embargo. Called the "Special Period in Times of Peace" (*período especial en tiempos de paz*), or "Special Period" for short, this moniker referred to the austerity measures taken by the state to try to overcome the crisis—including economic rationing similar to wartime, but in a time of peace. Cuban leaders enacted dramatic economic changes in an attempt to jumpstart the economy, with mixed results. For example, the state legalized the dollar, an act that encouraged more remittances from Cuban exiles wanting to support struggling family members. Leaders also opened the economy to international investment and joint business ventures that included building new hotels for the island's emerging tourist sector. Despite these changes, the economy recovered slowly throughout the 1990s. All Cubans faced dire economic instability that resulted in rolling electric blackouts, food shortages, and the absence of basic necessities during the Special Period, but black and *mulato* Cubans suffered these hardships even more than their white counterparts because of their limited ability to access foreign currency. They did not receive remittances from family members in the United States to the same degree, nor did they have the fair or white skin, the so-called *buena presencia* (good presence/appearance), needed to qualify for tourist jobs in Cuba's new tourism sector.[5] Black women in particular were denied sought-after positions in the newly opened hotels because of their looks, and many were assumed to be prostitutes as sex tourism expanded on the island with white male foreigners looking to explore sexual fantasies with women of African descent.

In the past three decades, a number of Cuban antiracist organizations have emerged to fight racial inequality in light of these new economic challenges.[6] The Afrocubanas group—founded by the book's editors Rubiera and Martiatu along with psychologist and blogger Sandra Álvarez Ramírez, poet Carmen González, and painter Paulina Márquez in the mid-2000s—is one of most prominent activist groups in Havana. It is also one of the few antiracist groups in Cuba that explicitly challenges racism and sexism together. The members of the Afrocubanas Project hail from a variety of professions, ages, and sexual orientations and meet regularly in each other's houses or available cultural spaces in Havana. This group of black women shares a collective interest in challenging negative stereotypes about black people and women in Cuba.[7] The *Estatutos* (bylaws) of the Afrocubanas Project state that the group's objectives are to "1) Recognize the contribution and the work of black Cuban women and 2) to stimulate the existence of a counter discourse to dismantle the negative, racist, and sexist stereotypes [that exist in Cuba] about black women." The *Estatutos* state that persons of any race, gender, sexual orientation, or political leaning can join the group, but they also emphasize that the project has been "created for afro-descended women and by afro-descended women."[8] Rubiera describes how the Afrocubanas group has both external and internal goals: "We want to make them [black women] visible in the core works of history and literature . . . but we also want to show them who they are and that they aren't just the simple stereotypes that have existed about them since the colonial period." The Afrocubanas Project produces intellectual and cultural works to meet the first goal and holds workshops and seminars (*tertulias*) in Havana that educate black women and men about Afrocubana history and experiences to achieve the second.[9]

This book is the inaugural edited collection from the Afrocubana working group, and it breaks the silence around black women's role in Cuban history. While many of the volume's contributors had been writing, publishing, and advocating for black and *mulata* women for most of their lives, this book serves as one of the first moments where they have come together to intervene into Cuban history, politics, and art in an interdisciplinary way. Few books in English or Spanish have centered black women's experiences in Cuba. The two closest works in English are Cherríe Moraga and Gloria Anzaldúa's *This Bridge Called My Back: Writings by Radical Women of Color* (1981) and Marta Morena Vega, Marinieves Alba, and Yvette Modestin's edited volume *Women Warriors of the Afro-Latina Diaspora* (2012).[10] In keeping with the radical tradition of *This Bridge Called My Back*, the *Afrocubanas* collection includes essays from both scholars and activists, both academic articles and personal reflections. While the two existing collections cover female voices from all of Latin America and the United States, this book centers on Cuba, one of the most important locations of Afro-Latin American thought.

In some ways this book is the culmination of the earlier works by each of the coeditors. Originally from Santiago, historian Rubiera has written essays and books about black women since the start of her career. She is best known in Cuba and abroad for authoring *Reyita, sencillamente: Testimonio de una negra cubana nonagenarian* (1996), a groundbreaking account in the Latin American genre of testimonial literature (*testimonio*) that chronicles her ninety-three-year-old mother's life in the eastern part of the island. Duke University Press translated *Reyita* into English in 2000 and it remains a signature book in US university classrooms.[11] *Reyita* is the first *testimonio* published in Cuba about a black woman, and the author's stated goals fit with ones she would later accomplish in *Afrocubanas*. Rubiera describes why she wrote the book: "I wanted to add the voice of a black woman to the national discourse. *Reyita* is the other side of what it means to be Cuban."

In Latin America, *testimonios* are seen as a genre of revolutionary literature that amplifies the voices of everyday people and their struggles.[12] One of the most recognized books in this genre is Miguel Barnet's *Biografía de un cimarrón* (1966), a *testimonio* about the life of a one-hundred-and-eight-year-old black man named Esteban Montejo who escaped slavery and fought in Cuba's wars for independence in the late nineteenth century.[13] This book is frequently taught at the University of Havana and has become canonical because of the ways Montejo, its protagonist, refuses to submit to slavery and ultimately finds liberation in the 1959 revolution. However, until Rubiera's *Reyita*, there had not been a *testimonio* about a black woman. Rubiera later collaborated with her good friend and fellow Afrocubana working group member Georgina Herrera to write *Golpeando la memoria: Testimonio de una poeta cubana afrodescendiente* (2005) about Herrera's life as a black woman poet in the second half of the twentieth century.[14] In each of these cases, Rubiera centered the voices of black women. By allowing Afrocubanas to tell their own stories, in their own words, Rubiera was not only a pioneer for black feminism in Cuba but also expanded the scope of Cuban testimonial literature. She continues this work in *Afrocubanas* by including primary documents, such as essays and newspaper articles, by black women intellectuals like Consuelo Serra and Úrsula Coimbra de Valverde from the end of the nineteenth and beginning of the twentieth century in the volume.

Martiatu broke similar ground in the fields of theater and literary criticism. Her specialties contribute to the interdisciplinary nature of the collection through the inclusion of poetry, short stories, and essays analyzing black women's creative works. Martiatu, who was raised in Central Havana (*Centro*), began her career working at the Cuban National Film Institute in the 1960s as an editorial assistant alongside famed black filmmaker Sara Gómez.[15] She later became a theater critic and is most well known for her books analyzing race and nation in Cuban theater, including *Bufo y nación: interpelaciones desde el presente* (2009), an account of the historical roots and contradictions of blackface theater in Cuba and an edited collection on the independent press El Puente's dramatic productions, *Re-pasar el puente: antología de teatro* (2010).[16] In *Over the Waves and Other Stories/Sobre las Olas y otros cuentes: A Bilingual Edition* (2009), Martiatu provides readers with a glimpse into her own creative work in an innovative Spanish/English side-by-side translated book. Martiatu's short stories feature black women protagonists and hone in on the ways black women live, love, suffer, and experience joy in Cuba. Her focus on black women as leading characters in her essays flows out of a desire to insert Afrocubanas as whole people into Cuban fiction:

> Not only in literature, but also in theater, black women almost always appear in folkloric or colonial caricature-like positions. But what I write is in relation to the people in my family, to the people I have known, with the stories that I heard in my house.... I have an obligation to these women to share their legacy. They are the histories of my grandmother, my aunts, my mother, who were black and *mestiza* women, but who were also professionals and self-directed women.[17]

For Martiatu, literature is a space for black feminist activism. She notes that in the early years of the revolution, leaders created openings for black women in the field of poetry, but that both then and now there were fewer opportunities for black women playwrights or fiction writers. Martiatu seeks to undo this erasure. One of the successes of the *Afrocubana* collection is its ability to uncover the work of black women, like Santiago playwright and director Fátima de la Caridad Patterson, who shares an essay about her all-black theater company in the book while also inserting black women's creative works into existing Cuban literature and theater.

While the attention the Afrocubanas group and this collection pay to black Cuban women's experiences is unique on the island, their work complements and is in conversation with transnational black feminism, especially movements occurring in Latin America and the Caribbean. In 2016, political scientist Sonia E. Alvarez, anthropologist Kia Lilly Caldwell, and sociologist Agustín Lao-Montes coedited a two-part special issue on African descendant feminisms in Latin America for the journal *Meridians: Feminism, Race, and Transnationalisms*.[18] According to Alvarez and Caldwell, "This issue grew out of our shared intellectual and political concern that academics and activists in the U.S. lacked exposure to critical insights and innovations offered by black feminist thought and praxis developed in the 'South' of the Americas." In their efforts to promote dialogue between scholars of black feminism in the United States and Latin America, the authors highlight both the similarities and differences between the respective movements. They note that in Brazil, like in Cuba, most black feminist organizing came out of the black movement rather than the feminist movement. This means that many of the activists in Brazil and Cuba "engage in mixed-gender anti-racist movement activism."[19] As I mentioned earlier, the Afrocubanas group emerged from a resurgence in antiracist organizing in Cuba that began in the 1990s. One of the most recent spaces for this mixed-gender organizing is in the Club del Espendrú (*espendrú* is another word for an Afro hairstyle in Cuba). The club not only holds workshops where children build and receive black dolls (which are rarely available in Cuba), they also host programming on black hair care and give out awards to influential activists like Rubiera. Women and men compose the membership of the club and like other antiracist activists in Latin America they are drawn together based on their desire to revalue blackness in Cuban history and culture.

Many of the Latin American black feminists featured in the *Meridians* special issue participate in regional collaborations, and Afrocubanas are no different. Throughout this volume, you will see references to the works of prominent Latin American thinkers such as Sueli Carneiro and Ochy Curiel. Significantly, essays by members of the Afrocubana working group and other contributors to this collection have been published in Latin America as well. Rubiera, Martiatu, and Carmen González all have essays in the Colombian publication *Hijas del Muntu: Biografías críticas de mujeres afrodescendientes de América Latina* (2011), and the Spanish edition of *Afrocubanas* is now a well-known text in Brazil, Colombia, and Ecuador.[20] Cross-regional collaborations highlight the importance of the early twenty-first century as a watershed moment in the embrace of black feminism in Latin America. As neocolonial regimes and economic hardships disproportionately impact black women's lives, activists are using new technologies to connect across state borders to build regional networks.[21]

Cuba's precarious economic situation means that Afrocubanas are forced to try to meet their principal goal of offering a counter-discourse to the grand Cuban narrative about black women in the midst of financial limitations. Due to paper and ink shortages, most Cuban presses publish only a limited number of books a year, and when a book is published, it is often released in small quantities and rarely reprinted. This situation means that many books run out within weeks of publication. Such was the case of the *Afrocubanas* edited collection. Within two months of Rubiera and Martiatu presenting *Afrocubanas* at the Dulce María Loynaz Cultural Center during Cuba's annual international book fair, the five thousand books published by the Editorial de Ciencias Sociales had sold out.[22] It is now almost impossible to obtain a copy of *Afrocubanas* in Spanish on the island or in the United States.

As the antiracist movement in Cuba enters its second decade, it too faces challenges of resources and time. On March 16, 2019, the Afrocubanas Project terminated the group amid an aging executive group—Rubiera who had been the director turned eighty in 2019 and Martiatu passed away in 2013. Stating that the executive board had voted to disband the project after over ten years of existence, Rubiera clarified that this move in no way indicated that they were abandoning their work or the goals of the group. In fact, she noted that the Afrocubanas Project was proud of what it had accomplished and that each member would continue "their constructive and revolutionary fight against racism and racial discrimination."[23] And the group's achievements are impressive. They succeeded in inserting two courses into the University of Havana curriculum; "Race and Gender" and "Hidden Histories: Black and *Mulata* Women in the Colonial Period" are taught by Afrocubana group members who are professors at the university. The project also built black feminist consciousness in local audiences through the monthly *tertulias* (workshops) and invited public radio and television broadcasts.[24] In addition to this first volume, the Afrocubana group published a second edited collection in 2016 titled *Emergiendo del silencio: Mujeres negras en la historia de Cuba* (*Emerging from the Silence: Black Women in the History of Cuba*). The flier for the new book's release stated that the book specifically aims "to fill gaps in the historiography . . . [and that it] provides another important step in the reconstruction of the historical memory of African descended Cuban women." The Afrocubanas Project used the book's release to commemorate the anniversary of Martiatu's death and to pay homage to her life and legacy. Noting that even a few days before her death in the hospital Martiatu was enthusiastically talking about the new book, Rubiera recounts how even though Martiatu was not physically present for the book's launch, she will always be present in their work.[25]

Members of the Afrocubana group are continuing the organization's legacy today. Significantly, black lesbian blogger Sandra Álvarez created and launched the *Directorio de Afrocubanas* (Afrocubana Directory), a digital archive with essays, photographs, and links to the works of prominent Cuban women of African descent, in 2016.[26] It currently profiles more than

350 women from a variety of industries, historical eras, and regions. In a 2018 interview for the radio station Caribe Nuestra, Álvarez described how the project evolved from a nugget of an idea she discussed with Martiatu in her home in Centro Havana to a website with hundreds of entries.[27] Georgina Herrera is working on another book of poetry, Gloria Rolando is fundraising and collecting footage for a documentary film about young black Cuban girls who attended the Oblate Sisters of Providence monastery in Baltimore, Maryland, and Fátima de la Caridad Patterson debuted a new play at the thirty-ninth annual Festival del Caribe conference in July 2019.

The Afrocubana group has served as a launching point for Cuban discussions about black women's lives, challenges, contributions to the nation, and so much more. In a variety of ways, the contributors to this edited collection persist in disrupting stereotypes about black women in Cuba all while offering a counternarrative to histories that have erased their experiences. This is not the type of work that ends because the group is no longer officially meeting. Rather, Afrocubanas today in Cuba are rising to meet new challenges with new opportunities because they recognize that "there is no feminism without Afrocubanas" and there can be no racial equality without gender equality.[28] As Rubiera states in a recent article summarizing the group's achievements and its future, "Afrocubanas is something more than an organization, it is an attitude towards life."[29] It is an honor to present the English edition of this groundbreaking book as another example of the lived legacy of black women's resistance.

A NOTE ON TERMS

Cubans express race in a multitude of ways.[30] Like other places in Latin America, there is a long list of racial terms to describe someone's skin color and their perceived closeness or distance from blackness. The history of Spanish colonialism and African enslavement led to racial mixing, often violently during the era of slavery and at other times consensually in more contemporary interracial relationships. Still, most Cubans recognize that they all have some African ancestry as highlighted in the common refrain, "The person who doesn't have Congo, has Carabalí," referring to different areas of the west African continent from where Cubans' ancestors were stolen during the cross-Atlantic Slave Trade.[31] In this collection, we had to decide how to translate Cuban racial terms like *negra, mulata, mestiza, trigueña, parda, morena, jabá, pasa, criollo, mestizaje,* and others. You will see that for the most part we left racial terms in Spanish (all Spanish words are italicized) and included the closest English translations in parenthesis. For example, *trigueña* is a wheat-colored woman usually with long straight hair, *parda* and *morena* are both used to express a type of brownness, while *prieta* and *negra* are reserved for dark-skinned black women. This is rarely a straightforward process, and words like *mulata* can be modified with *clara*, *mulata clara* (clear), to describe a lighter-skinned version of the term. Or take the term *pasa*, which literally translates as "raisins" but is a negative reference to kinky or nappy black hair in Cuban daily use. *Mulata*, referring to a black and white mixed woman, has been left in Spanish due to the negative connotations "mulatta" brings to mind for African Americans because it is tied to derogatory images of violent racial mixing and mules. Despite this explanation and our best efforts because racial terms in Cuba are different than those used here in the United States, there will always be some translation gap between how the authors express themselves and how we interpret it. As you navigate the book, what is more important than any one particular term is the lived experience of race and blackness that the authors are sharing with us. Regardless of the translated term, blackness impacts Afrocubana lives, relationships, employment, and education—as Afro-Cuban filmmaker Gloria Rolando stated at the book's launch in Havana, "This book is an invitation to traverse the soul of a forgotten part of our nation."[32] Let us remember together.

NOTES

1. See Fernando Ortiz. For more on the debate about the term Afro-Cuban, see Alberto Abreu, "Por qué me defino afrocubano," *Negra Cubana Tenía Que Ser*, June 25, 2017, accessed April 25, 2018, https://negracubanateniaqueser.com/2017/06/25/por-que-me-defino-afrocubano/.

2. I discuss the relationship between race and revolution in twentieth-century Cuba in Devyn Spence Benson, *Antiracism in Cuba: The Unfinished Revolution* (Chapel Hill: University of North Carolina Press, 2016).

3. Daisy Rubiera lecture to Williams College students, Havana, Cuba, January 16, 2012. Also see Rubiera Castillo, "Afrocubanas: un grupo, un proyecto, un sueño, un reto," *Negra Cubana Tenía Que Ser*, November 15, 2016, accessed May 1, 2017, https://negracubanateniaqueser.com/2016/11/15/afrocubanas-un-grupo-un-proyecto-un-sueno-un-reto/; Sandra Álvarez, "Las Afrocubanas ya tienen su libro," *Negra Cubana Tenía Que Ser*, December 16, 2011, accessed April 8, 2015, https://negracubanateniaqueser.com/2011/12/16/las-afrocubanas-ya-tienen-su-libro/.

4. For additional reading on contemporary Afrocubana activism, see Devyn Spence Benson, "Afro-Cubana Feminisms: Race, Gender, and Sexuality in Havana," in *Caribbean Migrations: The Legacies of Colonialism* (New Brunswick, NJ: Rutgers University Press, forthcoming).

5. Alejandro de la Fuente, "Recreating Racism: Race and Discrimination in Cuba's Special Period," in *A Contemporary Cuba Reader: Reinventing the Revolution*, ed. Brenner Phillip, Marguerite Rose Jimenez, John M. Kirk, and William M. Leo Grande (Lanham, MD: Rowman & Littlefield, 2007), 316–26.

6. For additional information on contemporary Afro-Cuban organizing, see essays in the special edition of *Cuban Studies* 48 (2019), including Maya Berry, "La movilización del tema afrodescendiente en La Habana, 2012–2014: Un estudio de las posibilidades del performance," *Cuban Studies* 48 (2019): 276–302.

7. Daisy Rubiera, "Grupo Afrocubanas. Reivindicarse a través del conocimiento," *Afroféminas*, October 7, 2018, accessed October 2, 2019, https://afrofem inas.com/2018/10/07/grupo-afrocubanas-reivindicarse-a-traves-del-conocimiento/co mment-page-1/#comment-7166.

8. Proyecto Afrocubanas, *Estatutos*, copy in the author's possession, received April 2, 2013.

9. Daisy Rubiera Public Lecture, "A Bilingual Conversation with Afro-Cuba Scholar-Activist Daisy Rubiera Castillo," Davidson College, April 19, 2017. Also see Rubiera Castillo, "Afrocubanas: un grupo, un proyecto, un sueño, un reto."

10. Cherríe Moraga and Gloria Anzaldúa, eds., *This Bridge Called My Back: Writings by Radical Women of Color* (New York: Kitchen Table-Women of Color Press, 1981), and Marta Morena Vega, Marinieves Alba, and Yvette Modestin, eds., *Women Warriors of the Afro-Latina Diaspora* (Houston, TX: Arte Público Press, 2012).

11. See Rubiera Castillo, *Reyita, sencillamente: Testimonio de una negra cubana nonagenarian* (Havana: Instituto Cubano del Libro, 1996); Rubiera Castillo, *Reyita: The Life of a Black Cuban Woman in the Twentieth Century* (Durham, NC: Duke University Press, 2000). For additional reading on *Reyita*, see Paula Sanmartín, *Black Women as Custodians of History: Unsung Rebel (M)others in African American and Afro-Cuban Women's Writing* (Amherst, NY: Cambria Press, 2014); and Karen Ruth Kornweibel, "Daisy Rubiera Castillo's *Reyita*: 'Mujer Negra' From Objectified Symbol to Empowered Subject," *Letras Hispanas* 7 (Fall 2010): 67–79.

12. For *testimonies*, see George Gugelberger, "Voices of the Voiceless: Testimonial Literature in Latin America," *Latin American Perspectives* 18, no. 3 (1991).

13. Miguel Barnet, *Biografía de un cimarrón* (Havana: Academia de Ciencias de Cuba, Instituto de Etnología y Folklore, 1966), Miguel Barnet, *Biography of a Runaway Slave* (Willimantic, CT: Curbstone Press, 1994).

14. Rubiera Castillo and Georgina Herrera, *Golpeando la memoria: Testimonio de una poeta cubana afrodescendiente* (Havana: Ediciones Unión, 2005).

15. For additional information about Martiatu and Sara Gómez, see Devyn Spence Benson, "Sara Gómez: AfroCubana (Afro-Cuban Women's) Activism after 1961," *Cuban Studies* 46, no. 1 (2018): 134–58.

16. Martiatu, *Bufo y nación* (Havana: Letras Cubanas, 2009); *Re-pasar el Puente* (Havana: Letras Cubanas, 2010). Ediciones El Puente (1961–1965) was a heterogeneous group of black, white, *mestizo*, and *mulato* authors and cultural producers who tried to push boundaries of Cuban literature and theater in the early 1960s. For additional reading on El Puente, see Jesús J. Barquet, *Ediciones El Puente en La Habana de los años 60s: Lecturas críticas y libros de poesía* (Chihuahua: Ediciones del Azar, 2011).

17. Sandra Álvarez, interview with Martiatu, "Inés María Martiatu: 'Sin las afrocubanas, el feminismo está incompleto,'" *Negra Cubana Tenia Que Ser*, August 2, 2013, accessed October 2, 2019, https://negracubanateniaqueser.com/2013/08/02/ ines-maria-martiatu-sin-las-afrocubanas-el-feminismo-esta-incompleto/.

18. Sonia E. Alvarez, Kia Lilly Caldwell, and Agustín Laó-Montes, "African Descendant Feminisms in Latin America, Part I: Brazil" and "African Descendant Feminisms in Latin America Part II: South and Central America and the Spanish-Speaking Caribbean," *Meridians: Feminism, Race, Transnationalism* 14, no. 1–2 (2016).

19. Alvarez and Caldwell, "Promoting Feminist Amefricanidade: Bridging Black Feminist Cultures and Politics in the Americas," *Meridians: Feminism, Race, Transnationalism* 14, no. 1 (2016): v–xi.

20. María Mercedes Jaramillo and Lucía Ortiz, *Hijas del Muntu: Biografías críticas de mujeres afrodescndientes de América Latina* (Bogotá, Colombia: Panamericana Editorial, 2011).

21. For additional reading on black feminist organizations in Latin America, see Agustín Laó-Montes, "Afro-Latin American Feminisms at the Cutting Edge of Emerging Political-Epistemic Movements," *Meridians: Feminism, Race, Transnationalism* 14, no. 2 (2016): 1–24.

22. Personal correspondence with Daisy Rubiera.

23. Personal correspondence with Daisy Rubiera, March 17, 2019, from an email addressed to members and allies of the Afrocubana group. A similar statement was published online the following month. See "Concluye Afrocubanas: Un proyecto antirracista de casi diez años," *Inter Press Service en Cuba*, April 7, 2019, accessed April 8, 2019, https://www.ipscuba.net/genero/concluye-afrocubanas-un-proyecto-antirracista-de-casi-diez-anos/.

24. Rubiera, "Grupo Afrocubanas: Reivindicarse a través del conocimiento."

25. Rubiera Castillo and Oilda Hevia Lanier, *Emergiendo del silencio: Mujeres negras en la historia de Cuba* (Havana: Editorial de Ciencias Sociales, 2016).

26. http://directoriodeafrocubanas.com. Also see Sandra Álvarez Ramirez, *Negra cubana tenía que ser*, https://negracubanateniaqueser.com.

27. "Entrevista—Conoce el Directorio de Afrocubanas—Sandra Álvarez—Marzo 2018" *Caribe Nuestro*, no. 142 (March 7, 2018), accessed April 23, 2018, https://www.youtube.com/watch?v=oPdpV6wHviU.

28. This quote is taken from the last interview Martiatu did before her death. Helen Hernández Hormilla, "Inés María Martiatu: 'Sin las afrocubanas, el feminismo está incompleto,'" *Negra cubana tenía que ser*, August 2, 2013, accessed October 2, 2019, https://negracubanateniaqueser.com/2013/08/02/ines-maria-martiatu-sin-las-afrocubanas-el-feminismo-esta-incompleto/.

29. Rubiera, "Grupo Afrocubanas: Reivindicarse a través del conocimiento."

30. For a more detailed explanation of racial terms in Cuba, including my own personal experience of racialization, see Benson, *Antiracism in Cuba*, 25–29.

31. This saying often also serves to deny the presence of racism by suggesting that all Cubans are mixed race and therefore could not perpetuate racism.

32. Gloria Rolando, "Mis Razones," presentation at the Afrocubanas Book Launch, published June 11, 2012, accessed October 2, 2019, https://afrocubanas.files.wordpress.com/2012/06/mis-razones.pdf.

Translator's Note

It has been my privilege to translate *Afrocubanas: History, Thought, and Cultural Practices* (2011) from Spanish to English. As a Central American woman scholar of color, I was affected and impacted by every word in this phenomenal anthology, by the lives, struggles, and victories of Afrocubanas. The anthology is vast in scope and disciplines as it travels through various historical periods. Therefore I focused on retaining the historical voice to each era and the individual tone of each piece. Because of the multiple voices, eras, styles, and types of documents or archival material used in certain chapters, there was as much codeswitching on my part as in the anthology. The anthology includes poetry and autoethnographic creative pieces; I was also tasked with the challenge of translating creative work that depends on connotative and not simply denotative meaning. Being a scholar and poet informed my creative choices as I attempted to do justice to the poetry, and creative voices, in the anthology. If the original work used fragmented language, intentionally using sentence fragments to replicate, for example, a fragmented psyche or a chaotic experience, I retained the use of fragmentation. My aim was not to correct the text but to retain the authenticity and originality of the many voices that make up this book as a body of knowledge.

One of the challenges that also came up was in the use of colloquialisms, especially when a piece integrated the language of rural Afro-Cubans. I have read works by other translators who in attempting to capture the vernacular colloquialisms in diverse Spanish-speaking cultures ended up creating a mistranslation that instead re-creates an English that reads and sounds like American slang. Frantz Fanon critiques the stereotype of formally colonized peoples, especially blacks, through language as heard by the dominant white or imperial culture, that is, "Sho' good eatin'" (1967, 112). The colloquialism to a specific region becomes mistranslated into nonstandard English that, even if unintentionally, can erase or mock the creativity, intelligence, and practicality that it took for a transplanted or colonized people to develop an internal language code in relation to the hierarchies of power embedded in the notion of "correct" versus "incorrect" language. For example, Herrera Cárdenas joyfully recounts stories as they were told to her by elder women as she grew into young adulthood. In telling the story of Congolese Benito and Matilde, she states, "¿Matilde, tu tá cuchá cosa así como suspiro de un ánima en pena?" If I were to have chosen to focus on sound, as "proper" Spanish adapted into colloquial speaking, I would have had to have written something like, "Matilde, dit'ya hea' somet'ing like a sigh of an anima in pain?" However, there is actually no direct translation for "tu tá cuchá," which actually means "tu escuchas," meaning Benito is asking Matilde if she has heard or is hearing a sigh of a suffering anima(l). In Spanish, "anima" has the same meaning and also has a similar sound in English. In both Spanish and English, "anima" means soul or spirt. However, because of the colloquial Spanish, I understood the author to also be playing with the word "animal," especially because the sound that Benito is referring to is that of Matilde's lover who lies in wait for Benito's wife. "Animal" is spelled the same in both Spanish and English. Rather than trying to capture the shortening of the words in this particular type of colloquial Spanish in rural Cuba to emphasize how "improper" it sounds, I emphasized the interplay between the couple: "Matilde, do you hear something like the sighs of a hurt anima?" "Yes, Benito, but I'll pray for that poor animal. You'll see."

Given the choice of translating the sound of the colloquial Spanish that is being spoken over the meaning, I chose meaning and content. For example, Chaveco Chaveco quotes a Guillén poem that in many ways intends to emphasize the dignity of the black male subject of the poem who has been mocked by a *mulata*, though Spanish readers or listeners of the poem would also be amused by the black man because of his "improper" Spanish. The line in Spanish is "mulata ya sé que dice / que yo tengo la narise / como nudo de cobbata." The first line is grammatically incorrect. In the second line, the man says "narise," though the correct term is "nariz," which means nose. The third line represents a mispronunciation of "corbata," which means necktie. The closest translation that would have captured the grammatical, mispronunciation, and inaccuracy of words would have been "mulata I knows yous says / that my noses / like a knot of a n'cktie." This would have represented an attempt at re-creating a vernacular that cannot be directly translated into English. Therefore, I chose to translate the lines as "mulata, I know that you say / that my nose / is like the knot of necktie." As the poem progresses, it becomes apparent that the speaker is speaking a local vernacular.

Other challenges arose related to specific cultural practices. The anthology's editor, Devyn Spence Benson, became indispensable in setting a standard for terms throughout the anthology. For example, see her explanation as to why she chose to use the term "*mulata*" rather than "mulatta" throughout the anthology. As an expert on Cuban history and culture, and as someone who collaborated with the writers in bringing the original anthology together, her editing of the anthology was indispensable, especially in making sure that the translation of racial and cultural terms was accurate. Whenever possible, we chose to keep culturally specific terms, for example, *porrón*, which would then be followed by a definition in context. Otherwise, the term was defined inside brackets. Both the editor and I used brackets to insert ourselves in the translated text; however, her insertions are noted with "Editor's note." We retained the writers' original use of parentheses. Moreover, while the Spanish version used italics to highlight terms in English, we inverted this act and italicized terms in Spanish for the purpose of clarity for English readers. Though we italicized words in Spanish, we also kept the words that were italicized in the original text. I participated in the editing process to the completion and final version of this anthology, and appreciate having been included in this collaborative effort.

I close in admiration of this anthology, of all the women involved, and how important this anthology will be in expanding our knowledge of Afrocubanas. I also close with admiration of Devyn Spence Benson and her dedication to this project, having been part of its process in the original collection in Spanish and now in its English version. I thank Jane Gordon and Lewis Gordon for their invitation to translate this text. It has been an honor.

REFERENCE

Fanon, Frantz. 1967. *Black Skins, White Masks*. New York: Grove Press.

Prologue
Throwing Stones and Breaking Heads:[1] *It Is about Undoing Erasures and Exclusions of Afro-Feminist Discourse*

Only until very recently have researchers in our country paid attention to women's studies or gender studies. Because these are always developed within the scope of the academy, the disinterest in black women is not surprising given the marginal space they occupy within these areas. Black women have been excluded by an academy that has historically held a hegemonic and patriarchal cultural discourse that inherited a classed character from the past. Academic discourse has served self-interests and functions within the social fabric.

Multi/pluri/transdisciplinary methodologies encouraged us from the first moment of the gestation of this book. Even though the anthology is fairly large, and though it is a collection of a heterogeneous number of works, all the chapters share the enunciation of a counter-discourse that opposes the dominant discourse that has been circulating historically on Afro-Cuban women.

> Black women's image in Cuban society has been built at all times on a foundation of negative stereotypes. Violence, scandal, vulgarity, disorder and sexual promiscuity have been attributed to them. From rumors, from malicious jokes, through the lyrics of popular songs, mass media has built a whole conceptual body that denigrates black women, which in the worst case, black women accept and reproduce. . . . She has also been demonized as a criminal. She remains the protagonist of a sexualized narrative that focuses on her body and has made it prone to all forms of sexual and class domination and paternalism.[2]

This treatment of Cuban and Afro-descendant women in the diaspora in general has been employed and claimed even by black people's own movements arising at the beginning of the twentieth century. For example, Afro-negritude in certain cases denigrates and insults. As Colombian researcher

Deisy Jimenez writes, "Why limit her presence to a sexual role? If the 'sensuality' of Afro-descendants in the Americas is highlighted as a positive feature and as a way to affirm their identity, then why place the responsibility on the female body? Where is the historical-social reality of the woman of color?"[3]

The negritude movement, except for rare exceptions, ignored black women. This was also the case in the Black Power of the 1960s and 1970s, in which some of its most important representatives placed women on a subaltern plane. Regarding this, the researcher Agustín Laó-Montes explains, "Most of the analyses of the African diaspora tend to marginalize the considerations of gender and sexuality."[4] These movements emphasize conflict, focused on the problems faced by black men. Additionally, many black men regard racism as an assault on their masculinity. When they talk about racism, they refer to black men, and when they talk about feminism, they refer to white women. In short, it is imperative to not only "blacken feminism," as Brazilian thinker Sueli Carneiro[5] would say, but also to feminize negritude.

All this explains, in part, why Afro-Cuban women have been kept in a subaltern plane. Subalternity is conceived "as the general attribute of subordination . . . whether this is expressed in terms of class, caste, age, gender and office or in any other way."[6]

This book has several purposes beyond offering a compilation of studies on the proposed topics; it also intends to intervene in the Cuban cultural field and the complex juncture in our society in which racial conflicts have emerged and monopolized the attention and debates about them. The documents and works presented here are intended to give readers the necessary information that will allow them to dismantle hegemonic discourses.

The book's multidisciplinary scope is expressed in the inclusion of historical, sociological, and musicological essays and literature, art, and other histories. We have followed the multidisciplinary criterion also in a generic sense. The anthology contains essays, articles, interviews, and genres, not only in literature but also journalism. The book presents other hybrid essays that are difficult to classify. These journalists, poets, artists, and thinkers have been working almost always independently, and the fact that we have brought them together in one book is already a very important step.

As early as 1888, two years after the abolition of slavery, black and *mulata* women from the pages of the journal *Minerva*, among others, "were able to articulate a discourse completely different from white women. Their texts addressed topics such as the vindication of their identity and Africanity, the experience of slavery, racial pride and the urging for cultural development."[7]

They expressed a clear understanding of gender, race, and class that can be considered the antecedent of Afro-feminism[8] among us. Prior to upper- and middle-class white women, Afro-Cuban women, whose work appeared in the magazines of their time, have been defined by the researcher Julio César González Pagés as proto-feminists.[9]

According to this author, "they reflected a world of private spaces where the landscape and family were their central themes. . . . The ample feminine literary production that was realized then, highlighted family roles. Mothers, wives, and daughters were the protagonists of their own texts."[10]

For example, is the discourse by the collaborators of the journal *Minerva* a counter-discourse opposed to those who attack black women? The poet África de Céspedes in her work "Reflections" stated:

> The black woman, cruelly treated by her vile exploiters, has become the most salient target for their poisoned arrows by those who trafficked with their noble blood in the sorrowful days of slavery. That is why . . . we prepare for our defense in the constant battle we are undertaking; And such we will continue to battle until we are recognized as we are and not as each pirate artist has wanted or as it has been convenient for their fearful ends. . . . If they invite us to fight, then we will fight . . . we, women of the black race, believe we are in the last stages of this infamous persecution."[11]

María del Carmen Barcia observes from this passage: "África de Céspedes's words imply that black and *mestiza* women who had undertaken the defense of their rights through the magazine *Minerva* were under attack."[12]

Since then, Afro-Cuban women's discourse has gone unheard, erased by scholars who have subsequently written the history of ideas in Cuba. The fact of underscoring it here can be considered a counter-discourse formulated from the present.

It is no coincidence that the journal *Minerva* emerged in 1888. The restoration of the Spanish monarchy brought changes in the civil society of the metropolis but also in the colonies. This is the timeline when the Law on Printing (1879), the Law on Meetings (1880), and the Law of Associations, among others, were passed.

Let us remember that the *lettered city* in the colony was established by white men, property owners, heterosexuals, and scholars. They controlled not only the artistic-literary production but also education and the dissemination of knowledge. However, the reforms produced an opening where new publications and associations of groups emerged, claiming their own space in civil society.

The transformation of blacks' *cabildos* into instruction, recreation, and mutual relief societies is perhaps one of the most illustrative facts of this process. These societies were founded throughout the Island, in large cities, and in smaller towns. In 1887, there were already 139 in existence. Many of them made up the Central Directory of Societies of the Race of Color.[13]

This text, from its title, informs us on its content. It is about rescuing the discourse of Afro-Cuban[14] women, of the Afro-descendants. We have divided the book into three parts, but the works included in each section are complementary and dialogue with each other.

The works gathered here could in some cases bewilder, due to their heterogeneity, or seem unexpected for the reader. They do not correspond to the ordered typologies established by Cuban institutional discourse. According to the critic Alberto Abreu Arcia in his essay "The Field of Social Sciences," institutional discourse "by the fact of having to lead officially and publicly as an authority, sanctifies some theses, gazes, and theories, while excluding subalternized ones."[15]

We have chosen a form of editorial "curation" that makes intelligible not only each one of the works in particular but also the focus of the collection in general. It is necessary that the book be understood as a whole, that it be comprehensible. We resorted to a combination in which we apply at the same time chronological order, thematic order, and an order moving from the macro to the micro in each subject, that is, from the general to the particular.

In the introduction, Daisy Rubiera emphasizes the location to which black and *mestiza* women have been relegated throughout time in Cuban society, the context in which this compilation appears, and its function today in the midst of conflicts and debates on the problematic of race and what remains to be resolved. In short, she establishes the purpose of this book. In the prologue, I get into the essence, intentions, and conceptual character with which this volume was conceived as a book.

The order that the book follows and the arrangement of each section were purposeful. The work is grouped chronologically but without losing sight of the themes of the essays and moving from the general to the particular.

The first part titled "History" presents histories that remain mostly unknown of black women as protagonists in history. They were women who had lives that differed highly from stereotypical ideas of slave and free women of color in colonial society. "Lawsuits by Slave Women in Nineteenth-Century Cuba" by Digna Castañeda Fuertes demonstrates how black women fought even as enslaved persons. They rebelled against inequality through judicial litigation to ensure that laws favorable to them were fulfilled. "Reconstructing Ex-Slave Belén Álvarez's Story" by Oilda Hevia Lanier and "Women 'of Color' in Santiaguera Colonial Society: A Commentary" by María Cristina Hierrezuelo rely on a foundation of documents, mainly from notarial archives, to reveal data that attest to the economic activity of black women in the cities, some of whom were born in Africa. The women achieved social and economic mobility in adverse circumstances in a colonial society that was foreign to some of them. Some of the women remained unmarried so that their success would not be attributed to their marriage.

The second part titled "Thought" opens with works on and from the poets and journalists of *Minerva*, a journal from the nineteenth century. "Women of *Minerva*" by María del Carmen Barcia Zequeira and "Gratitude: To My Friends and Colleagues of the Journal *Minerva*" by Úrsula Coimbra de Valverde follow a series of writings of Cuban women who participated very actively in public life during the turbulent first years of the Republic. The women of *Minerva* proclaimed a very clear consciousness of gender and race. Some of the works in the journal are journalistic essays and urgent texts very committed to political moments throughout the Republican period. Little has been written on the active and combative participation of women in the conflicts of the Independent Party of Color (PIC). Fragments of works by Carmen Piedra that were published in *Prevision*, a newsletter of the PIC, are an example of this. Consuelo Serra in her article "Our Ethnic Values," published in *Los ideales de una Raza* [Ideals of a Race], stresses the vision between blacks and whites and the dignity and pride of being Cuban and black. "What We Are" by Inocencía Silveira denounces how certain individuals are made to face daily battles simply because of the color of their skin. Gerardo del Valle's article "The Black Cuban Woman" justifies black women's situation as her own lack of interest in overcoming her condition. "The Black Cuban Women and Culture" is Catalina Pozo Gato's lucid response to Valle. In "Black Intelligence," Arabella Oña Gómez underscores black people's cultural advancement while facing society's scarce opportunities for black people.

Religious thought and women as protagonists in Regla de Ocha or Santeria could not be left out from this volume. "Women in Santeria or Regla Ocha: Gender, Myths, and Reality" by Daisy Rubiera Castillo analyzes this important theme.

Issues of racial identity, racism, racial discrimination, and complex interracial relationships are addressed by some of the youngest authors in the book. Even when they are articulated from very well-defined social sciences like sociology, anthropology, or history, their texts always contain a hybrid character as they sometimes deconstruct the very academic principles themselves. They draw from their personal experiences, which results in texts that are not easy to classify.

Some of these works have been presented in nonconventional spaces such as digital journalism and in the field of performance. The authors have collaborated with representatives of hip-hop and other alternative expressions.

The work of Yulexis Almeida Junco titled "Gender and Raciality: An Obligated Reflection in Contemporary Cuba" is a text halfway between the sociological essay and testimonial. It closes with aspects of the author's field investigation in the popular neighborhood of La Timba.

As a historian and anthropologist, María Ileana Faguaga Iglesias delves into the issues related to the distortions of the image of black women in her work "On Afrocubana Stereotypes: Construction and Deconstruction of Myths." In "Proposing an Inclusive and Nonsexist Gaze: *Mulata* Women, a Profane Invention?" Onelia Chaveco Chaveco explores how *mulata* women have been treated as social beings.

The symbolic representation of identity and the vindication of black beauty in the face of the Western canon are matters that appear in "Hairs" by Carmen González Chacón. "Passing for a White Woman" by Sandra del Valle touches, from the experience of the author, on two recurrent themes in the history of our country: racial intermixing (*mestizaje*) and whitening. "The Revolution Made Blacks into People" by Yusimí Rodríguez López shows the prejudices that prevail in the consciousness of some white people with power who impose their clearly racist conceptions. Yohamna Depestre Corcho in "Human Race? Ah . . . It Had to Be!" formulates, also from her life experience, questions that point to the awakening and awareness of her racial identity since childhood. "A Room of Our Own for Black Cuban Women" by Yesenia Selier Crespo is a reflection in which the author contrasts the reality of black women with that of women from the privileged classes of the first world in the globalized postmodern state.

In "Cultural Practices," the last part of the book, we have tried to cover the greatest number of cultural expressions. "Oriki for Elder Black Women of the Past" by Georgina Herrera Cárdenas opens the section. It is a text conceived in a space of negotiation between orality and writing. It represents the important traditions of *people without written history*. "The Black Female Imaginary in Cuba" by Aymée Rivera Pérez demonstrates how the racial condition has historically influenced the expressions of black and *mestiza* women in the artistic literary field. Works like "Contradictory Binaries in Nancy Morejón's *Octubre Imprescindible* and *Cuaderno de Granada*" by Lourdes Martínez Echazábal, "In Memory of Excilia" by Coralia de Mercedes Hernández Herrera, and "The Tough Skin of Teresa Cárdenas," an interview of Cárdenas by Leandro Estupiñán Zaldívar, particularize the shared subject with the other authors.

Theater is represented in the book with my piece, "*El Negrito* and the *Mulata* in the Vortex of Nationality." Not only do I deconstruct racist archetypes, but I offer "the other side of the coin," that of the real *negrito* [a diminutive for black man] and *mulata* in colonial society and their exclusion from the first projects of the nation. "Popular Theater and Collective Resistance" by Fátima de la Caridad Patterson explores her first-person account as a female founder of theater who in contemporary times took on the challenge to immerse herself in the lattice of traditional popular culture by always positioning Caribbean women at the center of her work.

In the field of music, we have "Catalina Berroa, the Audacious Trinidadian: First Female Composer of 'Cultured' Music in the Nineteenth Century" by Isabel González Sauto. She explores this extraordinary little-known persona who is no less relevant because she is unknown. An interview of María Elena Mendiola by Edelvis López Zaldívar, "The Marathon Exists for Both Men and Women," presents the persona and work of Mendiola, an orchestra director, pedagogue, musical producer, cultural promoter, and critic. On her part, María Elena Mendiola wrote "Making One's Dreams Come True Is Not the Same as Dreaming" on the public persona and career of one of the most prominent figures in our country, known in music internationally as the pianist, orchestra director, symphonic, and opera composer Tania León. Employing a feminist film lens, Sandra Álvarez Ramírez in "The Contributions of Sara Gómez" analyzes one of Gómez's documentaries. Lázara Menéndez Vásquez in "Belkis Ayón Manso, Between Heterogeneous Sensibilities" establishes how this singular artist was able to appropriate from a very original perspective what Menéndez calls great themes in the history of art. In "Black Women in Sports," Irene Esther Ruiz Narváez explores the field of sports in which black women have been widely featured. The anthology concludes with "A Lexical Semantical Analysis on the Discourse of Women in Cuban Rap" by Yanelys Abreu Babi and Anette Jiménez Marata.

We could not have ended this book except with hip-hop, which is the most combative and emancipatory expression of all the themes of race and Afro-Cuban culture in the twentieth and early twenty-first centuries. This movement did not emerge from the intellectual avant-garde [as did other movements] in the 1920s and 1930s and later the 1960s, but it has taken place (or grown) horizontally throughout the country and among young people of different social classes, but especially among the working class and blacks and *mulatos* from humble backgrounds.

Women rappers stand out not only for their Afro-feminist discourse but also as part of a movement that emerges and develops in a massive way. They carry out important projects that center hip-hop for the benefit of the community. Racism, discrimination, drugs, prostitution, domestic violence, mercantilism, and lack of spirituality are some of the issues that this discourse boldly addresses. This is a discourse that speaks to the present and the future. These women are resisting. They are making history.

This book, by making visible the texts that constitute it, is one of the first steps in recovering the place of Afro-Cuban women's discourse in the history of ideas in Cuba, of which black women were excluded, but the book also fosters the analysis and study about and by black women.

From here on, there will be many questions left to consider. Which path to take? What are the theoretical and methodological tools most appropriate in addressing our history, conditions, and needs? How to carry out interventions that promote substantial changes and improvements in the cultural field and in our society in general? These are some of the questions that we will have to answer collectively in the future.

Inés María Martiatu Terry
Havana, July 2010

NOTES

1. Paraphrasing the poet Georgina Herrera's poem "Elogio grande para mí misma" [High Praise to Myself] in *África* (Matanzas: Ediciones Matanzas, Colleción Homenaje, 2006).

2. Inés María Martiatu: "Chivo que rompe tambó, santeria, genero y raza en María Antonia" [Goat that Breaks the Drum, Santeria, Gender and Race in . . .], in *Una pasión compartida: María Antonia. Selección y prólogo Inés María Martiatu* [A Shared Passion: María Antonia and Prologue . . .] (Havana: Editorial Letras Cubanas, 2004), 55.

3. Deisy Jiménez, "Tambores en la noche, de Jorge Artel: La mujer de color y su imaginario sexual" [Jorge Artel's Drums in the Night: Women of Color and Her Sexual Imaginary], in *La casa de asterión* [The House of . . .], *Revista Trimestral de Estudios Literarios* 7, no. 25 (April–May–June 2006).

4. Agustin Lao-Montes, "Hilos descoloniales. Trans-localizando los espacios de la diaspora africana" [Decolonial Threads: Translocalizing Spaces of the African Diaspora], in *Tabula Rasa* (Bogota, Columbia), no. 7 (July–December 2007): 47–79.

5. Sueli Carneiro, "Ennegrecer el feminismo" [Blacken Feminism], in the *Movimiento* (Agencia Cubana de Rap, Havana), no. 7 (2009): 47–50.

6. Ranajit Guha, "Preface," in *Selected Subaltern Studies*, ed. Ranajit Guhua and Gayatri Spivak (New York: Oxford University Press, 1988). Cited by Ileana Rodriguez in *Hegemonía y dominio: subalternidad, un significado flotante* [Hegemony and Dominion: Subternity, a Floating Signifier].

7. Inés María Martiatu, "Mujeres, raza e identidad caribeña" [Women, Race and Caribbean Identity], conversación con Inés María Martiatu: entrevista por Sandra Álvarez Ramírez [conversation with Ines María Martiatu: interview by . . .], in *La Gaceta de Cuba* [Cuban Gazette] (Havana), no. 1 (January–February 2010): 42–45.

8. Afro-feminism emerged in the 1970s in the United States, Latin America, and the Caribbean. Black women established their own agenda, which had not been taken into account by white feminists who were almost always middle or upper class, nor by black men in the Black Power movement.

9. Julio César González Pagés, "Las etapas históricas del feminismo en Cuba: reflexiones, debates y experiencias (1878–1952)" [Feminist Stages in Cuba: Reflections, Debates and Experiences (1878–1952)], in *Cubaliteraria*.

10. Ibid.

11. África de Céspedes, "Reflexiones" [Reflections], in *Minerva*, no. 10 (February 28, 1889): 2–5. Cited by María del Carmen Barcia Zequeira: "Mujeres en torno a Minerva," in *La Rábida* [Rabid] (Huelva, Spain), no. 17 (1998): 9.

12. Ibid.

13. Oilda Hevia Lanier, *El Directorio Central de Sociedades de la Raza de Color* (Havana: Editorial de Ciencias Sociales, 1996).

14. Since the wise Fernando Ortiz coined this term, it has been controversial. There are a number of opinions that, of course, we respect. See Rogelio Martínez Furé, "Somos o no somos" [Are We or Aren't We], in *Briznas de la memoria* [Strands of Memory] (Havana: Editorial Letras Cubanas, 2004).

15. Alberto Abreu Arcia, "El campo de las ciencias sociales," http://www.afromo.

Introduction
Awaken Memory: Banish Forgetting

Given the invisibility of black women inside the general invisibility of women, it becomes imperative to reawaken historical memory and to begin to fill the current void in Cuban history and society about black women's images, actions, subjectivity, thought, and values.

Reawakening memory allows us to reflect on black women's historical experiences that have not been fully addressed by traditional discourse on women's oppression. In actuality, that discourse does not address the qualitative effect of women's oppression on an identity that intersects both gender and race. Black women have been part of a history of resistance at every era as protagonists in the course of Cuban history as they began to be regarded as human beings, with possibilities and opportunities, independent of their class, race, gender, sex, and religion. Her narrative must be brought to light, learned and relearned.

We must insist on the need for our historical texts to express the roles black and *mulata* women have played at every moment in our history. It is not enough to mention María Cabrales and Mariana Grajales as the wife and mother of Antonio Maceo and Dominga Moncada as the mother of Guillermón Moncada while ignoring their labor, role, and subjectivity in society as women, as well as their individual actions as black women.

Moreover, we must question the systemic absence that official discourse offers and possibly the deliberate forgetfulness by academia, with few exceptions.[1] This void includes black women from the sixteenth to the eighteenth centuries and also women that lived in Cuban society in the nineteenth and twentieth centuries who were part of lower, middle, and upper classes.

Understanding some of the major characteristics of their experience in each historical context explains their thought while bringing visibility to them. Black women exerted influence on the process of consolidation of national identity, regardless of whether their influence remained unrecognized: "in the moments when female stereotypes were solidified through liberal thought and the project of nation-building with its construction of the national identity . . . black women remained excluded from that model."[2] Invisibility became the foundation onto which black women's cultural absence was established, a significant absence that has historically characterized them.

Additionally, the constant aggression black women have been subjected to must be exposed alongside her struggle for recognition and acceptance. The ways in which our present society value her are detrimental to her self-esteem, as she remains the target of proverbs and racist jokes that are humiliating and malicious, such as "a white woman asleep looks like a dead dove; a black woman asleep looks like a dead turkey buzzard" or "better to have one white woman than twenty black women."

Hence to reawaken memory is to stay true to a discussion on the situation of black women in our society not only from a historical perspective but also today. Reawakening memory means coming to an understanding that the social significance of being a black woman is not the same as the social significance of being a white woman—not even a poor white woman—even when this claim seems illogical when said in a social project such as ours. While Cuba managed to break with multiple stereotypes, unfortunately it has not been able to deconstruct sexist, racial, and racist stereotypes that persist.

Afrocubanas: History, Thought, and Cultural Practices is meant to awaken memory. The anthology offers a selection of works that provide a comprehensive vision of the presence of Afro-descended Cuban women, *Afrocubanas*, through our history and in different fields, with the aim of endowing the new generations, especially black Cuban women and men, with paradigms that can contribute to, among other things, the development of their racial identity. In addition to rescuing Afro-Cuban historical memory, Afro-Cubans must be included in the history of ideas of the nation of Cuba, where the contributions of women from their own social group are barely represented. With this collection, we aim to contribute to the elimination of negative stereotypes of black women and to stimulate the study of the rich African heritage maintained through the contributions by Afro-Cuban women in history, literature, and art.

In one of my books, I posited that "every book must reveal a truth that was hidden because of fear, forgetting, censoring, because it is unknown or new; a book must be written to transmit a lesson of knowledge." With that in mind, all the works collected in this anthology not only awaken memory but they also banish forgetting.

Daisy Rubiera Castillo
Havana, June 15, 2010

NOTES

1. Some of these are included in this anthology.
2. Susana Montero, *La cara oculta de la identidad nacional* [The Hidden Face of National Identity] (Santiago de Cuba: Editorial Oriente, 2003), 62.

Part One

HISTORY

Chapter 1

Lawsuits by Slave Women in Nineteenth-Century Cuba

Digna Castañeda Fuertes

For the past twenty-five years, theoretical-methodological studies aimed at showing the role of slave women of African origin in the Caribbean colonies, mainly in the English or French possessions, have provided timely publications.[1] In the Hispano-Antillean Caribbean, however, the historiographic production dedicated to the topic is slight.

In Cuba, slave women of African descent have not been the subject of study. Their lives are known through literary works such as *Francisco* by Anselmo Suárez y Romero, *Petrona y Rosalía* by Félix Tanco, and the exceptional *Cecilia Valdés* by Cirilo Villaverde.[2] There are also historical or sociological studies that tangentially analyze aspects of the lives of these women.[3] For this reason, the work that follows aims to begin to cover the existing vacuum in Cuban historiography on the subject.

SLAVE WOMEN IN CUBA CONFRONT OPPRESSION

Slave women in the mills were scarce during the first centuries of slave trafficking in Cuba. Although since May 5, 1528, solicitors of established cities had expressed their interest in introducing slave women, landowners systematically refused to do so due to the relative ease with which they obtained slaves on the coasts of Africa, which made the sexual reproduction of slavery unnecessary.

Only in Baracoa did Belemitas monks introduce black women in their sugar mills and married them with their slaves.[4] However, the possibility of bringing women from Africa to increase slave stock by means of sexual reproduction began to be considered at the beginning of the nineteenth century after the restriction of the slave trade. The *síndico* of the consulate of

Havana[5] the criollo economist Francisco de Arango y Parreño underscored this line of action. He proposed to increase the number of slaves by adding up to one-third black women to each slave dotation; and to facilitate the process, he proposed exempting all import duties for their rights of entrance to the Island.

For a similar purpose, deputies proposed among other aspects "that the master of a male slave married to a female slave belonging to another master is obligated to sell him by appraisal if the owner of the female slave wants to buy him, counting also with the will of the male slave, and as agreed by the master of the male slave that does not have a third of female slaves in his hacienda, and also when the master of the male slave had not allowed his slave to marry."[6]

In this context, the Royal Decree of April 27, 1804, was proclaimed, which ordered: "That in the mills and haciendas that hold only black men, black women be included, limiting the permission to introduce black women until all those who desire to be married, do so."[7]

Although this was not completely fulfilled, by the mid-nineteenth century women slaves could be found in all the haciendas, sharing the harsh plantation work with their male counterparts. By obligation, the women carried out the performance of tasks with such effectiveness that some foremen said, "Black women are more resilient and of greater constancy than the men."[8]

This assertion was based on the labor of slave women, which was not confined to agriculture but also included other work, both in the city and in the countryside. They were used directly by their masters or rented out to serve as wet nurses or to do household chores (as cooks, ironers, seamstresses, etc.). They also served as midwives or birthing assistants.[9] Many of these tasks, mainly the last two, helped them to acquire their freedom, which they also obtained through common sexual relations with white males, which was often the case.[10]

Besides the rigorous work that women slaves were subjected to in the countryside and cities, they were also victims of the most cruel and outrageous punishments. They were whipped and sent to the leg stocks to be hung upside down, even when they were pregnant.[11] They were also their master's objects of sadism who manifested their sexual aberrations through inconceivable measures, unimaginable for people of sound minds.

An example of this is Don Ramón Saíz, in Havana, who promised a *mulata* slave Florencia Rodríguez or Hernández,[12] fourteen years of age, her freedom if she "lent him her body," which means she was made to have sexual relations with him. After achieving his goal, not only did he not release her but he also frequently punished her and forced her to work in chains in a blacksmith's workshop. According to her, the master even "tried to put silver rings in my most secret parts of nature."

Facing this situation, in October 1834, the slave girl complained to the mayor. Despite this, the mayor did not act and merely told her that he would speak to her master and that she should return to the master's house. The slave continued her claims elsewhere; everyone in the village ignored her because the master had money. She added that she sought help because if they returned her to him, she would die.[13]

Slave women were also victims of abuses such as their master stealing their belongings. For example, in the village of Guanabacoa, in March 1828, a complaint was presented to the chief mayor of the town by an enslaved African woman, María del Carmen Gangá, against her master because he had stolen twenty-one ounces of gold and several jewels that, according to her, were bought with her husband's savings. Although the master was cited on numerous occasions, he never appeared in court according to official documents and an inquest that form part of the case record.[14] Meanwhile, the fact that she remained in the hands of the *síndico* indicates the partiality of the colonial authorities.

THE DEMANDS OF SLAVE WOMEN AND JUDICIAL PROCESSES

In the legal battle carried out by the enslaved women, three types of lawsuits predominated, which reveal the most abusive violations. The main objectives of these lawsuits were to avoid family separation, to claim the right of *coartación*,[15] and to prevent the sale of freed blacks back into slavery. Some cases are illustrated here.

AVOIDING THE DISINTEGRATION OF THE FAMILY

Without a doubt, this type of abuse was very common at the time. For example, in mid-nineteenth-century Cuba, even when a slave family, with sui generis characteristics, was favored[16] by being theoretically recognized and protected by Spanish legislation applied to the colony,[17] their true situation was dramatic: having to survive in subhuman conditions.

The role of the black woman, whether enslaved or free, mattered in this slave colonial context. She fought to the extent of her abilities, even by legal means, to protect her relatives, help them gain their freedom or recover it, and to keep the family united. Theirs was an arduous and complex battle, especially because the family nucleus was habitually broken at the mercy of masters who with impunity violated the laws, almost always with the consent of the colonial authorities commissioned, supposedly, to defend the slaves.

One of the methods used by the slave owners to violate the laws that protected slaves and the integrity of their family was to send urban slaves to the countryside and hide them there. For example, a document from the Secretary of the Superior Government of the Island of Cuba dated September 12, 1837, involved a complaint opened in 1828 by María Dolores Frías, born in Africa, and who resided in the outskirts of the district of Guadalupe. According to the plaintiff's account, her daughter Ana María, a slave of Marcos Padrón, appeared before her fifteen days prior complaining that her master abused her. Consequently, the mother asked the trustee to find a new owner for her daughter.

However, when they went to buy her, the master accused the girl of being a *cimarron*[18] and of having multiple flaws, thereby discouraging the buyer. Achieving his goal, the master sent the slave to Alquízar where he continued to batter her and, although she was paying toward her freedom set at 350 pesos, he tried every way possible to block her sale to others. When in 1838 the court ordered Padrón to allow the slave to go to the capital to seek a new master, especially because she had an intended buyer, the master argued that he had already sold her to the administrator of the Dolores refinery.[19]

Another example of the abuse suffered by slave families is shown in the marriage of Hilario e Inés, belonging to the slave stock of the Nazarene refinery, owned by Juan de Dios Larrinaga, located in the district of Guanajay. This couple in 1852 claimed before the court the return of their small four-year-old son Juan Criollo. They explained that Don Juan Benítez on his own accord claimed ownership of the little boy and took him to another place and that they did not want to continue living without him because he constituted all their happiness. The court, based on the Regulation of Slaves of 1842, agreed that the law in all its articles tended to foment the principles of morality and of family for the slave class in article 31, which stated, "When the master of the husband buys the woman, he will have to also buy the children that they had together, under three years of age, because they have the right until the children reach that age for the mother to nourish and raise them."[20]

For this reason, the court asked Don Juan Benítez to present himself to the Captain General accompanied by the little boy Juan to sign the deed of sale with Mr. Larrinaga, after an appraisal by an administrator, because the parents wanted Larrinaga to buy Juan. Benítez refused, arguing that he had raised the boy as his own son. He stated that he would not sell him for any money because he was better nourished and cared for with him. Additionally, he wanted to grant him the letter of freedom so that when he came of age, he would inherit it. In short, everything seems to indicate that an arrangement was made between the owners. The authorities gave Benítez the possibility to buy the child, who was granted the letter of freedom. The court and owners decided to keep the boy in the shelter of Benítez, who continued to be obliged to feed him. In short, the family was torn apart.[21]

A practice that also led to the dismembering of the family was to rent out slaves, which sometimes led to the temporary or permanent separation of the family.

VALIDATING THE RIGHT OF *COARTACIÓN*

It was very difficult for slaves to obtain their freedom by legal means because they had to overcome many obstacles, especially because the process was fraudulent, dilatory, and generally did not resolve their demands. There are numerous cases that testify to that.

Jacinta, a creole slave of Don Jacinto Ferrer, presented her case to the authorities in Havana (1837). She argued that because of her advanced age, she sought to free herself with the money she had been able to save, 200 pesos plus 100 that had been given to her by a black individual. She hoped she would be assessed at 300 pesos. Her lawsuit was dismissed. Though the trustee General Procurator objected to the mayor's decision, the case was left unresolved.[22]

In other cases, the delivery of the document of *coartación* was interrupted. This happened to María Francisca Cañero, a freed woman whose daughter was in the power of Doña Loreto García for twenty-two years, of which she paid for twelve years for her freedom, almost in full. The slave got sick and was given to her mother to cure her. She remained with her for two years. In that period, the mother nursed the daughter back to health using her own money and without any financial assistance from the owner. Additionally, she raised a grandchild. In consideration of the small amount that remained on the *coartación* and the services rendered, the mother assumed that the letter of freedom would be granted to her daughter.

Instead, once the slave healed, she was captured and sent to the Malverde coffee plantation, located in Quivicán, where she was in 1849 when her mother presented the case to the colonial authorities. She demanded payment for her services and that the money owed be deposited to her daughter. The authorities applied the *coartación* to the daughter at 85 pesos, but the process did not continue because the slave did not show up. She could not, obviously, because she was being held captive.[23]

Additionally, to inhibit the sale of slaves who had *coartación*, owners used the method of continually increasing their prices. For this reason, relatives— usually female: mothers, wives, daughters—went to court to force owners to comply with the law.

In 1849, Damiana Montalvo, a black woman, complained to the authorities because Don Francisco Baños, master to her son José Victoriano Montalvo, abused him. Damiana wanted to find a new master. As she explained, it had been about a month since the current master had bought José for 400 pesos. Within that period, another buyer appeared, offering 500. However, the master now demanded 700 pesos, which was objectionable because the price of the slave could not have increased so greatly in such a short period.

The owner was forced to appear before the authorities to comply with the judicial process. However, he did so in the capacity of the "rightful owner" and expressed that he had sold the boy for 425 pesos. He also denied punishing the slave boy or asking 700 pesos for him. For this reason, he claimed that Damiana's lawsuit held no basis. In this situation the court decided to dismiss the petition for lack of evidence and because the slave had achieved his desire: a change of owner.[24]

PREVENTING KIDNAPPING OR THE SALE OF FREE BLACKS AS SLAVES

Slaves suffered this type of violation personally or through their children and other relatives. In this sense, mothers had to endure their free-born children being illegally sold as slaves. This is attested to in the situation of María Dolores Español, confronted as a slave of Don Juan Peraza. In 1851 she filed a complaint with the trustee for the unjust servitude to which her daughter, the *parda* Mary Francisca Librada, was subjected. This young woman was born free in Madrid in 1832, the year her mother traveled to the peninsula where the girl was baptized. When María Dolores returned to Cuba, her daughter was abducted as a young woman and sold as a slave for six ounces of gold, which the mother discovered after a certain time. Although the mother took pertinent steps to request her daughter's baptism certificate from the Spanish capital, she never received it. For four years the authorities of Bejucal maintained a lawsuit against Don Isidro Hernández, who had bought the girl; however, they only learned that she be sent to Real Casa de Beneficencia [Royal House of Beneficence, a charity house], where she was rented out like other slaves. This decision did not solve her situation because it did not return her freedom.[25]

Perhaps the most notable case of abduction in the nineteenth century was that of Plassy Laurence, which became an international lawsuit with a plot as if from an adventure novel. Known in Havana as María del Carmen, she was a slave of Don Pedro Pino when the claim was presented to the English Consul on February 15, 1851. She argued that as a native to the island of Nevis that belonged to the British Monarchy, she had been wrongly subjected to slavery for thirty years.

According to her statement, in 1819 or 1820 Juan Scabraugh directed her to flee from her mother who was a farm slave. This man led her to the island of St. Thomas, a Danish colony at the time, where they were detained and handed over by the governor to be returned to Nevis. However, because she did not wish to leave, she escaped from the officers where she was detained. She hid in the house of a native woman named Jane Huggins, who gave her to a black woman. From her house, Plassy was placed in a boat that took her to Puerto Rico. From there, she moved to another point called Cadgoa. She escaped from that place and presented herself to the judges of the township. However, officials did not grant her clemency and she was imprisoned by the mayor Don Victoriano Sancalo who sold her for 200 pesos to Don Joaquín Delgado. The master wanted her for farm work, which she opposed, so he exchanged her for a French cook. This new owner kept her enslaved for two years.

Confronted by Plassy's refusal to work as a slave and because she insisted that she was free, the master sent her to Havana aboard a brig with a group of slave African men with the warning that she should not disclose where she was from. For several years she was passed from owner to owner, sometimes sold, in other cases given or inherited, but always under protest that she was a free woman. Mary of Carmen, Plácida Lorenza, or Plassy Laurence, as her name appears interchangeably in the documents, wished to return to Nevis with her family.

For this reason, she went to the Consul General of England in Cuba who took charge of the case and presented the lawsuit to the government of the Island. As usual, while the investigations were being made, the slave was deposited at the Hospital de Paula, where she was forced to assist the sick and thus be exposed to contracting diseases. The consul argued against this and wrote to the Captain General asking that she be removed from there and be released, especially because she had not committed a crime. Six months after the proceedings were initiated, the consul wrote to the Captain General for a decision because in his opinion enough time had passed for a proper investigation. He added that at that time (February 2, 1852), Plassy was in the house of charity; however, the house tried to rent her to the Hospital of San Lázaro to work like the other slaves they subcontracted. The British consul insisted that the proceedings be expedited and that Plassy not be subjected to slave labor because she should be considered a free person and a British subject.

In May 1852, Fippo Laurence, a black male, arrived in Havana from Nevis as a family member of Plassy to officially identify her. He did and declared that he knew her mother, Elsie. Meanwhile, the English consul received the documents that confirmed Plassy's claims. Documents were reviewed, and dated July 14, 1817, the name of Plassy appeared, age fourteen, listed as number 70 in William Laurence's list of slave property. The slave registry of Nevis dated January 1, 1825, listed Plassy as missing from the island.

The British diplomat sent the evidence to the Spanish government of Cuba and explained that, being still a slave, Plassy was taken out of Nevis and sold illegally and that, by birth, she was a subject of Her Majesty the Queen of England, where slavery no longer existed. They also verified that based on the marks on her body, Plassy and Maria del Carmen were the same person. The consul requested monetary compensation for his client for her enslavement for more than thirty years in Cuba and Puerto Rico. With a calculation of 10 pesos a month, although she had won more for her masters, the compensation was estimated at 3,500 pesos, but the consul was willing to accept 2,000. However, the investigations carried out in Cuba show that some masters denied that Plassy had been their slave, while others had passed away. On his part, the governor of St. Thomas, a Danish colony, sent a statement in which he claimed to have no proof of Plassy having been on the island.

Under these circumstances, the English consul sent another letter to the Captain General on June 15, 1852, in which he expressed that having duly identified Plassy Laurence as such, and as a native of Nevis, that she be released immediately to leave on the steamship departing from the port of Havana on the 22nd of that month. He did not obtain a response to his letter or other communications addressed to the Captain General until the end of December 1852.

While the consul complained of the delay to the colonial government of Cuba, Plassy fled aboard the English ship *La Vestal*. In subsequent investigations it was shown that the British diplomat had interviewed Plassy in English shortly before her escape from the house of charity (Real Casa de Beneficencia).

This event constituted an international scandal, reflected by international presses. *The Morning Post* of London published an article on the case, which was reproduced by Havana's gazette (*La Gaceta de La Habana*) on February 23, 1853. One of the paragraphs stated:

> On December 1st, there was great excitement in Havana due to a kidnapping from the island of Nevis, belonging to Great Britain as a subject of Her Majesty the Queen, the black woman Plassy Laurence who was sold as a slave in Havana. The British government had demanded the return of this poor woman who found refuge on the frigate La Vestal, whose gallant captain regardless of being under the cannons of the Spanish batteries and surrounded by the Spanish squadron, kept her safe under the protection of the English flag ignoring proposals to return her to her masters.

The journalist of *La Gaceta de La Habana*, official newspaper of the Spanish government on the Island, argued that the delayed response by the Spanish authorities was not only fair but also indispensable in a country in which the sacred right to property was guaranteed by law and that the veracity of the facts on which the claim was founded needed to be investigated under the custody of loyal authorities before surrendering to the wishes of the government of Her Royal Majesty the Queen concerning the delivery of the aforementioned Plácida Lorenza. Additionally, it was pertinent, even after proof of origin of birth of the slave, to resolve a question of international law that would greatly transcend the interests of this island of Antilles.

Further on, it stated, "No less praiseworthy we believe is the wise judgement of our government to submit the proceedings to the resolution of the British Monarchy, for as we have said before we were attempting to resolve a question of international law, and in matters of this kind only a supreme power can make that decision." Another paragraph accused the team on the ship of committing a reprehensible act by favoring the escape of a person with a case before the courts and pending sovereign resolution. The journalist asked what could be expected of a woman capable of escaping from her home at the age of seventeen.

News of the case was also published by French and American newspapers such as the *Journal des Débats politiques et Littéraire* on January 18, 1853, *The Morning Courier*, and *The New York Enquirer*. The last two publications, under the title "Important from Havana," reported on Plassy's escape and characterized *La Vestal*, under the command of Captain Cospabrick Baillie Hamilton, as a naval ship that served North America and the West Indies. The position of these newspapers was favorable to Plassy. They even report that she was forced to prostitute herself and that her children were sold as slaves.

In consequence of the international scandal provoked by the Plassy case, the Captain General of the island suggested to the president of the Council of Ministers of Overseas the relevance of "declaring the freedom of the aforementioned black female slave, to give a clear example of impartiality and of respect for the sternest and strictest justice." He also criticized the conduct of the British consul, which, the Captain General stated, offended the dignity and good faith of the Spanish government and abused the impunities and advantages provided by his position.

By midyear 1853, the Spanish government in Havana was still interested in the whereabouts of Plassy, as evidenced by a letter sent from the Spanish consulate in Nassau on August 29 of that year stating that she could be found neither in Nevis nor in any of the immediate islands.

In short, this woman, unhappy but determined and daring, was in the possession of nine people, had eight owners, was sold four times, exchanged once, and inherited once. All transactions were executed fraudulently on four islands of the Caribbean. Her case reached a certain notoriety at the time, less for its human relevance than because it provided an extraordinary record to condemn the Spanish slave trade by England and France, where slavery had already been abolished.[26]

CONCLUSIONS

The judicial battle waged in Cuba by slave women during the nineteenth century focuses a new and important angle of African slavery on the Island. The documents analyzed indicate how, in addition to contributing their work in the plantations and residences of their masters in various and mostly harsh conditions, slave women were the center of the family. Organized in conditions of precariousness and dependence, women were fully conscious of their family's constant threat of disintegration, which they fought to the extent of their abilities in different spheres of their social lives. Because of the core status of that kind of family organization, perhaps women contributed more than men to preserving and transmitting their ancestral culture. Thus they prevented slaves from being reduced to mere biological fuel and rather imprinted their ethnic and cultural footprint in the Cuban context.

Although they rarely achieved justice, slave women waged what can be characterized as a true judicial battle in nineteenth-century Cuba. The documentation on their struggle provides new data on the horrors, abuses, and injustices of the slave institution and a consideration of slave women as forerunners of women's struggles for their rights.

NOTES

1. These are notable examples: Hilary McD. Beckles's *Natural Rebels: A Social History of Slaves, Black Women in Barbados* (New Brunswick, NJ: Rutgers University Press, 1989); and Marietta Morrissey's *Slave Women in the New World* (Kansas City: University Press of Kansas, 1989).

2. Anselmo Suárez y Romero, *Francisco* (Havana: Dirección de Cultura, Ministerio de Educación, 1947); Félix Tanco Bosmeniel, *Petrona y Rosalía* (Havana: Editorial Letras Cubanas, 1980); Cirilo Villaverde, *Cecilia Valdés* (Havana: Instituto Cubano del Libro, 1972).

3. Highlighted among these works are Fernando Ortiz, *Los negros esclavos* (Havana: Editorial de Ciencias Sociales, 1975); and Pedro Deschamps Chapeaux, *El negro en la economía habanera del siglo XIX* (Havana: UNEAC, 1971).

4. Ortiz, *Los negros esclavos*, 196.

5. A city civil servant assigned to protect the rights of slaves and to administer justice for them.

6. Ortiz, *Los negros esclavos*, 197.

7. Ibid., 198.

8. Anselmo Suárez y Romero, cited by Ortiz, ibid., 198–99.
9. See Pedro Deschamps Chapeaux, *El negro en la economía habanera del siglo XIX*, 169–84.
10. Ortiz, *Los negros esclavos*, 285.
11. Ibid., 230.
12. In the documents she appears interchangeably with either last name.
13. National Archive of Cuba (ANC), Fondo Gobierno Superior Civil [Superior Civil Government Reserve], file 936, no. 33047.
14. ANC, Fondo Gobierno Superior Civil, file 938, no. 33109.
15. According to Fernando Ortiz, "*coartación* gave the right to a slave to place a down payment to the slave's owner based on a fixed price applied to the slave's manumission, thus giving slaves the right to make payments towards their own freedom based on the difference between the fixed price and the down payment."
16. *La Real Provisión* [The Royal Provision] of the Emperor Carlos V and of Cardinal Cisneros, May 11, 1527, later reiterated that slave families were favored. (See Ortiz, *Los negros esclavos*, 401.)
17. *La Real Célula e Instrucción circular de Indias, sobre la educación, trato y ocupación de los esclavos* [The Royal Decree and Full Instruction of the Indies on the Education, Treatment and Occupation of the Slaves], and *el Reglamento de esclavos* [The Regulation of Slaves] are the titles of official documents by the Spanish Crown. Articles 29, 30, and 31 legally protected slave families. (See Ortiz, *Los negros esclavos*, 411, 446.)
18. Runaway slave.
19. ANC, Fondo Gobierno Superior Civil, file 938, no. 33087.
20. ANC, Fondo Gobierno Superior Civil, file 948, no. 33487.
21. ANC, Fondo Gobierno Superior Civil, file 947, no. 33431.
22. ANC, Fondo Gobierno Superior Civil, file 938, no. 33094.
23. ANC, Fondo Gobierno Superior Civil, file 946, no. 33365.
24. ANC, Fondo Gobierno Superior Civil, file 946, no. 33351.
25. ANC, Fondo Gobierno Superior Civil, file 946, no. 33376.
26. ANC, Fondo Gobierno Superior Civil, file 947, no. 33381.

BIBLIOGRAPHY

Beckles, Hilary McD. 1989. *Natural Rebels: A Social History of Slave Black Women in Barbados*. Brunswick, NJ: Rutgers University Press.
Deschamps Chapeaux, Pedro. 1971. *El negro en la economía habanera del siglo XIX*. Havana: UNEAC.
Morrissey, Marietta.1989. *Slave Women in the New World*. Kansas City: University Press of Kansas.
Ortiz, Fernando. 1975. *Los negros esclavos*. Havana: Editorial de Ciencias Sociales.
Suárez y Romero, Anselmo. 1947. *Francisco*. Havana: Dirección de Cultura, Ministerio de Educación.
Tanco Bosmeniel, Félix. 1980. *Petrona y Rosalía*. Havana: Editorial Letras Cubanas.
Villaverde, Cirilo. 1972. *Cecilia Valdés*. Havana: Instituto Cubano del Libro.

DOCUMENTS

Archivo Nacional de Cuba (ANC). Fondo Gobierno Superior Civil. File 936, no. 33047.
———. File 938, no. 33087.
———. File 938, no. 33094.
———. File 938, no. 33109.
———. File 938, no. 33431.
———. File 946, no. 33351.
———. File 946, no. 33365.
———. File 946, no. 37376.
———. File 947, no. 33381.
———. File 947, no. 33431.
———. File 948, no. 33487.

Chapter 2

Reconstructing Ex-Slave Belén Álvarez's Story

Oilda Hevia Lanier

INTRODUCTION

Studies on black women remain scarce, especially because only within the past few decades have women's studies emerged in Cuba's historiography, least of which involves research on women that deals with race.

The undeniable advances worldwide of research on women and race as shown in the theories that have been developed and on studies on the lives of women, as well as outside influence by researchers and an extensive bibliography on the subject, without doubt influenced the opening and visibility of women's topics on the Island in the past decades of the twentieth century. Since then, thematically and methodologically diverse research on women has been carried out, as well as on women in diverse historical periods.

However, creating space does not always imply a change of mindset. Until now, at least in Cuba, research on women and race remains underdeveloped. The field of historical studies reflects the prejudice, exclusions, and silences that black women have had and continue to face. Excluding a few exceptions,[1] most of the research on women does not mention black women or repeats old and harmful stereotypes lacking a thorough historical inquiry that could reveal new approaches and considerations. In other cases, black women are mentioned in passing as part of a social strata, focused on gender roles in the studies on families and sociability, or as mothers, wives, and daughters of a relevant figure, but rarely as the protagonists of their own stories.

The silence on black women contrasts with the trajectory they have had in the history of Cuba. As the researchers Levi Marrero and Alejandro de la Fuente, among others, have demonstrated, black women and *mulatas* held a notable presence in the economic, political, and sociocultural life of the

Island, especially in urban spaces since the sixteenth century. To this end, their laudable presence caused great concern among local authorities since that century, issuing successive measures to control black women's economic activities and restrict their social advancement.[2]

Their influence was, in certain periods, greater than that achieved by black men, although at the end of the eighteenth century and throughout the nineteenth century black women suffered the blows of the reorganization of colonial society that brought about the massive rise of the plantation slave system. However, women's influence was not fully diminished, especially in the economic aspect for those who remained in Havana, although their sphere of prominence and visibility changed throughout the colonial period and probably in the whole republic. Yet black women remained influential, among other reasons, because many of them were essential axes within the home, characterized by being carriers of the material and intellectual wealth harvested over the centuries from one generation to another.

Although traditionally they are better known at a popular level for their significant presence in most of Cuba's homes as slaves, wet nurses, domestics, or as poor black women, prostitutes, and beautiful *mulatas* whose goal was to be a concubine of a white man, that facet is only a part of their history. Besides these roles, very enterprising women whether through personal work or a stroke of luck managed to buy their freedom and build small- and medium-sized fortunes that enabled them to have a better life. They demonstrated that they were able to rise above the difficulties involved in living in a patriarchal and slave society.

They gained their goals most often through hard work. Taking advantage of the loopholes under colonial law, they inserted themselves in the economy of services needed in cities as owners of real estate, slaves, and small businesses. They emerged also in work sites and boarding houses in city neighborhoods and as owners of minor rural farms. Regardless of the importance of understanding the role that marginal businesses took in the cities, our historiography has not sufficiently dealt with this new area of study.

Although there is still a long way to go in examining the aforementioned issues, at least some inquiries have been made; however, in this chapter we will transcend the world of trades and social advances to approach a more susceptible universe: the family. We will not reconstruct the stories of those that individually or with their families were able to thrive on the Island, something that has also been strongly noted in recent years.[3] Rather, we will imaginarily travel from colonial Havana to Africa to learn how some of the families that thousands of Africans had to leave behind were constructed when they were brought to the Americas.

Approaching this history is extremely valuable because it allows us to, among other things, show that far from what some historians of slavery have claimed in the past, Africans had an affective family life and held stable kin relationships before reaching the New World. Among African peoples there were dissimilar human and cultural universes of extraordinary complexity, including relations and solidarity among clans and tribes that carried a fundamental weight.[4]

If when they were loaded onto the slave ships their affective values were almost always broken in human terms, from a spiritual point of view, without doubt, they must have retained the essence of their affective bonds in their memories, which they brought along with their bodies to the New World.

Though once arrived on the Island, they could not reproduce their customs and traditions in the exact same conditions; they could, however, forcibly introduce them into the new molds imposed on them by colonial society. From this fierce struggle between dominant and dominated cultures, negotiations were achieved that, although modified, retained much of their cultures of origin. These adaptations guided the new types of families and the affective-spiritual-religious relationships that were created with the course of time.

This explains why Africans and their closest descendants were able to create among themselves powerful networks of solidarity as a driving force to generate strategies of freedom and survival, as well as to face their greatest battles. Understanding more fully the roots and principles that nurtured their links is only possible when the limits of the New World are transcended to establish the necessary connections between Africa and America.

These reflections and many others arose from the invaluable and unusual information on the judicial case in the year of 1887 that the competent authorities opened to determine the claim made by the *morena criolla* Evarista González on her inheritance left by her aunt, the free *morena* of Lucumí ethnicity Belén Álvarez. To become her rightful heir, Evarista had to prove blood ties. It was then that she encountered an obstacle: her father and Aunt Belen (blood siblings) were born in Africa. The skein of this story that we will present emerges from this impossibility of people born on the Island to present legal documents that allowed them to establish origins with their direct ancestors born in Africa.

WHO WAS BELÉN ÁLVAREZ?

Belén Álvarez, free *morena* born in Africa of Lucumí ethnicity, single, without children, and of sixty-five years of age, died in the city of Havana on October 18, 1887, due to angina pectoris. Unfortunately, she did not leave a will, perhaps because her death was unexpected. Upon her death, she owned two masonry and roofing houses, one in Calle Rayos, no. 74, and an account of 6,500 pesos in the Spanish Bank of Havana.

Her estate reveals that Belén had good taste. Her home contained a long list of furniture: a living room set in the style of the Grand Duchess composed of small couches, two arm chairs, twelve chairs, a sofa, and a console table, including an antique sideboard with marble and a large extendable two-winged table, all of them of mahogany. In addition, her estate contained to two wardrobes, two iron beds with frames, a vanity, another dressing room with an antique washbasin, a mirror hanger to hang hats, a commode, a hospital chair, a washstand with its white earthenware basin, a three-light metal lamp, and silverware. This list does not represent great monetary value, but the quantity, quality, and state of conservation of this type of furniture were rare in houses of black women, even among those who were economically comfortable. Hence Belén must have enjoyed a certain level of distinction among her peers.[5]

Within nineteenth-century Havanan society, Belén Álvarez must have been an urban slave first because the cities granted greater access, particularly for women, to acquire the freedom and opportunities to be able to buy goods and to come to own small businesses. Although the redeemable conditions from the ignoble regime of slavery remain unclear, it is obvious that she was able to achieve her freedom and wealth before slavery and indentured servitude were abolished in 1886, especially because it must have taken her years between obtaining her freedom and building a small fortune.

It also seems that she managed to accumulate her wealth through personal effort because it does not appear that she received an inheritance by any means, won the Royal Lottery, or received large sums from loans. This information, for legal purposes, would have remained in court documents. Nor did she rely on parents, husbands, and children, who traditionally helped entrepreneurial freed black women in their efforts.

Those arguments and her heart condition tend to originate from a life full of great physical effort, daily tensions, or great sufferings, which suggests that Belén serves as one of many anonymous examples of black women who valued themselves according to their hard work and in doing so built for themselves a half-fortune. At least in Cuba, the information suggests that African women became commonly known for the notable investment that they put in their work. They brought this custom from their cultures of origin in which women began to work from a very young age, held ample knowledge of business, and were involved in commercial activities. In this vast African continent, women continued to contribute decisively to the family economy even after marriage.

Although not mentioned in the judicial case, Belén must have held several jobs, first to collect the money for the self-purchase and then if freed from slavery to have sufficient money to sustain herself. Otherwise, she must have been able to keep working the same type of job as when she was a slave to be able to save money. This would have allowed her to start acquiring property that would yield short-term earnings. Additionally, freed slaves counted on the possibility of borrowing money from people, especially close ones, a common practice at the time. Although there are several receipts for loans of significant sums of money made by a man during the decade of the 1870s, unfortunately the records do not offer the reasons for the loans. Whatever the motive, Belén recovered because at the end of her life she held no debts of any kind.

A distinguishable aspect of these women was their ability to save money, necessary to enter the world of investment and to cope with everyday life. Even when their gains were not very big, far from keeping it or settling, they always tended to reinvest it in the purchase of more properties. Hence they were able to obtain greater profits that would allow them to expand their patrimony. In that sense, Belén is an exceptional example not only in accumulating a large sum of money for a black woman but also in keeping her money in a bank of the colonial government, which was usually distrusted and thus not a common practice among her peers.

At the end of her life Belén rented several houses that she owned; however, this does not mean that she was always in this business. Because gender and skin color limited black women's possibilities, they tended to diversify their efforts. They dedicated themselves to buying slaves, establishing small factories of different products, and providing washing, ironing, and sewing services inside their homes. They also mounted street stalls for the selling and resale of edible products. Those who lived a little farther away from the city bought land, animals, and slaves to dedicate themselves to the planting of different products. In this sense, it is worth noting that as the economic life of the cities was increasingly expensive and dynamic, it became common for freed entrepreneurial women to devote themselves to several activities simultaneously. The most common was to have slaves earning daily wages and to rent houses.

Although not listed in her inventory of goods, the possibility remains that Belén came to own one or several slaves. Buying slaves, besides being a symbol of social prestige, was in economic terms a safe investment in the short term dependent on the various skills slaves held individually. Their levels of experience at a skill, at least in the cities, meant they would be able to find work with relative ease and on some occasions hold several jobs at once to increase their earnings and especially to be able to save. Hence the slaves represented to the slave holder a stable means to secure small earnings in the short term and an accumulation of wealth in the long term.

Being a slave owner under such a situation explains why slaves were not listed in her judicial case, primarily because slaves were not considered the type of property acquired for life. Slaves could die of different causes, flee, acquire their freedom, or be sold by the masters for any reason. But in addition, attempting to control slaves required a concerted effort on the part of their owners. Additionally, some slaves problematically came to involve their masters in judicial matters.

By the time of her death, Belén's age and health condition meant she could no longer have had the stamina to own slaves, which would explain why she was only dedicated to renting houses. Additionally, Don José Valero and Don Fermín Fernández were the caretakers of the rooms and of one of the houses, respectively. They were also in charge of collecting the rents for both properties. Interestingly, while Belén was an ex-slave, her two male employees were white men. This detail shows that contrary to what Cuban historiography has posed about the existence of rigid racial barriers in nineteenth-century Cuba, in the lower levels of society, the racial frontiers used to be more flexible and crossed frequently and with ease.

I mention all the possibilities in which Belén could have amassed her savings because she could not have accomplished this only from profits from rents. Rent payments were unstable and very often renters simply disappeared without paying, especially after the first half of the nineteenth century. Therefore short of having won the Real Lottery, she must have had other means to build and especially keep her small personal fortune.

Belén, although fortunate in business, did not form a family of her own. As already stated, she did not have and thus could not rely on parents, a husband, or children. Although the personal effects of a man were found in her house at the time of her death, she was never legally married. Did she break from someone or did that person die before the opportunity for marriage arose? Unfortunately, these types of details will remain unknown. However, it is pertinent to mention that some women when they enjoyed an important economic solvency avoided legal marriage to circumvent the husband from legally managing her properties.

Regarding children, although there is a myth about the excessive fertility of black women, it is worth noting that many of them ended their lives without offspring. This did not always happen by personal decision as is often argued. In some cases, there were affective and medical reasons. Deeper research must be done on the topic, at least for Cuba. Some day when studies come forth on the topic, Belén would be one of many examples to be considered.

In the absence of a nuclear family (father, mother, and children), her brother, sister-in-law, and nieces constituted her closest relations. The facts that two of her nieces lived with her, were present in the house when she died, and came to know the history of their ancestors and how to locate the friends and people close to their aunt indicate that Belén's family loved her. In addition, her ethnic compatriots helped her niece Evarista to rescue her aunt's heritage after Belén's passing. This shows that the affective relationships of Africans transcended the frames of the nuclear and blood family.

This is what I interpret from the scarce sources available on Belén. Only one last question still haunts me: Why does a woman that keeps her business so organized not have a will and testament? Although at the beginning of the text I suggested her death might have been unexpected, her property inventory contained a medical chair for ailing people, suggesting that she might have dealt with a heart condition for some time. There could be several reasons for her missing will: personal carelessness, did not believe in the religious Catholic significance of this document, fear of facing one's mortality, not wanting to assume the expenses and emotional exhaustion implied in making a will, or possibly the family had already agreed in advance what to do when the worst happened. This last variant was a reason frequently used by many black families.

Lacking sources, we will never know the motives. There is limited documentation for the reasons already expressed, coupled with the prejudices of sex and race at the time. Moreover, other reasons include the arbitrary selection made by the scribes of the information that was collected in the judicial cases and the fact that the majority of Africans did not know how to read or write. Being unable to generate documents for themselves contributed to histories lost in time or having only a few pieces of life stories survive of so many valuable women, like our protagonist Belén Álvarez.

THE FAMILY ACCORDING TO THE TESTIMONIES OF NATIONAL SISTERS AND BROTHERS

As the closest family member, Evarista González, who was legally one of her nieces, initiated the case.[6] For this judicial procedure, Evarista had to present to the competent authorities her baptism certificate, her parents' marriage license, and the death certificate of her father, Agustín González, who was Belén's biological brother, to legally prove the blood link between them.

In the course of trying to rebuild her family before the law, the disorder of the slave regime on the affective and legal life of Africans became visible. The first obstacle was that Belén's parents married in Africa, where they remained. There was no written record on the Island that their marriage had taken place.

As the children of that union, Belén and Agustín were born in Lucumí land. Therefore there was no evidence that they were biological siblings and, to make matters worse, once on the Island as slaves of different masters, they did not even have the same surname. Given this situation, the only way for Evarista to demonstrate the blood link between the two was with family memories that had been transmitted to her and the affection she witnessed between her father and his sister Belén.

Evarista hired a lawyer to at least deal with the legal issues. He explained in an eloquent statement:

> The circumstance of having been imported to this island in a slave expedition prevents the *morenos* Agustín and Belén to bring to this court documentary that verifies their origins and proves that they shared the same parents.
>
> ... by fault of our laws, the introduction of blacks from Africa was carried out by surreptitious means, being therefore logical that one did not leave trace of any of those who were imported by this trade, held by this flawed commerce or of whom are being taken advantage. Therefore, there is no case that is analogous to the present that makes it possible to prove with documentation the origins of individuals brought to this island with those individuals that remained or existed in Africa.
>
> But that circumstance does deny, nor can it be an obstacle to the confirmation of parentage itself, or to the recognition of the right of the descendants or of the right to their collateral succeeded abintestate by individuals of that origin. The same Law of Civil Procedure [*Ley de Enjuiciamiento Civil*] has been a constant previewer, having in its article 978—applicable to the present case with the precept of article 982—that the heirs abintestate can justify their kinship with the persons of whose succession is in question and obtain a declaration of their rights with the evidence that is possible to bring forth in the absence of the corresponding documents, with witnesses of the intestate death and to the character of the inheritor.
>
> In establishing such a principle, the Law has been consistent as to the character of the witness statement attributed in the article 577 in which it considers it one of the means of proof that can be used in a trial.[7]

The different articles of the Law of Civil Procedure allowed the lawyer to use legally as evidence Evarista's family memories and the oral testimony of people who witnessed her parents' wedding in Africa that allowed them to "reconstruct" a family history solid enough to prove their claim to the authorities.

Evarista was told that her Aunt Belén was the daughter of Elocun Esí and Dadá in Africa, who were married according to the ritual and customs of their Lucumí nation. Two siblings were born from this union, Agustín (Oyó) and Belén (Luoco), who were brought to this Island on the same slave expedition. Once on the Island, Belén was sold to a Mr. Álvarez and her brother to Don Guillermo González. Their respective masters changed their first names and claimed them with their surname, which they kept until the time of their deaths as was the custom among many in Cuba. She also explained that since they arrived and until they died, both continued to call each other brother and sister and were treated as such by all their companions and friends.[8]

The lawyer's convincing narrative motivates some reflections. The fact that the siblings came together in the same boat with other people from the same hamlet and that by the time of their departure both parents were dead suggests the possibility that this tribe had been involved in some kind of war in which they were captured, sold as slaves to traffickers, and brought to the New World. Once on the Island, they had the "luck" of having been bought by owners who resided in the urban environment, which allowed them like many other family members to stay together and to remain in contact with the members of their old hamlet. Belén might not have married because of the impact of seeing her family destroyed, coupled with the condition of slavery in which they were brought to the Island. Agustín married the *morena* Loreto Gómez, also of the Lucumí nation, after fathering two daughters.

The lawyer appealed to the provisions in articles 577 and 978 of the Law of Civil Procedure when the authorities delayed issuing a final resolution.[9] He sought five witnesses, as old as possible, who lived in Africa in the same hamlet as Evarista's grandparents to recount Elocun Esí and Dadá's wedding and thus demonstrate that they formed a legitimate marriage according to the customs of their country. Additionally, the lawyer presented three other witnesses who were not African to make declarations on the relationship of the siblings on the Island. Most likely, he used this last strategy to appease the possible doubts or resentment by those in charge in issuing a resolution based on so many testimonies of Africans.

One of the African witnesses of the Lucumí nation, sixty-seven-year-old Jorge Soto, testified, "Since they were small, their parents agreed that they should marry and when they grew up, the father of the male paid for the female with effects and in work as agreed upon. Then, the couple and their families went to a place where there was an elder who did and said several things; who knows what he said. He poured water on their heads and they were married. They spent the next eight or nine days celebrating."[10]

Another declarant, Luis Pastrana, free black of the Lucumí nation, day laborer, and seventy-seven years old, was more detailed in his testimony: "The elders met and after finding that they did not belong to a different nation nor had any contagious diseases, decided that their marriage would not inconvenience them. Then, an elder that is like a priest in this country, married them and advised them on their marriage. After, everyone celebrated with great amusement and at the end of eight or nine days the bride visited all of their acquaintances."[11]

Interestingly, all the witnesses were from the small town of Regla. Belén did not live there but her nieces did. Perhaps the witnesses knew her aunt but also had a close friendship with her three nieces. This hamlet had several community councils. This raised the question as to whether they belonged to any and hence the durability of their affective bonds.

The questions asked by the authorities were prepared and presented in advance by the lawyer. The witnesses might have already known them, which facilitated the similarities in their answers. However, there were some discrepancies; not everyone remembered Belén's true name in Africa. Significantly, they all mentioned that Belén and Agustín's parents were married, arguing that in their land only those who were husband and wife lived together.

What is observable in the judicial case is that the scribe selected details of their testimonies, eliminating some of their richness, as shown by his rushed notes. Regardless, the scarce lines still show some of the true traditions of their cultures.

Their witness statements could awaken doubt; however, they contain many details that are true. It is also very possible that Evarista was able to find several people who witnessed and remembered the wedding despite being so far away in time and space. Additionally, shipments of slaves that arrived in the ports of Havana often brought Africans from the same nation, tribe, and even from the same village or hamlet, as apparently happened in this case.

Due to the hustling movement in the cities, the presence of a significant number of Africans (free and slave), and the dynamic communication that existed among them, they were able to hear news when family members or acquaintances landed in Havana whom they would try to contact. If possible, they would attempt to help them at all costs. There are examples of free blacks who bought their relatives or asked someone to purchase them for a later payment. With luck, new arrivals would be bought by masters residing in the city, which would create the opportunity for their relatives to take it upon themselves to seek them out and restore the bonds that they believed had been broken forever.

Those details permitted many Africans to remake the family or friendship ties they had had in their homelands. Despite the rules imposed on them and the new living conditions in a country totally unknown to them, they created new family networks including with others of their own or different nations and to their descendants born on the island who became heirs and safeguards of their culture. The ability to create such strong ties between them is an aspect that relates less to slavery and more to clan solidarity, an essential characteristic for the tribes in Africa and that slaves and their descendants reproduced on the Island.

In the absence of documentation left by our ancestors about their customs and traditions in their lands of origin, testimonies such as these, which are very scarce, are deeply revealing for the details they offer.

The fact that Elocun Esí and Dadá's parents had agreed on the wedding because their children were small indicates that arranged marriages were a custom among the people of their nation. The children grew up with the certainty that they were destined to marry a person chosen by their parents. They accepted their decision. This included accepting the family that was chosen in advance with the consequent responsibilities that it implied and showing respect and obedience to their blood family, the clan or tribe, and the hierarchies within them.

The motives for the arranged marriage are not mentioned in the documents; however, probably both families had an interest in fixing the union. In such cases, economic interests weigh heavily, but there were also social, political, and religious reasons. On occasion, the agreement sought to establish alliances or to strengthen connections between different families to achieve peace at certain times or to be better prepared in the times of intertribal warfare.

The couple and their parents needed to meet certain premarital requirements before the wedding could take place. The witnesses probably did not mention everything, especially those related to the sexual preparation of women and men, but at least they mentioned the most important prerequisites. One of them was that the father of the male made the necessary payment to the bride's family in kind and in work, and the other was to verify that the bride and groom were of the same nation, held moral integrity, were physically healthy, and especially that they did not carry malignant diseases.

After a wedding date was set, they performed a bridal ceremony sanctified by the highest religious figure among them who also spoke about the foundation on which a marriage should be built. The wedding was followed by a celebration with their relatives that lasted for days, after which the new wife was presented in society to be accepted and recognized by all. A significant custom among them was that only after they were married could the couple live together and build their own family. Belén and Agustín's parents fulfilled this tradition, living together in their land until the moment of their death.

The history of Belén Álvarez's parents obliges a momentary digression to discuss the marriage practices in Africa. Unfortunately, documentation on the topic is very scarce in our country, not only the specific studies regarding customs and traditions in precolonial Africa but also literature that has been produced worldwide on the subject. Despite this limitation, we will outline the essential characteristics of marriage in West Africa in one of the geographical areas with the most human flow to the Island: the Yoruba. Belén and her brother Agustín were among them.

Though hundreds of Africans came from different nations and especially from different tribes with dissimilar cultural experiences according to the geographical environment in which they lived and the degree of socioeconomic development among them, they shared the most important requirements for marriage.

Statements submitted by Evarista's witnesses coincide to a great extent with the researcher Heriberto Feraudy's findings on the marriage practices between the Lucumí-Yoruba. He found that marriages were determined from an early age and in certain cases even before the birth of the girl. Despite this, the ages for marriage were late, ranging from thirty years of age for men and between twenty and twenty-five years of age for women. Men needed to remain with their family and thus wait to marry until their eldest sisters were married. Hence only wealthy people could afford to marry couples in their youth.

The "search for a maiden" was led by the male's female relatives on the paternal side: sisters, aunts, and cousins were in charge of finding a suitable bride. One of the most important requirements to be fulfilled was that neither party have hereditary diseases such as leprosy, epilepsy, dementia, or alcoholism, among others. Besides physical health, both families also investigated the moral qualities and social attitudes of the parents of the future husband and wife. Once the groom's representative presented the petition to the bride's family, they had up to three months to discuss the proposal. The definitive answer was provided by Ifá, the family oracle.[12]

After the family announces that Ifá had spoken well (acceptance of the suitor), they performed a very important nocturnal ceremony known as Ishihum (opening or lifting of the voice) accompanied by a great party attended exclusively by the bride-to-be and her relatives. During this celebration they drank beer and ate food. Kola nuts were also distributed among everyone present to serve as witnesses of the courtship. Without this activity, the commitment of the bride was not considered valid. The wedding would be carried out after a period of approximately ten years. During that time, the intended and their families dedicated themselves to getting to know each other and exchanging gifts during festivities and celebrations.[13]

After Isihun, the endowment to Aña is realized, which consisted of the bridegroom giving Kola nuts, crocodile pepper, and bitter cola to the parents of the bride, as well as a fine gown of good quality, a long length of fabric, a head tie, and a specified amount of money that varied according to the groom's economic possibilities. Additionally, the groom had to work for a while for the father of the bride.[14]

Weddings took place generally after the harvests and the festival of Égungun. They lasted about three days and before leaving to the groom's paternal house, the bride received the blessing and advice of her parents as to her duties, obeying her husband, and respecting her in-laws and his other wives.[15]

The most important point according to Feraudy is that women in Yoruba land seldom married without parental consent or rarely rejected the choice made by their parents. Additionally, virginity at the time of marriage was a factor of great importance, and the moment when the commitment became official gave the husband exclusive sexual rights of his bride-to-be. Nonfulfilment by the female was motive for public derision of the woman.[16]

It should be stressed that the Yoruba Lucumí practiced several types of marriage. One of them required the necessary parental consent to do so. Another required the father to offer the bride as a gift. There was also one that was carried out by mutual consent without family intervention. Last, another type of marriage occurred when the husband died without children; then the brother had to marry the widowed sister-in-law (Mosaic Law). Thus it can be inferred from the testimonies that Elocun Esí and Dadá were married according to the marriage codes that required family consent.[17]

Women in the villages, with the exception of the very elderly, did not remain single. According to their traditions, a husband was necessary for her protection and so someone could be made responsible for her. They were allowed to marry only once in their lives. Remarriage was not allowed under any conditions. They could divorce only under extreme and justifiable conditions. In this way, a woman would join the husband's family for life because in the case that the woman was widowed, she could only remarry her husband's brother. These same traditions, so strict on the women, permitted men to have as many wives as they wanted as long as they had the money to pay for their ceremonies and maintain them.[18]

The Yoruba were not the only people to follow these traditions. Similar matrimonial practices are found deeper into Africa and in other areas among other tribes. The Mandigas were another multiethnic group with an important presence in the country and whose nuptials shared similarities with the Yoruba peoples.

According to the researcher Madina Ly, among the Mandiga, matrimony was not an individual act but one that centered on the family. In their case, the chief—owner of the wealth and estate and the only person in charge of these—was the one who searched for brides for his men. Once he located one, then a ritual could be initiated in an attempt to establish an agreement to marry.[19]

The brothers of the father were petitioned. The family doing the petitioning sent ten Kola nuts to the relatives of the young woman, after which the uncles of the girl gathered the men of the family to inform them of the request. The uncles took their time to answer, making inquiries about the family of the suitor. They usually took a number of days to reply, ranging between one week and fifteen days according to their level of queries. Upon their decision, the family of the young woman would thus make an announcement that their Kola nuts had been accepted. Apparently, their decisions were more based on the human will than that of a divine oracle. As the bride was being sought, at no time did the groom have any knowledge of the acts of his family nor could he view his bride-to-be.[20]

However, once the proposal was accepted, the bride began to get to know her future family-in-law. She would spend three durations of time with them, in which she dedicated herself to getting to know her future in-laws and becoming familiar with her new chores inside the house and in the field. Once familiar with her future responsibilities, the families then agreed to celebrate the wedding.[21]

Two important formalities preceded the wedding ceremony. The first was the ablation of the clitoris.[22] This ceremony was accompanied by a great celebration if the families could afford it. The second was the payment that the groom gave to his bride's family.[23] The bride returned to her family with the dowry of baskets filled with rice or millet, cotton, gold, silver, cows, and even slaves if the groom's family was rich. As among the Lucumí-Yoruba, the wedding night was essential for the groom, thus family and community assured the virginity of the bride. Her virginity was proof of her morality and good manners. If a virgin, the grateful bridegroom would also give salt to her mother. If not, the other wives and family-in-law would subject the bride to all kinds of humiliation including tying her to a post and whipping her until she bled.

Likewise, among the Mandiga, women entered a family for life. Hence if she was widowed, she was married to a younger brother of the deceased. Infidelity and female adultery were severely punished. Divorce rarely occurred because marriages were arranged between families and divorce could cause family breakdowns. However, the man could have all the wives that his economic possibilities allowed him, although the family was in charge of fulfilling the formalities of marriage only in the case of the first wife.

These two examples are similar to marriage practices among peoples in Africa. In essence, they all paid a dowry for their future wives. While hunting, fishing, and raising small livestock constituted economic lines of considerable importance, agriculture remained their fundamental economy. Therefore payment was made with the products they harvested or raised such as Kola nuts, Auris shells, cattle (very important), and other objects of value. It was customary for the groom to work for some time before the wedding for the parents of the bride. Weddings included prenuptial and postnuptial ceremonies. Except for well-established exceptions, polygamy (the right of the man to have several wives) predominated, patrilineal in their affiliations and patrilocal in the postnuptial residence.[24]

These conditions point to the conclusion that among some of the ethnolinguistic groups that arrived on the Island, especially those that achieved greater numerical presence, they already knew the practice of marriage and held stable relationships of kinship before their arrival to this part of the world. African marriage, more than a simple tradition, was a whole institution from early on in these societies. Marriage went beyond the couple but also involved the material and spiritual interests of families (blood and political) and the clan or tribe. Because it involved the whole community, marriage necessitated economic, social, and spiritual preparation.

The need for several steps in this institution, the explanations of what these symbolized, as well as the rituality that accompanied each of these moments show that contrary to what slave traders reported during this time and what historians reproduced, Africans grew up under very severe, even rigid, values with respect for the family, paternal obedience, and moral-social precepts. These traditions were very peculiar to their different cultures and different, in turn, to those that existed in Europe or other parts of the world. These differences were used as a convenient pretext to disparage Africans and categorize them as savages before humanity. Unfortunately, this legacy has lasted in time, becoming myths, some of which are still used today as propaganda against the African origin population.

Regarding Evarista González, she was finally able to prove to the authorities with her memories and the testimonies of her African brethren that she was the legitimate niece of Belén Álvarez and the granddaughter of Elocun Esí and Dadá. In February 1888, she was declared the sole heiress and inherited the patrimony, including the savings in the bank, that her aunt built with so much effort.

NOTES

1. Among the most recent studies in Cuba are: María del Carmen Barcia Zequeira, "Mujeres en torno a Minerva" [Women on Minerva], *La Rábida*, Huelva, no. 17 (1998): 113–21; *Mujeres al margen de la historia* [Women at the Margins of History] (Havana: Editorial de Ciencias Sociales, 2009); Digna Castañeda Fuertes, "La mujer esclava en Cuba durante la primera mitad del siglo XIX" [Slave Black Women in Cuba in the First Half of the Nineteenth Century], *Anales del Caribe* [Annals of the Caribbean], Casa de las Américas, Havana, no. 13 (1993–1994): 53–69; Gloria García Rodriguez, *La Esclavitud desde la esclavitud: La visión de los siervos* [Slavery from the Perspective of the Enslaved] (Mexico: Centro de Investigación Científica Ing. Jorge L. Tamayo, A.C., 1996); Oilda Hevia Lanier, "Otra contribución a la historia de los negros sin historia" [Another Contribution to the History of Blacks Without History], *Revista Semestral de Estudios Históricos y Socioculturales: Debates Americanos* [Biannual Journal of Historical and Sociocultural Studies: American Debates], Havana, no. 4 (July–December 1997): 77–89; Daysi Rubiera Castillo, *La mujer de color en Cuba* [Women of Color in Cuba] (Havana: Editorial Academia, 1996); *Reyita, sencillamente (Testimonio de una negra cubana nonagenaria)* [Simply Reyita: Testimony of a Nonagenarian Black Cuban Woman] (Havana: Prolibros, Instituto

Cubano del Libro, 1996); and Josefina Toledo Benedit, *La madre negra de Martí* [The Black Mother of Martí] (Havana: Casa Editorial Verde Olivo, 2009).

2. Levi Marrero and Alejandro de la Fuente agree in their respective works that since the end of the sixteenth century, Havana became an important port city receiving annually thousands of consumers who needed to be fed, housed, and entertained. Slaves and freed *mulatos* provided these services and almost monopolized the important tertiary sector of Havana. In particular, women controlled many of these economic spaces because they managed taverns, hostels, and kitchens. Most of the taverns and hostels of the city, estimated at eighty in 1673, were owned or operated by women. As washerwomen, cooks, and street vendors, they also serviced a growing number of soldiers stationed in Havana.

3. María del Carmen Barcia Zequeira, *La otra familia: Parientes, redes y descendencia de los esclavos en Cuba* [The Other Family: Relatives, Networks and Descendancy of Slaves in Cuba] (Fondo Editorial Casa de las Américas, 2003); Aisnara Perera Díaz y María de los Ángeles Meriño, *Esclavitud, familia y parroquia en Cuba: Otra mirada desde la microhistoria* [Slavery, Family and Parishes in Cuba: Another Microhistorical Look] (Santiago de Cuba: Editorial Oriente, 2009).

4. According to Dr. María del Carmen Barcia in an article titled "The Ten Biggest Myths About the Black Family" published in 1990, among the ten great myths that have spread against slave families are the myth that the family is a product of white paternalism through the government's welfare program and the myth that black men are incapable of establishing stable parenting relationships (Lerone Bennett Jr., "The Ten Biggest Myths About the Black Family," *Ebony*, Chicago, no. 1 [1990]: 16, cited by Maria del Carmen Barcia in *La otra familia*).

5. National Archive of Cuba, Intestado de la morena Belén Álvarez [Intestate of . . .], Escribanía de Gobierno, file 864, collection folder 9.

6. Ibid.

7. The Law of Civil Procedure was published by Real Decreto [decree] of September 25, 1885, in Cuba and Puerto Rico by the cabinet of Amadeo Sagasta, and it was an adaptation of another law by the same name (LEC) that had existed in Spain since 1881.

8. National Archive of Cuba, Intestado de la morena Belén Álvarez [Intestate of . . .], Escribanía de Gobierno, folio 114.

9. Ibid., folio 120.

10. Ibid., folio 134.

11. Ibid., folio 132.

12. Heriberto Feraudy Espino, *Yoruba. Un acercamiento a nuesta raíces* [An Encounter with Our Roots] (Havana: Editorial Política, 1993), 68–70.

13. Ibid.

14. Ibid.

15. Ibid.

16. On the wedding night, two women slept outside the matrimonial bedroom to listen to the moans or cries of the bride losing her virginity. If the bride was not a virgin, they would leave immediately. The bride would be punished by being tied and whipped until she confessed who violated her. Additionally, a symbolic message

would be sent to her parents meant to reproach and disparage her and them because the family would also be shamed. However, a virgin bride pleased everyone. The white marriage sheet stained with her blood was used to announce her virginity as it was placed over a pumpkin. The next day, the groom would send the cloth to her parents along with a sum of money and a chicken to be sacrificed in the name of the bride. Later, he would visit her parents accompanied by his friends to show his gratitude and joy. Espino, *Yoruba. Un acercamiento a nuesta raíces*.

17. Ibid.

18. Ibid.

19. Ly claims that when the head of the family visited a place where the birth of a girl was occurring, the synchronicity of his visit with the child's birth was considered part of the child's destiny and his luck. The child was thus formally promised to his family until the girl was a young woman and ready for marriage. During that time of maturation, they remained unfamiliar to each other. Other ways the head of the family married his men was by turning to his sisters' daughters, a less costly alternative, or by looking for young women in other villages, in which case he had to find a respectable intermediary capable of making the request who lived in that village (Madina Ly, "La mujer en la sociedad mandiga precolonial" [Women in Precolonial Mandiga Society], in *La mujer africana en la sociedad precolonial* [African Women in Precolonial Society], edited by Achola O. Pala and Madina Ly [Serbal/Unesco, 1982], 188–89).

20. Though the men of the family appear to make the final decision, in practice, the girl's parents could oppose a request for marriage. The mother could contribute to the decision by giving her opinion but always through her husband (Pala and Ly, *La mujer africana en la sociedad precolonial*, 189).

21. The first visit was called *bolonda yira*. The bride-to-be would spend time with the eldest woman in the family learning small household chores. The second visit was the *sali deguesusu*, in which she learned how to make the *degue* (a type of mix of flour with condiments and milk) and participated in all of the household chores. The last visit was called *kolotomo*, which she spent participating in field work and in the harvest of *karité* (Pala and Ly, *La mujer africana en la sociedad precolonial*, 90).

22. The ablation or excision of the clitoris is a ceremony on the body as part of longer processes of initiation for young women in African societies. The ceremony initiated young women into womanhood and authorized them for sexual relations and motherhood. The ceremony excised sexual ambivalence, differentiating the initiated women as adults. The ceremony was conducted by women skilled in the act who also contained great knowledge of medicinal plants. The mother-in-law of the future bride would prepare everything necessary (that is, her gown and food) ahead of time. Both families would pay for this ceremony according to their economic capacities. The ceremony was celebrated a day prior to the event with food, music, and dance. The operation would take place the morning after. The initiated women would spend several days healing, cared for by a senior woman who educated them on sex and how they should conduct themselves in marriage. Once healed, a woman with great spiritual leadership would prepare a large dish of rice that the women would eat in the sacred wooded area outside of the hamlet. The women returned to their village

at night, swearing secrecy of everything they saw and heard during and after the ceremony. Their initiation was thus finalized. This ceremony was similar to one for men called circumcision. It included parallel practices (Pala and Ly, *La mujer africana en la sociedad precolonial*, 191).

23. According to the researcher Paly, the dowry is an institution that characterizes the societies in which the inheritance is governed by patrilineal principles and passed down to the sons. Women don't inherit and neither do their daughters. It was the husband's family that gave the cattle and other goods to the bride's family. This act fulfilled several social functions. It symbolized the transfer of the productive capacity of a woman (in the matter of work and procreation) of her family to that of her husband. It guaranteed the right of use of the daughters and the inheritance rights of the children of the marriage. It solidified the hopes and obligations among the families involved. The payment ensured the fate and protection of the woman to her family because the dowry was divided among the whole family. Additionally, it guaranteed that the husband would build her house and give her land to cultivate and farm. If the married couple disagreed, the wife could seek refuge in either her family or in-laws' home. Men did not have this right even in the case of divorce (Paly and Ly, *La mujer africana en la sociedad precolonial*, 88).

24. Jesús Guanche, *Componentes étnicos de la nación cubana* [Ethnic Components of the Cuban Nation] (Havana: Ediciones Unión, 1996), 56–57; Instituto Cubano de Geodesia y Cartografia [Cuban Institute of Geodesy and Cartography], *Atlas de Historia Moderna* [Atlas Modern History] (Havana: Empresa de Cartografia, 1986), 24; *Atlas de historia contemporánea* [Atlas of Contemporary History] (Havana: Empresa de Cartografia, 1985).

BIBLIOGRAPHY

Barcia Zequeira, María del Carmen. 1998. "Mujeres en torno a Minerva." *La Rábida*, no. 17. Huelva.

———. 2003. *La otra familia: Parientes, redes y descendencia de los esclavos en Cuba*. Fondo Editorial Casa de las Américas.

———. 2009. *Mujeres al margen de la historia*. Havana: Editorial de Ciencias Sociales.

Castañeda Fuertes, Digna. 1993–1994. "La mujer esclava en Cuba durante la primera mitad del siglo XIX." *Anales del Caribe*, no. 13. Havana: Casa de las Américas.

De La Fuente, Alejandro. 2004. "La esclavitud, la ley y la reclamación de derechos en Cuba: repensando el debate de Tannenbaum." *Debate y Perspectiva, Cuadernos de Historia y Ciensias Sociales* December, no. 4.

———. 2004. "Su único derecho. Los esclavos y la Ley." *Debate y Perspectiva, Cuadernos de Historia y Ciensias Sociales* December, no. 4.

Deschamps Chapeaux, Pedro. 1970. *El negro en la economía habanera del siglo XIX*. Havana: UNEAC.

Feraudy Espino, Heriberto. 1993. *Yoruba. Un acercamiento a nuesta raíces*. Havana: Editorial Política.

Fuentes, Guerra, Jesús. 2003. *Al sur del Zambezi. Un tratado de religión africana.* Cuba: Ediciones Mecenas, Cienfuegos.

García Rodriguez, Gloria. 1996. *La Esclavitud desde la esclavitud: La visión de los siervos.* Mexico: Centro de Investigación Científica Ing. Jorge L. Tamayo.

———. 2004. "Los cabildos de nación: organización, vicisitudes y tensiones internas (1780–1868)." *Del Caribe*, no. 43. Santiago de Cuba.

Guanche, Jesús. 1996. *Componentes étnicos de la nación cubana.* Havana: Ediciones Unión.

Hevia Lanier, Oilda. 1997. "Otra contribución a la historia de los negros sin historia." *Revista Semestral de Estudios Históricos y Socioculturales: Debates Americanos*, July–December, no. 4. Havana.

Hierrezuelo, María Cristina. 2006. *Las olvidadas hijas de Eva.* Santiago de Cuba: Ediciones Santiago.

Instituto Cubano de Geodesia y Cartografía [Cuban Institute of Geodesy and Cartography]. 1985. *Atlas de historia contemporánea.* Havana: Empresa de Cartografía.

———. 1986. *Atlas de Historia Moderna.* Havana: Empresa de Cartografía.

Marrero, Levy. 1983. *Cuba, Economía y sociedad.* Madrid: Editorial Playor. S.A., I-X.

O. Pala, Achola and Madina Ly. 1982. *La mujer africana en la sociedad precolonial.* Serbal/Unesco.

Perrera Díaz, Aisnara, and María de Los Ángeles Meriño. 2006. *Esclavitud, familia y parroquia en Cuba. Otra mirada desde la microhistoria.* Santiago de Cuba: Editorial Oriente.

———. 2009. *Para librarse de lazos, antes buena familia que buenos brazos. Apuntes sobre la manumisión en Cuba.* Santiago de Cuba: Editorial Oriente.

Rubiera Castillo, Daysi. 1996. *La mujer de color en Cuba.* Havana: Editorial Academia.

———. 1996. *Reyita, sencillamente (Testimonio de una negra cubana nonagenaria).* Havana: Prolibros, Instituto Cubano del Libro.

Stolcke, Verena. 1992. *Racismo y sexualidad en la Cuba colonial.* Madrid: Alianza Editorial.

Toledo Benedit, Josefina. 2009. *La madre negra de Martí.* Havana: Casa Editorial Verde Olivo.

Chapter 3

Women "of Color" in Santiaguera Colonial Society

A Commentary

María Cristina Hierrezuelo

Works such as *Blacks in the Havana Economy of the Nineteenth Century* by Pedro Deschamps Chapeaux and *Blacks in Colonial Society* by Rafael Duharte Jiménez offer valuable analysis of how, despite the discriminatory codes prevalent in Cuban colonial society, a significant number of blacks, *pardos*, and *mulatos* managed to achieve an economic solvency coupled with an undeniable social ascent even though it could never be equated with that of whites. Analysis and examples on the topic have relied on men in the context of ingrained differences between blacks and whites, rich and poor, free and slave. The daughters of Eve in whose veins ran African blood were presumed to share little to none of the socioeconomic mobility of the men of their race.

Diego Velásquez founded Santiago de Cuba in the summer of 1515, which received the first Africans in the year 1522. Manumission and *mestizaje* emerged with such celerity that before the sixteenth century ended, *pardos*, blacks, and *mulatos* who held the condition of free became a visible population in multiple productive activities. Among these jobs was commerce, which appears in the first municipal ordinances or as they were called ordinances of Cáceres established in the year 1573. Article 50 indicated "that no one can sell wine by way of black labor, nor can it be sold by a *negra horra* [free black], nor as Innkeeper, unless he was a person of trust who has been granted a license by the city council to do so."[1]

Free black women wine vendors whose reliability was authorized with a license required for the sale of drinks constituted the genesis of the group of free women of color that in the nineteenth century came to hold a protagonist role in many of the economic activities in the development of the city.

Other women of color entered the bourgeois class because of their various properties and from the position of owners contributed in a discreet way to the economic development of the jurisdiction of Cuba in general and the city of Santiago de Cuba in particular.

Regional historiography has not sufficiently recovered the social reality of the colonial Santiaguero past, which has prevented us from knowing with certainty the socioeconomic conditions under which women of color of Santiago de Cuba lived. This historiographic gap contrasts notably with the abundant information contained in the archive of documentation and the press of the time and that allow discovery of a small part of the psychosocial universe in which these forgotten daughters of Eve advanced. Thanks to this we can know, among other aspects, the economic resources that they managed to have and with opportunity allowed them to carve a small pocket of capital and— *"why not?"*—to develop their lives as good bourgeois women.

ECONOMIC RESOURCES ACHIEVED INDIVIDUALLY OR ACCOMPANIED

The protocol notary of the time collected innumerable operations of the purchase and sale of slaves, houses, roofing, docks, small plots of land, lowlands for tobacco, and haciendas by women of color, which provide a sample of what this population owned in the dynamic economy of the territory. Wills are also an irreplaceable source for knowing the properties that some of these black women managed to accumulate. Though often thought otherwise, a large number of women declared themselves owners of at least the property they inhabited, to owning slaves, gold and silver garments, domestic animals, a meadow, hacienda, or fine furniture. These inventories of black, *parda*, and *mulata* property-owning women, where in many cases the protagonists were ex-slave women, acquire greater significance. It is no exaggeration or impassioned claim to observe that this was an impressive feat given that they were sometimes able to accumulate superior estates.

To evade the monotony that enters any enumeration, I will cite only some examples, as in the case of María Gregoria Boza. Native of Africa, she was not able to notarize her will because she was not able to "name her parents who remained in their place of birth from where they sent her to this place at a very young age."[2] María Gregoria was married to Juan Manuel Boza who, like her, was a slave to Don Agustín Boza. Among her goods were a dock of wood and tile and a hut of similar materials. Both were located in the alley of San Bartolomé. She also owned an interior attic of wood and tile in the street of Providence, twelve slaves, two silver spoons and a fork, two gold rings, a copper pot, and the furniture sets of her house.

Similar to the case of María Gregoria was that of Mercedes Bosa from the Mandinga nation. She was married by law to Santiago Bosa. She did not have children before or after the marriage. She declared in her will to be the owner of a dock with its corresponding yard on Calle San Carlos. She also owned seven slaves, four of them grown and three boys.[3]

Antonia Sagarra, born also in a region in Africa, remained single, which did not prevent her from having seven children who, at the time of her will and testament, were underage. In her testament, she claimed a coffee plantation called San Pablo, located in the quarter of Damajayabo, composed of five *caballerias* [165.81 acres] of land with its farming equipment, farmhouse and other belongings, and an endowment of five slaves. Additionally, she owned a lean-to (*colgadizo*) with its own plot of land by the entrance of Caney.[4]

Antonia Palacios was also yanked from her native Africa and thrown into the city of Santiago de Cuba. She was stripped of the most precious thing a human being has: freedom. The assets she achieved and declared in her will must have cost her great effort, austerity, and sacrifice. She was married to Moises Palacios and the mother of five children. Both her husband and three of her children were enslaved at the time when she wrote her will and testament. She claimed a lean-to, a small plot of land with fruit trees, and two horses, which all constituted her small wealth,[5] achieved without a doubt with great personal effort given that her husband even after marriage and after having five children remained in a state of servitude.

Without a doubt, Victorina Bell is a formidable example of a former slave who accumulated significant wealth. A black woman of the nation Carabalí,[6] Bell was a slave to the Bell Irady family and married the slave Henry Bell. She declared in her will that she was able to acquire her freedom long before her husband, whose freedom she purchased in 1821. He did not bring any wealth or property to the marriage.

Victorina Bell managed to foster capital thanks to the work that she developed with constancy and dynamism since she became free and because of loans by her former mistress Dona Catalina Irady. Having been a slave once, Bell came to own a small coffee hacienda located in a half *caballería* of land [15.1 acres], while in another establishment she possessed four horses to carry loads and an appreciable number of domestic animals, besides another small plantation of coffee, with several small houses covered with guano, and equipment necessary for farming.

As for urban properties, she owned a lean-to where she lived in the wide street of the Enramadas, near the square of Plaza de Marte, built on someone else's land. She rented it for seventeen pesos a year, including the furniture. She also owned a house situated on land that she owned contiguous to her own home,[7] another lean-to on Calle del Cedro Street,[8] and an additional lean-to on the street of San Juan Nepomuceno, where she also had a plot of land that she rented out. At the time of testifying for her will (January 10, 1838), she claimed she was in verbal proceedings with Mr. Charles Delisle for the purchase of a small lean-to, located in the Street del Cedro for a price of 150 pesos, whose rent, as agreed, belonged to him since the month of November of the previous year when she established the agreement with the new owner.

As happened to many former slaves, Victorina Bell was caught in the network of the society in which she lived and became a slaver. On her small coffee plantation, she had an endowment of eleven slaves. They appeared as Tomás of the Apa nation; Antonio of Carabalí ethnicity; Ana, also Carabalí, with her three children named José, Cayetano, and Isidoro; and Loreto, from the Congo, with his son Jose de Santos. Dolores, mother of Juana, María Francisca, and Concepción, together with three more slaves were at Bell's service in the city.

The number of slaves destined for domestic service and the amount of clothing and accessories for personal use testify to the standard of living Victorina Bell achieved. Her will included a chain of fine gold, a pair of earrings of fine pearls and topazes, a pair of fine pearl earrings, a pair of gold cigar cutters, earrings of small corals, and some of ordinary corals. She also expressed that the title of possessions belonging to her husband be removed and that a list of slaves be excluded from the body of her private property: Isabel, Dolores, and her children Juan and Caridad, as well as Ana and her daughter named Socorro. They were all granted their absolute freedom the day following Bell's death. She named Dolores the heir of her estate. Thus, inheriting her mistress's wealth added a new page to the long history of women slaves who in reaching the condition of free came to possess goods. These former slaves ascended economically and entered into the controversial world of the black and *mulato* bourgeoisie of colonial Santiago.

It is almost certain that protected in her new economic position Dolores could not evade the trap extended by colonial society and became a slaver. A question can be raised: How is it possible that a person of the black race, a woman who was a former slave, could come to possess slaves and submit them to the regime of punishments, vexations, and humiliations that she herself suffered or that she saw her companions of misfortune suffer that included her own loved ones? There could be many answers. However, none should be formulated under a racial prism because then it might leave out the reasons used to justify these slavers of color as if their slaves had been white. The pigmentation of the skin of the slaver should never be an argument to wield when slavery is concerned. Doing so risks giving relevance to the racial aspect and minimizing the human. Therefore any response must start from an elementary principle: the position they assumed in their time to repudiate or not the validity of slavery and consequently the need to eliminate or maintain it.

Paulina and Eusebio Bell, both from the Carabalí nation, married when they were slaves of the family Bell Irady, which prevented them from attaining wealth during their marriage. In the testament of their will, they disclosed of owning a *cafetalito* [small coffee plantation] located in Guaninicum with twenty-six slaves of both sexes and of different ages and castes, a lean-to in Plaza de Marte built on its own property site, another in Enramadas No. 4, and a plot in Santa Úrsula along with household goods and furnishings.[9]

Given the opportunity, old slaves expressed truly interesting testimonies as shown in the legacies and declarations of their heirs. Occasionally, some former slaves reflected on their relationships that included the families they had once served. Their relationships show an almost mystical affection that rose above the rigors and cruelties of the regime of servitude, their sufferings, the vexations and ill-treatment received, and the grudges and fears that actually distanced the master and slave. In her will, Victorina Bell left to "my lady," the daughter of her former master, Doña Ana Maria Bell de Becerra, a chain of fine gold "as a small memory" of the affection she held for her since her tender age. She also decided to leave forty pesos to Eusebio Bell, fifty to Pedro Alcántara Bell, and fifty to Clemente Bell, black men, as a memory of the good friendship they had shared. Who were these men? What united them to Victorina? The presence of the surname Bell in all of them indicates a common trunk, the master, which reveals the affective relations that arose among the slaves belonging to the same owner, which logically were conditioned by their common coexistence and did not end when they obtained their letters of freedom. The affective bonds were passed down to the descendants of these former companions who had shared in the common misfortune of slavery.

María Agustina del Pozo's situation was different. She was born free unlike María Gregoria Boza, Merecedes Bosa, Antonia Sagarra, Antonia Palacios, Victorina Bell, Paulina Bell, and many others who would make this an unending list. She was married but had no children. At the time when she made her will and testament, she was the owner of a small fortune consisting of a house in the street of La Palma (San Basilio), a country estate named Tibisial in the Ermitaño region where she had three slaves and some birds. Additionally, she had five slaves in the city and a mare valued at half price.[10]

María Teresa Carvajal was also born free. She declared in her will that she possessed a wood and tile lean-to and a corresponding small plot of tax-free land, two slaves (one of them between twelve or thirteen years of age and the other a child of two months), house furniture, and various items, including a bracelet, a rosary and four gold crosses, four rings, a pair of cigar cutters, a pair of earrings, and a pair of yokes, all gold.

María Gertrudis Cruzata also came into the world as a free woman. She was the mother of ten children born in marriage with Carlos de la Rosa. In her will, she declared a small fortune composed of half of the lean-to where she lived, an estate located in the place called Aguacate with their houses, nine bovines, four horses, seventy beehives, two sows, and a slave.

Nicolasa Angulo, a *parda*, amassed a larger estatae.[11] She lived on Carnicería Street and was the natural daughter of Margarita Rizo. Nicolasa came to possess two lean-tos: one of wood and tile that served as her housing with an interior factory and a plot of land and the other also located on Carnicería Street, with its own tax-free plot of land. She owned a hacienda in Juan Angola, which was leased by a *mulato* named Felipe for seventy pesos a year. Additionally, she owned five mules, two horses, one hundred hens, three pigs, one sow, and a dozen ducks. Among the property of Nicolasa Angulo were twenty-eight slaves, thirteen of whom worked in the Juan Angola estate. Five worked as ranchers and two were rented out. The remaining eight were destined for the service of the lady of the house, which is an indicator of the conditions of leisure and well-being in which she lived, and which might have been common for women of color that reached a solid economic position.

There are not a lot of testimonies on this. Those left by travelers who visited the city during the nineteenth century, for obvious reasons, do not refer to the behavior of the black bourgeois in the domestic environment. However, their behavior must have been similar to other wealthy women, even those that were white. Without a doubt, Nicolasa would have rocked during the whole day fanned by a servant. She must have occupied her hands with weaving or embroidering that she would interrupt to take a nap, tend to herself, and attend the multiple festivities established by the church, visit friends, do some shopping in the city, stop by the house of the dressmaker, host those who visited her, or take the food produced by her slave cook to her friends. This slave, bought by a former slave, tended to her duties while the former slave slept peacefully on silk sheets while the city was idle and quiet.

María Josefa Olacuagas[12] accumulated a similar estate to that of Nicolasa Angulo. She was the widow of Martín Palacios, who left his inheritance to her upon his death. She was the daughter of Caridad Olacuagas and native of Santiago de Cuba. Her assets consisted of eighteen slaves of both sexes and different ages and castes. She owned four lean-tos with their respective buildings located on Enramadas Street No. 82, Cuartel de Pardos No. 16, San Agustín No. 4, Enramadas No. 93, a property on the corner of Cuartel de Pardos that served as her lodging and whose value was 3,249 pesos, half a dozen old silver spoons, half a dozen silver forks, a gold rosary with its medal set in corals, and a gold rosary of filigree and green stone. Because María Josefa did not declare land in the countryside, she must have dedicated her slaves to the service of the house, while she probably rented the rest in the city or the field, which must have provided her with considerable income. As Deschamps Chapeaux points out, by renting out slaves in jobs as diverse as street fruit sellers, day laborers on the docks, or domestics, the slave owner obtained an annual income, in his case study of Havana, that could be calculated to 20 to 25 percent of the slave's value.[13]

These cases—both those of Cuban-born black women and African-born women—are a small sample of the many that existed in the city of Santiago de Cuba and are sufficient to corroborate the economic status achieved by many women of color rather than considering these as isolated circumstances.

UPWARD MOBILITY, SOCIAL MOBILITY?

The riches that these women came to own, whether single or accompanied, constituted only part of the matter in colonial society. Some of them were able to amass as much or more wealth than many of those who lived in the city or jurisdiction. Additionally, the concept of the cleansing of blood (*limpieza de sangre*) was decisive to their social mobility wherein a drop of African blood circulating through their veins condemned them to marginalization, humiliation, and contempt. The drop determined whether they had to see a concert from the atrium of the cathedral, view dances of the Philharmonic Society from the street, or step aside and make room for a white person on the streets of the city, and whether they would be emphatically rejected when aspiring to marry a white person.

The imbalance between the economic mobility of the population of color and the state of social marginalization to which it was subjected is a consequence of the social ordering established by the metropolis. Hence, as the historian Rafael Duharte has pointed out:

> Blacks and *mulatos* could build up an important capital, owning land, workshops, slaves, etcetera, but this did not guarantee access to the halls of the whites, the universe of public posts, the colonial army or the world of the pedigreed. In front of him stood, like an impassable wall, the barrier of color, the prejudices instilled by slavery over several centuries.[14]

As Duharte emphasized, the black and *mulato* bourgeoisie solved this issue by constructing a social universe of their own, parallel to that of whites, which turned out to be a kind of copy of the society that rejected them. The battalions of *pardos* and *morenos* and the sumptuous dances in the coffee plantations of the Cauto valley were replicas of the colonial army and the lavish dances organized by the slavers and the wealthy sugar aristocracy.[15]

The mimicry that existed in the social sphere became unnecessary in the religious field. Each migratory group that settled in Santiago de Cuba brought an ingredient to the great religious complex that constituted the city. Hence many of them practiced with more or less discretion syncretic cults in which there were abundant African elements. Some were oriented to Vodu [voodoo] introduced by the Franco-Haitian immigrants. Catholicism was the official religion and its practice was associated to a greater or lesser practice of prestige in the social order. The church, however, in its undelegated function of ruling the destiny of man from the cradle to the grave, charged everyone the same for weddings, baptisms, and burials, and both blacks and whites could access these services. The sumptuousness that could be exhibited in these acts was not determined by the coloration of the skin but by economic power. A person of color could marry, be baptized, or be buried in a simple way or with wasteful ostentation, which without doubt—and because of the social connotation that this implied—could be exploited by those individuals of color who ardently desired to show off the riches they had come to obtain to whites and blacks.

The act of baptism was accompanied by a number of ostentatious acts. The Santiago population by then paid close attention to details such as the attire worn by the participants, including the baby; the number of coins thrown into the multitude of curious people—usually children—who waited impatiently on the outskirts of the church; and the gifts that were given as souvenirs and that showed the filial bond or the level of friendship with the family and the child's godparents, which could be a gold shield, a peseta, or silver coins. The feast and banquet that followed the religious ceremony was attended by family and friends and included alcoholic drinks such as *agualoja*, sangria, and Catalan claret, an exquisite red wine from Bordeaux, as an essential companion to the variety of dishes that were presented to the guests.

The accoutrements of the funeral honors, whose characteristics the interested person specified in his will, stand out in the competition to have the greatest show of wealth. Thus Nicolasa Angulo asked to be buried in *cruz alta* [the economic category of the high cross], cloaked, and accompanied by eight ecclesiastics. *Acompañados* was the name of the clergymen that the mourners paid to accompany the burial and whose number constituted a demonstration of the social rank of the deceased and the importance of the funeral.[16] She also requested that a mass be sung with the clergy present, and in case they were not available, that the mass take place the following day.

Nicolasa Angulo's requested funeral honors that showed the high economic level she had reached resembled those of María Josefa Olacuagas. She was buried with high cross, cloak, public lamenting, vigil, a mass with the congregation, and twelve clergymen to accompany her burial. Victorina Bell's funeral was superior to that of Maria Josefa Olacuagas. Once a slave of the Bell Irady family, she was buried with high cross, cloak, public mourning, vigil, mass with the congregation, and sixteen clergy accompanied her burial.[17]

Maria Josefa Olacuagas's and Victorina Bell's funerals were not isolated cases. The economic ascent achieved by many women of color allowed them to undertake the final journey surrounded by the same pomp and sumptuousness that white ladies who lived in those halls they could never access. A cursory review of the burial books that exist in the churches of Santiago de Cuba confirms this. The records of Santísima Trinidad [Most Holy Trinity Church] contain a total of ninety-two wealthy women in the short period between 1804 and 1810. But life is not summed up to a supreme moment of frankincense and myrrh. Even at that moment of mourning and in spite of the funerary honors, the women remained marked by laws and social norms. For example, the burials of people of color, like baptisms and marriages, were not registered in the same book where those of whites were, even when whites were poor and their ceremonies of low means.

A witness of the time, Hipólito Pirón, a *criollo* from Santiago, educated and based in France, gave an insurmountable testimony on the subject of color-based prejudices that provides a glimpse of the knowledge acquired from his own *mestizo* roots even when these were not recognized. In referring to a walk in the Alameda, Pirón testifies to what Duharte claims, but in observing the experiences of women of color. Regarding racial prejudice he points out that "among the riders and the people who strutted in the vehicles there were hardly any people with dark skin. I made this observation to someone who was by my side, and I found out something that had been a mystery to me: Racial prejudice. . . . In this way, any person who was not of the white race, even if rich and honorable, does not have the right to walk or ride a horse or carriage in the Alameda."[18]

To illustrate his claim, Pirón inserts the following anecdote representative of racial discrimination against women of color:

> I was told that on a Sunday afternoon, a lady of color who was very well considered among her own, known for her wealth, for her beauty, for her elegance, rode a carriage with her family and had the thought of driving to the Alameda. Upon seeing her, the white ladies trembled with indignation. Faced with such a situation, their husbands, parents and brothers who accompanied them, did not even know how to punish such imprudence. However, the women took care of it and agreed among them that they were all to leave slowly, thus abandoning the profaned place. After a few minutes, the lady of color realized that they were walking along a deserted promenade. Agitated, she commanded her carriage to return, muttering: "Apparently, I seem to be the plague!"[19]

Following this story, whose eloquence makes any comments unnecessary, the author reflected on the racial prejudice as supposedly assumed by the female sector of the so-called white class. He pointed out: "Women tend to be intolerable in matters of prejudice, their pride has no mercy with those who are not of the white race. Men are more tolerant. It often happens that young people of color, when their skin is not too *trigueña* [not too dark], slip in mounted on beautiful horses among the male riders who pay them no attention when they see them, nor do they feel offended."[20]

In the same direction, the English painter Walter Goodman who lived in Santiago de Cuba between 1864 and 1869 left a formidable testimony through the *mulata* Herminia (a character in his work *An Artist in Cuba*). A daughter of a *mulata* and white man, she recognized herself "as white as it was possible to be in my caste."[21] Herminia, by being born free and as a goddaughter of a white male from a comfortable economic position, received an education and humane treatment. Recalling the most relevant aspects of her life, she said that "the white women who visited the house of Don Benigno sometimes deigned to greet me in consideration of my presence, but secretly hated me and despised me, and while they did not dare to criticize me openly, they did not waste, however, the opportunity to remind everyone of my origin and the great difference that existed between them and me."[22]

The observations made by Pirón and Goodman reveal an interesting angle of the reality of the time, of which there are few available testimonies: racial prejudice of white women on women of color. As Pirón proposes, women seemed intolerant in the matter of race and their pride had no mercy, however this should not be seen as a supposed expression of tolerance on the part of the men. Both Goodman and Pirón peeked at the sultry spectacle of racial discrimination with the gaze of a male spectator. However, this does not mean that men of color were treated more favorably than women. "White merchants and landowners were willing to tolerate the presence of black and *mulato* men in the business world and even to make transactions with them. However, it was inadmissible for them as people of 'broken color' as it was said in good colonial prose of the last century for them to enter into their social world."[23]

Intolerance against women also existed as Pirón's testimony observed. When the lady of color was seen in her carriage strolling down the Alameda, "The white women trembled with indignation. Faced with such a situation, their husbands, parents and brothers who accompanied them, did not even know how to punish such imprudence."

Any attempts by women of color to rise socially was condemned to shipwreck in the sea of prejudices of colonial society. The obstacles that society imposed on them included education. A brief analysis of the development of this sector in Santiago de Cuba shows that at the beginning of the nineteenth century, schools that existed in the city taught women only to write, count, and pray, besides being instructed on gender-based labor. Over the course of the century, many school principals introduced varied subjects in their numerous curricula. These innovations served a purpose: to accustom women with the refinement that was imposed in the halls of high Santiaguera society, which was closely related to the customs and manners introduced by French immigrants.

The women of the "white class" had to overcome only the prejudices that existed in terms of educating the so-called beautiful sex. Those of comfortable means had the alternative of public schools—private schools and private tutors. In the case of those of very humble extraction, they had the possibility of attending public schools financed by the city council. To attend, they only needed to prove their condition of poverty. They could also attend one of the few free spots that were offered in the private establishments of the city. An example of this is the case of María Josefa Agostini of Prince who offered five openings in the Colegio Santa Rita de Cascia. These were filled by the same number of poor girls of the white race.[24]

An analysis of the enrollment of the schools of Santiago de Cuba shows that they favored males. For example, 1865 shows a total of 1,053 males and 875 females of the named "white class" who attended public schools and lived in the city and whose ages ranged between five and ten years old. Whereas 463 boys and 273 girls in the city attended private school. Respectively, 43 percent of boys versus 31 percent of girls were enrolled in schools.[25]

For girls of color, the situation was more difficult and complex. Before them stood the barrier of sex and also of color. By way of illustration, in the school enrollment of the city in the year 1849 was of a list of 373 girls, only 48 of who were girls of color.[26]

Pezuela provides a more totalizing view of the disadvantages for young women of color in comparison to young white women and males in general. Pezuela points out in his analysis that in the year 1861 in the city there were twenty-one schools for boys and only eight for girls. Their enrollment was 1,053 for boys and 353 for girls. These figures clearly reflect the discrimination that existed in terms of sex. As far as the composition of matriculation when considering skin color, 892 boys were white and 161 of color, thus respectively 85 and 15 percent enrollment. The percentage disadvantage rises in the case of girls who were not white, which shows the double barrier of race and sex that impeded their cultural ascent. Of the 353 girls who attended thirteen schools in the city, forty-eight were of color, representing 13 percent, and they were concentrated in five institutions.[27]

The colonial government's obligations for the education of girls of color were below those for white girls. The General Plan of Instruction for the islands of Cuba and Puerto Rico, approved in 1845, stipulated that in the regions where populations required a school, separate schools be established for free children of color according to the judgment of the governor. Despite the legislation, in many public schools in the city, children and girls from different races attended the same classrooms. A governmental disposition changed this situation: in 1863, two of the six schools for boys were for boys of color and one of three schools for girls were for girls of color. These schools were financed by the city council that existed in Santiago de Cuba.[28]

As can be seen, the number of schools designated by sex does not favor the girls and as far as race does not benefit students of color.

The limitations for free young black, *parda*, and *mulata* girls to access education were very similar to those that they had to face to practice teaching. Until the adoption of the General Plan of Instruction for the islands of Cuba and Puerto Rico in 1845, primary education was not the government's primary interest. This made it possible until the decade of the 40s of the nineteenth century for women of color to devote themselves to teaching with relative ease and, although in very small numbers, to reach the role of teacher.

The number of those who graduated on the island during the 1836–1837 biennium demonstrate this. From 149 people who received credentials, 84 were men and 37 were women belonging to the white class, representing 56.3 percent and 24.8 percent of the total, respectively. Of the "free of color," 18 men and 10 women were credentialed, who represented, in the case of the first, 12 percent and in the second 6.7 percent.[29] As you can see, the last rung was occupied by the women of color. Even though the figures refer to the entire island, they allow us to deduce the situation that black and *mulata* women faced in this regard in Santiago de Cuba.

The approval of the aforementioned Plan of Instruction made it more difficult for black, *parda*, and *mulata* women to access the Magisterium. The Plan envisaged the possibility of creating schools attended only by children "of color." But the faculty of these establishments were governed by the norms established for the schools for whites, that is, in addition to confirming the future teachers' good conduct, they needed to certify *la limpieza de sangre* [purity of blood].

This provision made the Magisterium a profession inaccessible to men and women of color. In the case of women, in the year 1849, just a quadrennium after the Plan of Instruction was approved, a total of ten women served as teacher-directors in the city of Santiago de Cuba. Only two of them were *pardas*: Antonia Núñez, native of Maracaibo, and Emerantine Bailly,[30] native of the Guarico. Table 3.1 shows the enrollment of girls of color in their schools in the 1849 school year.

An analysis of the official document indicates that starting in 1857, all the teachers-directors of Santiago de Cuba were white women. As table 3.1 shows, young black and *mulata* women who belonged to the bourgeois Santiaguera society were given the opportunity to educate themselves in the most privileged schools led by white women. The school's cloister was composed of professors and teachers of the white race. The case of the school Santa Rita de Casia run by María Teresa Irizarri serves as an example. In 1849 the school consigned six girls of color in its registrar. More than a decade later in 1862, an estimated twenty-seven girls obtained outstanding scores in the annual general exams, twenty-three of who were *mestiza*, representing

Table 3.1 Enrollment of girls of color in the 1849 school year

School of	Matriculated	Blacks	Whites
Juana Pelet	39		39
María Antonia Monier	47		47
Emerantine Bailly	25	18	7
María Josefa Agostini	41		41
María Teresa Irizarri	14	6	8
María del Carmen Romana	14		14
SEAP	3		3
Hildebrando Martí	15		15
Agustina Hernández	24	5	19
Gumersindo Martinez	70		70
Antonia Núñez	15	12	3
Catalina Acosta	23		23
Josefa Portillo	43	7	36
Total	373	48	325

85 percent of the total.[31] This does not mean that the doors of access were opened to their classmates in the noble task of contributing to their education. Through the character of Herminia, Walter Goodman left another insurmountable testimony about the discriminatory situation faced by girls and young women of color, in this case of the impossibility for them to dedicate themselves in the education sector. Herminia, the subject of his piece, states, "Many times I wanted to take advantage of the education that I received thanks to the kindness of Don Benigno, and in turn, teach other girls.... But unfortunately, in Cuba it is not customary to appoint governesses to children, and what respectable lady would have sent her children to my school in the event that I could have established one?"[32]

Herminia could not establish a school because she was a person of color, and this impossibility was determined by the existing racial prejudice of the time, which was codified by the established laws. In the case of the Magisterium, only those who proved their *limpieza de sangre* [purity of blood] could become teachers-directors. Young women of color, like Herminia, had only one alternative to entering the Magisterium, which was the "Schools for Friends." These schools were created in homes by someone who by petition of her friends and neighbors could register students as young as three years of age. Lacking methods and using punishment to a great extent, these schools offered lessons, writing, and instruction of the catechism. In 1848 in Santiago de Cuba there were nine schools of this type, four of which were led by women of color: Ramona López, María Nicolasa Ramos, María Feliciana Portuondo, and Antonia Núñez.

The limitations to access education were a consequence of the discriminatory political logic of the time, influencing the labor spectrum to which women of color were destined to a narrowness as one of their fundamental characteristics. Her status as a woman deprived her of the right to venture and stand out in the practice of music or in the visual arts, unlike men. Lino Boza, clarinetist and composer, and Baldomero Guevara, painter and portraitist, exemplify this. Women who did not belong to the bourgeoisie and who lacked resources had to make products or offer services, perform domestic work, as well as be sellers, resellers, weavers of hats, and in lesser quantity porters or housekeepers. The sea of information that appears in the press of the time includes requests and notices that constitute a sample of the tasks with which they earned their sustenance: "A *parda* of good qualities seeks a job by month, knows how to sew perfectly and attends children with care"; "A free *mulata* wants to be placed with a family to wash and iron with great perfection"; "A *parda* asks for accommodations to care for children and other domestic services"; "A free *morena* seeks work in washing and ironing"; "A *parda* wishes to give lessons on gold and silver embroidery with all perfection and since this is such a brilliant branch of education for the ladies of these establishments, she seeks that the women teachers hire her for two hours: The price will be friendly"; "A *parda* of good manners that knows how to sew with perfection, she wants to be accommodated in the service of a lady, either in this city or to accompany her to any part of the island or outside the island, with the only condition that she is not to be occupied in street chores."[33]

The performance of these activities in the face of great scarcity, and fate materializing with a winning lottery ticket, an inheritance left in the will by a godmother, godfather, grandmother, grandfather, a white father, or other relative, whose social conventions prevented them from recognizing a black girl as their daughter, but later left something in their will provided some black women the necessary resources to buy the goods that they would someday declare in their wills and leave as a legacy or inheritance bequeathed to their friends and loved ones. In the case of former slaves, their lives in bondage were also marked by signs of saving. The capacity to save money in the first instance was shown in their ability to buy their freedom when they did not receive their freedom by some other way. Buying or receiving their freedom was followed by the acquisition of property or the freedom of a family member, including parents and children. Many used all of their savings in that transaction as was the case of María Rufina Colás. Born in Africa, she was married to Cirilo Colás with whom she had seven children. At the end of her life, her will showed that she had no possessions.

She transferred the lean-to that she owned in the low street of San Bartolome, valued at three hundred pesos, to her freeborn children José Bonifacio and Evaristo, born after she and her husband had obtained their freedom. María Rufina Colás intended to make them equal, as far as the inheritance was concerned, to her siblings Irene, Manuel, Patricio, Lucía, and Aniceta, who were born slaves. She paid three hundred and fifty pesos, four hundred pesos, two hundred fifty pesos, three hundred and fifty pesos, and two hundred and fifty pesos, respectively, for their freedom. The possibility of acquiring goods and entering the bourgeois world gave way to the immensity of her maternal love. Giving their children the status of free men and free women was without a doubt their greatest wealth.

A NECESSARY REFLECTION

Women of color achieved economic mobility as shown in the examples despite the multiple obstacles imposed by the legal and social framework that prevailed, despite the prohibitions, limitations, and vicissitudes that they had to face throughout their lives. When women were married as was the case for Victorina Bell, María Agustina del Pozo, Paulina Bell, Mercedes Bosa, and María Josefa Olacuagas, their great effort, sacrifice, and constancy resulted in a decisive economic rise that affected them personally and affected the matrimonial community. The economic rise for women of color was greater than that for men. However, it granted them lesser social mobility in comparison to men, though both were restricted as people of color. This point is important to recognize given that women of color were a social sector living under total adversarial conditions confronting the double discrimination through race and sex. As shown in relation to education, they were limited to extreme measures, thus restricting their potential in labor.

The social order of colonial society could not be modified and with it offer social equality, which was denied to people of color. This would have required political change that the cities did not want to concede as shown by the failed *Junta de Información* [junta of information]. The only option was the armed struggle. The founding fathers of the Cuban nation prepared this struggle against their material interests and stemming from the love of the homeland. They initiated the struggle for independence in the morning of October 10, 1868. Women of color from Santiago were present such as Mariana Grajalas, María Cabrales, and Dominga Moncada, who are well known for their participation. Yet we should also recognize the heroic labor associated with these women of color as mothers and wives.

The revolt ended without achieving the abolition of slavery, but the winds of change it brought forth in the Cuban economy showed that this terrible institution was no longer viable. The first population to understand this was the plantation owners so that by 1886 this embarrassing institution was finally abolished. The whips and chains disappeared, but the prejudices remained as a fated sequel.

Despite the time that has transpired and the measures taken to know our history, stereotypes persist. The subject matter of slavery attracts artists, writers, directors, and producers. The histories of the use of leg clamps, *bocabao* [hanging upside down], and slave women that live in pursuit of or by the luxuries of slave owners and overseers are exposed to the detriment of the rich pages in our colonial past with women of color as protagonists. Their daily struggles for economic and social betterment, their roles as mothers and wives, how they consecrated their families, their efforts to purchase the freedom of their loved ones and to liberate them from the painful prison of slavery, their histories of love, and their insertion in the machinery of Santiaguera society constitute historical realities that must be known, centered, and disseminated because who we are today is closely tied to who we have been in the past, which cannot be delinked from who we want to be tomorrow.

NOTES

1. Hortensia Pichardo, *Documentos para la historia de Cuba* [Documents on the History of Cuba] (Havana: Editorial de Ciencias Sociales, 1971), t. 1, p. 111.
2. Archivo Histórico Provincial de Santiago de Cuba [Historical Archive of Santiago de Cuba] (AHPSC), Protocolos notariales 384, folio 233.
3. Notary protocols 385, folio 443, year 1839.
4. Ibid., 488, folio 108, year 1856. Editor's note: In this chapter, *colgadizo* is translated as "lean-to"; however, there is no easy English translation for the word. A *colgadizo* is a structure in Santiago not necessarily attached to a building that can stand alone or act as an entry way to a building or *solar*. It has two posts and a slanted roof and provides a shaded area for resting or selling goods.
5. Ibid., 550, folio 334, year 1868.
6. Ibid., 384, folio 12, year 1838.
7. It was probably the house made of wood and tile on a piece of land approximately 10 varas [about .002 acres] in the front yard and 34 varas [.0059 acres] in the back, situated on the street Enramadas purchased from Fortunata Sanchez with 700 pesos (see AHPSC, Protocol Notary, 393, folio 586, year 1837).
8. This was probably the *colgadizo* with a small plot, 7.5 varas [.0013 acres] in the front, and 15 [.0026] in the back, situated on Cedro street that she purchased for 350 pesos from Nicolás Plutín (see AHPSC, Protocol Notary, 382, folio 176, year 1836).
9. AHPSC, Protocol Notary, 281, folio 55, year 1851.
10. Ibid., 281, folio 149, year 1851.
11. Ibid., 13, folio 88, year 1814.
12. Protocolos Notariales, Juzgado de Primera Instancia [Notary Protocal: Judgment of the First Court], file 716, record 3, year 1867.
13. Pedro Deschamps Chapeaux, *El negro en la economía habanera del siglo XIX* [Blacks in the Nineteenth-Century Havana Economy] (Havana: Instituto Cubano

del Libro, 1971), 50. The case of Nicolasa Angulo to some extent indicates that the calculations estimated for Havana were common also for Santiago de Cuba. Juana Angula was paid seventy pesos per year by the *mulato* who tended her hacienda in Juan Angola. This figure represents 25 percent if the slave had cost 280 pesos, or 20 percent if the price was 350 pesos.

14. Rafael Duharte Jiménez, "El ascenso social del negro en el siglo XIX cubano" [Upward Mobility for Blacks in Nineteenth-Century Cuba], in *Nación y nacionalidad* [Nation and Nationality] (Santiago de Cuba: Editorial Oriente, 1991), 34.

15. Ibid., 89.

16. In 1836, the French Clara Bonne paid sixteen pesos and six reales for the parochial right to be buried with high cross, cape, public mourning, and the opening of her husband's burial ground and sixteen pesos to pay for sixteen *acompañados*, which means that one peso was paid per clergyman.

17. Archive of the Santa Lucia church. Burials of *pardos* and blacks. Book no. 4, folio 50, no. 25.

18. Hipólito Pirón, *La isla de Cuba* [The Island of Cuba] (Santiago de Cuba: Editorial Oriente, 1994), 28–29.

19. Ibid., 29.

20. Ibid.

21. Walter Goodman, *Un artista en Cuba* [An Artist in Cuba] (Havana: Editorial Letras Cubanas, 1986), 254. In the racial stratification of colonial society at the time, the children of whites and *mulatos* were deemed *cuarterones* [quadroons].

22. Ibid., 256.

23. Jiménez, "El ascenso social del negro en el siglo XIX cubano," 88–89.

24. AHPSC, Gobierno Provincial [Provincial Government], Instrucción Pública [Public instruction], file 791, section 11, year 1856.

25. Archivo Histórico Oficina del Conservador de Santiago Cuba [Historical Archive Conservation Office] (AHOCSC), Fondo Gobierno Municipial (Colonia) [Municipal Government Reserve] Materia Instrucción Pública, file 82.

26. Biblioteca Provincial Elvira Cape (BPEC) [Provincial Library], "Register of Statistics of Public Schools of Santiago de Cuba," year 1849. Calculations by the author from the data gathered from the various schools.

27. Jacobo de la Pezuela y Lobo, *Diccionario geográfico, estadístico, histórico de la isla de Cuba* [Dictionary of the Geography, Statistics, History of the Island of Cuba] (Madrid: Imprenta del establecimiento de Mellado, 1863), t. II, p. 198.

28. Emilio Bacardí Moreau, *Crónicas de Santiago de Cuba* [Santiago de Cuba Chronicles] (Barcelona: Tipografía de Carbonell y Esteva, 1908), 310–11.

29. Maria Elena Orozco Melgar, "La educación de la mujer en Cuba en el siglo XIX: el caso de Francisca Gispert de Méndez" [Women's Education in Nineteenth-Century Cuba: The Case of Francisca Gispert de Méndez], in *Mujeres de Cuba* [Women of Cuba], Coloquio Internacional Burdeos, April 1998, Editorial Oriente, Santiago de Cuba, 2002, 207.

30. See María Cristina Hierrezuelo, *Emerantine Bailly: una francesa singular* [Emerantine Bailly: A Unique Frenchwoman], paper presented at the VI Taller Francia y el Caribe [French and Caribbean Seminar], Festival de la Cultura de Origin Caribeño [Festival of Caribbean Origin Culture], Santiago de Cuba, 2002.

31. Their exam performance was as follows: in the superior class, one white girl and seven *mestizas*; in the first class, one and five; in the second, one and nine; in the third, one and two (*Diario of Santiago de Cuba*, December 16, 1862, 3).

32. Goodman, *Un artista en Cuba*, 256.

33. Samuel Hazard left an interesting testimony on the matter. He referred specifically to "the gorgeous *mulatas*, as they are called, even when their skin is white, in the majority they are descendants of *criollos* [first generation born in Cuba] of Spanish or French origin. They work in domestic services or if they are free, sew to earn their subsistence" (Hazard, *Cuba a pluma y lápiz: la siempre fiel isla* [Cuba by Plume and Pencil: The Ever-Faithful Island] [Havana: Cultural, Havana], t. II, p. 293). Walter Goodman referred to the youth of color that worked in the dressing room of the Philharmonic Society (Goodman, *Un artista en Cuba*, 145).

BIBLIOGRAPHY

Archivo de la Iglesia de Santa Lucía. Burials of pardos and morenos. 1851, 1856, 1868.

Archivo Histórico Oficina del Conservador de Santiago Cuba (AHOCSC). Fondo Gobierno Municipial (Colonia). Materia Instrucción Pública.

Archivo Histórico Provincial de Santiago Cuba (AHPSC). Gobierno Provincial. Instrucción Pública.

———. 1867. Juzgado de Primera Instancia.

Bacardí Moreau, Emilio. 1908. *Crónicas de Santiago de Cuba.* Barcelona: Tipografía de Carbonell y Esteva.

Biblioteca Provincial Elvira Cape (BPEC). 1849. "Register of Statistics of Public Schools of Santiago de Cuba."

Deschamps Chapeaux, Pedro. 1862. *El negro en la economía habanera del siglo XIX.* Havana: Instituto Cubano del Libro.

Diario de Santiago de Cuba. December 16, 1862.

Duharte Jiménez, Rafael. 1991. "El ascenso social del negro en el siglo XIX cubano." In *Nación y nacionalidad.* Santiago de Cuba: Editorial Oriente.

Goodman, Walter. 1986. *Un artista en Cuba.* Havana: Editorial Letras Cubanas.

Hazard, Samuel. 1928. *Cuba a pluma y lápiz: la siempre fiel isla.* Havana: Cultural.

Hierrezuelo, María Cristina. 2002. *Emerantine Bailly: una francesa singular.* Paper presented at the VI Taller Francia y el Caribe [French and Caribbean Seminar], Festival de la Cultura de Origin Caribeño. Santiago de Cuba: Unpublished.

Part Two

THOUGHT

Chapter 4

Women of *Minerva*

María del Carmen Barcia Zequeira

The changes produced in Cuban society at the end of the Ten Years' War were multiple, diverse, and transcendent. In part they were a logical consequence to the long war and the positions taken in both Cuba and its metropolis at the end of the conflict. Moreover, it cannot be ignored that the historical era that emerged was qualitatively different as a traditional society transitioned to a modern one. This was reflected in all the areas of society, economic, political, and social, which included objective and subjective aspects.

In the 1880s, the reform movement drew new spirit. While the long process of struggle had defined positions and criteria, it was now a matter of sustaining and developing them in a new context. All the classes, segments, sectors, and groups of society, from those who enjoyed an economic dominance to those who were unfortunately subjugated, assumed a precise position of what each of them had to do to safeguard their interests whether collective or individual. For these reasons the end of the century was loaded with homogeneous and contradictory actions and reactions, conservative and revolutionary, which made this timeline one of the most interesting in the history of Cuba, although very little studied from a social point of view.

In 1876 Spain decreed the constitution of the Spanish monarchy as a product of the restorative process. Although it was strongly conservative politically, it covered a series of individual liberties that did not threaten the sectors of the peninsular bourgeoisie who held power. The constitution was endowed with a democratizing tone. For example, article 13 states, "all Spanish people have the right to associate for the purpose of human life." These licenses, apart from the significance they held for the peninsula, had important consequences in Cuban society.

In 1879 the Law of the Press was approved, in 1880 the Law of Public Meetings, and in 1886 the Law on Associations. Cuban civil society acquired a new dimension from these laws. Until then, corporations, associations, and entities had emerged circumstantially and were not backed by specific legislation. From the decade of the 80s emerged societies of all types while others were transformed. Political parties, charities, and recreational or culturally based groups were created. The old black *cabildos* became societies of instruction, recreation, and mutual aid. They all met to project and disseminate their interests and used their right of free press.

Open and closed spaces, private and public proliferated in this new society. The analysis of the abolition of slavery shows a new dimension to the organization of the black and *mestizo* classes in the public and private spheres. Never had anything like this been seen before. Only on the occasion of the Feast of Kings and with prior authorization of the respective masters and the government could black *cabildos* freely go out into the street. Everyone attended the curiosity, especially foreigners, who detailed that spectacle of blacks with their erotic dances, their multicolored costumes, and their atavistic *diablitos* [little devils].

Processions commemorating the abolition of slavery were another thing. Blacks celebrated the social conquest while practicing their right as citizens. Parades included blacks on horseback, bands of music, various orchestras, brotherhoods, religious fraternities (*cofradías*), and *cabildos* with their typical costumes coming from Havana, Matanzas, Cárdenas, Santiago de Cuba, Puerto Príncipe, Santa Clara, Bejucal, San Antonio de los Baños, Santiago Las Vegas, Guanabacoa, and Regla. They walked the streets with banners dedicated to political figures such as Labra, Portuondo, Vizcarrondo, Cortina, and Gamazo. Recognition was also made to the Spanish Sociedad Abolicionista [Abolitionist Society] and the liberal press, represented in this case by the newspapers *El País* [The Country], *La Lucha* [The Struggle], and *La República Ibérca y El Radical* [The Iberian Republic and the Radical]. The demonstration was closed by a wagon, protected by a cordon of carriages, and drawn by four horses. The carriage included a young woman who represented freedom dressed in the colors of the Spanish flag. The mobilizing and economic power of the black and *mestizo* urban strata were objectively demonstrated. In the subjective plane, something more important took place: the legal authority that blacks had to claim their rights as citizens and the possibility of using public spaces to manifest their actions.

According to the Cuban historiography, the free sectors of people of color, a very important class from an economic and social perspective in the first forty years of the nineteenth century, had been crippled after the repression of the slave rebellion, the Conspiración de la Escalara[1] [Conspiracy of the Ladder]. Upon closer inspection one deduces that this sector became subversive with the purpose of sustaining and safeguarding its essential interests. The silent mass became stronger and reached an appreciable degree of organization, which was manifested in the creation of multiple societies that in 1887 reached 139. Some of these were integrated in the Central Directory of the Societies of Color,[2] gaining a greater force.

The black and *mestizo* societies existed in the most important cities as well as in the smaller towns. They played a transcendent role in the development of blacks and *mestizos* against all manifestations of racial discrimination. Many of them were old *cabildos* [fraternal guilds] that were abolished according to the provisions of the Real Orden [Royal Order] of October of 1880 and had to adopt new organizational forms. *Cabildos* that were not turned into mutual societies had to distance themselves from civilian life, although in many cases they adopted the image of a new organization and maintained their old content. They were extremely persecuted by the authorities.

Sometimes the older *cabildos*, who generally did not want to mingle with other ethnic groups or admit black *criollos* [blacks born on Cuban soil], solicited for permission to dance "in the style of their country." Many educational and recreational societies considered that this practice did not contribute to the advancement of the race.

Initially the societies of instruction and recreation only admitted women as daughters or wives and not as associates; their exclusion therefore motivated the creation of women's groups that excluded men, as for example Our Lady of Carmen or Lady of Charity.

Women also made their demands known in those years. Many had war experiences because they had shared the stage of war as mothers, wives, daughters, sisters, friends, or simply as companions of the struggle, dangers, risks, and vicissitudes of the long conflict. Others, long before the war, had taken responsibility for supporting their families by working outside and within their homes. Their experiences allowed them to gain particular awareness of their social importance and the need to acquire for their sex the rights and possibilities that they had been denied. In this process of social consciousness, black and *mestiza* women had a very active part because they merged to the demands on gender, those of race. The urban middle class of color demonstrated the maturity and relevance they had achieved in those years on the basis of a collective effort.

The Law of the Press was one of the freedoms obtained from Cuba's new constitution. Because of it, newspapers and magazines of various kinds and different political tendencies proliferated during those years. Some were specialized from an artistic, literary, scientific, or professional point of view, and although the press was not applicable to all—only 27.7 percent of the population read—new ideas and knowledge were disseminated. In this sociopolitical context, newspapers and magazines of color came to play an interesting role that expressed diverse positions such as the pro-Spanish sentiment headed by Rodolfo Hernández de Trava and Blanco de Lagardere, *mulato* descendant of the slave driver Pedro Blanco. Blanco was editor in chief, among others, of several newspapers, among which *El Ciudadano* and *El Hijo del Pueblo* stand out [The Citizen and The Son of the People]. Casimiro Bernabeu and Manuel García Alburquerque also shared this position. However, most of black and *mestizo* journalists were in favor of the separation from Spain. These figures included Juan Gualberto Gómez, editor of *La Fraternidad* [Fraternity] and *La Igualdad* [Equality], and Rafael Serra, Margarito Gutiérrez, and Martín Morúa Delgado.

Women's presses occupied a very special place that although limited was able to show the spirit of their struggle and the intellectual development attained by women, in particular black and *mestiza* women.[3] These constituted 33.8 percent of the female population. It should be noted that only 12.3 percent of people of color were able to read. In this context an interesting magazine came to the fore that featured women's freedom and intellectual growth. Its promoters titled it *Minerva* with a note that described it as a "fortnightly magazine dedicated to the woman of color." The chosen name was highly allegorical and representative of the magazine's intention because the goddess Minerva had been for the Romans the personification of wisdom and the protector of the arts and sciences. Unlike the biblical Eve—born of a vulgar rib from the first common man to serve and obey him—Minerva emerged from the head of Jupiter, supreme divinity of the Roman pantheon, and thus from his intellect. She was also warlike and therefore decidedly courageous and combative.

The symbol was evident in the magazine's goal to "stimulate our women to study,"[4] which appeared as its sole objective, yet an appreciable number of articulates were dedicated to divulging their rights and attributions. *Minerva* was published fortnightly in Havana from November 1888 to July 1889. In small format, the magazine's presentation was very modest. Miguel Guala was its first director and Enrique Cos its first administrator, who was soon replaced by Américo Arenosa. It should be noted that in Cuba, except in the case of widows, women had no legal right to hold public positions. The first issue was sold to the public at the price of 75 cents in Havana and 60 cents in the rest of the country. The loose pages could be purchased at the price of 30 cents. An appreciable number of Cuban women in and out of the island were in charge of promoting it: 39 in Cienfuegos, 6 in Cruces, 5 in Corral Falso, 6 in Güines, 58 in Havana, 5 in Lajas, 17 in Matanzas, 14 in Placetas, 3 in Rodas, 11 in Santiago de las Vegas, 13 in Sancti Spiritus, 14 in Sagua, 11 in Trinidad, 19 in Bejucal, 19 in Cardenas, 14 in New York, and 58 in Key West.[5]

The magazine was edited by a group of women who, although they only appeared listed as collaborators, were actually in charge of preparing the different sections. The articles highlighted topics of special interest for black and *mestiza* women on news, poetry, commentaries, critical and social assessments, and artistic and sporting reviews.

A prominent role was played by Úrsula Coimbra de Valverde, who signed her articles under the pseudonym of Cecilia. She had been an enslaved woman who later became a teacher of piano, English, and French. Her family came from the city of Cienfuegos in the central part of the country. Her collaborators agree on her importance, describing her as "the heroine of our race that inspired by the ideas of the century, raises our sisters up from the deep sleep of withdrawal" and as the "genius that has spoken for our sisters."[6] At the beginning of the year of 1889, she became severely ill as a result of a difficult birth. The child was born dead and Cecilia took a leave from writing for the magazine. This situation evidently affected the publication and because of it numbers 8 and 9 were prepared by a group of editors who supported the work of the women's group. Various articles show the appreciation that everyone had for Úrsula Coimbra.[7] When she rejoined her duties, Cecilia would write thankfully, "I am proud to belong to a race that although alone, and at the cost of sacrifices, tries to rise to the height of others and fights, works and studies to overcome. . . . For too long, we lived through the noose and the gag, we had to keep quiet for so long that the spirit of the century demands that we raise our voice."[8]

Other outstanding collaborators from the magazine were América Font, María Ángela Storini, África Céspedes, Lucrecia González, Pastora Ramos, María Cleofa, Onatina, Cristina Ayala, and Catalina Medina, also known as K. Lanita and Catana, who was also an enthusiast of the dramatic arts. She acted in *La Pasionaria* by Leopoldo Cano, which was shown in the Irijoa theater. She was well respected among the black and *mestizo* segments especially because Antonio Medina was considered "the spiritual father of the Havana youth of color" and as "the black Don Pepe that if he was not as illustrious as a white man, it was because of his time."[9]

The social demands of women, particularly black and *mestiza*, without forgetting those concerning the legal emancipation of ex-slaves, of whom an appreciable part were urban women, were prominent in *Minerva*. The journal expressed through its articles or other contributions such as letters, poetry, or notes not only what slavery had meant in the individual plane for women, their family members, and friends before slavery was abolished but also the consequences that gendered racism exerted on society. Doubly dismissed, black and *mestiza* women dragged a past of consensual unions, illegitimate children, and social and cultural marginalization that they were determined to change at all costs.

Racial discrimination, drawn from the strong root of slavery, manifested itself in different treatments of people based on the color of the skin, which in the case of women was added the category of sex. The term Cuban *mulata* according to some contemporaries had a pejorative origin because it was derived from the hybrid character of the mule, offspring of the donkey, and the mare and was product of the crossing between the white man and the black woman. *Mulatas* favored the paternal lineage and tended to whiten successive generations.

In colonial society, the *mulata* was usually a woman of exceptional beauty and seen only as an object of pleasure: "Everything about her is soft, everything about her is ductile, everything about her is morbid."[10] However, the social situation that could be reached with these physical characteristics was brief and lasted only with the presence of beauty: "The time of my greatness, to last along with my beauty, dulled by no other than the *mulata* Julia, daughter of black Juana."[11]

Among the various articles found in *Minerva* are works by ex-slave María Ángela Storini, who was also educated, which interestingly reveals the focus of the magazine. She was fortunate, exceptional for her class, to have belonged to a cultured and generous family. During the Ten Years' War (1868–1878), she had resided with her old ex-owners in the United States, France, Germany, and Italy, which gave her an opportunity to become of aware of how women developed in other societies.

Her work was published under the title of "A Letter."[12] She proposed that most of the ills afflicting women were due to the belief that education for women was an adornment that could be dispensed with, thus she expressed with concern: "We follow those who belong to my race, to my sex, without examining the steps they took to the path of enlightenment ... it makes sense that black women hold no greater use in Cuba than for the delights of the dance." The last point dealt with a particularly sensitive aspect of that time for *mestiza* women that referred to a generalization by men who considered that dance was the place where *mulata* women unfolded and showed their sensuality.

Actually, the hobby of dance was quite widespread in nineteenth-century Cuban society, which influenced different types of situations centered on the undisputed rhythmic capacities of blacks and the special circumstance that it was a cheap and permissible amusement, capable of distracting the slaves and distancing them from subversive intentions. The other's vision curiously observed this phenomenon: "Everyone dances in Havana without regard to age, class or condition, from the old man who can barely take a step, to the old women, from the Captain General to the last employee. The same dances are danced in the palace as in the huts of blacks."[13]

Collaborators and members of *Minerva* were extremely concerned with the appearance and the hobby of dance. The principal black and *mestizo* education and recreation societies also focused on this trend, which they considered a disruptive factor capable of curbing the cultural development of their members. The journal referred to some girls whose parents took them to rehearse "the dance of the cuadro to stage later" and did not attend classes regularly, which was allowed by their parents. "Dancing is one of the main causes of our moral and physical decay. . . . It seems everyone's affected by the results that dance has brought to the present generation that wants for the next one . . . to also have the dance as their sole patrimony."[14]

The poet África de Cespedes was a woman of special human sensibility, well known on the Island for her artistic and literary values. Despite her almost white skin, she was *mestiza* and did not hide it. The social place she occupied and the recognition she received for her literary work never led her to be unaware of her black roots. She usually collaborated with the magazine and in the work titled "Reflections," she stated:

> The black woman, treated cruelly by her vile exploiters, has become the most salient target for their poisoned arrows by those same ones that trafficked with their noble blood in the sorrowful days of slavery. That is why . . . we prepare for our defense in the constant battle that we are undergoing; And as such we will continue to battle until we are recognized as we are and not as each pirate artist has wanted or as it has been convenient for their fearful ends. . . . If they invite us to fight, then we will fight.[15]

In the words of África de Cespedes, it follows that black and *mestiza* women were being attacked who had undertaken to defending their rights through the *Minerva* magazine. In another part of the article, she adds, "We, of the black race, are stigmatized in the bottom sector of this judgment."[16] The poetess made very progressive considerations on those women who were obligated, because of their economic situations, to practice prostitution. She explained that in those cases the women were only victims and reinforced this thought by quoting the well-known verses of Sor Juana Inés de la Cruz:

Stubborn men that accuse
women without reason
without seeing your situation
the same as what you judge.

África de Cespedes concludes the article by stating that "polygamy has not been imposed by women. . . . But by the wantonness of men."[17]

Another article, titled "To Cuba,"[18] reaffirmed patriotic sentiments. Cuba, at the height of these years, had already undergone two wars and transitioned to national liberation. The first, known as the Ten Years' War, was fought between 1868 and 1878. The second is known as the Little War for having lasted only sixteen months, from August 1879 to December 1880. Though independence from Spain in this intense period of struggles was not achieved, the wars helped to reaffirm the patriotic and nationalist spirit of the Cubans in the later years, especially among women.

In the fourth issue of the magazine América Font, another important collaborator published an interesting work titled "My Opinion,"[19] dedicated to the education of women. Boldly revealing of the times, the author dared to go much farther than those who defended female instruction and education framed in the narrow limits of the family. Counter to those who felt that women needed only three things, virtue of the soul, modesty on her forehead, and work on her hands, the author believed that women's virtue would always weaken women if it was not accompanied and protected by the endowments of their intellect and culture: "The instruction must be for woman to be as wise as a tree . . . for where there is no instruction, there is no freedom."[20] With incredible audacity for the time, she expressed that domestic chores had been entrusted to woman by a custom that had been turned into law.

In other articles, for example, in "The Instruction" written by Lucrecia González Consuegra, who was also a poet and essayist, the author insisted on the need for women to better themselves. "We need to educate ourselves and to study a lot so as not to vegetate as useless plants."[21] Also, "I Adhere," by Cristina Ayala,[22] addressed the significance that teaching had on black and *mestizo* men and women. It states, "As long as the individuals of our race . . . do not educate themselves and by way of education moralize themselves, we will not be able to enter into the concert of societies that are considered cultured."

The concern, not only for education but also specifically for learning, was also one of the topics that was repeatedly addressed. Natividad González, for example, exhorted black and *mestiza* women not to allow their children to lack "that beneficial and interesting bread of instruction." She insisted on the need for black and *mestizo* children to "study, learn, be a model of virtue and selflessness and forgive those who so badly treated our poor and disinherited race."[23]

With sharp observation, María Ángela Storini, the erudite ex-slave, applied to herself the judgment of Concepción Jimeno de Flaquer: "The prosperity and increasing strength of the people is due to the intellectual superiority of their women."[24] Additionally, Felipa Basilio expressed that "neither studies nor learning will make women lose neither of their virtues nor of their delightful weaknesses and that by having an educated woman the husband could count on having a companion instead of a slave."[25]

Laura Clarens published the article titled "Women in the Academy"[26] to support the role that educated women could hold in society and the equality it granted of possibilities between women and men. The same article referred to Gertrude Gómez de Avellaneda's denied admission to such a prestigious institution and to the article published in the *El Eco* [The Echo] *of Galicia* by the outstanding feminist and writer Emilia Pardo Bazán.

The article recounted the situation that occurred in 1853 when the already eminent and recognized Cuban writer who had won two awards in poetic competitions and successfully released no less than thirteen dramatic works was denied admission to the academy for the mere fact of being a woman. The rights of white, black, or *mestiza* women and the need to acquire an educational level that would allow them to assume and develop their social responsibilities as citizens, mothers, and wives was a primary concern for this group.

Certainly not all women of color were willing to collaborate with the magazine, especially because it involved assuming positions that attracted attacks from the retrograde sectors. Several issues mention the case of Felicia Valdés, who apparently stood out for her literary work. She was invited to collaborate with the magazine, but she declined, saying that the "multitude of intruders, of petulant ones and of madmen, who become fond of being the nightmare of well-acquired reputations will come to disturb her tranquility."[27]

The editors' attempts to recruit her failed because Felicia Valdés, fearful of losing a public who accepted her as a *mestiza* but could reject her if she took positions to rescue and reaffirm the rights of women, never collaborated with the magazine. It is possible that África de Céspedes referred to her when she pronounced, "the maidservant of low sphere battles their judgment."

Family occupied a special concern for women of color, which also served as motivation. The legal marriage was more than a goal for the group of women occupied with the defense of their rights because it constituted differences between slave and free women. The negative experiences inherited from servitude were numerous and widespread. How many children had not been recognized? How many were disinherited in favor of their brethren, sons of legal marriages, even violating testamentary provisions? Many cases had been mocked because the legitimate white children used their influences against those who did not have that status and were unaware of their rights.

These situations led the columnists to express crudely: "Slavery has never produced wives but concubines." The essential concern was not so much in the social position that the marriage brought but with the situation in which concubinage placed the single mother and the children born of illegitimate unions. In the biweekly notes section, this criterion was expressed with clarity: "The age of children of the womb, of children unknown by their parents has passed. That time of insult and shame . . . had its raison d'être when our slave status limited our aspirations toward the greatness and sublimity of marriage."[28]

Without a contractual union there was no legitimate offspring, nor the possibility of the child having a "clean" surname, that is, paternal or inheriting the riches of the father. In order for women not to be deceived, the advantages of civil marriage were required over the religious. For this reason, the magazine explained to the readers that the second was not substitutive of the first one because only the first was able to regulate the formation of the family in a precise way that granted legal advantages that the church could not resolve because the ecclesiastical marriage was not valid without the civil contractual union.

Social and cultural activities were also covered in the section of biweekly notes. In this regard, the editors imitated, formally, the ridiculous "Social Chronicles" of the press of "the whites." The wedding of Concepción Humames was commented on extensively by the race of color that the magazine was commissioned to review.[29] It described the dress of the bride, those of the guests, the style and quality of the wedding cake, the food and beverages that had been offered to the guests, etc. The review proudly stated that everything had been made by artisans of color.

Similar observations were made in great detail with the baptism of the son of the marriage Diago-González, whose surname connotes slave roots.[30] After describing the festivities, the magazine expressed that the father of the child was a famous *mestizo* pastry chef. This section was also used for charity, requesting help for sick and helpless blacks or *mestizos*.

The biweekly notes exercised criticism as another very different function. In this direction, the editors expressed that it was extremely difficult for them to carry out this task because many of those critiqued cried to the sky when they were pointed out.

For a long time E. T. Elvina led this section. She even reviewed sports, something unusual for a woman of that time. The sports comments made readers doubt whether the pseudonym belonged to a woman. However, it is not difficult to deduce that it belonged to Etelvina Zayas. The two baseball teams were Cuba and the Universe. The journalist complained about the scarce female presence at the ball game because the event was attended only by two women, the wives of the president of team Cuba and of the treasurer and deputy secretary of team Universe.

An article stands out titled "The Match of the 19"[31] that reviews a party designed to raise funds for a school that held two societies: La Bella Unión Habanera [the Beautiful Havana Union] and the Divina Caridad [Divine Charity]. Two issues call repeated attention to the ball clubs, a custom that was transplanted by emigrants such as Cuban ladies who resided in New York and in Key West. They supported the publication of *Minerva* and their presence is evident in the magazine's use of English terms, for example, gentleman for *caballero*.

The magazine also published some translations of articles relating to personalities or prominent figures. For example, Number 10, corresponding to the year 1889, appears in successive numbers of the translation of the portrait on Alejandro Pushkin, written by Henry Jywell. Also published were the biographies of Mrs. Harrison and Mrs. Morton, wives of the president and vice president of the United States, respectively, in that year.

Minerva frequently covered goals of education or fundraising for societies of color. The magazine echoed the initiative of the Divine Charity Society, which wanted to build a school that had created a committee that included Concepción Morales de Gualaba, the wife of the director of the magazine, and Julia Molina de Gálvez, Paula Oquendo de Carmona, Carlota Lebefre, Micaela and Francisca Moya, Gertrude Heredia de Serra, and Francisca Infanzón. Publications on fundraising were frequent and generally the members of the fundraising committees were related in one way or another to the editors who worked with the magazine.

Another topic covered by *Minerva* was poetry, thanks to the constant collaboration of some of its members or the editors' relatives. In this aspect, Onatina stands out, whose surname we do not know because it does not appear in any of the issues. Possibly the magazine used a pen name. According to Lino Waal de Crees in an article titled "Open Letter,"[32] Onatina had achieved through self-teaching the necessary knowledge to write poems of great beauty, like "Morir" [To Die], "Lágrimas" [Tears], and "A María Cleofa" [To María Cleofa]. The poetry of Lucrecia Gonzalez and Cristina Ayala also stood out.

The following is part of Onatina's poem "La inconstancia"[33] [Inconsistency]:

I saw a butterfly
in the chalice of a flower
fluttering on its soft petals
with the sweetest love.
In contemplating his rhapsody
I said, Butterfly,
How is it you kiss all the flowers
simply and with ecstasy?
You are the inconsistent faithful wanderer
who swears eternal love
to all who brush beside him
like you on every flower.

Minerva magazine had notable collaborations with prominent black or *mestizo* journalists, such as those of Martín Morúa Delgado who published in successive numbers his booklet "La mujer, defensa de sus derechos" [Women, in Defense of Their Rights]; that of Rafael Serra, a recognized supporter of José Martí who edited poems; and that of Antonio Medina Céspedes, father of K. Lanita. He was the first man of color who directed a

Cuban newspaper, *El Faro* [The Lighthouse], in 1842 and whose activity as a teacher we already covered.

It should be noted that the magazine's newsroom was also used for cultural events. They held an opening when the book *La Mujer, defensa de sus derechos e ilustración* [Women, in Defense of Their Rights and Betterment] was released, for example, by Margarito Gutiérrez, who also collaborated with the group of editors.

Minerva could not continue because of economic hardship. Since the beginning of 1889, the situation was publicly expressed through the magazine itself. However, in the two years it reached the public, it was able to establish the positions, criteria, and aspirations of black and *mestiza* women who took advantage of the possibilities of the moment to advocate for the defense and dissemination of their social and civil rights. While enhancing the possibilities of achieving their goals through education, bypassing forms of struggle more organized and effective, it should be noted that both the publication of the magazine and the collaboration of its editors to defend the interests of their race and sex showed readers a path to follow, thus setting a positive precedent in the social and political struggles that Cuban women began to undertake.

NOTES

1. This thesis was developed by Pedro Deschamps Chapeaux in *El negro en la sociedad habanera del siglo XIX* [Blacks in Havana Society in the Nineteenth Century] (Havana: Premio Ensayo UNEAC 1970, 1971).

2. The directory was formed in 1887. For further details, see Oilda Hevia Lenier, *El Directorio Central de las Sociedades De La Raza De Color* [The Central Directory of Societies of Color] (Havana: Editorial de Ciencias Sociales, 1996).

3. It should be noted that the press acted as an instrument of defense for some marginalized communities, like prostitutes. See "Entre el poder y la crisis: las prostitutas se defienden" [Between Power and Crisis: Prostitutes Defend Themselves], in *Mujeres latinoamericanas: Historia y cultura, siglos XVI al XIX* [Latin American Women: History and Culture, Sixteenth to Nineteenth Centuries], Serie Colquios, Havana, 1997, no. 35.

4. "A Don Próculo" in the magazine *Minerva*, May 30, 1989, no. 16, p. 3.

5. The data were offered on the back cover of some issues, for example, no. 14 on April 30, 1889, and no. 16 of May 30, 1889.

6. "To Cecilia" in *Minerva*, March 16, 1889, no. 11, p. 4.

7. Among these is the article by África Céspedes titled "For Cecilia," which was published February 28, 1889, no. 10 in the magazine.

8. "Gratitude: To My Friends and Colleagues from the Magazine *Minerva*," in *Minerva*, no. 9, pp. 1–2.

9. E. T. Elvina, "Notas quincenales" [biweekly notes] in *Minerva*, March 16, 1889, no. 11, pp. 7–8. Don Pepe Blanco was Don José de la Luz y Caballero.

10. Eduardo Esponza, *La mulata* (Havana, 1878).

11. José María Quintana, *La mulata de rango* (Havana, 1891).

12. "A Letter" in the magazine *Minerva*, November 30, 1888, no. 4, pp. 3–5.

13. Nicolás Tanco Armero, "Voyage to New Granada to China and from China to Paris, France, 1881," in *The Island of Cuba in the Nineteenth Century as Seen by Foreigners*, by Juan Perez de la Riva (Havana: Editorial de Ciencias Sociales, 1981), 125–27.

14. E. T. Elvina, "Biweekly Notes" in the magazine *Minerva*, February 15, 1889, no. 9, p. 8.

15. "Reflections" in the magazine *Minerva*, February 28, 1889, no. 10, pp. 2–5.

16. Ibid.

17. Ibid.

18. "To Cuba," article written on the root of the abolition of slavery in *Minerva* magazine, March 13, 1889, no. 11, pp. 2–3.

19. *Minerva* magazine, November 15, 1888, no. 3, pp. 2–3.

20. Ibid.

21. Ibid., June 15, 1889, no. 17, pp. 1–2.

22. Ibid., pp. 2–3.

23. *Minerva*, June 15, 1889, no. 17, pp. 1–2.

24. Ibid., pp. 3–4.

25. "La mujer antes de la razón" [Women in the Face of Reason] in *Minerva*, May 15, 1889, no. 15, pp. 1–2.

26. Ibid., May 30, 1889, no. 16, pp. 5–6.

27. Ibid., May 26, 1889, no. 7, p. 4.

28. Ibid., May 15, 1889, no. 15, pp. 4–5.

29. Ibid., December 15, 1888, no. 5 pp. 6–7.

30. The Diago were slave traders and then owners of slave plantations. It should be noted that usually the surname of the masters was assumed by the slaves.

31. *Minerva*, May 30, 1889, no. 16, p. 2.

32. Ibid., February 7, 1889, no. 8, pp. 3–4.

33. Ibid., December 15, 1888, no. 5, p. 5.

BIBLIOGRAPHY

Barcia, María del Carmen. 1997. "Entre el poder y la crisis: las prostitutas se defienden." In *Mujeres latinoamericanas: Historia y cultura, siglos XVI al XIX*, no. 35. Havana: Serie Colquios.

Deschamps Chapeaux, Pedro. 1971. *El negro en la sociedad habanera del siglo XIX*. Havana: Premio Ensayo UNEAC 1970.

Hevia Lenier, Oilda. 1996. *El Directorio Central de las Sociedades De La Raza De Color*. Havana: Editorial de Ciencias Sociales.

Tanco Armero, Nicolás. 1981. "Voyage to New Granada to China and from China to Paris, France, 1881." In *The Island of Cuba in the Nineteenth Century as Seen by Foreigners*, by Juan Pérez de la Riva. Havana: Editorial de Ciencias Sociales.

Chapter 5

Gratitude

To My Friends and Colleagues of the Journal **Minerva**[1]

Úrsula Coimbra de Valverde

Dear compatriots: my heart pounds with so much pleasure that I fear that it may explode with the pure joy that it experiences and . . . how could it not be so? Why not say that you have corresponded in the most gallant way to the invitation you directed, thus receiving the homage that I am credited for your talents and virtues? Thanks, incomparable sisters, MINERVA will occupy a favorite place in the pages of history, since its columns have been decorated with your elaborate and filigreed writing, even more beautiful than the innocent butterflies that flutter around the flowers. We will not wither; today, our objective should be only to make us even more worthy to aspire to the life of our rights.

Until yesterday heinous because of ignorance, today we work and when we rise to a height that exalts us, we give palpable proof of the wisdom that presides over our actions.

When I proclaim these truths, I am proud to belong to a race that alone and at the cost of sacrifices tries to rise to the height of the others and overcome a lot with much work and study. No doubt, following the flight of my enthusiasm, will displease those who still see us as sad pariahs, subject to the slavery of silence and plunged into the clumsy distribution of ignorance. For quite some time we have had the noose and the gag so long we have kept quiet, so the spirit of the century demands that our voice be lifted. Until these last days, our fates were shrouded in a dense fog of uncertainty, our well-being was a great problem whose solution we did not decide to tackle with unfounded and vague fears, but with the astonishing advancement of the time we are in, the veil was drawn, ideas progressed, modern human progress gained ground toward our improvement, infiltrating gradually in the development of the intellectual and philosophical world. It became time to also reveal the desire for a sheltering beauty as well as to improve our condition alongside the civilizing impulse of the time. Each of us are required to carry out a small contribution with our grand thoughts.

The mission that we have voluntarily undertaken is sublime; that is why even my voice echoes around you to encourage you not to break your pen. Work is the virtue that adorns us, and enlightenment is the powerful lever that, do not doubt, formed the cornerstone to cement our aspirations. These are worthy, so our position is already defined; the bounty of the law of progress that we will welcome.

In conclusion, rest assured the renewed gratitude given me with all of you who in your beautiful writings have greeted with real delight the wrong thoughts that I have dedicated to everyone. I encourage you not to faint as I make you partakers of the gratitude that I hold toward you; your names have been sculpted with bright letters in my heart. Moving forth, then, is the way of our regeneration and glory.

Yours,
Cecilia

NOTE

1. This is a faithful copy of the original. The author utilized the pseudonym Cecilia during the whole first phase of the magazine *Minerva*, published in Havana from 1888 to 1889.

Chapter 6

Black Voices in Favor of the Independent Party of Color[1]

Carmen Piedra

HAVANA

"Shame to the state of inhibition of most of the black race of this location. It seems that they have us metamorphosed so that they do not understand the reason for us to form our own Party and claim the rights that by justice is ours."

WE MUST BE CALM

"Cruel persecutors threaten to destroy the Party that bears the beautiful title of Independents of Color, but fear not: Could a few weaklings have more power than a plethora of strong men?"

HORROR TO THE LIE

"The black man knows how to carry the pains of life, armed with the love he professes for his race and his homeland. And he also knows that the only fear the Independent Party inspires is in not lending itself useful to the ambitions and vain pleasures of those concerned who do not reward nor appreciate great works!"

NOTE

1. These fragments are from the writings of the activist Carmen Piedra taken from the newspaper *Previsión*, an official part of the Independent Party of Color (April 7, 1910, p. 5; April 15, 1910, p. 5; April 24, 1910, p. 5, respectively). These articles came to us as a collaboration from Tomás Fernández Robaina, the writer and researcher of the National Library José Martí.

Chapter 7

Our Ethnic Values[1]
Consuelo Serra

"Union among races is the beautiful ideal that seizes our social consciousness today with stronger intensity than ever, since it increases by a great necessity from the natural product of our exuberant Republican life. It is necessary that we call ourselves Cuban because we look to our land solely, but that for the betterment of all of humanity, democratization is necessary and must be elaborated until forming in great principles and beautiful ideals, that vivify the whole world, the universal necessity because it emerges from life itself, which is everywhere.

"The sublime ideal of union among all those born in this blessed land developed more intensely out of the natural consequence of our national life, exemplified admirably in our day with the gestures of true democracy carried out by the first Magistrate of the Republic of General Machado, where everything is in concert and harmony in nature and where there is only thing lacking once and for all, let's all agree, the descendants of Quintín Banderas, the Maceos and Carlos Manuel of Céspedes, for the consolidation of a homeland: 'With all for all.'

"But it is important not to lose sight that great ideals must be accompanied by great means as well, capable of making these very attainable.

"In favor of the union among all Cubans of both races, we offer to the common fatherland this double contribution, which is necessary for it touches our ethnic group, that we strive to keep our values always in the public light, understanding that the liveliness in which we make them shine depends our triumph, no other than that of the fatherland itself.

"We must spread our values among everyone; fortunately, we do not have to create them because they always existed justifying our pride in the mind and in the heart of our elders. We can see in the acts of life written with salient characters these irresistible virtues: *dignity, moral focus*. Dignity with which we feel the legitimate pride of being Cuban and being black, because black Cubans have done many good and dignified things, in all phases of Cuban life, and this not always mediocrely but also in a distinguished and noticeable way. Moral focus, in order never to divert any force, to never lose any opportunity that leads us to the unwavering intellectual-moral grandeur that we have not only the right but the duty to aspire.

"Our elders have bequeathed to us these virtues, these ethnic values. It is up to us to pick them up and elevate them high for the whole world to see, so that they may serve for peace and union among all Cubans who will recognize in them *national values, Cuban values.*"

NOTE

1. This and the following essays belong to the Sunday column "Proyecto Ideales de una Raza" [The Ideals of a Race Project]. This specific piece is found in *Diario de la Marina*, January 27, 1929, VI (third section). The "Ideals of a Race" column was born a cultural effort from the initiative of architect and journalist Gustavo Urrutia (1881–1958). From its inception, it presented itself as a platform from where they raised and discussed the serious issues affecting the black Cuban population. Urrutia was able to count on the collaboration of important black and white intellectuals in the broad debate opened in the fight against racism, discrimination, and prejudices. (For more information, see Tomás Fernández Robaina, *El negro en Cuba* [Havana: Editorial de Ciencias Sociales, 1990].)

Chapter 8

What We Are[1]
Inocencía Silveira

To the brother in ideals,

Dr. José M. Carbonell

"We are not racists because consistent with our duty, we raise our voices to express that there are many cases of individuals overlooked and combated, exclusively and solely for the reason of the coloration of the skin.

"We are not racists because we express our feelings in a frank and determined way, nor because we proclaim that these postponements are unreasonable, unfair and extremely detrimental in a country like ours, given its ethnic, political and social composition.

"We are not racists, we are an entity conscious of our duties and our rights as free citizens. And since we are free and aware, and we know, can, and want to expose our grievances and our aspirations in our collective life, we write, talk, and work in a practical manner, so that it results in reality and not a myth of the ideal of our freedoms of the apostle José Martí, who extolled and wanted a cordial republic 'with all and for all.' That is why our pen is sincere, our word persuasive, and our conduct diaphanous.

"We feel we speak and proceed as sensible, noble and fellowship-loving people: attributes that no one can argue against.

"Most of our brothers of the race have many reasons to be aggrieved with some representative of the white race. And not only in terms of the benefits that are obtained from the public treasury but also in what concerns the exclusions observed in many of the manifestations of social life. Because after all, man does not live by bread alone, as was wisely said by our unforgettable Don Pepe de la Luz.

"We must, can, and want to also enjoy our country, the same satisfactions enjoyed by our brothers of the white race, in regard to the moral and material benefits that are obtained in the progressive development of the nation.

"We have the right to equality, and we request it. It does not matter that we proclaim it in a low voice, or by giving rumbling cries so that it is heard better. The question is that our brothers give a warning sign that if they try to put a thick but flowered veil to our right, or to call us without reason, racists, because we try to improve our condition as pariahs.

"We would be worried and reprehensible racists if we wanted all the privileges only for ourselves: all material benefits and all the enjoyments of the spirit. We are not racists, and we know that those who know us also know that we are not. And we can show our history to all those who ignore who we are and let them know our daily behavior.

"We are not racists, we are conscientious citizens."

NOTE

1. *Diario de la Marina* [The Marina Daily], February 10, 1929, VI (third section).

Chapter 9

The Black Cuban Woman[1]
Gerardo del Valle

"The black Cuban woman is characterized by two transcendental qualities: a great maternal love and innate and passionate patriotism.

"There are two ways to know, without mirages or sophisms, the truth of things: statistics and the study of the terrain in the environment where life develops. Both guide our work, whether sociological and literary. The people are not studied from the desk nor by references: you have to live with them to capture their spirit and thought.

"Cuba's statistics proclaim the negligible amount of infanticide committed by black women and the small number of children of color thrown into charitable organizations and other institutions. Rare is the case of a black woman getting rid of her children for her own development in life and who does not care about the problems that the excess offspring can cause. She brings children into the world and then for better or worse takes care of them and keeps them with her. Anyone who visits the abhorrent '*solares*,' shameful tenements of our Republic, can notice how in one room there is a woman of color with four, six, and up to ten youngsters around her, while she fights heroically on the washing pan and the iron to give them a bite to eat, without lamenting the cruel and selfish fathers, 'spoiled' following fillies with their campaigns of Don Juanism. Within this poverty and the thousand difficulties that she finds to work, her only resources are washing and the kitchen because she's not allowed in the stores, despite the pseudo-feminists. She does everything possible so that when the children are ready, they can go clean to school, learn a trade, or enter the Normal schools. Only she knows the sacrifices that it costs for that beautiful spectacle of the daily attendance to school campuses!

"Energetic, optimistic, and full of faith, she drives and stimulates her children that excel in any activity. She runs from here to provide for them to reach the top of the arts, sciences, or sports. We know of many prestigious blacks who rose on the strength of the pulmonary impulse of their mothers.

"Black women have pride for their Cuban nationality and proclaim it to the four winds. They never allow women foreigners who live in the same apartments displeasure or insult to the fatherland. With her primitive rudeness, she jumps like a lioness and defends her own with all the picturesque aggression of the prohibited vocabulary. Each one embodies a Mariana Grajales, mother of titans, who wants to make their children instruments of glory and national exaltation. Within her ignorance beats a rare instinct of social concern, rebellious, and audacious: she worries every day of 'the situation,' is aware of the politicians who betray and exploit the country, and is one of the first to rejoice for those who sacrifice out of loyalty or succeed in their work.

"The number of girls who study at all cultural centers has long been drawing attention. Girls of the people, daughters of extreme poverty and much more admired for their eagerness to excel, to arrive quickly to the goal and join progress.

"No social class has more need to overcome the dark jungle of ignorance in which it has been mired for as long as the black woman. In doing so, she advances by leaps and bounds: from the Normal schools emerge skillful and affectionate teachers, conscious and possessing modern pedagogy, who know to water equally the seed in the daughters of the people, black and white, banishing from their spirits the ignominious chain of backwardness. It is she who can and has the imperious duty of humanity against idolatrous beliefs. The majority of black women, naive and simple, is an easy believer of perverse suggestions hidden under the veil of the mysterious. A thousand-tentacled octopus perennially threatens her life: that bastard combination that is formed with witchcraft or black magic and false spiritism, adulterated especially to reach the bottom of their souls and the bottom of their poor purses.

"The black woman lives in perennial fear of the unknown, pending spells against her, slave of a complicated net of superstitions. Sometimes the product of two or three weeks of ungrateful labor is used to combat 'bad influences' that could drive away her man, make the children sick, or bring a decrease in her economic income. There is a nucleus of practitioners from both sexes and of the same race that prosper, joyfully maintaining that state of alarm and fear of which they get an optimal result.

"The remedy of these evils is found only in school and in the rational eloquence of good teachers to dispel those shadows that cover the happiness of black Cubans, worthy of all respect and prosperity."[2]

NOTES

1. *Diario de la Marina*, November 2, 1930, V (third section). Catalina Pozo Gato responded to the article by Gerardo del Valle in the following article.

2. There is another type of woman of color whose attributes include being cultured and having social distinction. The challenges that she faces will some day be dealt with on these pages. (Explanation written by Gustavo Urrutia.)

Chapter 10

The Black Cuban Women and Culture[1]
Catalina Pozo Gato

To the writer Gerardo del Valle, an inquiry:

"I read with particular interest your latest article 'The Black Cuban Woman' in the section written by our distinguished and cultured compatriot and architect Gustavo E. Urrutia in the *Diario de la Marina*. Your article is full of sad truths and with it you have achieved your desire to reflect on a part of Cuban society affected by its inhumane results and the discouraging consequence of their unfair prejudices. I cannot underline the sentimental praise made by the women of my race, but if I can, with my right in sight, make some minor notations between the lines of your admirable writing.

"You arrive at the overview of cultural expansion. We agree, but when you investigate the 'modus vivendi' of the black woman, you forgot to refer (and a drafting note confirms this) to the insurmountable obstacles, systematized and organized, with which the black educated woman, overwhelmed by a reality with the same level of misery and defeat as the uncultured black woman.

"There is a notorious percentage of white educated women. There is a high number of black women that rose to the struggle from the university classrooms, institutes, Normal schools, homes, academies, schools, and countless educational and cultural centers, the same where white women are prepared and enabled.

"However, while both groups of women may be equally capable and prepared, black women hardly find opportunities to show their skills and knowledge and less to live decently. Because the reality is that the racial prejudice gnaws at Cuban nationality, nullifies its efforts, sterilizes its management, and makes lives bitter. Then the imperative to subsist makes them descend from their scale, to reduce them to the most rude and sad jobs—if she finds work—with such paid scarcity, which only allows living in those stables of moral torture that are the tenements, where as you have pointed out, they are exposed at least to confusion—and this is nothing compared to other consequences. Because numerous black women including university graduates, women with diplomas from diverse schools as academics, typists, stenographers, language teachers, embroiderers, dressmakers, etc., and countless girls suitable for decent service work in shops, workshops, and offices are forced to live and die in the frightening apartments and attics.

"I know of young women of my race with an impeccable education, languages, diplomas, titles, etc., working as domestics after being exhausted of chasing a modest position in state office or in a public establishment for a long time. There are dentists, pharmacists, lawyers, and doctors working as dressmakers (barely meeting their practical aspirations), earning an exasperating salary in shops owned by 'the Poles.' Because, poor things, they do not have the same opportunities as their sister, the white woman, who is less prepared.

"There are many who were determined to leave their role behind a counter that does not require scientific or technical knowledge and nevertheless, she arches over the counter because in our lavish and dazzling shops, a girl of color cannot find a place of employment that will pay her more than minimum in designer stores. And even in this line of work, the most skillful and most intelligent does not go beyond a simple operator.

"Neither those shops nor the private offices, Cuban or foreign, provide employment to our prepared girls, mocking those ingenuous Cubans, who were our ancestors, and believed in equity and justice when the revolutionary ideal preached by Martí and realized by Maceo spoils in today's reality.

"How many young women of color do you see serving in the big shops or the torturous Ten-cents? In what proportion do you find them in public offices? (I do not speak of specific offices.) How many in the buildings of the state? And yet we meet the criteria for these occupations. What is ironic is that there are a number of associations here in Cuba founded for the protection of women.

"They never achieve a job that is dignified to them as women and to their personal aptitudes in the workshops, factories, etc. I'm not talking about exceptions, because I want to say it like you, in general. Is all of this human, fair, patriotic? And this is happening in front of our eyes to the women of my race, cultured or uncultured, educated or not, by our own Cuban brothers of the white race!

"If women influence greatly the spiritual structure of the child, what will the children come to think of their mothers? And when this happens, what will be the future of Cuba?

"The urgent thing is not to inflate these moral miseries, but to demand the goodwill of good Cubans and the action of the government by doing reparation work (I allude to all the organizations and writers who deal with these matters) and others by legislating in such a way that we may all feel affection for this debased land, upon which ran the blood of our parents and grandparents.

"Yours truly with the outmost consideration."

NOTE

1. *Diario de la Marina*, November 30, 1939, VI (third section).

Chapter 11

Black Intelligence[1]

Arabella Oña Gómez

"If we meditate on the time that has elapsed since blacks were admitted to the centers of higher education to date, we will notice how their intellect has improved with surprising quickness. Every second elapsed, they are drawn in the light of wisdom, throwing off the poisonous tiller of ignorance. The number of intellectual blacks is increasing, showing a clear understanding of their unwavering faith to be triumphant.

"Our country for years has been the cradle of blacks whose fame has filled the pages of history. For example, we have Maceo whose technique and bravery are largely owed us having won our war of independence. His heroism and abilities demonstrated in front of the invasion earned him the comparison by historians with the greatest generals of all time. We have the poet Plácido, the martyr of the first moments who with practically no education knew how to compose several famous poems among which include 'Plegaria a Dios' [Prayer to God], and the eminent violinist known in Europe and America, among many others who belonged to the time when blacks were slaves and therefore it was almost prohibited for them to cultivate their intelligence.

"With all this, even today with blacks being at the cultural level of most civilized races, they are repudiated from the bosom of society. But it is time for equality to be established for all, that justice not be determined by the color of the skin but by the quality of the people. To this we must give our all, black and white, completely united like in the fields of the revolution to conquer the independence of the fatherland.

NOTE

1. From the publication *Adelante*, March 1938, no. 34.

Chapter 12

Women in Santeria or Regla Ocha
Gender, Myths, and Reality
Daisy Rubiera Castillo

For several years I have dedicated myself to investigating the position and condition of women in Santeria or Regla de Ocha. My intention to write on this topic did not emerge out of thin air but from the lack of information due to a lack of existing literature. I also was not satisfied with the justifications given based on mythology in response to questions of gender in Santeria or Regla de Ocha presented at different international congresses about the religion of the Orishas and other cultural events that I participated in, both inside and outside the country.

If men's roles were clearly defined, why was it that in the majority of ceremonies—to not generalize absolutely—women seemed to be subordinated at almost every level of ritual life? Who or what regulates relations among male initiates and female initiates in religious practice?[1]

Santeria, in my eyes, has a very well-defined gender structure. Hence the diversity of criteria in relation to the position and condition of the initiates that maintain both Babalawos and Babalochas, and the same *iyalochas*, convey the idea that the limitations and prohibitions that are allocated according to the sexes are related, fundamentally, with the prescribed and proscribed behaviors through the oral tradition in terms of myths, legends, taboos, etc.

Hence to locate that difference requires unmasking from that mythology the roles of gender that serve as a basis for the discrimination of women. This is a great challenge due to the nonexistence of any antecedents in this respect and to the sexist prejudices and the machismo present in the believers in relation to his gender identity and religious self-image.

It is also complex because of the nonexistence of a single sacred text that is admitted as common by the whole of the believers, whether initiated or not. It is logical to think that for that reason, there is a large variety of interpretations.

The *Corpus* or *Tratado de Ifá* is a text with various versions in different languages that come from abroad, although the authorship of some of them is unknown. Literature from Nigeria and Benin, written in Yoruba, has also arrived in the country, which makes it possible for those who know Yoruba to make an adequate translation of its contents and to be able to match them with the *criollo* essays. Even Babalawo researchers collect the rare texts from different backgrounds in order to enrich their knowledge of Ifá. For this reason, any inadequate interpretation of these texts could harm women's religious rights as the ideological messages that enter and mark women's activities appear "natural" and "inevitable." In keeping with it, today many female initiates assume their status as something that should not be questioned. Others consider the position they occupy to be theirs, according to what is intended for their sex. There are those who never question it because "as it has always been, so must it always be." However, some admit to the place that "corresponds" to them, aware of the lack of equity that it entails but without proposing a change of values that would imply transforming the situation.

Contrary to this, we find through different sources[2] references of women who not only emerged as transmitters of ideas and religious values but who also enriched women's roles as believers. The women pioneers were African of Yoruba origin who did not allow any of the negative factors imposed on their status as slaves to prevent them from defending their religious beliefs and to transmit them to their *criollo* offspring, slave or free. In this sense, they took advantage of every space that they could "tear away" from the colonial authorities. A space of great importance was that of the *cabildos*, which were independently created as a means of control and segregation of the slave population but became centers of conservation of much of the beliefs and traditions of the African culture, in this case Yoruba. In the *cabildos*, they established their roles as transmitters of religion from their positions as queen, godmother, or head of house, positions for which they were elected, fundamentally, according to their religious hierarchy, advanced age, and economic importance within the African community. They shared roles with the king, and the hierarchy of both prevailed according to each other's ability to solve religious problems. These positions also granted them social prestige within the group. Example of these include Inés Flores, of the Cabildo of Our Lady of the Rosary and the Animas; Ña Caridad, best known for Iguaro of the Cabildo Changó Tedún; María Josefa Cárdenas, of the Royal Congos, who upon her death, in addition to her religious knowledge, left the organization several properties; and María de Jesus Soto, renowned for her knowledge of the rituals and ceremonies of the Cabildo Carabalí Isuama of Santiago de Cuba.

Due to the prohibition, in 1880, of the creation of new *cabildos*, the existing ones were transformed into foundational houses where specific male or female deities were worshipped that retained individual and collective gender stereotypes and the extensive knowledge systems pertaining to the original cultures of its members. Some *olorishas* [gender-neutral term for a santero/a; a Santeria priest], considered pioneer women who remained active more or less at the start of the nineteenth century, were Malaké *la grande* [the great], Malaké *la chiquita* [the small or smaller], and Dadá. Other than that they were associated with the Cabildo San José 80, many details remain unknown about these women.

Other women who developed their religious activities during the second half of the nineteenth and the beginning of the twentieth centuries were the following:

Ña Rosalía. Efunshé Warikindó, founder of the religious lineage Egbado.

Ña Matilde Zayas. La Gemí. A free black woman from the Eguado nation. In the middle of the nineteenth century, she pompously celebrated the festivity for Olokun in her temple on Perdomo Street in the town of Regla.

Ma Monserrate González. Obá Tero. She was one of the first women consecrated in the last quarter of the nineteenth century. Founder of the religious lineage Egbado.

Oní Changó. Obá Tero is the source of many Egbado orishas in Cuba: Olokun, Oduduwa, Bromu, Yewa, and others. Her religious lineage is very well marked in Matanzas.

Fermina Gómez. Ochabí, ordained by Ma Monserrate González, *ochabí*. Of great capacity and deep religious knowledge, she was known as the most reputed source in Cuba of Orishas de Egbado, such as Olokun, Yewa, and Oduduwa, until her death in 1950. She stands out for having given the fundamentals of Olokun to people not initiated yet. She also blessed the first Orisaoko in Cuba. Ferminita inherited all of her knowledge from her *iyaloricha* Oba Tero.

Arabia Oviedo. Priestess of Oyá founded a religious lineage in a new town, Matanzas. Their line is probably the second largest in Matanzas.

Ña Belén González. Apoto. Founder of the branch of La Pimienta. It is not clear if she was Oló Ochún or Oní Yemayá. She was ordained in Cuba by an *iyaloricha* known as Teresita Ochún Funké, probably the same Teresita Ariosa. One source says that she was ordained by China Silvestre, Ochún Miwá, and others say that Apoto was the one who ordained (sacrament) Ochún Miwá.

Rosa Rodríguez. Ochún Kolodé (white).

Ña Margarita Armenteros. Ainá Yobo. Founder of another important religious lineage in Havana.

Tiburcia Sotolongo. Ochún Mewá and Obá Oriaté; descends from Ainá Yobo.

Panchita Herrera. Consecrated in the cult of the divinities of Yemayá. Her name of consecration was Atiponlá.

Timotea "Latuán" Albear. Ajayí Lewú Oní Changó and one of the first Obá Oriaté. She was one of the most prominent Lucumí in the beginning of the twentieth century. She dictated most of the narrative of Osha and Ifá in Cuba. She trained Octavio Samá, Obadimejí.[3] It is told that she taught the language of Oyó to her religious line.

Calixta Morales. Odé Dei. Some sources believe that she was the daughter of Efunché. She is considered to have been one of the most brilliant women *apwón*, meaning caller of saints, in her time. An informant of Lydia Cabrera said about her: "when Odé Dei called the saints, not one remained in heaven."[4] She might have been the first *olorisha* of Ochosi ordained in Cuba.

Renowned *Maria Towa* also stands out, historically considered as the queen of the Lucumíes. She was at that time the only Lucumí who could read and write. In this religious practice she was Oriaté. It is said that she was the one who introduced the knife (Pinodo) and the possibility of killing (sacrificing four legged animals) to all Santeros and babalawos who followed.[5]

Josefa "Pepa" Herrera. Echubí, daughter of Adechina and possibly the first *olorisha* ordained in Elegba in Cuba. Supreme *iyalocha* of Town of Regla in the first half of the twentieth century. Queen of the Cabildo Our Lady of Regla, which she directed from the time of her father's death until her own passing in 1947. She left behind a religious family of more than a hundred godchildren. Fernando Ortiz gave her eulogy.[6]

Ña Inés Flores. Yenyé T'Olokun. Consecrated on the last quarter of the nineteenth century. Queen of the Cabildo Our Lady of Rosary and the Animas.

Mercedes. Known as Ogún Toyo and Mercedes la Balogún. By being initiated in the cult to the orisha Ogún, she was allowed to sacrifice plumed animals and four-legged animals, thus decreasing the criteria that limited women from sacrificing because of lack of physical strength. She held great knowledge of *dialogún*.

Aurora Lamar. Obá Tolá until 1959. She was probably the most prolific *iyaloricha* in Cuba. She ordained over two thousand people. She introduced the religion in Santiago de Cuba in 1940. Her religious lineage is probably the most extensive.

Susana Cantero. Omí Toqué. Born in Trinidad, initiated in Cienfuegos. She resided in Regla beginning in 1913 where she founded her *cabildo* in 1914. The *cabildo* disappeared after her death in 1947. She made contributions not only with the religious education of her family of ritual but also her *cabildo* brought great splendor to the religious festivals celebrated in her town. Her influence was so great that her cadaver was maintained unburied for forty-eight hours. Her farewell was given by the mayor of the town. Omí Toqué had a religious family that included more than one hundred godchildren.

That shared knowledge, combined with the regulations as to the ways of relating to nature, enabled their descendants to assume the appropriate attitude and behavior at the time of putting them into practice. The cognitive method of this knowledge, in addition to selective oral transmission, necessitated direct observation through ceremonies, offerings, supplications, chants, prayers, and other rites in the moments and places that allowed for this practice to develop despite the discrimination and rejection to which this religious belief was subjected. In that religious field, some of these women led the ceremonies for certain deities that are now considered to be exclusively for the babalawos.

It is known that during the prerevolutionary period in the activity of Oriaté, the well-known women of Olosa, emerged: Aurora Lamar Olo Obatalá, Delia Espinosa Omitoké of Malecón No. 15, Dulce Calderón Osungunmí of Marianao, Carmen Acosta of 5th and Fernandina, Carmen Miró Ewinletí of the Positos, Asunción Bruselo Ilarí of the district Atarés, Candita Obosujón of Cotorro, María Magdalena Peñalver, and Yomiyomi de la Palma, among others.[7]

Popular sayings also played an important role in the transmission of this knowledge and the moral and ethical content implicit in it that refers to unity, discretion, reciprocity, mutual help, good behavior, and morality. We are familiar with many of these teachings today in hearing them from the mouths of our great-grandmothers and grandmothers. Example:

A dog has four legs but picks only one path.
One stick does not make a forest.
If it's known, it's not asked.
A good listener needs few words.
A tree born crooked can never have a straight trunk.
Big talkers end badly.
Not everything that shines is gold.
When the cat's away, the mice will play.

Among female domestic slaves, some nannies also played a role in transmitting knowledge because they communicated some of their religious beliefs to the children they looked after whom they reencountered as adults. All of these African women and their Cuban-born descendants deserve our highest homage and remembrance for their perseverance and courage that they raised in defense of their religious traditions and practices during the difficult conditions in which they lived.

Today, looking at Santeria from the outside might lead observers to believe that *iyalochas* and *babaloshas* had the same roles and endeavors.[8] But this is not so; the existing gender structure does not permit it. Not only does sex limit the roles of the initiates but so does their gender as a result of an ideological socialization assimilated with the oral tradition (myths, legends, taboos, songs, prayers, etc.), reinforced in the religious activity that includes numerous attitudes and practices that then justify that socialization. This materializes prohibitions and limitations that position subordination as something seemingly innate or inescapable.

In this sense, the initiates find themselves subjected to interpretations as well as limitations and prohibitions present in *odu of Ifá*,[9] which impedes the equality among the sexes, independently of some women closing some of these gaps. The gender gaps are entrenched in tradition especially when considering that the *odu* refer to the creation of the world, men and women, and everything that exists. Half of everything is masculine and the other feminine. The content of each is accorded to what is born and what is marked in each of them. Some of the masculine *odu*, among other meanings, include the head of the earth, strength, harshness, justice, the law, the rays of the sun, etc. The feminine includes sacrifice, vanity, enslavement of women, and desperation.

The *odu* contain the origin of ceremonies, rites, taboos, uses, customs, flora, fauna, and associations of the original habitat. Generally, they reflect a patriarchal society that mainly recounts masculine tasks in which men hold power and that subordinate women's position. The rules of established conduct must be accepted and respected by the believers. The *odu* represent the explanation of the world in the Yoruba religion and are considered marks, signs, energy, and essence that imply the wisdom and knowledge of the Yoruba world. They are considered divinities. Its total integration is in the Ifá oracle. The content of its representations reflects the undervaluation of the feminine and the difference between the sexes.

WOMEN AND MYTHOLOGY

Feminine representation is broad in Yoruba mythology as in Cuba's reality. As with any traditional oral narrative, transmission corresponds with the cultural history that served as a foundation and that is therefore deeply masculinized. In this sense, the masculine scope of the traditional Yoruba helps to understand that even in those *pataquies* in which women and deities occupy a leading role, they reaffirm the deeply hegemonic macho sense enclosed in them. For example:

> Orúnmila and Yemaya lived together; they were married. Many people visited their house to consult with Orúnmila. She observed how her husband worked with the cowry shells, and like that, without him noticing, she learned the art of interpretation of the sacred signs of Dialogún.

On one occasion, Orúnmila had to leave on a trip and was detained longer than expected. Without food or money, Yemaya was starving.

One day, a man arrived at the house looking for Orúnmila and Yemaya decided to take care of the task herself. In time, she became an expert. The fame this brought her reached Orúnmila's ears and he decided to return home. Upon confirming the news, he couldn't permit for his woman to be as intelligent as him, so he broke his relation with her and threw her out of the house.[10]

It is logical that her transgression would carry a price in the vision of the cultural world of oppositional sexes that this myth reflects. In this case, she pays a high price. Yemaya breaks the established norms and thus alters the equilibrium that maintains the patriarchal order in the communitarian cosmos in which her intelligence, ability, and valor are characteristics only of men that cannot be assumed by feminine subjects. Thus condemnation, sanctions, and punishment must fall upon her.

Although differences between biological sexes determine a certain distribution of gender roles, that allocation is not defined as a natural but as a social fact. In this sense, "difference" becomes inequality, which can be exemplified by menstruation, a biological fact in which the religious sphere prescribes that women behave differently than men.

An explanation can be found in the fact that the ancient civilizations could not give an adequate interpretation of the female menstrual cycle. It was not until 1827 with the discovery of the egg that menstruation became a biological fact as part of women's reproductive processes. Prior to this, menstruation was considered the purification of the female body of evil humors, of negative vital energy that provoked misfortune and that made the female body impure during that time of menstruation.

For that reason, religious texts (Bible, Koran,[11] Rules of Ifá) contain norms on menstruation that regulate the attitudes of believers. The stigma inherent in the sexual condition of women is found in every religious expression according to an intrinsic negative value granted to the conception of life. Those fanciful musings on menstruation that obviated everything that connected it with life while granting it negative values turned it into an impurity that increased the exclusion of women already attributed to their sex. This ethic of differentiation marked women's destiny through rules and taboos that sought to justify the existing gender gaps.

Traditional Yoruba society did not escape that social conditioning; neither did ours during the colonial period. Regla de Ocha incorporated those beliefs in its normative principles. Relating to how these are valued in the traditional Yoruba religion is a well-known babalawo who states:

> The most archaic texts give a profound mystical sense to menstruation. . . . It is believed that it was Órisá Odú who provoked menstruation in all the women of

the world (narration of the Ódu of Ifa Ótrúpón Meji and Ogúndá Ósé); Another of the details suggest a distancing between women and this divinity to prevent women from being victims of very prolonged menstrual period. The Ifa narrative reveals that Orisha Odú is the keeper of all female blood. She is superior to all the women in the world. Women cannot touch her symbols nor inherit them, since she is women's own inner representation, she menstruates eternally. Therefore, her influence on women could damage women's biological nature and their reproductive organs.[12]

Among different myths on menstruation that incorporate elements that discriminate against women is the following:

It happened that a woman, Nana Burukú[13] was of marrying age but did not have a husband. So, she pleaded to Olofi who replied, "You want husband? You'll have one." Olofi looked for Ogundaché who was sitting on a rock in the middle of the mountain thinking that the whole world held everything except food for him because he had no *aché* [divine gift, energy, wisdom, life] for hunting. And with the bow and arrow he meditated on his situation when Olofi arrived and told him that he wanted to marry him to Nana Burukú and he agreed and they got married.

Days went by and Ogundaché said, "And how am I supposed to keep my woman when I never catch anything?" Olofi replied "From now on, you'll have *aché* in hunting, only that you cannot kill the animals, but take them to where I instruct you."

The place was a cabin in the middle of the woods, and since that day with *ibbó-ozain*[14] given to him by an *egún*[15] that lived there in the Ceiba. Ogundaché would take the live animals and as they got nearer, *ibbó-ozaín* would paralyze them. He'd take the animals to the cabin Olofi had indicated and he would suck their blood, returning their bodies to Ogundaché, who would then take them home.

His woman, Nana Burukú thought it strange that the animals did not have blood and her female curiosity led her to following her husband. But once in the woods, she lost sight of him. She kept walking and came across the cabin and looked through the window seeing Olofi suck the blood of the animals. She was so entertained when *egún* who lived in the ceiba and guarded the area, took her as prisoner and to Olofi who said, "You asked for a husband and I gave you one. Today for being curious, what you saw today, you will see every month." So, the woman returned home and upon arriving saw herself hemorrhaging, meaning the release of the human body through women.[16]

I reference this story of the origin of menstruation as an example of a punishment of women for their curiosity. It is significant to consider that the context of the story develops in a world of obedience in which through symbolism women's search for knowledge is negatively valorized. Another negative quality associated with women also appears, curiosity, as the cause of ills and punishment for impulsivity. Blood must remain in its own body! Menstruation, shame, punishment, and her subjection to total repression.

Bearers are credited with impurity that cause malignant effects and are therefore surrounded by limitations and taboos on the purity of the sacred. Some examples include menstruating woman cannot get near the Saints, cannot go under Osain, cannot prepare the food of Añá, and cannot kill quails.

These popular myths and taboos, inside of the religious expression, appear as unconscious or natural, but are to a large extent a factor excluding initiates through rules and prohibitions oriented toward them but also as a test of their faith. The initiates' belief of the credibility of the religious account and its plot is shown in its influence on the initiates, which explains why some of them accept the prohibitions that are assigned to them during their menstruating period, considered as a disadvantage during those days. This drawback, in a certain way, is legitimized by the myths concerned. The testimony of one Omo Yemaya who has been initiated for fifteen years serves as example: "What I know is that my elders told me that while I am on the period [menstruation] I cannot do an endless list of things. Since that is what they established, I don't do those things."

The limitations are exercised according to the mythology and determine behavior. Religion establishes difference and exercises its dominance accordingly. It favors inequality and makes it part of religious practice, enabling the reproduction, transmission, and reaffirmation of sexism.[17]

Contrary to the previous testimony, examples of certain *iyalochas* exist that deconstruct, through their practical experience, the symbolic order. By "dispelling" the narrative myth, they reveal how the phantasm of the stereotype of menstruation is itself mythical. This is attested by another devotee of Yeyama:

> I am religious by faith. I did not get initiated because of health problems, nor issues of justice. I practice my beliefs in my way especially since I have proof that men try to limit us so that they may be the ones with greater power.
>
> One of the proofs was when I was given my *kofá*.[18] I received my period on the day scheduled for that and I told myself: If it's a true impediment then why can't others see I'm on my period? Nothing happened; I received my *kofá*.
>
> At the conclusion of the ceremony, I decided that if I needed to take care of something during my time of menstruation, that I'd take care of it. That's how it's been for all these years. I have never suffered anything and everything I do comes out well.

Testimonies like hers are exceptions. Generally, female initiates do not commit any type of transgressions against what has been established. Their religious identity makes their beliefs understandable and helps them manage the incomprehensible, which prevents them from seeing or disqualifying the obvious. It is representation in mythology and not the biological that is responsible for how female and male initiates act and what happens between the two genders.

In religious practice, women have their own domestic and ritual activities.[19] Songs and prayers are sung in rituals. The *Iyalochas* have learned them through oral transmission, but many of them ignore the meaning of them due to the lack of knowledge of the Yoruba language. In the same way, the changes of intonation, rhythm, and cadence can alter the significance of the ritual. They can also perform the role as godmothers in Santeria, a position that grants them a major role. As such their identity, in addition to religion, is formed by other identities such as gender, class, race, political militancy, profession, or occupation, which can at any given time complicate their religious performance. I interviewed several godmothers in Santeria, and we tried to examine to what extent they could or could not affect their religious practice. The following fragments exemplify this:

> It has taken me twenty-two years to create my religious family. I have 47 godchildren, men and women. I am a professor at the nursing school and when some of my students find out that I am a santera, they look at me with a certain suspicion. On occasion, they've told me that they don't understand how someone so well educated could practice such a primitive religion. Although my beliefs don't influence my work in any way, I've had difficulties for the same reason with other professors.

Another *madrina* [godmother] stated:

> I have been an initiate in this religion for a very long time. I have a small religious family. In twenty-two years, I've only had 10 godchildren since my work blocks me from developing my religious commitments. I am a principal of a primary school and I have to dedicate most of my time to my work. I do so with pleasure though I consider it a negative thing that because of my position, that I have to keep my faith almost a secret. As such, I have never tried to influence anyone in any way.

An official of a company explains:

> It's so negative that because I work in this so-called emergent economy that I have to hide my religious beliefs. The Communist Party has allowed this religion since the opening up of religion in the '90s, so there hasn't been a political opposition between this religion and the State. I received my militancy four years ago but, even though in my nucleus, I am not openly discriminated, it feels like my colleagues don't accept it. I have fifteen godchildren and my religious role has nothing to do with my role as leader and militant of my Party.

A godmother in Santeria, resident of Miramar commented:

Aside from the meetings of the Committee, Federation and the Delegate's Report, my neighbors treat me equally. I know they do it because of their political commitment, because outside of those spaces their attitude towards my religion is very biased, problematized further by my race and class, I'm black and poor.

The godmother in Santeria is supposed to be a symbol of her ritual family. Her authority and power must serve the benefit of her godchildren due to her responsibility to them, not only in the reinforcement of the faith through the values and paradigms that she must transmit but also in support of the traditional knowledge and principal custody, especially in its house temple, of the inherited African legacy. However, it is not always so. Some of them fail to fulfill these functions for different reasons. Among them is the shallowness in their true role as such and in some aspects of the ceremonial ritual, to which are added the contradictions that are created in their attitude and conduct in social practice by assuming taboos and prejudices as part of their knowledge and integrating these in her religious family. We cannot fail to mention the use of suggestion and coercion for lucrative purposes.

There is a diversity of criteria in relation to the different positions[20] that women can aspire to, besides Apetebí (an assistant of the babalawo), which is the highest position[21] in almost all religious branches of the country. Professor and babalawo Wande Abimbola in a public talk titled "Ifa Mending Our Broken World" said on this point: "The Apetebi in Cuba and America has always been utilized to cook, serve the table and to attend the babalawos. They've been denied access to the literature of Ifa, to touch the ikines of their spouse . . . she merits respect and her participation in every ceremony is indispensable, as is her need to hold great knowledge."[22]

Victor Betancourt Estrada referring to the Apetebí stated:[23]

Women receive the name of *apetebí* automatically after receiving their preinitiation in Ifa, known in Cuba as ikofá. This new position gives her the capacity to invoke the spirit of Ifa through the handling of the sacred seeds. She can take care of and actively maintain, spiritually, the altar of Ifa. She can recite and convoke the spirit of Orúnmila mediated through the sacred chants. . . . Symbolically, she's engaged in the preparation of the nest or the cradle, or the new abode on earth, allowing for the future being to be born. She can also be initiated in Orisa and for that reason, she receives the authority to summon the rest of the 199 divinities of the Yoruba pantheon. She is the guide of the devotee at every step in their initiation of Ifa. *There are many rites that represent a new engendering where the Apetebí must and can function.*[24] In a mythical sense, she is the one that plants the sacred seeds or Ikin Ifa.

Apetebí ayafá. After an Apetebí supports a Babalawo in an initiation, like a liturgic annex, she acquires the rank of Apetebí ayafá (wife of Ifa) and represents the fundamental base in the later activities of the babalawo. Symbolically, she represents the woman who got pregnant and holds in her womb the seed of Ifá. She carries the sacred pumpkin (elegegé), symbolic of Osun's womb. She represents this divinity when she became pregnant by Orunmila. She participates in all the ceremonies conducted for the new adepts. Without her involvement, it is believed that the results of the rites would be lacking in spiritual potentiality. The Apetebí ayafá accompanies in officiating the sacrifices and preinitiations. *Philosophically, she represents all the care that mothers should follow in the prenatal period.*[25] The service that they must provide to the priests is symbolic of the services given by Osun to Orúnmila. Totally separated from the pejorative sense that alludes to servility, she is truly made present in the performance of the care of a seedling in the germination period.

The function of "wife of Ifa," independent of its importance in the ritual, identifies *apetebí ayafá* as belonging to the feminine realm to fulfill the role of woman-mother in care of biological reproduction—in this instance symbolic—in the transmission of established religious values. Her personal identity is suppressed to integrate the identity of the other: the babalawo. All the "symbolic" services that she offers draw her nearer to the traditional pillars of femininity through which her experiences as a subordinate then develop meaning from the perspective of someone who holds less power and privilege than men.

Another great issue pertaining to gender in Regla Ocha Ifá is the consecration of women as priestesses of Ifá or Iyaonifá. Only until recently were women allowed that possibility. However, some babalawos considered it a woman's right and started to carry out the corresponding ceremonies needed to consecrate women as priestesses. The turn of events was not seen positively by religious devotees from various branches and religious families and surprisingly by some *iyalochas*, which unleashed a strong debate among the believers. Researchers and other people interested in the subject joined the debate, extending to babalawos residing outside of Cuba. Such was the case of a well-respected Nigerian who took it upon himself the role of global Ifá inspector, who said on the topic: "There is no taboo prohibiting women from Ifa, women that are diviners of Ifa are called iyaonifás, but they serve as babalawos."[26]

A Cuban babalawo recognized that the role of the *iyaonifás* is similar to but not equal to the babalawos, whereas the Council of Major Priests of the Yoruba Cultural Association in Cuba spoke against it. However, the debate did not enter the public arena.[27]

A document issued by the Cultural Yoruba Association, as indicated in the corresponding note, shows the statements made by the teacher Idowu

B. Odemayí Balogún, Awo Agbaye, and president of Ifa International Religion Council based in Nigeria. He states: "It is prohibited that any woman from any spiritual extraction take possession of, manage or have a vision of Orisha Odu. This is by no means discriminatory against women, but rather, is pure and strictly consistent with the dogmas of Ifa expressed in Ofún Meji 16:4, in Irete Osa 22:8, in Irete Ofún 226:18 and in Otrupón Irete 192:11."

Despite the paternalism of these approaches, the stories accompanying the *odu* of Ifá collaborate a vision that maintains and accentuates the lack of existing equity, regardless of the advanced religious thought of the members of the branch or branches who agreed to the consecration, a lack of equity that is also observed in the functions that the consecrated perform. Victor Betancourt, whose work I already mentioned, posits:

> Iyáonifá. Signifies iyá-mother, possess-ni, Ifa-sacred elements of the cult, meaning, the mother that possesses the secrets of Ifa. She is considered a priestess with the same range of the Babalawo therefore she also performs divination through the Oracle of Ifá. She can officiate initiations, carry out sacrifices, so, she handles a wide spectrum of ritual work, *except those that could harm her spiritual and biological nature*.[28] Symbolically, she represents women postpartum. Her role is similar to that of the babalawo in respect to the rest of the religious community just like a mother and father are equally responsible for the care of a child in all familial relations. It is believed that the devotees that belong to the congregation of an Egbé (religious house) will not fully develop without the presence of at least one babalawo and one Iyáonifá the same way that a child will surely not develop integrally with an absent mother or father. She also represents women that after collecting the fruits of a good harvest, turn these into food for the community; such are her multiple roles in the liturgy. Iyáonifá is the mother, Ifa herself, who can be incarnate in any woman that has given birth. . . . An Iyáonfá, like any woman who has born a child, can assist in caring after other women and through her experience, contribute to the maternal proliferation of the rest of the community and of the Egbe or similarly, all women whose religious service and counsel are under an Iyáonifá can bear the fruit of life.[29]

The consecration of women in Ifá is accepted in different parts of the world, such as Benin, Nigeria, the United States, Venezuela. Some babalawos in Cuba followed those examples. Fifty-two initiations were realized between 2000 and 2009.[30]

Orisha Odu is an important female figure of Regla Ocha Ifá. She has served many generations of women initiated as a model of anti-dentification, by the distance that had to be kept from her "to avoid being 'victim' to prolonged menstrual periods."[31] This claim is highly charged, ideologically reflecting a society that grants women roles that guarantee their subordination to the male. But at the same time, we find a clear example of the way in which this religious expression solved the problem of "equity" between women and men, which is the same between babalawos and *apetebís* for some religious branches and between babalawos and *Iyaonifás* for others. Orisha Odu arouses much interest as a symbol, though she has been interpreted from a male reading.

What has worked as the "the fruit of discord" among the different babalawos is one of the *pataquíes* [allegories] of the *odu* Ireté Ogbé (Ireté Untelú), which is not universally recognized, of uncertain and suspect origin. Versions of it are limited;[32] regardless of this there is also a diversity of criteria about the authenticity of its message. Some interpreters posit that it prohibits the consecration of women as priestesses of Ifá; others counter, showing three interpretations. First: those who are totally opposed to consecrating women in Ifá. Second: those who accept the consecration of women but do not present[33] them to Odu (Igbá Iwa). Third: those who accept the consecration of women and present them to Odu (Igbá Iwa).[34] These are the trends derived from the babalawos' interpretations of the aforementioned *odu*. We could talk about a fourth trend by those who naturally accept the female consecration in Ifá because they simply do not know of any *odu* that forbids it.

Deconstructing allegories, myths, histories, and legends permits the unmasking of reality: tradition, taboos (considering that behind each one there is a secret) while the interpretation of the *odu* allows us to understand the conservatism, ethnocentrism, and misogyny of those who oppose the consecration of women in Ifá. A more inclusive attitude would unify the interpretations of sacred messages to reach a new mentality based on the deep conviction of equality between men and women, illustrated by the following fragment of the *odu* Otura Osun that in its translated version states:

I say to each, their purpose:
Men cannot listen to
the purpose I give to each.
Women cannot listen to
the purpose I give to each.
Women must be initiated
they must know my designs
they must speak out Ifa.[35]

A new mentality will be a step forward not only through innovative contributions by men and women in relation to their absolute and equitable integration but also in that it will open a path to developing unity among the varying religious tendencies, a concern that has been discussed for many years. I am not going to dwell much more in this area of discussion, but I hope that my attempt has been useful. My only aim has been to motivate reflection.

GLOSSARY

Adimu: The name signifies "to transform by absorbing." It refers to the various food offerings for the deities who absorb them until they consume the spirituality they contain. It is a supplementary offering after the sacrifice.

Añá: Drum. The deity that lives inside of the batá drum, its foundation. It is also the mate seed that is introduced to the sacred drum.

Apètèbí: Women who possess the preinitiation of Ifá known as akofá (messenger of Ifá). She convokes to birth in the ifismo.

Àse or *Ashé*: The name means "[the one] who realizes or causes." It is the cause of everything that is done in creation and the perfection of what is created. It is the dynamic principle of realization that it possesses and protects. A specific gift given to a particular person, it is the creative energy and neutral principle that is between the active and passive forces of the universe.

Apwon: Interpreter of religious chants and songs. "Caller of the deities."

Bàbálawo (babalawo): Diviner of the Ifá system. He is called Oluwo when he reaches a high degree of wisdom above his peers. His name means "father who possesses secrets."

Bàbálòsà or *Ìyátòsá* (babalocha o iyalocha): Father or mother of Òsá. Persons who have initiates under their custody and control.

Broma and Bronciá: Twin Orishas that live in the desert. They represent the bones of the dead and the secret of Oyá. Messengers of Orúnmila. Bronciá is a messenger of Oyá. Both are forebearers of Obatalá and Odudúwa. There are stories in which they appear as female, daughters of Yewá begotten by Changó. It is posed that Bronciá was born and Broma was not.

Balogún: A person consecrated to the deity Ogún.

Dialogún or *Dìlógún*: The name means "to transform by use of the dead." Another definition is "converted in the presence of an ancestor." The *dialogún* consists of sixteen eyo (cowries), which have two faces or parts that according to the number that fall face up or face down when thrown correspond (to the mystic number) with an *odu* of Ifá. It specifically serves as a base to establish communication with the ancestors through which the person asking for divination may receive the course of action to take.

Ebbo: This word is confused with corporeal cleansing and always gives the sense of purification and detachment of negativity. Ebo means simply to remove the soul of a sacrificed animal so that it may travel to heaven for two purposes: as our substitute searching for a new behavior or as a carrier of some negativity.

Egún: Spirit of an ancestor or dead person.

Egbado or *Egguado*: Lucumí tribe or ethnicity.

Ifá: From a philosophical point of view, Ifá is considered a complex system of divination that comprehends the foundation of everything that exists in the world. Expressed by 256 symbolic figures, known as *odu* Ifá, they appear during the manipulation of certain elements that make up the paraphernalia of the oracle. There is a vast literature that using a poetic language tells legends, fables, myths, and stories, with a structure based on poems, verses, and proses known as Ese Ifá, verses and poems are the key to the divination system. Expressions of the deep knowledge and appreciation of nature are an important part of them.

Ikin: Seed for divination. It is obtained from the fruit of the corojo palm (*Elaeis guineensis*). A set of Ifá is composed of eighteen ikin. During the process of divination and of certain rituals, sixteen are used to represent the sixteen olodu.

Iyáonifa: Woman consecrated to Ifá.

Igba Iwa: Another name for the Orisha Odu.

Ibbó-ozaín: Magic protection.

Olokún: The name means "owner of the sea." Orisha of the fishermen and mariners. He resides, according to the people of Ifé, at the bottom of the ocean. In Cuba, this orisha sometimes functions as Yemaya. Devotees go to the sea to make offerings to Yemaya, believing that she is the ocean. Some say: "She—Yemaya—is the surface of the ocean and Olokún its depth.

Odùdúwà (Odúa): The name signifies "who researches behaviors." He is the maker of righteousness, justice, and equity who developed the Empire of Ife unifying the thirteen peoples of the ancient Yoruba. He is the first deified king of Ifá and the supreme representative of ashe on earth.

Omo: Son or daughter.

Osun (Ochún or Oshún): Her name means "caregiver." Owner of the sweet waters and waterfalls, this orisha symbolizes fertility and the beginning of natural reproduction. She protects pregnant women and women who have just given birth. In Cuba, she is syncretized with the Virgin of Charity of el Cobre.

Orishaoco: His name means "possessor of the force of life." The productive honeybee and his servants and messengers. They indicate fertility. He is a guardian of secrets and costs. Arbitrator of disputes between women. In Cuba, he is syncretized with San Isidro Labrador.

Oyá: The name means "the one that opens paths." Orisha of the rain, tempest, lightning, and the winds. Tornadoes and violent storms are attributed to her. Patron saint of the dead. She symbolizes the strength of women who loyally accompany men. She controls the energy of the spirits so that it does not disturb the world of the living. Owner of marketplaces. She is part of a trilogy with Oba and Yewá in charge of the dead. In Cuba, she is syncretized with Our Lady of Candelaria and with Saint Teresa of Jesus.

Ògún: The name means "who battles." Owner of metals. Establishes the balance between positive and negative energies found in humans. Marks the limits of what is just in everything that is measured. Responsible for making tribal marks, tattoos, and surgeries. Protector of the orphans. He presides over oaths, alliances, and covenants. In Cuba, he is syncretized with San Pedro, San Pablo, San Juan Bautista, Santiago apostle, and San Miguel the Archangel.

Oshosi: His name means "the one who looks out for someone." Owner of the forest and hunting. He is never separated from his bow and arrows. He is the patron of family unity and is considered an excellent healer. In Cuba, he is syncretized with Saint Norberto.

Òríaté: The name means "the one that scans wicker basket where they throw the divination shells." Leads initiations and readings of the oracle of *dialogún*. When he excels above the rest of the Oriaté, holding maximum responsible in the direction of a ritual, it is called Oba (monarch, king).

Odù Ifá: Are the figures or ideograms that contain all the laws in the universe and all the possible existential situations of human beings. They are considered to be fractions of the body of Olodumare sectioned into sixteen pieces that match up to produce 256 sections. Each one of these figures or sections encloses the lives and works of all our ancestors, which are taken as a reference to establish the correct patterns of behavior and human coexistence. They represent the explanation of the world. Bank of all the data of the history of the universe, presented in full volumes subdivided into numerous chapters known as Ese Ifá, which explains fractionally the laws that integrated and intervened in the formation of the universe and nature at the time of creation. In addition, they contain the destiny of human beings and the patrons who govern it.

Òbàtála: His name signifies "resplendent in the limit." Owner of creative powers. Creator of human beings. Orisha of purity and intelligence. Sir of the white clothing. Protector of deformed beings. In Cuba, he is syncretized with the Virgin of las Mercedes.

Yémojá (Yemaya): Her name means "mother of the seed of the fish." Protector of maternity. In Cuba, she is syncretized with the Virgin de Regla.

Pínódó (Pinaldo): A ceremony through which the person who successfully completes it is empowered to sacrifice four-legged animals.

Yèwá derived from yè, to be alive and wá, to exist: It is the ocha that governs our existence in the world. It is also one of the names to denominate Ile Aguere, or Mother Earth. It is an orisha of death and presides in pits and graves. She owns desolate sites and the graveyard. In Cuba, she is syncretized with Our Lady of the Forsaken.

Òrúnmila: The name means "the one in heaven knows those who are saved." Is the maximum expression of the dialogue with nature. He knows, by reading the *odu* Ifá, the explanation of the world and all possible existential problems of humans.

Pàtaki: Word used to refer to stories, narratives of the ancient times, orishas, the *odu* of Ifá, and the *dialogún*.

NOTES

1. I believe there is a need to undertake a gender differentiation in the discourse given the abundant references to both genders in the writing referring to the male gender marked in Spanish, which subsumes the feminine.

2. From conversations with distinguished babalawos and from the personal archive of Aníbal Argüelles, researcher of CIPS. See also Yrminio Valdes Garriz, *Dilogún* (Havana: Ediciones Unión, 1995), 135.

3. There is a diversity of criteria related to the person who unified Yoruba cults to give rise to Santeria. Natalia Bolivar in *Los Orishas en Cuba* (p. 10) proposes, "Sama who took the name Obadimeyi (King crowned twice) became inseparable of a Yoruba black woman that embarked for Cuba in 1887, daughter of Changó, called Latuán. They conceived of the idea together of unifying the different Yoruba cults into a single liturgic body that they called Regla de Ocha. Obadimeyi enjoyed great prestige and his ideas gained a general acceptance." Victor Betancourt Estrada states in the book *Las Santeria una tradicion en decadencia* that "according to popular history, it was not until the end of the nineteenth century that the so-called Santeria was popularly instituted. It was stated that Remigio Herrera (Adesi-na-Addeshina awo Òbárá méjí) who stands out during the period from 1872 to 1890, contributed to the conformation of the Òsá rule as it is known to this day. For the second time, he rebuilt the Bata drums for the initiation of *criollos* in those mysteries and formed most of the "branches" that today exist in Cuba.

4. Lydia Cabrera, *El monte* (Havana: Editorial Letras Cubanas, 1989), 39.

5. Victor Betancourt Estrada, *Las santeria, una tradición en decadencia* (Venezuela: Edicion Orunmila, C.A., Gráficas Reus, no date).

6. Among his many words for her, he said, "Pepa was an honest woman whose honesty could not be betrayed to any type of exploitation, a purity of belief, and charitable spirit. She was my friend for more than thirty years whom I spoke to with great trustworthiness on the Lucumí tradition (taken from the personal archive previously cited).

7. Filhio Fernández Portugal, *Guia pracico de lingua yoruba em quatro odiomas*, first edition (Havana: Editorial de Ciencias Sociales, no date).

8. Bird sacrifices, purification ceremonies, the ritual of the medio asiento, the giving of Eleguá and the hand of cowry shells, making ebó, making omiero, taking on the roles as godfathers and godmothers of beaded necklaces, of the warriors, of asiento, or of both, among others.

9. The *odu* of Ifá are sixteen Meyis with 256 combinations. Each *odu* includes a description of each sign accompanied by one or more *pataquíes* or myths that play a decisive role in the divination process serving as an intermediary that fulfils a specialist function in that divination system of the Orishas that together with the ancestors can establish direct or indirect communication with their devotees.

10. Rosa Maria de Lahaye Guerra and Ruben Zardoya Lauredo, *Yemaya a través de sus mitos* [Yemaya through Her Myths] (Havana: Editorial de Ciencias Sociales, 1994).

11. In the Koran, book I, Surah Al-Baqarah 2:222–23, states that Allah said to Muhammad: When they ask you about menstruation, say: "It is filthy; so, keep away from women in the state of menstruation and do not approach them until they are cleansed" (pp. 173–206). Book 28 also states, "Say to the Believers: "When you repudiate women, you reject their prescribed menstrual periods." In Leviticus 12–15 appears: "When a woman has a discharge, and the discharge in her body is blood, she shall be in her menstrual impurity for seven days, and whoever touches her shall be unclean. . . . But if she is cleansed of her discharge, she shall count for herself seven days, and after that she shall be clean."

12. Estrada, *Las santeria, una tradición en decadencia*, 190.

13. Nana Burukú is a very ancient orisha related to the waters of creation. She is associated with water that contains dirt. Male and female simultaneously, she is also associated with life and death. She is present at the moment that the egg is fecund for the sperm in the instant of procreation in order to imprint in that moment the energy that the new being must assume. In that sense, it is a supreme energy associated with fertility. Its association to death is found in its function to accompany the dying in their last moments, not only to help them depart but to collect their last breath, like someone who detaches from his bones when the coffin is opened to carry out an exhumation. This determines the category of this orisha as a Major Orisha.

14. Guardian shield.

15. Spirit.

16. Daisy Rubiera, "La mujer en la Regla Ocha: una mirada de genero" [Women of Regla Ocha: A Gendered Gaze], in *Revolución y Cultura* [Revolution and Culture] (Havana, 1999), no. 2–3, p. 75.

17. Sexism is the belief system—founded on a series of myths and mystifications—of the superiority of the male sex, which results in a series of privileges for the male sex, making it believe its superiority (Alda Facio, *Cuando el género sueña, cambios trae* [When Gender Dreams, It Brings Changes] [Caracas, Venezuela, 1992], 36).

18. Ceremony by which the initiated is consecrated as an apetebí. Until recently, this greater charge was something the Iyalochas could only aspire to in the Regla de Ocha.

19. Prepare the room where the rituals take place, plucking and butchering birds of sacrifice, serve the *adimu* (innards) of the sacrificed four-legged animals to the deities, keep all of the ceremonial vessels clean, serve food to the major officiators among others.

20. An example is how they're impeded from leading the ceremony of presentation of their godchildren before the drum, sacrificing four-legged animals even if they've received the knife in the ceremony called "Pinaldo," playing the drum of batá of foundation or sacralization of the deity Añá, etc.

21. I must point out that, as such, they perform an important role in the ceremony of the Iyoyé, one of the ceremonies that is made in the consecration of the babalawos, the only ceremony in which the Apetebí can participate.

22. Taken from a copy provided by a babalawo dictated by professor Abimbola at a public talk.
23. Estrada, *Las santeria, una tradición en decadencia*, 184–89.
24. My italics.
25. My italics.
26. Interview of Ivor Millar a Wande Abimbola.
27. Regarding the debate, see Declaraciones del Consejo de Sacerdoes Mayores de la Asociación Cultural Yoruba de Cuba, September 11, 2004. Also see *Boletín Lukumí*, numbers 1, 2, and 3 of the temple-house Ifa Iránlowo, September 2004, www.ifashade.com.
28. My italics.
29. Estrada, *Las santeria, una tradición en decadencia*, 186–87.
30. The babalawos that were responsible for them were Frank Cabrera and Victor Betancourt.
31. Estrada, *Las santeria, una tradición en decadencia*, 201.
32. According to the compilation of documents that the previously named researcher from CIPS helped me to obtain.
33. Taken in its essence from the collection previously cited.
34. Ibid.
35. www.Ifachade.com/Iyaonifa.Htm.

BIBLIOGRAPHY

Argüelles Mederos, Aníbal, and Ileana Hodge. 1990. *Los llamados cultos sincréticos y el espiritismo*. Havana: Editorial Academia.

Angarica, Valentin. No date. *Manual del oriaté: Religión Lucumi*. No publisher.

Betancourt Estrada, Victor. No date. *Las santeria, una tradición en decadencia*. Venezuela: Edicion Orunmila, C.A., Gráficas Reus.

Bolivar Arostegüi, Natalia. 1994. *Los Orishas en Cuba*. Havana: P. M. Ediciones.

Cabrera, Lydia. 1974. *Yemayá y Ochún*. Madrid: Ediciones C.B.

———. 1989. *El monte*. Havana: Editorial Letras Cubanas.

Centro Islámico. No date. *El Sagrado Corán*. Translated by Ahmed Aboud and Rafael Castellanos. First edition. Valencia: Centro Islámico de Venezuela, Valencia.

De Lahaye, Rosa Maria, and Ruben Zardoya Lauredo. 1994. *Yemaya a través de sus mitos*. Havana: editorial de Ciencias Sociales.

De Souza Hernandez, Adrian. 1996. *Las dieciséis esencias basicas del ifismo*. Vol. 1. Venezuela: Ediciones El Cataruro.

———. 1998. *Echu-Elegguá: equilibrio dinámico de la existencia*. Havana: Ediciones Unión.

Donrbarch, Maria. 1993. *Los orichas en sopera*. Editorial Szeged.

Elbein Dos Santos, Juana. 1975. *Os nago e la norte*. Fourth edition. Petrpolis, Brazil: Editora Vozes.

Facio, Alda. 1992. *Cuando el género sueña, cambios trae*. Caracas, Venezuela: Escarcha Azul.

Lachatanere, Romulo. 1992. *El sistema religioso de los afrocubanos*. Havana: Editorial de Ciencias Sociales.
Lagarde, Marcela. 1997. *El cautiverio de las mujeres: Madresposa, monjas, putas, presas y locas*. Mexico D. F.: Universidad Nacional Autónoma de Mexico.
Mestre, Jesús. 1996. *Santeria, mitos y creencias*. Havana: Edicion Prensa Latina, World Data Research Center.
Ofún Yemiló, ed. No date. *Tratado de Oddu de Ifa*. No Publisher.
Portugal Filho, Fernández. No date. *Guia pracico de lingua yoruba em quatro odiomas*. First edition. Havana: Editorial de Ciencias Sociales.
Ramos, Arthur. 1949. *Las culturas negras en el Nuevo Mundo*. Pamica, Mexico: Fondo de Cultura Económica.
Rubiera Castillo, Daisy. 1999. "La mujer en la Regla Ocha: una mirada de genero." In *Revolución y Cultura*, no. 2–3. Havana.
———. 2001. "Genero y mitología en la Regla Ocha." In *Del Caribe*, no. 35. Santiago de Cuba.
———. 2002. "Lo femenino y lo masculino en la cosmovisión Yoruba: su influencia en la Regla Ocha." In *Del Caribe*, no. 37. Santiago de Cuba.
———. 2007. "La Iyáonifá: un problema de género en la Regla Ochá/Ifá." *Afro Hispanic Review* 26, no. 1. Vanderbilt University, United States.
Sociedades Bíblicas Unidas. 1960. *La Santa Biblia: Antiguo y Nuevo Testamento*. Mexico D. F.: Sociedades Bíblicas Unidas.
Valdes Garriz, Yrminio. 1995. *Dilogún*. Havana: Ediciones Unión.
Verger, Pierre. 1982. *Orisha: Les dieux yoruba en Afrique et au Noveau Monde*. Metailie, Paris: Editions A. M.

Chapter 13

Gender and Raciality

An Obligatory Reflection in Contemporary Cuba

Yulexis Almeida Junco

INTRODUCTION

The concept of race has no scientific validity. Developments in anthropological and genetic studies show that there are no pure races, that racial classification is arbitrary and impossible. The renowned Fernando Ortiz stated on this subject, "With scientific rigor, the race is taxonomically imprecise or illimitable. . . . The typical characteristics perceived as racial fade from individual to individual in a multitude of variations."[1]

Yet race continues to function in society operating like an objective category that traverses every aspect of human relations. The idea is difficult to banish because people look different and attribute those differences to a natural state that determines personal and cultural features. Nature is problematically part of the term because it holds an association between a subjective component at its base that sustains it and the expression of tangible, visible, external elements, such as phenotype, nationality, language, traditions, cultural symbols, etc.

In this sense, the notion of race shares a genealogical logic with gender in making a social condition dependent on biology because in both apparent physical differences overlap social constructions that become anatomical extensions and make up the symbolic universe of each culture.

Consequently, gender and race constitute social constructs that through their interaction shape specific social hierarchies. The nexus between them is not unidimensional and does not imply a relation of cause and effect. They are not two isolated systems that clearly and distinctively intersect in all cases. We are speaking about two categories related in complex ways whose comprehension is not possible from a single theoretical and methodological frame of reference. Both act at every level (micro and macro) and interact with each other and other axes of oppression that produce a combination of intersected social structural inequalities.

Societies have developed on the foundation of hierarchical relations that have been considered natural forms necessary for social organization. Patriarchy rises as one of the first systems in constructing structures of clear domination whose hegemony has been perpetuated across time. The success of patriarchy has undoubtedly been based on its capacity to establish alliances with other systems of domination while it changes their character by executing ways of implementing itself according to the time and terrain in which it operates.

Different factors attenuate or accentuate the weight of the constructions of gender and race or the interweaving of both in certain situations. Discovery of the key points of the reciprocal construction between gender and race and how the sociopolitical conditions that propitiate it remain the fundamental challenges for the studies responsible for exposing the links between them in order to narrow the gaps among different social groups on the basis of sex and skin color.

GENDER AND RACE: A THORNY BUT NECESSARY ENCOUNTER

Race becomes important for social and power relations in certain areas or moments. Power and domination adopt multiple forms of expression. In this regard Foucault reflects, "power is not something that is divided between those who hold it as exclusive property and those who do not have it and suffer it. . . . It is never located here nor there, it is never in the hands of someone. . . . Power works and is exercised through a network. Individuals not only circulate in its mesh but also are placed in the condition of suffering or exercising it."[2]

Consider black men and women as subordinated groups. Since the nineteenth century, science has established an analogy between them as beings with inferior intellectual abilities. As Sabrina Brancato stated, "the inferior races were represented as a female type among human species and women represented an inferior race between the genders." However, the relations within each group are also hierarchical.[3]

Myths on women hold different connotations for white and black women, for example, women as objects of beauty. The aesthetic canon is founded on a white typology that challenges black women's physical features, continually devaluing and burdening them with a pejorative symbolic system. When women are spoken about as objects of beauty, the focus tends to be on white women. This myth places demands and holds implications for all women yet doubly impacts black women. Besides positioning them at a disadvantage, it places limitations on them from a social and personal perspective.

Due to the sexism that predominates the labor market, women hold greater mobility not only in activities that have been traditionally assigned to them but also in those jobs that implicitly carry requirements related to physical appearance, creating greater competition for black women to access those jobs versus white women than between black men and white women.

Additionally, the assumption and adaptation to the predominant cultural models on aesthetics, cultural expressions, representations, and symbolic systems compel many black women to continually redraw, oppose, or deny themselves which produces ailments, anxieties, and frustrations that mediate between what is expected of them and the place that society gives them as women.

Black men have not been exempted from these conflicts. They also face aesthetic requirements that usually attenuate sexist valuations that limit them from caring for their bodies, which is considered a feminine attitude, not disregarding current tendencies like those of metrosexuals[4] that constitute a rupture with these values. Apart from this, although black men may be positioned more favorably with respect to black women, the hegemonic male model also places social demands on them that measure and hinder the success they could achieve.

Black men have been stereotyped as slackers, brutes, and failures counter to the social mobility of white men, representative of the status quo. Researcher bell hooks[5] explains how these stereotypes represent an effective way for racists to hide the meaning of the labor of black people from public awareness, and later the same stereotypes are evoked as reasons to deny them the right to work.[6]

These ideological devices work in reality. Black men have a harder time in the job market. This translates into greater limitations to fulfill the role of provider assigned to men, which is reflected in family dynamics and in the general stability of the social construction of class linked to the color of the skin. However, this does not mean that we cannot speak of a homogeneous black masculinity.

All these conceptions also impact the terrain of sexuality in which black is associated with the instinctive, primitive, and savage. Once these characteristics are accepted as part of negritude, they are used to identify black women and men as people with an exacerbated sexual appetite.

For a long time, women were denied pleasure as part of their sexuality. Pleasure became trapped in the sphere of the perverse, made deviant and illicit through an extensive manipulation, and associated with anti-values like promiscuity and immorality, reserved for prostitutes, homosexuals, and black people. These ideas have changed over time due to the struggles of women as protagonists of their sexuality. However, the essence of these ideas remains, continuing to hyperbolize the sexuality of black women and men.

In largely *mestizo* societies, it has become increasingly urgent for an explanatory and action-based paradigm. This paradigm must contemplate a multidisciplinary approach that includes a historical perspective in all areas that allows knowledge on the specific situation of different ethnoracial groups pertaining to the relations between men and women.

GENDER AND RACE IN CUBA: BETWEEN CONTINUITIES AND PERMANENCIES

Black men and women belong to a population that has had to contend (with the concrete particularities of each country) with situations of discrimination, marginalization, and devaluation legitimized socially on the ideology of racism that seeks homogeneity as ideal. It has found a fertile ground in a system of patriarchal social relations that positions the paradigm of human to mean man, white, heterosexual, and economically solvent.

Cuba has not escaped this social ill. The Cuban *ajiaco* stew has among its fundamental ingredients the meeting of two nonhomogeneous cultures that converge in Cuba with very different conditions. On the one hand, Spaniards who came looking for fortune and hogged, a good number of them, important socioeconomic positions within Cuba's classist social structure; and on the other, an African black population brought to Cuba in the most inhumane conditions as part of slave labor.

From its beginnings, Cuban society was characterized by a stratification of classes that corresponded to racial grouping in whose lower strata blacks were overrepresented. A foundational element of this social organization constituted racism as an ideological system that disseminated a primordial role legitimizing the superiority of some groups over others, that is to say of whites over blacks. Therefore race throughout history has been intimately linked to the class struggle and the overcoming of racial inequalities as a latent revindication in all struggles undertaken to achieve a democratic and just republic. The decisive Revolution for National Liberation in 1959 marked the beginning of a social project that envisaged a series of transformations in the political, economic, juridical, and social order that led to profound structural changes that allowed the transition to a different social order. These changes, although benefiting society in general, included proposals aimed at the most vulnerable groups, including women and broad sectors of the black population.

With respect to women, they were successfully incorporated as an active force in the construction of the new society. Actions were taken in different sectors that ruptured the division between public and private, although this division was not evident for broad sectors of black women and poor white women who constituted pillars in the sustenance of their families, some because the father figure was absent and others because the family budget was very small, and they had to contribute to the livelihood of the household. For the majority of these women, the possibilities of work were in precarious conditions with meager salaries and at times they extended the roles traditionally allocated to women.

Keeping this reality in mind, the revolutionary process increased and made sustainable the opportunities for women to improve their scientific, technological, and professional preparation. In this context, the Federación de Mujeres Cubanas (FMC) [Federation of Cuban Women] achieved an important role in creating an organization in 1960 to represent women's interests in all segments of society with the objective to direct, elaborate, and organize on policies that further social change for Cuban women.

This allowed the percentage of women in education to increase in general, especially in areas of specialization, although their presence in vocational training linked to occupations directly tied to production, such as qualified workers, continues to be limited. At present in Cuba, women are the majority in the educational system not only as students but also as teachers. Notwithstanding, this process has not yet had an equally proportional impact on the structures of management. However, changes in the educational situation of women and their progressive incorporation into this area led to their gradual access to the working world. They were incorporated into the country's economic developmental projects while the demand for an active and integrated female workforce grew ostensibly during the decade of the 1960s in the twentieth century. The changes were supported by a series of measures that laid the foundations for the successful insertion of Cuban women in the sphere of labor.[7]

These transformations throughout the revolutionary period have had suppressive barriers, typical of a country that on its way toward the construction of a more just society for its citizens maintains in its essence a system of relations deeply rooted in patriarchy. The phenomenon is reflected in the composition of labor differentiated by sex as it relates to branches of activity and occupational categories. Professional groups offer accounts of being subjected to the feminization and the masculinization of some occupations even today in the labor environment.

Regardless of barriers, gender focus from the 1990s to the present gradually increased, converting itself into a central category in the treatment of different social problems from a multiplicity of scientific disciplines in the country. This allowed a consolidation of studies and debates on the subject in different spaces: informal, academic, and media, among others. In this way, I contribute to deconstructing many of the concepts that support the assignment of roles, attitudes, and activities according to the biological sex of men and women in an arbitrary way.

These investigations have exposed the impact of sexist stereotypes on the social lives of men and women and the need to avoid unjust disparities, as well as their determinants. The gradual, complex, and contradictory process has favored the reconstruction of cultural patterns that have become more flexible and have promoted an increasingly favorable situation for women with respect to men. Nevertheless, they live with new acquired values and old values that remain hegemonic and keep us within a patriarchal cultural pattern.

Regarding racial discrimination, despite advancement on its eradication, the process has been slower and has included limitations that have thwarted the solution of a central problem in our context. In this regard, the commander in chief Fidel Castro Ruz at the closing of the Congress Pedagogía 2003 expressed:

> Having radically changed our society, women, formerly terribly discriminated and whose scope was only the most humiliating work, are today in themselves a decisive and prestigious segment of society that constitutes 65% of the technical and scientific force of the country. However, though the Revolution achieved and guaranteed the rights for all citizens of any ethnicity and origin, it has not achieved the same success in the struggle to eradicate the differences in the social and economic status of the black population of the country . . . , even though in many areas of great transcendence, including education and health, they play an important role.[8]

The changes experienced in the social panorama of Cuba in the early years of the revolution managed to dismantle in the public order and, at an institutional level, discriminatory policies based on the color of the skin. Subsequently, racial inequalities were addressed, not so much in their specificity but as an expression of class differences. Therefore its solution was implemented on the basis of creating policies aimed at improving the socioeconomic conditions of the poorest sectors of the country. Racial equality was reached in the middle and long term shown by the range of important socioeconomic indicators such as education, culture, sports, and life expectancy. The latter reflects very broad economic, educational, and sanitary conditions. As for the occupational structure in the early 1980s, there remained differences associated with skin color, but blacks and *mulatos* had managed to enter massively in the most attractive sectors of the labor market, including technical and management sectors.⁹ Undoubtedly, the policies that were applied demonstrated their effectiveness in achieving standardized conditions at a social level and in the promotion of opportunities that have limited the emergence of exclusionary processes.

This was achieved by shortening the racial divide as a result of a more favorable and uniform socioeconomic situation for the different population groups. Despite this, the changes undertaken failed to directly affect the social disadvantages faced by the black population. In this regard, political scientist Esteban Morales was explicit: "Inside the Revolution, there was no social policy project aimed at balancing the asymmetries that the different racial groups that make up the Cuban society faced in 1959."¹⁰

The universal guarantees of social rights for citizens from all spheres of society created the illusion of a solved problem. The access to education and employment by all the sectors of the population without distinction of class and color of the skin allowed old racist conceptions to change, which made the racial issue lose visibility and thus become left out of the focused interests of the social sciences in the country.

The public debate on race was believed to be out of place in our society, a judgment that was legitimized in science with works of this period that gave an account of a problem that had been overcome. Such is the case of works such as "Racial Discrimination in Cuba Will Never Return" (Felipe Jose Carneado, 1962), "A Bad Past, Aspects of Racial Discrimination" (Juan Sanchez, 1972) in the journal *Bohemia*, the work by Juan Rene Betancourt *The Negro Citizen of the Future*, and of Pedro Serviat *The Black Problem in Cuba and Its Definitive Solution*.¹¹ All these works in some way highlighted the role of the revolution in overcoming racial inequalities. A silence emerged that favored the displacement of racism that remained latent in the social consciousness in the field of everyday life and interpersonal relations. According to a Marxist theory, the changes that take place in the economic base are not reflected at the same time in the superstructure. Racism is not only a problem of unequal distribution of resources of all kinds, it also constitutes a system of ideas, values, and social representations greatly rooted in our culture. These are transmitted through the processes of socialization in which the family, school, media, and community play a fundamental role. Yet these are spaces that have not been used in all their potential as pathways to direct action to influence society.

Additionally, racism as all systems of domination has multiple ways to perpetuate, transfigure, and reinsert itself. The difficult economic situation created in the 1990s, aggravated by the Período Especial [Special Period], highlighted significant disadvantages confronted by some population sectors during the crisis. These unequal material conditions, together with inherited leucocratic conceptions, served as a foundation to re-create and revitalize stereotypes, representations, and images that had remained dormant.

Although the impasse of almost three decades conditioned a theoretical-methodological delay in treating the problem of race from the social sciences in Cuba, evident in the limited number of works that exist on the subject, the effects of the crisis catalyzed interest on the crisis. Recent research conducted by the Institute of Anthropology revealed that the black population has less access to the emerging sectors of the economy, faces more limitations of social mobility in the labor force, receives less remittances from the exterior, and resorts more than the rest of the racial groups to do extra work after a full work day. The majority of black women are single mothers, heads of households, with limited social mobility also in the work environment.

The socioeconomic disadvantages linked to the historical gaps of the black population with respect to other racial groups have not been able to be radically overcome, so it becomes necessary to address the problem in its specificity, deepening the macro structure and micro character that are conjoined in the social reproduction of the same. Critical analysis is necessary to allow for a policy rethinking. These must explicitly include the racial dimension in order to achieve greater social effectiveness in achieving equitable and sustainable human development.

This analysis deserves an integrative perspective for the understanding of processes in the field of interpersonal relationships, family, and everyday life explained by real people from their life experiences that build and re-create their particular worlds according to their racial, class, and generational belonging, among others. This makes it possible to influence the processes of the formation of stereotypes and prejudices. This is an important element when we take into account that the racist expressions that had remained latent in the field of daily life were moving more and more from the private space to the public sphere, being articulated in the spaces where concrete subjects act, regardless of the laws that are meant to guarantee equal rights for all people irrespective of the color of their skin.

A recent case study investigation explored the nexus among social, gender, and racial representations[12] in a neighborhood in Cuba and revealed how individuals through processes of communication available in quotidian life exchange knowledge that reflects stereotypical views of the different racial groups in Cuba. It showed how race continues to operate as an instrument for stratification of social relations articulated with other variants such as generations and social classes of the community.

The group selected for the study was composed of twenty women and twenty men. For each sex, ten whites and ten blacks were chosen. Similarly, heterogeneous groups in relation to age, education level, origin, and social occupation were found so that the study could collect a variety of information from all segments, generations, and social groups in the community.

The study highlighted some of the most significant ideas that were part of the social representation of the group. First, both blacks and whites referred to themselves in relation to whites. This signified the internalization of white as the norm, pattern, and measure of being human. It also indicated how the white population translated the hegemonic cultural and aesthetic values associated with the white color as superior, legitimized by an economic, political, and socially dominant position for centuries. In turn black people did the same, reproducing power, not for them but for those who have held it throughout history. About this, Fanon expressed: "The Negro enslaved by his inferiority, the white man enslaved by his superiority alike behave in accordance with a neurotic orientation."[13]

Most of the white women of the study pointed to hair as a significant element for the condition of black women and referred to it in terms of a disadvantage. Hair is a relevant attribute in the construction of femininity. It is a decisive element in the aesthetics of women, who from an early age, without distinction of color, are educated in the cult of long and straight hair. This is reinforced through different socializing devices such as fashion magazines, television programs, and images of commercial products of all kinds. The exclusion or undervaluation of a racially different type of hair has led to its disqualification. Thus the hair of black women has not been considered ideal; on the contrary, it is pejoratively referenced, referred to as *pasa* [likening the tight curls of short afro to dried raisins], and is depreciated as ugly and bad. This has been internalized by both white and black people.

These valorizations impact other areas of social reality. Black men and women agreed that they encountered more limitations in the workplace, an idea that was not claimed by white respondents. Life experiences were considered an important element in the construction of concepts that they held based on the racial group to which they belonged. In this sense, black people recognized the role that skin color can play as a catalyst for social mobility in certain spaces as they exemplified it, drawn from situations in their daily lives.

White people, however, did not emphasize racial embodiments. Though racism is multidirectional and under certain circumstances any racial group can be an object of it, as shown throughout Cuban history, racism has predominantly been anti-black. This explains why in a general sense black individuals shared in greater proportion experiences in which they had been victim to racist expressions, while white people focused on elements that disqualified black people whether because of their physical characteristics or the social behavior attributed to them.

White people's responses coincided in their views that black women and black men have inferiority and prejudicial complexes. Black people since birth are valued as incomplete beings either because of their physical characteristics or by the qualities that are socially assigned to them. This triggers multiple responses that are not always expressions of complexes and prejudices but rather of the racist ideology that places whites as an icon in society who gain greater valuation of themselves by pointing to complexes and prejudices to neutralize any reactions to racist attitudes. In turn, black men and women respond passively to situations in which they are denigrated and disqualified for fear of being labeled as "complainers" because in some cases, if they do not respond passively, they will be converted into victims while simultaneously being responsible for discriminatory actions against them.

However, there is no doubt that belonging to a color that has a marginal place in language, cultural symbols, and different communicative technologies builds in the social imaginary an imperfect being that recognizes itself as secondary in a society that devalues their body constantly. The distance between the paradigm of the human and real black women and men generates ailments, anxieties, and frustrations that have an impact on their physical and mental health.

As far as interracial relationships, the study found a favorable response for relationships among all groups, which aligns with a success of the revolution intended to eradicate racially stratified spaces, the elimination of institutional racism, and the integration of all social groups in Cuban society. However, an analysis of the responses of the white group revealed that the majority of the women rejected interracial relationships that involved formal marriage, parenting, cohabitation in neighborhoods, and businesses. Race configures a social hierarchy that is perpetuated through the control of sexuality as a means to maintain racial difference. Thus latent expressions of racism are embedded in the field of interpersonal relations and the family that emerge and are strengthened through economic junctures that in turn accentuate social inequalities.

The attitudes of the group toward black people based on gender differ for men. In terms of business, they expressed their refusal to establish business relations with black people. This relates to social constructions of gender. Businesses are activities considered historically more typically male than female, as they imply a display of qualities understood as masculine: rationality, audacity, authoritarianism, and self-control. It is also a recurring activity for men in their role as economic providers and protagonist figures within the public sphere.

People are involved in business relations when they ensure certain conditions that become guarantees for the success of their businesses. A fundamental element is, without a doubt, the existence of a climate of trust and security. The attributes generally associated with black people discredit them as trustworthy beings, being labeled as treacherous and transgressors of moral values accepted by society.

Simply put, people in their daily lives need to understand and explain the reality around them; it is much easier to simplify and select the information available based on old values and inherited racist beliefs, which are sometimes reinforced from particular life experiences that become widespread. The difficult thing is to try to understand all the complexity of social factors that intervene in the reproduction of behaviors and attitudes assumed by different social groups. "It is simpler to attribute differences to heritage than to decipher all the complex social reasons that determine these differences."[14]

Throughout history, wide sectors of the black population have lived in the worst conditions, which generates cultural patterns and lifestyles that are transmitted generation to generation. None of this results from racial affiliation but from socioeconomic status, educational, and cultural levels and opportunities for social mobility, among other factors.

CONCLUSION

Deepening the study of race in Cuba increasingly demands more investigative efforts, especially in overcoming obstacles, given the results of studies that demonstrate the permanence of racist expressions. The theory of social representations constitutes a valid approach to this problem, which raises an indissoluble nexus between the individual and the social. The nexus reflects a social consensus that gives account not only of a social reality but also of processes that intervene in its elaboration, an aspect that has not been valued in terms of what it potentially represents to the transformation of sexist and racist values greatly rooted in our culture.

The project of social justice in the current Cuban context requires perspectives from vulnerable groups to whom social policies are oriented. In this sense, it is necessary to articulate strategies that intentionally include the racial component in areas of great social influence, such as education, employment, and culture, as powerful tools to promote equitable social development that will gradually minimize the socioeconomic disadvantages faced by the black population who remain the majority in the worst-paid jobs and with limited access to opportunities for economic improvement.[15]

The subjective character of the phenomenon, its foundation in the lived experience, limits its social recognition framed in a society in which the universalization of education and conditions for full employment were achieved, granting social guarantees in indicators like health, sports, and culture. In this context, cliché phrases are frequent that conceal the real thoughts of people as a result of the internalization of the discourse of equality and also of the level of consciousness reached in a negative sense, from an ethical point of view, that does not openly expose racist attitudes in Cuba.

Efforts should be directed at converting the negative and unacknowledged valorizations that the complex interplay of racial and patriarchal systems have made invisible. The persistence of discriminatory behavior in different social fields, combined with the permanency of stereotypes and racial prejudice in our society, demands a critical lens reflective of reality that allows us to articulate precise actions if we intend to annihilate a social ill that agonizes but refuses to die.

NOTES

1. Fernando Ortiz, *El engaño de la razas* (Havana: Editorial de Ciensias Sociales, 1975), 130.

2. Michel Foucault, *Genealogía del racismo* [Genealogy of Racism] (Madrid: Editorial Piqueta, 1992), 39.

3. Sabrina Brancato, "Masculinidad y etnicidad: Las representaciones racistas y el mito del violador negro," in *Nueva masculinidades*, edited by Marta Segarra and Angels Carabi (Barcelona, Spain: Icaria, 2000), 109.

4. This term was coined in 1994 by Mark Simpson in England to refer to men who break from models of dominant masculinity and turn to the care of their body and an aesthetic based on attributes considered feminine.

5. Bell Hooks (bell hooks) is the pseudonym of Gloria Watkins, who signs her work in lowercase letters.

6. Marta Segarra and Ángels Carabi, eds., *Nuevas masculinidades*, 111.

7. Some of the principal transformations were: profound renovation in the structure and system of jobs that allowed women to overcome some barriers and to occupy positions of labor traditionally assigned to men; the creation of a diversity of jobs covering a broad range to include women; women's interests for cultural, technical, and professional betterment were stimulated; the labor rights of these women in the Constitution of the Republic and the labor codes, advanced revolutionary laws guaranteeing equal rights for men and women; in 1961, childcare was created for working mothers.

8. Kali Argyriadis, ed., *Las relaciones raciales en Cuba: Aportes empíricos y nuevas interpretaciones, Documentos IDYMOV* (Xalapa: CIESA-Golfo, 2006), no. 10, 28.

9. See Alejandro de la Fuente, "Raza, desigualdad y prejuicio en Cuba," *América Negra*, Bogota, Columbia, no. 15 (December 1998): 27–30.

10. Esteban Morales Dominguez, "Un modelo para el análisis de la problemática racial cubana contemporánea," *Catauro. Revista Cubana Antropología*, Fundación Fernando Ortiz, Havana, 4, no. 6 (2000): 61.

11. "La discriminación racial en Cuba no volverá jamás" (Felipe Jose Carneado), *Cuba Socialista*, Havana, 2, no. 5 (January 1962): 54–67; "Un mal pasado, aspectos

de la discriminación racial" (Juan Sanchez, 1972), *Bohemia* (1973); Juan René Betancourt, *El negro ciudadano del futuro* (Havana: ONRE, 1959); and Pedro Serviat, *El problema negro en Cuba y su solución definitiva* (Havana: Editora Política, 1986).

12. Yulexis Almeida Junco, *Género y racialidad: Un estudio de representaciones sociales en el barrio "La Timba,"* dissertation, Cátedra de la Universidad de La Habana, 2008, unpublished.

13. Frantz Fanon, *Black Skin, White Masks* (1983), cited by Rocio Castro Kustner in *Relación género-ethia: Reflexión sobre la genealogía del poder* [Gender-Ethnic Relations: A Reflection on the Genealogy of Power], http://www.desafio.uba.br/gt7-006.html (accessed October 2007).

14. Antonio J. Martínez Fuentes, "Antropología, variación humana 'raza y racismo'" [Anthropology, Human Variety "Race and Racism"], in *Revista Universidad de La Habana*, II Semester, no. 258 (2003): 167.

15. See Rodrigo Espina and Pablo Rodríguez, "Raza y desigualdad en la Cuba actual," *Temas*, Havana, no. 45 (January–March 2006).

BIBLIOGRAPHY

Almeida Junco, Yulexis. 2008. *Género y racialidad: Un estudio de representaciones sociales en el barrio "La Timba."* Dissertation. Cátedra de la Universidad de La Habana. Unpublished.
Amorós, Celia. 2006. *Hacia una crítica de la razón patriarcal.* In *Documentos IDYMOV*, no. 10. Xalapa: CIEZA-Golfo.
Argyriadis, Kali, ed. 2006. *Las relaciones raciales en Cuba: Aportes empíricos y nuevas interpretaciones.* In *Documentos IDYMOV.* Xalapa: CIESA-Golfo.
Bordieu, Pierre. 1996. "La dominación masculina." In *La ventana. Revista de estudios de Genero de la Universidad de Guadalajara*, no. 3. Guadalajara.
Brancato, Sabrina. 2000. "Masculinidad y etnicidad: Las representaciones racistas y el mito del violador negro." In *Nueva masculinidades*, edited by Marta Segarra and Angels Carabi. Barcelona, Spain: Icaria.
Carneiro, Sueli. 2001. "Ennegrecer el feminismo. La situación de la mujer negra en América Latina, desde una perspectiva de género." In the International Seminar on Racism, Xenophobia and Gender organized by Lolapress in Durban, South Africa, August 27 and 28. http://www.lolapress.org/artspanish/carns16.htm.
Castro Kustner, Rocio. *Relación género-ethia: Reflexión sobre la genealogía del poder.* http://www.desafio.uba.br/gt7-006.html.
De la Fuente, Alejandro. 1998. "Raza, desigualdad y prejuicio en Cuba." *América Negra*, no. 15 (December). Bogota, Columbia.
Espina, Rodrigo, and Pablo Rodríguez. 2006. "Raza y desigualdad en la Cuba actual." *Temas*, no. 45 (January–March). Havana.
Foucault, Michel. 1992. *Genealogía del racismo.* Madrid: Editorial Piqueta.
Ibañez García, Tomas. 1998. *Ideología de la vida cotidiana.* Barcelona: Ediciones Sendai.
La Gaceta de Cuba. 2005. "Nación, raza y cultura." January–February. Havana: Unión de Escritores y Artistas de Cuba.

Lagarde, Marcela. 1996. *Género y Femenismo. Desarrollo Humano y Democracia.* Madrid: Horas y Horas.

Martínez Fuentes, Antonio J. 2003. "Antropología, variación humana 'raza y racismo.'" In *Revista Universidad de La Habana,* II Semester, no. 258.

———. 2003. "Siglo XXI: Antropología, 'razas y racismo.'" In *Revista Universidad de La Havana,* II Semester, no. 258.

Martínez Heredia, Fernando. 2002. "La cuestión racial en Cuba." *Caminos,* no. 24–25. Havana: Editorial Caminos.

Morales Dominguez, Esteban. 2000. "Un modelo para el análisis de la problemática racial cubana contemporánea." In *Catauro. Revista Cubana Antropología* 4, no. 6. Havana: Fundación Fernando Ortíz.

———. 2007. *Desafíos de la problemática racial en Cuba.* Havana: Fundación Fernando Ortíz.

Morales, Sandra. 2004. *La representación social del negro en Cuba.* Dissertation thesis for the Department of Psychology. Havana. Not published.

Moscovici, Serge. 2002. "Racismo, prejuicios y discriminación." In *Psicología Social II.* Spain: Editorial Paidos.

Ortiz, Fernando. 1975. *El engaño de las razas.* Havana: Editorial de Ciensias Sociales.

Pérez Álvarez, Maria Magdalena. 1996. "Los prejuicios raciales: sus mecanismos de reproducción." *Temas,* no. 7. Havana.

Segarra, Marta, and Ángels Carabi. 2000. *Nuevas masculinidades.* Icaria, Barcelona.

Stolke, Verena. ¿Es el sexo para el género lo que la raza para la etnicidad y la naturaleza para la sociedad? Presented at I Conferencia de asociación Europea de Antropólogos Sociales en Coimbra. Accessed May 2007. http://www.xoc.uam.mx/~pol-cul/pyc14/25-60pdf.

Chapter 14

On Afrocubana Stereotypes
Construction and Deconstruction of Myths
María Ileana Faguaga Iglesias

There are two essential moments regarding stereotypes about Afro-Cuban women and the construction and deconstruction of prevalent myths about them. I refer to them with greater precision so as not to create disaggregated concepts of Cuban black women. The two moments are the moment of the deconstruction of racialized discourses and the moment of deconstruction of racist discourses. Both moments form a holistic interrelation involving different elements from language to political power structures. It is essential to emphasize that first the deconstruction of racialized discourse cannot happen if the second one does not occur, which is the deconstruction of racist discourses, nor vice versa. When there is no possibility of practicing racial discrimination, discourses of racial content become lost insofar as they are useless and thus lose interest. When there is a real possibility of attacking and tackling racialized discourses, the space to exercise racial discrimination becomes constricted and shortened.

Both discourses constitute elements of the panorama of power relations in which societies move. In the case of societies being formed by various nationalities or the result of the mixtures of nations and of different ethnoracial groups, these discourses have solidly incorporated differences between black and white as mechanisms of domination and not as an instrument of sociological, economic, political, and social enrichment, thereby imposing the dominant ethnoracial group as the model group. Any group considered different is marginalized and even excluded on which the vision of the model group is imposed, sometimes so flimsily that it does not exceed the category of label. Thus this discourse positions the nonwhite as *the inferior, primitive, and uncivilized*,[1] establishing a long chain of qualifications that are left in the collective imaginary, creating deep and bleeding wounds in them that the undervalued pretends on several occasions to forget.

A complicated and perverse game of power is thus expressed that works from the point of a psychic process in response to the violence exerted on the subordinate groups. They in turn reproduce it in a trance that goes from the conscience to the unconsciousness, being able to concurrently express both positions: the stereotypes that the dominator has built and that from that moment on the dominated contributes to by disseminating, reproducing, and rooting these constructions of artificial character in a historicity that should not correspond to the dominated and a false legitimacy of which neither should possess.

Afro-Cuban women's national and gender identity share several elements with their fellow compatriots in general, but due to their different ethnic origins also have distinctive characteristics that can be seen in their perspectives, expectations, and needs, trauma not excluded. Unfortunately, the only existing women's national organization has not considered an analysis of black women's particular situation. Nor has the rest of society considered their differences, or when they have done so, it has not been usually done in a positive manner. The social structure has not tended to study differences. It has been ignored, as in other things, that society is not a monolith, least of all in countries composed of ethnoracial mixtures like all of Indo-Afro-Hispano-America, the Caribbean, and inside these, the Cuban nation.

Recently, and generally *in informal ways*—to use the language that has accompanied these cases—black Cuban women on the Island and abroad have initiated an attempt at feminist theory and praxis. The theoretical foundation of Cuban feminism is located in the late nineteenth century, although in practice it appeared much earlier. That is, beyond Cuban women breaking with more or less happy appearances, for multiple reasons, in the arts in general, or in the struggle for independence, but even earlier chronologically, since female slaves rebelled, where they would free themselves as female *cimarrones* (*cimarroneaban*) or they would leverage themselves, all of this gives our Cuban feminism, in my opinion, as in the rest of Afro-America, an Afro origin.

That is why the topic of Afro-Cuban women, in a space like this panel, would find a place in dissimilar moments. The theme of Afro-Cuban women transverses and in turn is transversed by the topics of slavery, maroonage and resistance, marginality, culture, identity and othering, transculturation, and syncretism, relationships of interethnic affiliation that restructure the social sphere among others.

Culture, economy, politics, and biology shake hands in a complex thematic that given its polysemic character can hardly be approached only from an area of specialization because it needs the complementarity of the sciences as well as of transdisciplinary work. It is a necessary methodology that can hardly be exclusively the conventional one because it must go and return again and again on orality and do the exhaustive work of observation, as well as to take history, philosophy, and cultural studies, anthropology, sociology, and psychology into account. These have to be fused with economics, politics, linguistics, archaeology, and medicine if one tries to disentangle the web of the problematic of Afro-Cuban women.

The Hispanic colonialist discourse that built racialized content and of racist character has not been deconstructed. The idea of Cuban black women as sensual and sexual is effective and alive in the collective imaginary, with many believing that black women are more likely than their other compatriots to participate in prostitution. This presents the stereotype of black woman as vulgar and prosaic, given freely to violence, women who have children irresponsibly and are negligent mothers, unstable in their relationships, and as one white interviewee said, and warned: *"I am not racist but . . . they don't like to better themselves in life."*

This discourse declares black women practically inept for anything positive in that it continues to assume that black women who cannot be placed comfortably in that schema have been civilized. This idea introduces that if they are civilized, it is because they *think* (and act) *like white women*, a proposition deeply embedded in the imaginary of all ethnoracial groups that comprise the nation. A high percentage of white, black, and *mestizo* people are carriers of these ideas in a conscious or unconscious way because one of the characteristics of racism, remember, is that once enthroned in subjectivity, its reproduction is often alien to our consciousness. Hence the transcendence of these constructions in the social organization through which relations are established and therefore the social functioning of these ideas.

White families repel *the black* even when it might be present among them through rising numbers of interracial marriages, which is not an indicator of the absence of racial prejudice nor of racism. They coexist with the *mestizo* families that reflect more or less a concern for the imitation of the pattern imposed as positive that is clearly a white one, and with black families that meet the same criteria, some of whom express one of the national traumas of the belief of the *superiority* of whites.

We lead our lives for better or worse individually and irrespective of the racial component. However, race counts in the social environment. Being black can be *a career*, although in reality we are taught that we are a *sack of coals*.[2] Trauma that on women finds manifestations, for example in the excessive importance that is usually placed on the texture and length of hair, color of the eyes, in short, on appearance.[3] For example, little black girls who will grow up ashamed of their hair, learning to straighten it at all costs—not as an option but as an imposition that is converted into an obligation—because *they have to suffer to show off* and moreover, *they look more beautiful that way*. Little black girls who will soon learn, if their skin is lighter, they must do so to be *well-groomed and look like white girls*. Little black girls so often despised by their brothers because *you don't have* [long] *hair* or because *your hair is not good*.[4] Violent reproduction of imposed beauty codes.

All of these are the first lessons on the path to learning self-negation that society, convenient for the macro dimension and regardless of individuality, applauds—*she always has such pretty hair*—or blames them—*you are the ones who discriminate against yourselves*—and will speak behind their backs—*look at how she wears fake hair extensions*—because for us, hair functions as an added value. Black mothers who teach their sons to marry—despite their feelings—white women so that they may have daughters in close proximity to whiteness *because I don't want to keep combing pasitas [kinky curls]*.[5] Future grandmothers living in a trance of racial self-genocide and worst being proud of it because society made them believe that to do so is *intelligent.*

These are a few examples of the *performance of whitening*—physical, cultural, ideological—and an expression of the asymmetry established in the economy fundamental to power that is also expressed racially in a complex and ambiguous way by sectors that are excluded politically and economically.[6]

This psychological manipulation imposes a miseducation on "others," in this case black women, inculcating us with the feeling of impairment and contempt against ourselves. It amounts to an imperceptible social crime that is very rarely identified as such, curious and naively considered *normal* in Cuban society today because it ensures that *there is no racism here only prejudice, it's not so serious, there are only jokes*, and after all, *it is mostly black women who do it*, and *not all blacks are thieves, but every thief is black*. There are *mulatísima*[7]—an educated, white, Cuban friend tells me—*leave that alone. Isn't it true that black women are super good in bed? Feel proud of that*. My friend barely reproduces the stereotypical constructions of race-sex-gender despite the past existence of the Cuban Color Project, eliminated in 2009, and the recent creation of the National Commission Against Racism and Racial Prejudices in the National Union of Writers and Artists of Cuba (UNEAC).

Bringing whitening creams to sell in Cuba in the so-called *foreign dollar stores* could have been an idea of the Spaniards who supplied the product, and as usually happens with traders, the idea of obtaining profit prevailed. Besides, the case of Spaniards included their historical racial traumas and having been our colonizers and one of the ethnoracial roots of the Cuban people, they also imposed it as a national trauma, something we need to consider further and in greater depth. The idea of whitening is accepted in Cuba that includes daringly commercializing it with a stylist behind the counter blatantly trying to promote sales among black and *mestizo* people on the

Island by saying things like: *Imagine, you that are mulata, how you are going to look after using this cream*, adding emphatically: *You are going to look white!* This act should not be taken lightly because the implications of the propagation of the Michael Jackson model among black and *mestizo* Cubans reflects a trauma of great depths that cannot be neglected and that continues to expand, regrettably.

It is not just for fun that teachers, some of whom may themselves be black or *mestizos*, express preferences, mostly expressed as favoritism, for white children or children who appear whiter.[8] This also happens inside black and mixed families among their own children. This scheme is reproduced throughout society.

Black women who appear in Cuban media, especially on TV, transit among the copycats of the Janet Jackson model.[9] This globalized mixture seems to spawn this model, totally folkloricized and equally artificial for not corresponding to the average person, whereupon the topic Afro-Cuban women could also be addressed from other thematic statements present in this workshop, that is to say, of the *symbolic flows as strategies of globalization*, in a monopolizing attempt of power that extends to the imaginaries present in all social orders, including ethnoracial identity, gender, etc. These monopolistic attempts that—with or without conscience—are aided from the attitudes and patterns that have been imposed or induced have been acquired by the injured themselves, repeaters of colonialist schemes, as the racialized and racists within their own communities.

The racialization of the stereotyped construction of black women enters the Afro-religious world as well. One of the things we see is a very simplified understanding of the Orisha Ochun, in which women embrace her playful, sensual, and festive side rather than her other avatars where Ochun manifests as a faithful mother, passionate wife, and protector, or as the auxiliary of Orula, the deaf old woman and weaver or intellectual, or any other characteristics or identities that fail to gain traction in the collective imaginary. There are many women who, eager to stand out for their sensuality, revelry, and conceit, claim themselves as Omo-Ochun [daughter of Ochun] even when they are not.

The social pyramid reveals a complicated and traumatic ethnoracial relationship that for too long has been neglected and has placed many black women in a bad situation. If in times of economic crises it is women who together with children and the elderly suffer the most around the world, in societies in which black women are not representative of social mobility or in which this representativeness is not directly correlated with their deserved merit—as could happen with any other emerging social sector—in these times of crisis, it is black women who endure not only more prejudice but also more trauma. Black Cuban women after the drastic structural changes that occurred in 1959 were able to achieve secondary school and university studies. With equal aspirations, they educated their children and perhaps grandchildren, whereas today, in greater measure compared to their white compatriots, black women's aspirations are frustrated. Racial problems, some already partially recognized, that exist throughout our society, especially in the foreign exchange areas, affect black women in greater proportion because in addition to discrimination due to anti-black racism, they are impacted by gender and, to a large extent, class discrimination as well, even without considering the disastrous contribution of *sociolismo* [friend-ism].[10]

DECONSTRUCTION OF THE MYTH

Deconstruction of the myth of black women with its colonialist character, racialized content, and racism is a more difficult, arduous, and complex process than its construction. The myth imposed on black Cuban women by the colonizers that was institutionalized with the collaboration of white *criollos* extended the attitude that reproduced stereotypes about black women and became part of the trauma of *mestizos* who were inculcated with the illusion of *whitening*.

For deconstruction to be effective and thus real, it must be multilateral and on two fundamental levels, the social structure objectively organized on which stereotypes are institutionalized not through laws but by the established social order, and the collective imaginary which repeats, reaffirms, and spreads it. It is fundamental also that all the social sectors participate, always rejecting and undoing the position and the idea that it is others who think prejudicially and act for them. It is one thing to attend, help, and accompany the process, and a very different one to rescind the right of thought while the maneuvering of others, inevitably and even with the best of intentions, leads to manipulation.

In the past three decades, representatives from the world of hip-hop and some scholars on the Island and abroad have emphasized their theory and practice.[11] The deconstruction of discourse from theoretical feminism is a difficult task. Not having been a phenomenon completely understood in the decade of the 1960s, feminism tended to remain identified among us as a bourgeois phenomenon; it was believed that in societies like ours differences and discriminations would be determined by class struggle. Time showed the usefulness of facing some socially sensitive subjects from other broader, more multifaceted viewpoints, the need to delve into the study and treatment of these with more ductile positions, which allowed greater possibilities of flexibility. Race, with all its implications, including its relationship to gender and in turn gender in its entirety, with its multiple facets, would be some of these topics, which certainly continue to require deeper and more panoramic treatment.

Memory, silence, and forgetting are great at invisibilizing the worst, what is often forced from the construction of male, white colonial power, and are mixed in with a history that has a lot of resistance and stability, permanence and pride, continuity and rupture. As our dear teacher Leyda Oquendo Barrios was accustomed to saying, we are the daughters of the strongest, torn and tossed from their soil, from their families and customs, and whose languages and much of their cultures were mutilated; but we survived. Yet it is fitting to question: At what price? What has been the price to pay for future offspring?

In the search for answers to these questions, we would simultaneously clear paths to our historical reconstruction, transitioning to paths toward the deconstruction of myths. To challenge an official history, a history that from the beginning of the Republican era owes us these and many other answers—work that has begun to be done, with a feminine gaze, in recent years, albeit timidly—is an urgent task and part of our contribution in the process of deconstruction of the patriarchal and white discourse. The black Cuban woman has to be an active part of this process, and to do so, she must be stimulated to perform her best instead of being urged to participate from the least good, including inertia and submission.

We share with the region our history as *new peoples*, the fictional literature being published in Cuba, which is not the only type being produced, however other parts of the Caribbean do not always reflect for example the collision of conquest, the imposition of colonial regimes, the system of trafficking and slavery, Christian evangelization and the processes of transculturation and syncretism, alongside other elements with a gaze that is usually male and not always the result of adulation.

For example, *Príapos* by Daniel Chavarría is a dangerous work because it is written by a good writer. It is a very well-developed work with a dynamism that seduces and traps the reader and in which stereotypes abound. Among others, we are interested in the *mulata* woman: "with white skin" (p. 98, paragraph 1), "monumental" (p. 103), a Santeria practitioner, rumba dancer, heartbreaker, cabaret dancer, who loves a black Abakua man. Coincidental? He is trapped in the margins in which he seems to wallow in the "paradigm of manhood and loyalty" (p. 66). He does not want to leave the *solar* [tenement housing] nor to take advantage of an attitude as an excellent musician. He goes to prison for *honor* and has a tragic death, while the *mulata* finds happiness in the arms of a blond, white man, also a ballet dancer, but again we have to ask: Coincidence? It is not that none of these characters is truly an existing social type. It is the insistence on the coming together of these characters in a work of fiction that does not present different black, *mulato*, white, or other characters, who also exist.

The fact that *Príapos* as a literary creation re-creates social models of a white educated man matters. Subjectivities are marked by the interrelations that are produced sometimes at a profound level with a class or group of people who hold personal characteristics and belonging—voluntary or inherited—to that group or class. The will and levels of consciousness and unconsciousness mark subjectivities that also hinder but do not impede the deconstruction of the racialized and racist myth in general, with all its negative imprint on black Cuban women.

Once the party is over and the effects of the hangover are overcome, whoever had it knows how bad it feels; counter to what we heard through our ears, life is not *a carnival* and not all *sorrows can always be sung away*. Even if denial has become fashionable among us that does not allow confrontation and for people to go through the process of catharsis, we should sooner rather than later recognize that suffering and pain do not vanish because we wish it, nor can they be eternally hidden behind the carnival, alcohol, and the appearance of being totally carefree. As with every living organism—and we will agree that these include all human groups—the identification and acceptance of suffering and pain is the only thing that allows their confrontation to initiate a true process of social healing.

It is not about *self-victimization*—a word that has also become fashionable to say as an attempted insult—but about recognizing that at some point in history, we find ourselves as the heirs of victims and others as heirs of perpetrators, and some even as heirs of both, and that this has left manifest traces in everyone embodied in social structures and in the repercussion that this implies today. It is no coincidence that while so many black women deny their family history and their origins of survivors—which should imply pride—there are Cuban women who are proud to come from slaver families who also consider themselves *revolutionaries*. It is not necessary to deny the family past if it has not been pleasant, dignified, and honest, yet it is a very different thing to exalt it.

"For the black woman to know herself," explains Neusa Santos, "is to live the experience of having been massacred in her identity, confused in her expectations, and subjected to demands compelled by alienated expectations. But it is also, and above all, the experience to commit herself to rescuing her history and recreating herself in her potentialities."[12]

Female Cuban rappers, most of them black and *mestiza* women living in slums, know this—euphemistically classified as *differently favored*. Many of them have to fight to survive their material poverty. Moreover, they struggle to defend their particular aesthetic taste, by erecting themselves as black women outside the stereotypes imposed upon them, and by imposing themselves on the machismo that is also part of the world of hip-hop, all of which can result, for a few, as subversive. Some of them stated responding to their national identity:

I,
Mariana
make the world know
that Cuban women
know more than just
how to move in bed.[13]

They respond from their identity as Afro-Cuban women—making it known that national identities do not pretend to include the others—with rap that equally manifests from Afro orality, and a rhythm that moves between the lament of African American spirituals and Yoruba prayer, musically accompanied by the Bata drums. With a punch to the gut, they tell us:

I.
Crude.
Black.
. . .

I am always going to talk to you
about the same topics.
Of sisters, cousins, and grandmas
and of our great riches.
Of our mother, nature.
. . .

I am the virtue
left by our ancestors.
I am poetry.
I am this that passes through me.
. . .

I am rebellion
to everyday life.
. . .

I am proud of my *bemba* (full lips).
I am proud of my color.
I am identity.
I am culture.
Black!
Crude!
Cuban![14]

NOTES

1. Editor's note: These words (and all forthcoming *italicized* words) are emphasized in the original.
2. "Being white is a career. Being *mulato* is a profession. Being Black is a sack of coals" is the popular refrain that synthesizes the national imaginary regarding racial valuations.
3. It is not about cementing positions that could become fundamentalist, denying each person the possibility of rearranging his or her appearance according to fashion and personal tastes. It is a question of claiming the possibility of choosing changes as an option not an imposition. For years, white people, especially women, have changed the color and texture of their hair without being severely criticized for it, but they—despite the publicity by aestheticians and other specialists—have a greater chance of choosing because they do not suffer the strong criticisms and mockeries that black women do for wanting to change their appearance or who have been historically pressured to do so.
4. White hair is considered "good hair" or *pelo bueno* in Cuba.
5. *Pasa* is what tightly curled, thick, black, or Afro hair is called in Cuba. (While it literally translates to raisin, it means and is used to signify kinky or nappy.)
6. In the popular neighborhoods, it is said without questioning that poverty merged on the surface of skin color, it is common to hear women be called *la Negrita* [little black woman] and *la mulatica* [little *mulata*], differentiating them from white women even when they share the same social conditions. The following two statements illustrate this: "She is a studious *mulatica*," and "I am poor, but I am not black."
7. *Mulatísima*: a name for a *mestiza* woman who is flattered and presumes herself to be "superior."
8. As part of an investigation on the topic, the Center of Anthropology examined schools in Havana and Santiago de Cuba, and among its results found something that is part of the daily experience in the lives of blacks and *mestizos* in Cuba. The researchers cataloged it as a complex "that black children . . . are rarely chosen, independent of the racial group of the selectors, and they verified the use of verbal expressions embedded with stereotypes and racial prejudices" (see Rodrigo Espina and Niurka Núñez, *A propósito de las desigualdades: una propuesta de estudio desde la Antropología de la educación*, no. 9, Workshop of American Sociocultural Anthropology, 2005, Casa de Africa, Havana, Cuba).
9. The images we receive from the media and the countervalues transmitted in schools present these as cultural spaces for us in which the myths and collective fantasies that tend to be at the service of social production are manifested unconsciously. According to Erdheim, "These symbolic cultural manifestations respond to a double movement. . . . They tend to distort and recognize conflicting life projects for social consensus, which can jeopardize the order established by a system of socially shared values whose function of disclosure and outsourcing through the staging of forbidden worlds of life, subvert the prevailing norms, junctions and taboos in a given historical epoch" (see Mario Erdheim, *Die gesellschaftliche Produktion von Unbewusstheit* [1984], in Roxana Hidalgo, "La otredad en America Latina: etnicidad, pobreza y

feminidad" [Othering in Latin America: Ethnicity, Poverty and Femininity], http://antroposmoderno.com/antro-articulo.php?id_articulo=1013 [accessed May 11, 2007]).

10. Editor's note: *Sociolismo* stemming from the term "*socio*" meaning friend or partner is an informal term used in Cuba to describe the reciprocal exchange of favors by individuals. Black people are frequently excluded from these relationships.

11. For example, Blog "Negra cubana . . . tenia que ser" [It Had to Be a Black Cuban Woman] by the Afro-Cuban psychologist and journalist Sandra Álvarez. Work by a group from the Faculty of Psychology (University of Havana, UH) with a focus on lesbians. Historical investigations by Dr. María del Carmen Barcia (Faculty of History and Philosophy, UH), from the researcher, narrator, and advocate Inés María Martiatu, writer Nancy Morejón (Casa de las Americas), and the researcher and narrator Daysi Rubiera. Martiatu has centered women of African descent, Cuban or not, protagonists in her narratives and important subjects of her research. Barcia studies women's role in enslaved families. Morejón writes on *mestizaje* and black women are central subjects in her poetry. Rubiera has studied Afro-Cuban women in the arts, religion, and *testimonio* literature. *Revista Movimiento*. Agencia Cubana del Rap. Black feminist theater, director Xiomara Calderon and dramaturgist and actor José Acea. Part of the theater of the dramaturgist and director Eugenio Espinosa. The work realized by the poet and researcher Carmen González Chacón with female rappers. Works abroad by the essayist Ileana Fuentes and the artist of plastic arts, Victoria Ruiz-Labrit.

12. Neusa Santos Sousa, *Tornarse negro* [Becoming Black] (Rio de Janeiro: Ediciones Graal, 1983), 8.

13. "Mujeres," rap lyrics, performers: Explosión Femenina, Yula y Atómicas.

14. "Madre natura," Las Krudas.

BIBLIOGRAPHY

Chavarría, Daniel. 2005. *Príamos*. Barcelona: Ediciones B, S. A.

Erdheim, Mario. 1984 (1992). *Die gesellschaftliche Produktion von Unbewusstheit*. Frankfurt am Main: Suhrkamp. Cited in Roxana Hidalgo, 2006, "La otredad en America Latina: etnicidad, pobreza y feminidad" [Othering in Latin America: Ethnicity, Poverty and Femininity]. http://antroposmoderno.com/antro-articulo.php?id_articulo=1013.

Espina, Rodrigo, and Niurka Núñez. 2005. *A propósito de las desigualdades: una propuesta de estudio desde la Antropología de la educación*. Workshop of American Sociocultural Anthropology, no. 9. Havana, Cuba: Casa de Africa.

Santos Souza, Neusa. 1983. *Tornarse Negro*. Rio de Janeiro: Ediciones Graal.

Chapter 15

Proposing an Inclusive and Nonsexist Gaze

Mulata *Women, a Profane Invention?*

Onelia Chaveco Chaveco

They say that the best inventions of the Galician people were the *porrón* [wine pitcher], *espadrilles* [thick jute braided-soled sandals], and *mulatas*. This absolute and pejorative assertion suggests that just as Eve who was taken from a man's rib, *mulatas* seem to have been born from the sternum of the Galician, without a black mother, without Cuban roots, and without an identity demonstrated for centuries and consolidated to this day. For some, the term still contains a dose of racism in the claim that to say *mulato* reveals a tendency to soften the hardness of the word black, which since its arrival in Cuba was articulated in a derogatory manner.

Early reference of the dark-skinned woman is found in Hebraic literature: The Song of the Songs, Songs of Love of King Salomon and Shulamite, which evidence the beauty of a dark-skinned woman. In fact, she is a woman with dark complexion who somehow justifies the color of her skin, according to her, as a result of the sun. She offers this justification because feminine beauty was associated with a white complexion.

From then to now, the treatment that *mulatas* have received as social beings leaves much to be desired. One aspect of this has to do with the invisibility of these women. Titled *La Mulata*, the first known painting by the painter Diego Velasquez of a *mulata* appeared between 1617 and 1618. It is an oil on canvas that belongs to the Baroque movement. According to Wikipedia, the work represents the moment when a maid approaches a table and takes a jug to serve the diners, who are seen in the upper right of the painting. The Wikipedia explanation covers the whole structure of the painting, the quality of the objects that appear above the table, the brilliance of the metal and the ceramics, and the realism that points to the artist's later works, in which the handling of the brush is simply exceptional. However, there is no reference to the central character of the canvas. The image of the main figure, the *mulata* woman, was lost in the description of objects and the technique of the painting, which disappears the *mulata* female figure. *Mulata* becomes only the name of the oil painting. In another order, and perhaps the most preposterous, is the erotic and sexist approach with which these women are seen.

The famous legend of the *Mulata* of Cordoba emerges from a discriminatory and lustful lens through which she has been perceived since the Inquisition. The legend tells of the persecution of a beautiful woman with cinnamon-colored skin, a resident of the city of New Spain where she is captured so that she may be burned alive. She escapes on a boat that she painted in her cell, thus establishing a link between her and magic, witchery, and other diabolical involvements that surround women of color from that moment until the present.

The presence of *mulatas* impacted lettered individuals and artists of the visual arts. Federico García Lorca, on arriving to Havana, was captivated by that singular woman, and said: "This Island has more feminine beauties of original types, due to the drops of black blood that all Cubans carry. And the blacker, the better. The *mulata* girl is the superior woman here in terms of beauty, distinction, and delicacy."[1]

On his part, the muralist Diego Rivera, a man who framed his life with the tonalities, claimed, "a great luck to know the covered Havana streets, with carriages occupied by beautiful ladies . . . , while the wonderful *mulata* in robes were on foot fanning themselves and throwing off lightning bolts of sex as they walked."[2]

ALWAYS CECILIA?

There has always been a halo of eroticism and legend around *mulatas*. The most famous *mulata* in Cuba, Cecilia Valdés, was the incarnation of all the virtues and defects that the authentic part of our *criollo* polychromy foisted on her. Cirilo Villaverde's book, titled *Cecilia Valdés* after the protagonist, is considered among scholars one of the most significant *mulato* epics and has become our unique literary myth.

It is important that the most important novel in nineteenth-century Cuban literature stars a *mulata* woman as the protagonist. There is no denying, therefore, the strength in the antecedents of these women, in an ironic era of slavery, of such entrenched racism.

The *mulata* emerged from active *mestizaje* initiated during colonialism, the mixture of two races that resulted in a stereotype of beauty and sensuality in which the rhythm, magic, and sexuality of the African tradition unites with

Spanish tradition in the *mulata*. Her value is granted in the context of pleasure. She is a lover or prostitute but is not conceived of as a wife for white or black men, nor is she included in the religious Christian practice because her beauty and attraction have been associated with the diabolical (remember the *Mulata* of Cordoba).

As such, the *mulata* moved people enough to constitute a source of inspiration in the artistic currents of Latin America, to the point that the exuberant sexuality ascribed to her is described in poetry and narrative through images and metaphors that associate her within a paradisiacal space.

From Romanticism forward, the theme of blackness acquired a different connotation; poetry became the expression of a national consciousness in which the search for origins and the protest against the injustices of the colonial system took place. Within this context, the black theme began to become important, and blacks were conceived of as members of society who had suffered the oppression of colonialism. However, the poems that speak of the *mulata* woman contemplate her from an aesthetic and sensual point of view but at the same time give continuity to a negative valuation within the social environment by considering her a hybrid lacking identity.

The resources that poetry uses are metaphors relating to color, textures, aromas, and movements in which the landscape and the musical rhythm are characteristic of hot territories. However, the social problems that afflict these women are not included.

They appear haughty, proud of their beauty and qualities. *Mulatas* do not reflect feelings of inferiority; on the contrary, their presence has an air of superiority drawn from their sexuality because their prey is the white man, who dies and surrenders to their charms.

And we arrive to our Nicolás Guillén, who wrote several poems about the social situation that dark-skinned men lived. The black poetry, or *negrismo*, movement (1928–1940) was integrated within poetry of the nation, and from that poetic basket, the black was seen "from inside," which implied speaking like him, pronouncing Spanish like him, feeling, mourning, and laughing like him. Guillén has been one of the greatest proponents of this genre. His work has been considered the height of the *negrismo* movement for representing the transformation process from African negritude to "Latin Americanism." His poetry has a new vigor. It is *rumba* and *son* that sings and dances to the lyrical rhythm. But the poet also surrenders to the full and lustful hips of that beautiful woman. He wrote the following poem about the *mulata*:

Enough, I found out *mulata*,
mulata, I know that you say
that my nose
is like the knot of necktie.

And pay attention that you
isn't so advanced,
because your mouth is real large
and you pass on color

You bring a lot with your body,
bring a lot;
you bring a lot with your mouth,
bring a lot;
you bring a lot with your eyes,
bring a lot.

But if you knew the truth
mulata;
that me with my black woman I have enough,
and I don't want you for noth'n.[3]

In this poem, the black woman is the wife or companion, while the *mulata* is the object of desire, foreign to the black race, her *mestizaje* is a product of other social values, and her presence disturbs family integration. She is looked at as primitive and savage, in opposition to the culture and civilization of white men, and she reproduces the myth of the sexual superpotency of the black race.

In the case of Cuban theater, we have the *mulata* woman with the Galician and the *negrito* [diminutive for black man], interpreted by the great Rita Montaner and Candita Quintana.

It is true that the work established a leading role, but with the same sexual focus of the phenomenon. The *mulata* was an important ingredient in theater as an aphrodisiac symbol and therefore she played a basic component as an article of luxury and an erotic object in the recipe of any creole work.

Cinema presented the first staged roles for *mulata* women interpreted by white actresses that coated the face or body with brown paint. Certainly no *mulata* women in those times could become an actress, with few exceptions. *Mestizaje* was made a type of transvestitism.

Paradoxically, the first movie with sound in Cuba was a short fifteen-minute film titled *Maracas and Bongo* (1932) about a *mulata* woman that does not give in to the pretensions of a suitor. Meanwhile, there is a festival in the *solar* (tenement house) in which everyone sings and dances.

WOMEN IN IMAGES

The first edition of *Palante*, published on October 16, 1961, had on its cover a caricature by Luis Felipe Wilson Varela (Wilson). A few days later in a speech, the commander in chief, Fidel Castro Ruiz, praised the image that depicted black Cuban women integrating into society as laborers.

The image on the cover represented a rich woman, symbol of the bourgeoisie defeated by the popular revolution, who went to the bank a few months after the first of January 1959 and found that the bank attendant was a young black woman who had been her maid until the triumph of the revolution.

The young black woman illustrated by Wilson had all the physical features of a *criollita*, though at that time the artist's illustrations of these women were not called that. It was not until August 6, 1962, that Wilson's new section *Criollitas* appeared, which continued for several years until the artist's death in December 2006. The *criollitas* had a long life. The artist depicted their beautiful anatomy but would also showcase them doing voluntary work, in mass mobilizations for social projects, in education, and as healthcare workers.

Photography, however, has linked *mulata*s to eroticism and demons. This occurs in the advertising of products, and we notice this without having to talk about the bottle of rum that bears *Mulata* as its name, even if that rum is our well-known Cuban rum. Additionally, faces of *mulatas* appear on the covers of magazines, but not in the content of their articles, and if so, only when linked with the folklore of Cuba, images published by vendors of these women wearing colorful handkerchiefs knotted on their heads, selling flowers through the streets of Cuba. However, nothing compares to musical expression in depicting all the voluptuousness of these women. Sometimes we hear music with such strident and scandalous lyrics that it fails to treat these Cuban women with delicacy and respect. One wonders, why do we distance ourselves from that mysterious language that Manuel Corona discovered in the mouth of Longina that highlighted sensitivity?

In most of the cases, our media support Cuban women's struggle for equality and emphasize women's rights and duties and their role as builders in constructing a new society alongside men. Although, in so many cases, the media unconsciously support, through their communicative products, the reaffirmation of existing archetypes built around these women.

One hundred and forty years after Carlos Manuel de Céspedes summoned the union between blacks and whites to fight Cuba's war for independence, the hedonistic vision about their descendants, specifically related to *mulatas*, continues to have life. It is time to see *mulatas* not as sexual objects but as they are, in a broader and more complete spectrum. To remove them from the greater context, fragment their projection, and envelop them in a crippling frivolity means to also leave our women's history incomplete, which in turn is part of another history, that of Cuban nationality.

Mulatas are combatants, teachers, doctors, economists, researchers, jurists, writers, cooks, seamstresses, and journalists, and they are mothers, wives, and revolutionaries. In short, they are able to contribute their bit to any just cause.

Half a century cannot be transformed in a stroke, but right in the middle of the centenary meeting between two cultures, the European and American, it is worth turning and restarting how we write about the roles of *mulatas* with more appropriate prisms. This becomes even more important when one considers the current and growing *mestizaje* in Cuba. The last population record at the beginning of this millennium attests to this. The Population and Housing Census of 2002 Cuba registered 11,177,743 persons with permanent residency in comparison to the census of 1981. The population increased by 1,454,138 inhabitants. For the purposes of the censuses, the population was stratified into three groups based on the color of the skin: white, black, and *mulato* or *mestizo*. The categories refer to concepts that are commonly understood by the population and do not reflect actual races. Of the first cited figures, 5,580,510 are women: 3,653,577 white women, 1,393,915 *mulatas* or *mestizas*, and 533,018 black women. These results in their equivalence were comparable in the provinces as well. Of course, statistics do not move the world, but they illustrate how the world moves.

In conclusion, and without wanting to prioritize *mulatas* above the rest of Cuban women, I call attention to the need to find other eyes to look at *mulatez*. The occasion is conducive to reflect and reconstruct the approach from the significance of gender on these women who are not only a product of Spaniards but also of Africans and who carry within them whole generations of culture in the process of the formation of our *criollismo*, that *aijaico* stew in which Don Fernando Ortíz mixed us all.

NOTES

1. Leonardo Depestre Catony, *100 famosos en La Havana* (Havana: Editorial de Ciencias Sociales, 1999), 121–24.
2. Nicolás Guillén, "Mulata," in *Obras poética 1920–1958* (Havana: UNEAC, 1974).
3. Humoristic seminary *Palante*, October 16, 1961. [The original poem plays with the man's enunciation of Spanish words and slang.]

BIBLIOGRAPHY

Depestre Catony, Leonardo. 1999. *100 famosos en La Habana*. Havana: Editorial de Ciencias Sociales.
Guillén, Nicolás. 1974. "Mulata." In *Obra poetica 1920–1958*. Havana: Union de Escritores y Artistas de Cuba.
Humoristic Seminar *Palante*, October 16, 1961.

Chapter 16

Hairs

Carmen González Chacón

A NEEDED RETROSPECTIVE

The sea at ten years old; La Concha, El Nautico, El Ferretero, waves, sand, salt, hardboiled eggs, lentil *congris*, sweet fruit water, and the return. Crammed buses, washing hair, grease (animal, vegetable, or car), plastic comb, burner, hot comb, and the little chant:

You have a hard pasa.[1]
Hard and rebellious.
You have a hard pasa.
Pass the comb through it.

The cinema at twelve years old; Olympic, Trianón, Radio Centro, candied orange or mandarin, chocolate bits and little chocolate eggs, an exchange of looks, half-light, nearness, touch, smell, sweat, Koniec, The End, and the little song:

The negra mora,[2]
I carry in my feelings.
But the negra pela'
I take to carry cement.

A morning like any other between twenty and twenty-one years old: washing hair, scissors, grease (animal, vegetable, or car), hair comb (conditioned fork), headscarf to round the edges, small taps with the right hand, small taps with the left hand, hair comb again, headscarf, hair comb, head scarf, head comb . . . , the stairs, and the little chant:

I saw a negra pela'
with the black hand style.
Negra pela',
who cut your hair?

You hear it, but it no longer matters to you. You still don't know why. Simply, time is not enough, nor money for the hair *processing*. You sit at *parque de G* [Park G] and see the leaves of the trees recently pruned. No one asks them, who trimmed you? Nor your friend Miriam Negrin de Céspedes who every week has the pleasure to spend a fortune at a beauty parlor to get those bizarre *haircuts* that practically expose the green skull of white women.

The lady at two hundred and seventy-seven on your street, the one with the wiener dog, biting and scandalous, she looks at you without disguising the contempt that runs through her veins. Until yesterday, she hid behind the degenerate corners of her lips, simulating a polite greeting. Today, that is to say this morning, you gave her reason to justify her frankness. She passes by dragging her evident disdain, protected in the superiority she assumes from the purity of blood: "*Marimacho*—tomboy," she tells you, and you smile at her with that ridge of white even teeth that Olofi gave you.

After, maternal despair as you try to locate that mistress, your father's, she's a psychologist by profession. Some friends ask if it was because of lice. And you: "Black people don't catch. . . . Shh." You smile again and throw yourself to the conquest of the eight blocks that separate you from the Tuff club, enjoying the inauguration of this hair freedom. You go in, ask for a telegram, and while the bartender curiously tries to guess between any possible *deviation* in your sexual preference, you hum the Pata pata. Happy for that first practice of the decolonization of your hair. Relapses will ensue; extensions, silicone. . . . A universe of complete possibilities in the free will that began this morning like any other between your twenty and twenty-one years.

THE ALTAR OF THE GREATS

Through the colonial history of the island of Cuba, black women's hair has been a prison, precipice, labyrinth. . . . Bad hair, *pasas* [kinks], *alambre* [wire], *tornillo* [screw], *moñito* [bun], and *clavo* [nail]. . . . Words that denote their representativeness in the socialization of this physical attribute, making it a symbol of invalidation and injury.

In the exercise of walking, the first step we must take is backward.[3] Otherwise, we will face emergencies, doubling back and extremes, forcing us to walk in circles for another two hundred years. The advantage of this maneuver leads us to the origins of an organic thought that crosses the Eurocentric and racist sites from which our historical consciousness has been erected, articulated, and stimulated. It is necessary to make use of that thought. Turn it into an active voice to raise spaces for self-definitions and listening.

Walterio Carbonell, Manuel Moreno Fraginals, Rogelio Martínez Furé, and Inés María Martiatu Terry will be my guests. I will not ask questions. This time I am here to listen to them through their texts.

> They turned the male into common goods, an earthly thing, object of trade, a commodity, and the female an object of double possession, possession for work and sexual possession.[4]

> It began there and this drama of interracial relations and the racist practices that have lasted for more than five centuries. In our continent, that is a trauma of millions of men and women because from that moment on, the European powers implanted a caste structure according to the color of the skin, the shape of the hair, the nose, and lips that would determine whether the being was human or livestock, an object.[5]

> Housing, clothing and food were satisfied with exclusive productive purpose, trying to erase the entire African cultural world.[6]

> If blacks have been an object of all sorts of deformations in the imaginary of a society historically racialized, it is indisputable that black women have carried the largest role. The image of black women in Cuban society in every era has been constructed on a foundation of negative stereotypes. Violence, scandal, vulgarity, disorder, and sexual promiscuity have been attributed to them.[7]

> Slavery distorted the sexual life of slaves, and racists justified those distortions by inventing the myth of blacks' sadistic sexuality, immorality of black women and the lustfulness of the *mulata*.[8]

> In Spanish, white is purity, luminosity, creativity, height; black means darkness, filthiness, corruption; *mulato* means the son of the mule, sterile. Thus, these are denominations invented by the dominant classes to humiliate, subordinate, and constantly remind this sector of our population of its origins: the slave barracks, whip, leghold trap or the violent mating of the black woman with the dominators.[9]

> It follows that black women have been excluded and insulted by the discourse of those who have historically held the economic and cultural power in our country, a white, male and heterosexual minority who from positions of undisputed power have imposed a vision of beauty, aesthetic, cultural, and religious projections on black women who remain unrecognized, despised and systematically invalidated.[10]

> As long as confusion on our ideological past remains, we will continue suffering from, as Karl Marx said regarding the French Revolution in 1848, not only the evils of the present, but also of the past.[11]

We insert ourselves in this dialogue thanks to the relevance of remaining in acute dexterity, startling the enclosed spaces of the established symbolic violence. Thinking about raciality, and its asymmetries in Cuba, as part of a strategy of additions and subtractions determine the detonation. The absence of an aesthetic self-definition, of a cultural and intellective support that decodes the political relationship between appearances and the assimilation of acculturation patterns, leads to a close analogy between racist oppression and arguments that lose objectivity of subjective factors that close and displace the emancipatory discourse in favor of black women and men.

The identity markers of Afro-descendants who were discharged in these lands as a type of livestock highlight difference, indicate otherness. The slaves were part of the patrimony of the colonizer and his successors in the same way as their horses, beasts for ploughing, domestic animals, and their prosperous lands in which they planted their coffee plantations, mills, and homes. Cubanness depends on the purification of the impurities of the germ of blackness and its genealogy. Citizens who freely display these identity traits continue to be victims of intolerance and insults of a popular imaginary that affects institutions such as tourism, government-owned "dollar" stores, television, etc.

Joining all these postulations together allows a discussion on causes, conditions, effects, and consequences. Enslavement conditioned the entire racist structure we inherited. Nationality was established on a base indebted to a colonial cultural and economic inheritance. Thus we received the republic amended and fractured by a colonizing philosophy of exclusion. Or else how can we explain why after gaining political independence from Spain, black Cubans continue to exist at the bottom of the social pyramid, even after the revolutions of '33 and '59?[12] How do we explain why exclusionary stereotypes continued to be reinforced in which the hair of black women is still being evaluated in the same way that one evaluates the mane of a beast of burden, and even worse why hair must be mannered socially until it is turned into a lie, a dead attribute? Why has the hair of black women and men become attributes of reaffirmation and confrontation? There is only one answer for all these questions: the conditions have been key in the thought of José Antonio Saco, Domingo del Monte, and company as a way of thinking about nationality or the aesthetics of what is considered Cuban.

The consequences *are gathering around us, daily, invincibly.* A nomadic ethnic group, which does not find among the advantages of being Cuban the dignity of being represented in its essence. A group waiting for economic and social improvements, distant in political decision making. A patch attached to the popular consciousness, uncomfortable when it comes to defining ourselves as Westerners.

NOT WHITE, NOR BLACK, BUT I EXIST

Miriam, Alberto, and you have taken multiple extremes since your parents forced meetings in the intense precariousness of the basements of El Vedado. They don't live that close now. Two or three times a year they come, they shake the little space of your intimacy, they drink, they scream, and leave. One, to her *little house* at the *Casino Deportivo*.[13] The other, when he is in Cuba, to his two-story *bajareque* [shack], near the tunnel of Fifth Avenue.

He makes use of the faculties that have been conferred to male uniformity, piles up the words, grips bombastic arguments, distributes the pauses . . . he orders. Today, he fixates on debating social asymmetries.

She establishes her advantages from birth, desperately looking for excuses to submit (in her favor) the attention of the audience, tries to impose a discourse on, and a call for, racial equality.

You. You serve them another round of tea with lemon, you wait one, two, three more minutes and intervene. Your eyebrows are in that peculiar gesture that they know from childhood: "I think . . ." Miriam and Alberto agree for the first time: "Shut up and listen." It is not said in words. It's a smile without warmth, an unusual blink, a look over the shoulder. "I've been reading something . . ."

They know about you. "Have you finished writing that book of essays?" That simple question shuts your mouth like a punch with silk gloves. You return to slicing the lemon, the cups, note the marks of humidity on the front wall. But those hands of yours seem to be declaring war. They sweat so much that they end up revealing the state of anxiety accelerating the neurons located beneath your dreadlocks. "Statistics show that after 1959, women in Cuba blah, blah, blah. . . . Ana Betancourt . . . sixty percent of the workforce. . . . Prostitution eradicated as an industry . . . women have been made blah, blah, blah, Now, for blacks, nothing." He is sure of his parliament.

She interrupts. "In this country, racial prejudice is not a law nor a foundation. You are my brothers, my guys, never in my house blah, blah, blah . . ."

When you manage to appease the compulsion of your neurons, you intervene passively as a hostess would: "Are you both being serious about this?"

She barely hears you and begins to profusely announce a listing of those *liberated* through social mobility, good manners, and media negotiations.

He interrupts her: "Cuban women since the twenties of the past century (twenty also) . . ." She: "Racism here, among us, is soft, of low intensity, subjective . . ."

Him: "Women . . ." She: "Black men, black women, look at her, she looks more like me than a damn African black woman . . ."

You decide to positively end the ping pong to which your neck has been submitted, forcing your neurons to get out of that digression, you begin to weave your dreadlocks; separate the hair, twists to the right, you pass the braid through the opening, another twist to the left, you pass the braid through the center and . . . "Can you leave your kinky hair alone?" Alberto and Miriam finally agree. "NO!" You scream, "I don't want to. Miriam, honey, when you say black, you're not including me. I won't reply to your comment about me resembling you because you don't deserve it. Alberto, dear, show me any of your statistics where I feel represented; hairs, nose, big lips. . . . As I am with dignity and respect, without negotiation, without adding to the forced mutilation of my nature. Shut your mouths once and for all. That door goes straight to hell. And see you never again."

From this moment forward, you will have to continue alone. You just mismanaged five hundred years of godparenting and marriages. Never mind, roads were not made by themselves alone. You go out to the balcony. The neighbor facing you undertakes his conditional freedom shouting something he learned in his frustrated certainty that all women are equally despicable:

. . . *and now about those moñitos [little hair buns]*
All black women are moras [Moors]
All black women are moras [Moors]
All black women are monas [monkeys].
Don't listen to him sister, we have come a long way.

MY PRICE IS HIGH

Today is day twenty-two in the last month of summer. Then the heat will come for no reason. You walk around looking for some handicraft that you can hang on the moisture stain on the *front wall*. You welcome the idea of the artistic center in Cathedral Square. "So, looking at everything all at once I can find something worthy to cover my spot," you reason, "I'll go first for the paintings . . ."

A black man interrupts you. Tall, a strange combination between the inordinate blue of his shirt one hundred percent sheer nylon; red Lee jeans and leather shoes. He says I know you from somewhere. You are about to believe his story when an immense black woman arrives imposing her religious omens. You decide not to get bothered. At this temperature and with your emotional background you can explode, you feel it, it runs through your knots. You breathe deeply; the hot air fills the space of the lungs that has not yet been touched by damn vices, and leave.

"At last, the paintings. I'm going to peruse them one by one, no compromise. I have been told. . . . But what is this? I've come here to flee from mediocrity and the waste accumulated in the racist network of engineered stores (hard currency stores, thrift stores, stores only for tourists, etc.); the impressionist egocentrism of the galleries; and the creative delinquencies of my sisters of faith. This is worse . . ."

Now you are going to explode. You are tenser than the string of a bow in the middle of an archery contest. You get some pieces of paper and a blue pencil from your green *handbag*. "Where are you going in such a hurry? Wait for me." You choose a painting, then another, and another, and another, and another. . . . Faces of black women that you interpret, while you wield the HB-2 with your hand like a pulsar.

"In that image I see the essence of a black woman amalgamated in the twist of a frightful smile that pretends to be a kind gesture impelled by gigantic lips. Red, as the shame that is quenching the sense in me of measuring consequences. In this other sheet, the old woman seems to be sucking a penis. The veins and the corolla on the Havana cigar leave no room for doubt. There is another, repeated in many others, disproportionately black women in the position of slaves, sold next to baskets of fruit. Look at this, gentlemen! All the features decomposed in an endless grimace, this black woman has her eyes tightly closed and her legs flaccidly open, from her vagina hangs jungles. Until when!"

The until when is born from the center of your brain. It was almost a scream; you have given yourself away and make yourself visible. A seller approaches you. Your maneuvers baffle even me that I've known you for so long. You dig for information on the smuggler and happen to find out that he never leaves the port. He stays on the boat securing new merchandise. They, the dealers, think you'll end up buying a painting. You ask the price, you look at her belly, breasts, her teeth. . . . You want to know what they have *accomplished*. The little woman dressed in yellow walks over. "I don't understand. The pictures or the models?" You don't answer. The silver bearded man comes: "*Whereyoufrom, Whatyouneed?*" You move your head; you still don't want to reveal yourself. You enjoy stretching the moment to make your revenge greater. They don't know to what propose. They surround you and offer assistance. . . . Not all of them are white skinned. Although all of them act like whites. You return to the first piece. The dealers run after you. "*Bomdiasenhora*" [good day]. And moving the arms like they are mills inside of communication: "*Vocefalaportues? Representasón alfolclordenustropaish. Vocegustare.*"[14]

I like black women
but only when they're pretty
since I've been in Cronita
My price is high[15]

You escape the siege and reach the second picture amid the bewilderment of the dealers.

But if the negra cries
What am I gonna do!
She kneels in front of me
What am I gonna do.[16]

"Where are you from, princess, don't leave, look, these are three for fifteen. All of them are good . . ."

She washes, irons, sews,
and above all, gentleman
how she cooks!

"Are you Cuban?"

Walk on negra, and don't cry.
Go over there;
Walk on by and don't cry negra.
Come over here.
Walk on, negra, walk
When there's a will, there's a way![17]

"She's Cuban. She's not going to buy anything . . ." Who knows where the silver-bearded man with tortoise shell glasses went; now I swear, you better not explode. "Sadly, for you, I'm Cuban. We never went to the beach together, nor the movies. I have never seen you sitting in Park G; we never met in the M-1, but I am Cuban. I don't believe it. You leave. Even worse, you're laughing. At least explain it to me. What has changed?"

It is not worth it. I only wanted to join two languages from the same trunk and make them conscientious of their lack of originality. Life is a sum of bonds and consequences. Besides, I had the pleasure of ridiculing traffickers, dealers, smugglers, slave hunters . . .

They are left validating the nature of your satisfaction. They look at you and become entangled in the intricacies that point to the meaning of your dreadlocks. They don't understand you. Tomorrow they will talk about your dementia or of the fundamentalism found in the latitudes of the northern part of the continent.

"I pray because my brothers of the nation understand my causes, but I will not rest from doing. Fortunately, the continent is being shaken again. It was sleeping, but the dawn is here . . ."[18]

ATONEMENT

To them, the maltreated ones; ever since from her foster home in San Luis de los Yeros, Ma' Juliana Chivas, *ayoyo*,[19] muzzled their ways imposed by a gag of the master's will. Those who connect me to the existential past of Manuela Savigne and Esperanza Cárdenas, my elders. The thousand times trapped, reaped, and humiliated, again by their own hand. To them, a thousand times more intelligent because they refused to grow under the domination of the superstructure of colonization. Thank you to them who finally came down my back, free, without hatred, or frivolity to stop them.

It has been a long path in making amends with my hair. It did not begin in the safety of filial protection, nor in the construction of a social personality, or as part of the aesthetic foundation of personal growth. Slowly, very slowly, they began appearing; behaviors, commitments, alliances, readings. . . . It was not an organic process either. We had to deconstruct, repair, build without tools.

Every morning a showdown. First, against the painful memories of childhood: the classic towel on the head representing goddesses, fairies, and martyrs of the European literature to which our popular imaginary was subjected. Clashes against the voices of the tough ape, no hair, black monkey or shit, bald *cocotimba*; repeated almost always to confirm some social, economic, or cognitive advantage. Second, against the need for research associated with adolescence framed in an effervescence of struggles and social achievements in Cuba and Latin America. The mobilizing gestures of a pan-Americanism headed by the middle class that accommodates an aesthetic of avant-garde thinking: literature, music, the dramatization of a continental reality . . . , moving away from our own being and existence.

Rarefied contacts with the African diasporas and the conceptual revaluation of their representation, distorting, displacing. . . . Enunciating from a subordinate subject, folkloric. Finally, at the forefront of major resistance and risk; against other prejudices, raising awareness from our intellectual autonomy. Systematically, advanced intellectual Cuban thought has built a discourse parallel to racial colonization suffering from slaver ideas.

My hair is a protagonist of a history hidden by the falsehood in how events occurred. They nobly resisted the onslaught. They utilized their own defense mechanisms: insubordinate to the murder[20] of black women, breaking from the root before the invasion of sodium hydroxide, silicone, or other chemicals were applied to them, or disappearing forever in certain areas of the cerebral convolutions as a result of molds and hair and scalp treatments. . . . "Black women continue to be obsessed with their hair, and the straightening of hair is still a serious matter that takes advantage of the insecurity that black women feel about our self-value in this white supremacist society."[21]

Although it was relegated in my own racial conception, I was satisfied with the color of the skin, but I would have liked to have changed my hair. They showed me the way to solidifying a critical conscience that sustained the appropriation of necessary tools. It is not about using it as a vindictive weapon. Nor of conformity. It is not a question of recognizing and (re)establishing an ethical value of the existential past of Esperanza Cárdenas and Manuela Savigne, my elders. To accept who I am: beautiful, black, and legitimate as Ma' Juliana Chivas (the eldest of my elders), loving me in freedom, against all processes of *refinement*. Especially if the process of refining makes docile the integrity of my hair, displaces ancestry and descent toward submission or subjugation.

To come to terms with my hair is important. Through dialogue sustained by its definitive emancipation, I have been able to restore the identity of five generations of hair. My daughters have a few years left of tongs, silicones, stretcher plates, and extensions. They are aware that the outward appearance appeals to the fool, and that where knowledge commands there are few things *to fix*. Free will begins with the responsibility of becoming part of a community that contributes invaluably to the economic, social, and cultural development of the nation. Moreover, just in case, the strategy does not end with a defense of my dreadlocks. There are the photos that tell the family past, the (de)dramatization of reinforcing self-esteem, and the links I offer from *hip-hop* culture.

UNTIL *HIP-HOP* ARRIVED

One of the more tangible liberties feminists within *hip-hop* culture show, undoubtedly, is the emancipation of their *hair*.

Men (black and white), white women, and *mestizo* men and women use black women's hair to offend in their rap replies and counter-replies. The gradations used by the popular imaginary demonstrate this: good hair of white women (straight), medium hair of *mestizas* (wavy), bad hair of black women (kinky). Interestingly, black men and *mestizos* devalue black women's hair the most, assimilating the deculturation that makes them more or less inferior. The racist chants collected in this work were carried by word of mouth and came to our realities, accompanied by the rhythmic phraseology of our brothers with the same skin.

Every attempt to seek and restore our dignity as an individual or as a group has been attacked, discredited, and converted into something to joke about. For those who think upon reading this essay that I am exaggerating, despite the previous examples discussed, consider the following jingle directed at blacks when between the 1960s and 1970s blacks decided to grow out their hair: *Roon, roon, roon, roon. / Does not flatter your espendrúm [afro]. / With that ball of nappy hair, does not flatter your espendrúm.*

We crushed our intention with the beat of the conga and mediating English phonetics to explain our most elementary conception. *Black is beautiful*, in Africa or in the United States. In Cuba we are equal all citizens; your *espendrúm* does not flatter you.

No artistic movement has put its finger on this sore, until *hip-hop* came along. The voices of some of the women, driven by the avant-garde of alternative thinking, who travel horizontally alongside communities, are cleaning up the national culture of *Saquilegios* and *Delmontinos*.[22] They respond to this outburst in the popular imaginary: *"Negra pelá, who cut your hair?"*

"Ignorance, subjugation, and abuse were the causes," they respond with existential legitimate authority. The effect has been built like a brick wall: subject to subject, in a proposal of the individual toward the community, marking the recognition of a critical consciousness, formulated from the demands of a female discourse responding to the racial problematic evidenced in *rap* lyrics (written mostly by males), from the decade of the 90s to today.

I would like, however, to focus on two musical themes: "Los Pelos" by Obsesión and "Mi piel oscura" [My Dark Skin] by La Negra del Momento. Both topics speak to the community from which they emerge as individuals aware of the need to expedite a system of ideas rooted in the related perceptions of racist supremacy. They are not political denunciations or an extreme anarchism. Their work *responds* to those who doubt the imprint of female discourse within hip-hop culture. They transcend a legacy that has served to underpin their self-esteem by examining on equal terms the dialogue of race, culture, and nation with autonomy, without the need of marital amulets or cronies.

"Los Pelos" is a beautiful and daring musical composition, enclosed in the sonority of African percussion, enriching the island, complicated in the agility of the verb, forceful intellective and popular flavor and suppositions that characterize the flow of the rappers Magia and El . . . tipo . . . este.[23] The first intention of the text is a proclamation to freedom and free will. *Loose hair and the road / Look there's no desriz [hair straightener] / I realized what for / since I was not born like that.* Her language communicates directly with the community, ensuring the message is well received (*look*, I am not an academic, nor Santera, or *jinetera* [prostitute], nor manager, I am like you: *why am I speaking to you from the reality that consumes us; I realized*).

Critical consciousness begins when a black woman decides not to contaminate her head with chemicals. It is not simply a clinical process; first we must establish a nexus with the historical truth (we know that it is a hidden plot within the story of national historiography). *With me they sleep for more than four hundred years / dreaming with the "until when."* Before establishing a relationship; I have to know my body, consciousness, and the need for self-expression as a black woman and man. We, blacks, did not arrive to Cuba only fifty years ago.

Interaction with divergent thinking that fosters a new relationship with our historical processes is essential. This leads to discussions and exchanges that reformulate dissimilar points of view, which requires the systematization of knowledge, taking as a starting point our own life experiences to develop a theoretical body that supports the enunciation of reality and could effectively serve the collectivity.

How many times must Magia López have felt on her scalp the harshness of chemicals, whose use was unfair even to women's economic budgets. Remember that the best hair salons specializing in black women's hair are established in clandestine locations. All this translates to exorbitant prices and no control over the products used. It is a complex process, in which of course black women are again in a state of helplessness. Hair straightening processes external to government subsidy are very costly. Maintaining our hair, in particular within the norms of racist aesthetics that mark us, constitutes paying rent.

Magia sings: *Processing stretches your hair / it makes it a liar....* She is an embodied testimony of what happens a few months later: *[racial] roots in the form of [hair] roots appear . . .* And everything starts all over again. Processing or perming hair must be done five to six times a year. The chant and uncomfortable question arise: *Negra pela' / who cut your hair?* Magia does not care: *the man who loves me / accepts me as I am.* She does not need to straighten [her hair] for her self-esteem nor to well manner her passion. Love is found in other parts such as in the responsibility of plentitude and in the pleasing of spirits. It is not a dogmatic nor narrow formula. Persons who accompany each other in existential communion, without reinforcing egocentrism, can be initiators and founders.

Ultimately, I think analyzing the poetic foundation born of social commitment appreciated in "Los Pelos" is a high point. The most important message is aimed at understanding the *reasons why*. The essential cannot be observed with the eyes, it goes beyond to that blessed muscle that poets abuse, known as the heart. *I carry the Afro in my blood / Wherever I go,* she sings, facing the complexity of a social structure that tries to turn it into shadow, who observes it as a transplanted tree whose roots and its tomorrow must be reshaped.

With "Mi piel oscura," La Negra del Momento channels a look at the evolution of the feminine in juxtaposition to the traditional stupidity that deals with emotions, granting the roles of nurses (breast/belly) or exotic sexual priestesses (belly/sex) to black women. She is not presented as smooth nor docile. Nor does she appeal to clichés where dramaturgy is accompanied by the folklorization of founding entities that accentuate a dying *Afrocubanidad*, limiting the development of new subjects that rise up from the defamations of the slave barracks and achieve structuring themselves as the citizens of a *mestizo*, complex, and underdeveloped nation. *Reject a whole story / sacrifice it / to adopt a role / that does not belong to you.* As we read in the *Altar de los Grandes* [Altar of the Greats], they turned the male into common goods, an earthly thing, object of trade, a commodity, and the female an object of double possession, possession for work and sexual possession. To be turned into something is not a natural, spiritual, nor emotional state of being for a human being. For this vanguard of thought the primary objective is not to become a Moor woman and be carried off in the feelings of a disrespectful male. Her role, the one she has identified, demands a lot of sacrifices, confrontations, and disagreements that banish the discourse of victimization. It replaces it with a keen tone of an empowered, future-making woman. *Why desire dead hair / when your hair is living / like the vegetation of the narrowest forest.*

Know the marks where the obligation to renounce hides, converting you to a dead letter by denying what is considered ugly, violent: *I realized / that it's better to wear dreadlocks, braids or buns / than to process or perm [my hair] with chemicals that blister my head, damn.* The same as Magia advises, self-legitimizing speaks on the physical damages without making it a clinical matter. On the contrary, *that my color not be white out of ignorance.*

These are phrases taken at random from the very well elaborated lyrics of La Negra del Momento that contain two fundamental thematic bodies: one deals with history and social disadvantages and the other raises the question of until when? Undisputedly, before reaching the chorus, which is another topic, she imposes the representation of women who do not ask permission to disagree with traditionalism. The lyrics speak of everything that autonomy touches, symbolizing the recovery of self-esteem and knowing its place. "My Dark Skin" is one of the topics contained in the album *Respuesta* [Response] by Asere Productions, the record label of the Cuban Agency of Rap. *Respuesta* is a compilation of topics written and sung by women. The album did not do well despite being nominated for the Cubadiscos Prize in its 2008 edition. Its distribution, marketing, and socialization depends on the anomalous structure of national labels for promotion and sales. However, it has traveled to alternative spaces, academia, and even the international market bustling to the point of *quemao'chando humo* [smoking fire]. Applying popular wisdom to this point implies that as much as the album's aura increases, the album is nitpicked in an attempt to silence and hide it.

The refrains make up a theoretical body that devastates, in which music is a pretext to propose emancipation and social commitment. The rapper Obsesión states it in her own words:

Hey, up with our hair
Let dreadlocks grow
Those who like them, good
and for those who don't, good too[24]

La Negra del Momento also introduces a polemics on gender through the compulsory gaze of women that reproduce a male gaze that results in shaving our roots or depriving the senses contained in the idea of *advancing the race*.

My dark skin
like the darkening night,
with nothing to tie us down.
This nappy hair and this race transcend,
a truth we project.
There is no punishment for this negra
that shuts up her bemba [big lips], no.

Rap has benefited displaced populations living in precarity from an economy in crisis well over a decade. Rap invents solutions for mobility and formulas for success in the exchange of other existing realities in the country. It has been the musical genre that accompanies the hip-hop culture, its aesthetic and ethical avant-garde. It allows itself to cross avenues and drive against spaces designed by power, to prosecute those who accept being a chair philosopher as a status of life, in short, contemporary rap is one of the most critical phenomena within the national culture. This debate for the vindication of black women and their right to exist without marriages or paternal patronage began when back in the decade of 1970s Sara Gómez, Nancy Morejón, and Inés María Martiatu Terry, among others, delinked themselves from the colonizer language that still remains in power.

NOTES

1. Editor's note: *Pasa* translates directly as raisin but is commonly used to refer to kinky or nappy hair.
2. Translator's note: *Negra mora* means black Moor woman; for line three, *negra pela'* means short-haired black woman. It is also used in the saying in the next paragraph.
3. Conversation with Tato Quiñones.

4. Walterio Carbonell, "Cómo surgió la cultural nacional," in *Raza y racismo*, edited by Esther Pérez and Manuel Lueiro (Havana: Editorial Camino, 2009), 110.
5. Rogelio Martínez Furé, "El racismo proteico," in *Raza y racismo*, 216.
6. Manuel Moreno Fraginals, "Aportes culturales y deculturacion," in *Raza y racismo*, 39.
7. Inés María Martiatu, "Nuevas voces, nuevos reclamos en la canción cubana. Discurso femenino en el *hip hop*" [New Voices, New Reclamations in Cuban Songs: A Feminist Discourse on Hip-Hop], *Movimiento*, no. 7, Havana, (2010): 5.
8. Fraginals, "Aportes culturales y deculturacion," 32.
9. Furé, "El racismo proteico," 217.
10. Martiatu, "Nuevas voces, nuevos reclamos en la canción cubana," 2.
11. Carbonell, "Cómo surgió la cultural nacional," 118.
12. Editor's note: Here the author is referring to revolutions that overthrew sitting Cuban governments in 1933 and 1959 and later implemented social reforms.
13. Editor's note: Casino Deportivo references a neighborhood location in Havana.
14. You speak Portuguese? They represent the folklore of our country. Do you like them?
15. Nicolás Guillén, "Me vendo caro," in *Motivos de son, Libro de los sones* (Havana: Editorial Letras Cubanas, 2001), 61.
16. Ibid., 61.
17. Ibid., 55.
18. Fragment from a song by Pablo Milanés. I am referring to indigenous and Afro-descendant movements in which Americans are dialoging from their communities toward an opening in the struggle of all Americans to save the planet against racism, sexism, and any other form of exclusion.
19. Grandmother, in the imaginary of the family.
20. This is said about the hot comb [straightening iron] because it straightens the rebelliousness out of black men and women's curls.
21. Bell Hooks (bell hooks), "Hair Straightening," *La Gaceta de Cuba*, no. 1, Havana (January–February 2005), 71. See note 5, on bell hooks, in chapter 13, "Gender and Raciality," this volume.
22. The name refers to those who follow the thought of José Antonio Saco and Domingo del Monte.
23. Editor's note: The hip-hop duo Obsesión is composed of Magia López and Alexey "El tipo este" Rodríguez.
24. Obsesión, "Los Pelos."

BIBLIOGRAPHY

bell hooks. 2005. "Alisando el cabello" [Hair Straightening]. *La Gaceta de Cuba*, no. 1 (January–February). Havana.
Carbonell, Walterio. 2009. "Cómo surgió la cultural nacional." In *Raza y racismo*, edited by Esther Pérez and Manuel Lueirol. Havana: Editorial Camino.

Guillén, Nicolás. 2001. "Me Vendo Caro." In *Motivos de son, Libro de los sones*. Havana: Editorial Letras Cubanas.

Martiatu, Inés María. 2010. "Nuevas voces, nuevos reclamos en la canción cubana. Discurso femenino en el hip hop." *Movimiento*, no 7. Havana.

Martínez Furé, Rogelio. 2009. "El racismo proteico." In *Raza y racismo*, edited by Esther Perez and Manuel Lueirol. Havana: Editorial Camino.

Moreno Fraginals, Manuel. 2009. "Aportes culturales y deculturacion." In *Raza y racismo*, edited by Esther Pérez and Manuel Lueirol. Havana: Editorial Camino.

Chapter 17

Passing for a White Woman

Sandra del Valle Casals

Today, I must feel proud. It was not an ordinary praise: A man decided to take the opportunity to reaffirm his standing as a belligerent male before a group of other men by calling to a woman who crossed in front of him: "Look at that white woman there . . ." But in reality, there was no white woman. Or rather it was just I; I am *mestiza*, biracial.[1]

White skin, "refined" features,[2] slender figure, and seemingly straightened hair whose brilliance undulated with the wind and made it look natural drove this black man to choose and emphasize among my external attributes the qualifications that would make me a "good white woman," meaning "that she's fine." I mean, "fine and a white woman."

For this man, after I turned the corner, I was just another woman who could boost the performance of his ego in front of the group. However, I could only think of the process of existential simulacrum that women who have this kind of racial duality suffer more aggressively, in which they often become rootless and lacking the ability to define themselves racially. The discovery of a false whiteness always tends to be described as "she is white skinned, but with curly or 'bad' hair."[3] Hair becomes the differentiating element for biracial women.[4] This is why all the efforts and anxieties are concentrated in the *blanqueamiento* [whitening] of the hair [trying to make one's hair more like whites' hair] because all the models of beauty and feminine sensuality exalt straight hair over *pasudo* [kinky or nappy] hair.[5]

I remember the time when I tried to have my hair natural, so I cut it for it to grow out. I felt as if I stopped being attractive to men. I felt this way because I had broken with the canon of dominant femininity that centered hair as a tool of feminine eroticism.[6] Audiovisual media depict the sexual rite between a man and a woman in which she unties her hair—if it was not loose already—in the climactic moment of seduction when the female image is erotically exalted or as an erotic domination of the other.

In fact, hair should be tousled during the sex act to accentuate feminine "savagery" or subordination to the male who grabs it. This imaginary creates a feeling of a lowered or inferior femininity, which compels biracial women to straighten their hair[7] to satisfy the hegemonic white canon of beauty,[8] illustrating the old refrain "you have to be willing to suffer to look good." These words are aimed at psychologically alleviating the burning of the scalp that the hair straightening chemicals [*desriz*] produce, a product and process that helps women to pass as white. I am not sure when I used that straightening cream for the first time. Evidently, I had not developed a consciousness yet or perhaps I internalized the process as part of women's initiation rites that hooks[9] discusses. I have a black cousin who superficially applied the product to her two-year-old daughter so that she could look like a "little *mulata* with good hair." The process is part of the anguish of "advancing the race" and of having a child endure less social stigma, though the child does not yet see the world in black and white.[10]

I imagine—and I am sure—the satisfaction that my black grandmother and *mulata* mother must have had when I was born in seeing that I looked white, that I was white. In fact, it appears to be part of the identity of my flesh that authenticates my skin color, and of which my grandmother does not get tired of repeating as an additional (false) quality. The playwright Abelardo Estorino knew from the title of his play *She Appears White*, the existential and social conflict that functioned as an attribute and anathema to Cecilia Valdés, central character of the homonymous novel *Cecilia Valdés* by Cirilo Villaverde, which inspired his piece, extending the projections of biracial women on the condition and desire to be white.[11]

Cecilia goes through an apprenticeship of her raciality and the privilege of whiteness. It is precisely her black grandmother who teaches Cecilia as a child on the culture of race and racial discrimination. The racist and self-flagellating discourse of the grandmother becomes evident in a passage in which she weighs the significance of being almost white:

CECILIA: I was playing a game with Nene.
CHEPILLA: Isn't that great! A ragged *pardita* [little brown girl] who wears cheap sandals. . . . You shouldn't mix with those blacks.
NEMESIA: This old woman hates blacks as much as if she had been born in Galicia.
CHEPILLA: You look white. Look at yourself. Look at your face. Do you see your skin? White. And notice your nose, fine like that of a young lady. And that hair, it means you have white blood.
CECILIA: Good skin and good hair are of no use to me.

CHEPILLA: When you are a grown woman and it becomes time for you to find a husband, a white gentleman will come and ask for your hand in marriage and he will take you to a new house with floors that shine like mirrors and you will have a carriage.
CECILIA: A carriage!
CHEPILLA: ... and dresses ...
CECILIA: From Paris!
CHEPILLA: ... And I will never tell anyone that I am your [black] grandmother. I'll watch you from afar, always from a distance.
   [...]
CECILIA: But I want to live with you always.
CHEPILLA: Oh, if you only understood what it means to be white in this world.

This short fragment of the screenplay based on the nineteenth-century literary classic illustrates the conjoined ideologies and practices in which women who look white or who can pass for white operate. The grandmother rejects and then denies the black race, making it inferior, while celebrating her granddaughter's white appearance. Mixing with blacks would, according to Chepilla, function as a type of contamination, a lowering of the status that white skin confers even when the person is not white.

In the novel,[12] the *niña* Cecilia—*niña* [girl] was a term used during that time only for white young ladies—is insulted when a black man denies her whiteness: "I must tell the *niña* even if she despises me. She thinks that because her skin is white that she is white, but the *niña* is not white. She can fool others but not me."

I remember with frustration when I was called "*jabá*" [yellow] for the first time by those objecting to me being perceived as white, but I also remember the contradictions that came later when I tried to show my black roots to those who thought I was white. Being called "*jabá*" is, without a doubt, a way of calling attention to my fraudulent whiteness, my white mask. This act of unmasking acts as a devaluation of my perceived status. In fact, black women are the ones who most often have detected my false image as a white woman.[13] Because they also straighten their hair and are trained in the cultural codes that circulate among people who use hair-straightening creams, these women recognize that I am infiltrating whiteness, or that I am "passing for white," or maybe they are people who know my *mulata* mother and my black grandmother.

Hair demarcates the frontier of whiteness, which is why it becomes the primary obsession of biracial women because it establishes the parameters of appearing white. A black woman with straightened or processed hair will feel whitened, and a biracial woman with straightened hair becomes white.[14] Every time I process my hair, the hairstylist exclaims admiringly, "Now you are really white."[15] My black grandmother proudly narrates an anecdote told to her by the hairdresser when she went to straighten her hair: A client arrived at the moment when I was leaving and asked her curiously, "And what was that white woman doing here?" Having an almost white granddaughter who can pass for white is my grandmother's racial vindication. In the novel, Cecilia's black grandmother also admires her granddaughter: "Even though it might be wrong to say, she is the most beautiful incarnation of woman that I have seen in the world. No one would say that she has even a speck of color. She appears white."

Without a doubt, the quest and longing for straight hair are associated more with black-skinned women. Some Cuban cinematography has shown this imaginary though images such as in the feature film of Enrique Colina, *Entre ciclones*[16] (*Between Two Hurricanes*). Although the scene is part of his satirical and ironic discourse, the film shows the hot comb[17] being passed through a black woman's hair, constituting that moment of female socialization that bell hooks[18] explains as part of a subjectivity that assumes that her hair is not beautiful nor attractive. One of the women tells the hairdresser, "You know well that I am pro-black with absolutely everything, but I can't handle *pasas* [nappy hair] . . . "; another woman with her elongated hair, thanks to braids made with hair extensions, projects her longing for straight hair while browsing a foreign magazine in which the models exhibit long, blonde, and silky-looking hair attributed to the products being promoted. The character is satisfied and feels beautiful when her friend the hairdresser hides her braided hair under a blond wig. Not only does she compare her to a sexual icon ("You look like Madonna"), she also assures her that she will be victorious in her sexual-romantic conquests ("That little doctor is going to be eating out of your hands"). It reaffirms a pattern of racist beauty that exalts straight and blond hair as paradigmatic.[19]

However, it is that singular association of stretched *"pasas"* [naps] with black women that leaves biracial women in a state of ambiguity, lack of definition, and invisibilizing of their racial conflicts. Hair stretching by biracial women works mostly as a form of concealment of black ancestry and the valuing of white power. However, these strategies of whitening are not based on sexual practices[20] but have a more symbolic and therefore transgressive meaning: it constitutes disobedience of the racial order.

Our culture views *pasas*, nappy hair, as backward, described as "crude" hair rather than natural, and in need of "softening" treatments. Crudeness is prosaically identified with the black race. Pejorative words like *greñas* [tangled mess] or *pasas* [raisins] to refer to kinky or nappy hair or *bemba* for thick lips contribute to the construction and reaffirmation of an imaginary that identifies the beauty of black people, and generally of nonwhite people, as inferior[21] and part of an imaginary that valorizes white as beautiful.[22]

Cirilo Villaverde describes Cecilia's gorgeousness in a positive sense based on values of white beauty: harmonious enchantress, regularity of her features, symmetry of her form, and slender shape. In 1959, Juan Rene Betancourt, a black Cuban intellectual explained in a public talk titled, "El concepto racial de belleza" [The Racial Concept of Beauty], from an economic perspective on the white supremacy of white beauty norms, "women of any race, and even females of any species, always seek strength and power in males, thus there is no doubt, that this characteristic is found even more so in the victorious race than in the defeated race." As for men, "They seek in women, among other things, refinement, exquisite and expensive perfume, elegant dress, etc., attributes of which black women are deprived from having."[23]

Being white is more so a position of power and privileges rather than a racial condition. Hence the writer Estorino's Cecilia is already endowed with a consciousness of race when she tells Nemesia, "White is not a color: it is that they see you as white, they greet you as white, they think you are white." It is the social and cultural distinction bestowed by the norms of white supremacy.[24] Whiteness grants impunity. Being white is a social status in itself.[25]

We are still functioning under the Aristotelian proposition that there is a direct relationship between ethnicity and social status. Women and blacks, as groups, have had to live under the axiom "It had to be this way." The appellants, white men, are excused. They have the advantage of sex-gender and race. However, a certain moral whitening functions over some black people, either because of their economic status, intellectual level, or simply by a sentimental proximity, which exempts them from the negative stereotypes imposed on the black race, found in expressions like "You don't behave like the blacks," "You are not like them." Negative racial stereotypes associate the body with morality. For example, because I appear to be a white woman, it is common for me to be included in phrases like "let's do things like white people," as well as make racist remarks by assuming that I am white.[26] There is a racial morality that regulates behaviors, the system of values, and (pre)judgments.

Having white skin and good hair served Cecilia's future; in fact, it was these characteristics that allow her to dream of a fate as a white woman and in turn a white future.[27] The white future as the longed-for paradigm is meant only for white people. Cecilia dreams of living in "a house with floors that shine like brilliant mirrors," of wearing clothes "of black chiffon and laces," and of freeing her descendants from discrimination, of having a daughter who would not have to pass as white: "she will have his skin [that of Leonardo], rosy cheeks and smooth long hair."[28]

Cecilia interpolates a sexual politics that naturalizes women's bodies as a mechanism for social mobility to ascend to white status. Her grandmother had already forewarned her about the contradiction between a white future versus a black future in relation to beauty or ugliness of the house they occupy or will occupy: "Daughter, contemplate what you will be and be wiser." The racist and classist education advises her to live "in the shadow of the white, even if by false means fusing a union, I believe and hope that Cecilia will always ascend out of the humble sphere in which she was born, and if not her, then her children."[29]

However, Cecilia suffers her hybridity in her very flesh, as Cirilo Villaverde calls in his novel, it is from his feminine protagonist's biraciality that she declares, "I am not of your condition Leonardo. I am poor, and worse, I am not white." Since her childhood, Chepilla had planned the trajectory of socioracial mobility for her granddaughter. After reprimanding her for playing with her friend Nemesia, "a poorly bred, ragged *pardita* from the street," she tells her, "You are better than her. Your father is a white gentleman and one day you will be rich and travel in his carriage. Who knows? But Nemesia will never be more than what she is now. She may marry and if she marries, she could possibly marry a *mulato* just like her because her father is after all, more black than anything else. You, however, are almost white and you can aspire to marrying a white man." As an adult, Cecilia tells her friend Nemesia one day, "I can't deny that I like white men better than *pardos*. My face would fall off from shame if I married a *pardo* and if I had a child that was *saltoatrás*."[30]

Like Cecilia, I have been raised and cultured as white, in negation of all evidence of my black patrimony. Since adolescence, I have heard and been told that I must marry white and especially that I must reproduce a "legitimate"[31] white child so that the generational lineage from me forward will be white. In her story on the process of racial whitening, Reyita, the protagonist of Daysi Rubiera's book, states that "blacks and especially the older blacks, always consider the union with white males very important, because the whiter we became, the less we would have to deal with variations of discrimination."

In my maternal side of the family, a similar sequence is reproduced as the one that Chepilla outlined in *Parece blanca* [She Appears White]: "Black Magdalena had a child, Chepilla Alarcon, with a white man, she was a *parda*; and Chepilla Alarcon had a child with another white man named Charito Alarcon, a light-skin *parda*; and Charita with another white man then had Cecilia Valdés, white woman."[32] These fragments reveal the genealogy of *passing* in the sexual exploitation of black women slaves by white men, slavers, and colonizers.

The mechanisms of *passing*—in this case of *passing* for white—were historically related with achieving freedom, as a way to become free, and were part of an antagonism of "races" (white versus black) associated with a legal condition (free versus slave). In the beginning in the United States, the "almost white" were permitted to leave their slavery and move from a state of subordination and oppression to freedom and privileges. Whiteness has thus been constructed on that signification.[33]

Passing—as explained by Elaine K. Ginsburg[34]—is all about identities, their creation and imposition, their ascension or negation, their reward and penalties. It also takes shape on the frontiers between identity categories and the anxieties of individuals and cultures induced to crossing those frontiers.[35]

Even though the cultural logic of *passing* implies that it is driven by the desire to move an identity from one oppressed group to another to gain access to economic and social opportunities (which is important in the face of a persistent racism), rationalizing *passing* can be more or less complex and ambiguous and motivated by other perceived gratifications.[36]

Passing, however, is a subversive act of manipulation in which individuals can remake their identities by using strategies that employ the body. Above all, *passing* is more than falsification or fraud; rather it represents the fallaciousness of race itself, its crisis.

We stand before transracial beings, extra-frontier, of mobilized, transitory, and cyclical identities—especially because skin color is itself an unstable element—that has a contingent, performative, volatile character and that is politically and ideologically relative in how races have been constructed, assumed, negotiated, and negated. However, the cultural inheritance that allocates race operates on a subjective level.

My skin is white, but my race is not. Black is invisible on my skin. It is physically present only in my hair, and in my cultural inheritance and the genealogy of my family.[37] The conflict is not located in a presumed legal condition because my white flesh elevates me as white woman[38] but in the cultural legacy that I claim defines me.[39] In the novel, Cirilo Villaverde asks, "To what race does this young woman belong?" Through a biracial character, a speculative exercise is embarked upon on the ambiguities of her race in a society in which to be white or black is unequivocal and in which vagueness is unacceptable. Biraciality alludes to racially illegible bodies.

The biracial subject not only complicates boundaries—frontiers that have been established—but the subject itself has to live in those conflicts. More so, the biracial subject problematizes the certainty of identity categories and their borders, in doing so creating a possibility for new identities and mocking established margins. The process and discourse of "passing for" is an interrogation, a questioning of the ontology of identity categories and their construction.

"I feel white" is what Cecilia proclaims by abandoning the physical plane and planting herself on psychological and moral grounds. The reality is that even if a woman can pass for white, she lives and experiences internal conflicts similar to those of black women, from the mutilation of the body with the stretching of the hair to the construction of racial myths that promote the longing for whiteness.

NOTES

1. Biracial is a term I use to highlight a state of duality in racial identity in which belonging to the black race or the white race places the individual outside of the established racial order. Being biracial means existing in an intermediate state and therefore undefined.

2. I use the quotation marks not because I do not have a Latino profile (Greek) but because of the semantic discriminatory connotation that hides behind the adjective: it is not simply the slenderness or narrowness of the physical appearance but that it is distinguished and distinguishable and consequently socially superior.

3. Like the adjectives describing fine or refined features, the phrase "bad hair" signifies more than hair texture because a repugnant quality is ascribed to wavy and *pasa* [kinky or nappy] hair in contrast to the position given to smooth and long hair.

4. I am referring to female gender as the focus of my study, but men contend with the same reality. For them, a close-shaved head is equivalent to "whitening" or trying to make your hair look more like white hair.

5. Other physiognomic features are associated with the black race like a wide nose and thick lips. However, these other features do not blacken, while hair does whiten.

6. Especially because the texture of the newly grown hair subverted the beauty norms traditionally hoisted by white supremacy.

7. I prefer the term straightening (*estirar*) rather than relaxing (*alisar*) that scholars like bell hooks or Paul C. Taylor use. I believe that straightening does not propose smoothness and creates a certain stiffness specific to curly hair. See note 5 in chapter 13, "Gender and Raciality," this volume, to read further on bell hooks.

8. Wearing curly hair today is assumed as a return to one's origins, an "afro" trend; it is especially more apparent in women who are more visibly black. However, in many cases, beyond countering the dictatorial nature of white femininity and achieving the consequent self-rectifying and self-validation of the condition of black, wearing hair like this is fortified by a social sphere that receives this difference as a cultural and political action.

9. bell hooks, "Selling Hot Pussy: Representations of Black Female Sexuality in the Cultural Marketplace," *Criterios*, no. 34, Havana (2003). Without a doubt, hair-straightening products function as an act of initiation, as bell hooks proposes, indirectly associated with patterns of white beauty because young women learn that is necessary to stretch their hair "to be beautiful," to "look good," and to be "well-groomed."

10. A Cuban paradigmatic book on "racial advancement" is *Reyita, sencillamente* by Daisy Rubiera, daughter of the protagonist who narrates the process of the whitening of the family as an ideological project for her daughter. "To advance the race" means to not suffer for Reyita: "I did not want the children that I would have one day

to suffer what I have suffered. That is why I wanted to advance the race, which is why I married a white man." Her voice is a symbol of an imaginary that continues to perpetuate the idea of "backward" versus "advanced."

11. Estorino's attention to the question of racialization and whitening are striking. As part of a description of interracial relations in the context of slavery, literary critic Salvador Bueno analyzes Cecilia's character from the conflict of class struggle in the novel (see Salvador Bueno, "Esclavitud y relaciones interraciales en Cecilia Valdés," in *Ensayos cubanos* [Ediciones Unión, 1994]).

12. My use of the imaginary contestation in this novel, works derived from it, as well as later pieces of Cuban culture is not fortuitous because it is one of the first works that incorporates and reveals the conflicts of female *mestizaje* besides the theme of blackness. The very foundation of the Cuban nation seeks conformation by the very nature of the *criollo*, although mixed and subsumed. The novel has been recognized in the history of the national literature as a top work that captures the customs, tensions, and class conflicts of nineteenth-century society. (Needless to say, I am using the final version of this work originally published in 1882.)

13. I think here of Richard Dryer's explanation in "La cuestion de la blancura" [the question of whitening] that "race in and of itself refers to some intrinsically insignificant geographical/physical differences among people; it is *the images of race* that are in operation" (see Richard Dryer, "La cuestion de la blancura," *Criterios*, no. 34, Havana [2003]).

14. Though hair straightening can be seen and lived in a nonideological order, as a cultural process, it reflects a certain anxiety and desire for "the other"—curiously signaled as superior—which is the focus of this chapter.

15. The "fixing" of hair type becomes a moment of female socialization among women who relate to similar cultural hair codes. The work of the hairdresser that uses *desriz* [hair-straightening cream] has held an invisible, secret, and veiled role behind closed doors working by very subterranean channels meant only for the initiated.

16. This film also explains the biraciality of a male character, Tomás: "He came out a . . . '*jabao*' *capirro*, white-washed *mulato*, that looks white but isn't."

17. In the documentary *Los del baile* (1965), Nicolás Guillén Landrián documented black women "passing the hot comb" [though their hair], a tool that was popularized in the twentieth century by Madame C. J. Walker, and in *Retornar a Baracoa* (1966) a black woman is shown using rollers as a beautifying ritual.

18. hooks, "Selling Hot Pussy."

19. bell hooks makes a notable demonstration regarding the image of the music artists Diana Ross and Tina Turner.

20. The phrase "washing the womb" has been used to signify the process of racial "advancement" by women when a black or *mulata* daughter marries a white man.

21. In his notable text "¿Hay razas o no hay razas?" [Do Races Exist or Not?], Gastón Baquero highlights the perception that black turns things ugly and desensitizes by narrating an anecdote that took place in a religious school for poor girls when a visitor in not seeing any black girls asked a nun if black girls were denied admittance: "It is not that we do not admit them," replied the nun. "We don't have racial prejudices. You know, it is just that I kill myself preparing the chorus of angels. Have

you seen how cute it looks? Well imagine a black girl there in the middle or anywhere in the chorus, she would ruin it. She would diminish my work. . . . The girls look so cute and the chorus is so perfect!" (see Baquero in Rafael Hernández and Rafael Rojas, eds., *Ensayo cubano del siglo XX* [Cuban Essays of the Twentieth Century] [México: Fondo de Cultura Económica, 2002], 282–303).

22. However, it is important to note the phenomenon of *mulata* women's association with voluptuousness drawn from stereotypes of black women and the beauty of white women. The *mulata* is recognized as "the best invention of the Spaniards," which is a phrase that enunciates a colonialist and sexual smirk.

23. Cited by Victor Fowler, "Estrategias para cuerpos tensos: po(li)(é)ticas del cruce interracial" [Strategies for Tense Bodies: Politics/Poetics/Ethics of Interracial Crossing], in *Ensayo cubano del siglo XX*, 658–88.

24. It is interesting what in reality are privileges and power are assumed by many whites as something natural, inherent to their humanity and not to their whiteness; however, nonwhites clearly highlight the difference. Therefore those who do not enjoy these concessions simply for not having the right hair look for all the possible means to pass as white.

25. A refrain circulated in the popular imaginary that says, "to be white is a career."

26. In her essay "Passing for White, Passing for Black," Adrian Piper narrates the multiple conflicts that she faced when she was assumed to be white (see Elaine K. Ginsberg, ed., *Passing and the Fictions of Identity* [Durham, NC: Duke University Press, 1996]).

27. I would like to refer to the semantic counter position established by a "black future" associated with the condition of being black. The black future is clearly seen in the play when the grandmother instills in Cecilia the fear of black people and blackness: "The gentleman took her hand and they walked, kept walking and crossed the fence. And as they kept walking further away, the man began turning black: his blond hair became kinky black hair and he grew fangs. The black man was the devil. He dragged her, the *niña* [the girl], all the way to the bell tower of the church of the Angel, a bell tower that did not have a cross, and from there he threw her in a well that would grow deeper and deeper and deeper. A bottomless pit, abysmal where she would never be able to leave." Frightened Cecilia responded, "Grandmother, I don't want a black man to take me away." Thus black men and blackness are demonized in the novel.

28. The gesture to define her descendants in terms of the feminine line of lineage no doubt documents that it is women who mostly must contend with racial conflict because she is also stigmatized by belonging to the "weaker sex." In fact, many times, being black overrides being a woman. In a conversation with a black friend, she confessed that in her professional and personal development, she has had to confront many more devaluations for her black skin than for her gender, in addition to her voluminous body, which excludes her from every pattern of femininity that is regulated by white supremacy.

29. Men in the seventeenth century were allowed to purchase under certain circumstances the "Title of Whiteness" or "Letter of Whiteness" that granted them privileges such as being considered officially white, the right to dress like gentlemen, to be named sir, and also inherit their families' wealth. Another certificate of the racial

order during that era was the "purification of blood" (*limpieza de sangre*), a document that would prove that the person did not contain any black blood, similar to the one drop rule in the United States.

30. Editor's note [in the original Spanish anthology]: a caste designation that translates to "leaping backward" in racial terms from the perception of almost white back to black.

31. This vigilance over the legitimacy of the white race has continued to be transmitted in the reference to "real" whites; people's "real" race is observed when someone goes to the beach and becomes sunburned rather than tanned, whether or not their scars become keloid, to checking newborns for the "*jabá*" or mark on the butt cheek or observing if their external genitals are darker. Cirilo shows Cecilia's *mulata* quality when it is revealed that "her red lips had a dark lip line, and the illumination of her skin was like a penumbra that darkened at her hairline."

32. This genealogy reproduces almost textually in the novel Maria de Regla's explanation (p. 242).

33. See Ginsberg, *Passing and the Fictions of Identity*, especially Adrian Piper's essay titled "Passing for White, Passing for Black."

34. Ibid.

35. An important element in the logics of passing is the geoterritorial dislocation of individuals to places where they will not be recognized. Cecilia, for example, curiously argues with her grandmother that if Leonardo "marries me, fills my life with riches, gifts me many silk dresses, and makes me a lady, and he will have to *take me to another land where no one knows me*. What would your mercy say about that?" (emphasis added).

36. Ginsberg, *Passing and the Fictions of Identity*.

37. Victor Fowler had already underscored the character of cultural heritage in his memorable essay "Estrategias para cuerpos tensos: po(li)(é)ticas del cruce interracial." He states, "What duality is this other than the same one that underlies the root of the Cuban nation, split between its two counterposed inheritances, African and Hispanic."

38. The voice of the literary character alludes to the following point: "how easy it is today to put a white color on the flesh of identity, which is a revolution in the field of genealogy." See Fowler, "Estrategias para cuerpos tensos: po(li)(é)ticas del cruce interracial."

39. With acuity, in one of his radio broadcasts about blacks in Cuba, Gustavo Urrutia highlighted the topic of "color prejudices": "Note that I did not say racial prejudice, since in Cuba everything that does not appear black is white."

BIBLIOGRAPHY

Baquero, Gastón. 2002. "¿Hay razas o no hay razas?" In *Ensayo cubano del siglo XX*, edited by Rafael Hernández and Rafael Rojas. México: Fondo de Cultura Económica.

Bueno, Salvador. 1994. "Esclavitud y relaciones interraciales en Cecilia Valdés." In *Ensayos cubanos*. Ediciones Unión.

Dryer, Richard. 2003. "La cuestion de la blancura." *Criterios*, no. 34. Havana.
Fowler, Victor. 2002. "Estrategias para cuerpos tensos: po(li)(é)ticas del cruce interracial." In *Ensayo cubano del siglo XX*, edited by Rafael Hernández and Rafael Rojas. México: Fondo de Cultura Económica.
Ginsberg, Elaine K., ed. 1996. *Passing and the Fictions of Identity*. Durham, NC: Duke University Press.
hooks, bell. 2003. "Selling Hot Pussy: Representations of Black Female Sexuality in the Cultural Marketplace." *Criterios*, no. 34. Havana.

Chapter 18

The Revolution Made Blacks into People

Yusimí Rodríguez López

Three years ago, I still worked at a national newspaper. On the afternoon of July 31, 2006, the Cuban people were told about the sudden illness of President Fidel Castro, at least it was sudden for the majority of us. The newspaper had scheduled a party for the following day, which was, of course, canceled upon hearing the news. By midday, after translating some news for the newspaper website, I found myself seated at a reception alongside a group of coworkers. It was something we did whenever we had free time. Everyone was talking about the commander in chief, speculating on the seeming uncertainty of the country's future.

A coworker that joined us related that some of his neighbors held a party the moment that they heard the news of the leader's illness. It was unclear whether the party coincided with the news or if the news was the reason for the party. What happened, however, is that my coworker, taking on the dignified attitude that we have been instructed to have in circumstances like these, went over to his neighbors' party to send them all to hell.

The colleague who holds one of the most important positions in the newspaper and is a member of the Cuban Communist Party had fought clandestinely against the dictatorship of Fulgencio Batista and risked his life even though he held a privileged position in the country because he was the "white son of rich parents."

I found all of this out while the colleague dissertated, offering details as he stood in the reception room of the newspaper's office. His support included having walked several miles daily from his home to his work center to fulfill his social duty during the hardest years of the Special Period, just like many Cubans did at that time, not because they were heroic but because they lived (?) off their salaries and the other options consisted of spending hours at a bus stop or commuting on a bicycle, if they had earned enough merit to deserve a bicycle from their work centers, or if they had enough money to purchase one.

The high point of my colleague's story was the moment when he said, if he, being a white son of rich parents, was able to sacrifice, then blacks should have done the same because the revolution made them into people.

I do not know if the coworker had anything else to add because I interrupted him in a very aggressive way and I called him a racist, among other things. It was a very disagreeable discussion from which he chose to excuse himself to his office.

It was a good decision because I do not know how that discussion would have ended otherwise. I now lament not having had the necessary calm, including the maturity, to have held that debate in a more civilized way. We are not going to gain respect with violence, not only black people, but everyone who because of their skin color, gender, sex, sexual orientation, or ideological orientation are deemed incorrect by the dominant spheres and submitted to any type of discrimination.

IGNORANCE IS POWER

We have been told since we began studying Cuban history that we have had only one revolutionary process and that it began October 10, 1868, with the uprising of Carlos Manuel de Céspedes in La Demajagua, the same moment when he also gave his slaves their freedom, inviting them to join the struggle for liberty. However, could Carlos Manuel de Céspedes have kept his plantation, and with it his slaves, in initiating the war? Wasn't it, without negating his just and abolitionist character, a strategic decision by Céspedes to liberate his slaves, having realized that they could represent a significant amount of the Liberation Army and that these slaves could fight for everyone's freedom and that they had very little to lose and much to gain? What would have happened if the slaves had decided to decline the invitation, as well as all the blacks and *mestizos* who took part in the struggle; what would have happened if the independence forces would have been composed only of the white landowners of the island? Blacks had to fight barefoot and seminude in the war while suffering signs of racism even within the Liberation Army.

In 1898, when the North American government decided to intervene in the Spanish-Cuban War, blacks and *mestizos* constituted eight-tenths of the Liberation Army according to Howard Zinn's book *A People's History of the United States*. He offers this fact as an anxiety held by the North American elites considering the possibility that if Cuba succeeded because of the Mambises, they might have established another black Republic like in Haiti.

In the history of Cuba that I studied in high school and pre-university, the Independent Party of Color, founded August 7, 1908, was mentioned in passing mainly due to the contempt to which black and *mestizo* veterans of the War of Independence were subjected in the neocolonial Republic. The party was directed by Evaristo Estenoz and one of its main actions was the Armed Uprising of the Independents of Color. They had the most advanced political platform at the time. I returned to studying Cuba's history in college, and I do not remember the professor mentioning it. Perhaps there was not enough time to cover the subject. We received only one semester of the course in the first year, and I guess it was necessary to condense the content and impart what was considered most important, but according to whom?

On November 27, the whole country memorializes the execution—carried out by the Spanish colonialists—of eight Cuban medical students that occurred in 1871. On that same day, a group of black members of the African-inspired secret fraternity Abakuá were killed in an attempt to avoid that same massacre. But this is not a fact offered by the country's sources of information, at least to this day. I was not taught these facts when I studied history at any level of my education. To date, I do not see it as part of the program *Este dia*, dedicated to daily events in history.

I learned about them a few years ago because a friend of mine commented that he had been invited to participate in an exposition organized by a youth group to commemorate the occurrence. My friend also knew about the Abakuá. I never found out if the exposition took place. A person involved in the idea of this exposition was Mario Castillo, and it was through one of his articles published in the journal *Caminos* that I gained more detailed information on the Abakuá who also died November 27, 1871.

THE BURDEN OF THE REVOLUTION

What do black people owe according to the commentary of my ex-coworker, fighter against the Batista dictatorship, eminent journalist, and member of the Cuban Communist Party? What was he actually saying? That black people only possess dignity thanks to the triumph of the revolution? That whites were already people before the triumph of the revolution? Or that whites were able to choose to oppose the government, able to decide to sacrifice or not to sacrifice, but that blacks could not because "the revolution made them into people"? I keep thinking of questions that could fill up pages, but this is not the point.

Owing something or someone limits our freedom of thought, judgment, and action. It is a way of restricting our rights. A debt is a stone on our neck, but what happens if we are inculcated with believing that we owe being a person to someone else or to a determined process?

My ex-coworker's affirmation implies that not only all blacks who lived in the country during the revolution but also all subsequent generations who had fewer opportunities to choose the revolution because they had not been born when it triumphed are people thanks to the revolution. And thereby, before even entering the world, we [blacks] are in an inferior position to the rest of the nation. We hold an eternal debt and therefore have less or no right to protest or to disagree with power.

There are realities though that we cannot deny. The facts are that the majority of people in jail are black men and women, that the patterns of marginality remain dominant in the black population of the country, that the most economically and socially disadvantaged people remain black, and that the majority of the citizens from whom the police ask for their identity cards on the street without any reason are black (the police do not need a justification to ask for an identity card). Moreover, any black man or black woman accompanying a foreigner is considered a *jinetero* [a hustler or prostitute] and it is not necessary for the person to be a foreigner, it is enough that he or she is someone with white skin. Once I was on the beach with a Cuban friend whose skin is white, and a policeman asked me for my ID because he thought that she was a foreigner. Besides these realities, the living conditions of most people are better than before 1959. However, this improvement did not happen only in the black sector of the population. Would someone feel that it is right to say that Cubans became people thanks to the revolution?

On many occasions, the leaders of the country have been obligated to recognize that despite their struggle to eradicate racism in our country, and notwithstanding the gains made regarding this aspect, racism has survived in Cuban society. It is understandable that it is impossible to eliminate its practice in fifty years given that it was present for four centuries. What is really frightening is that a member of the Cuban Communist Party would make that type of statement because it raises the question: What is the vision of our leaders in regard to us black people? Which includes asking: What was the true motivation for bettering the quality of life for this sector of the population?

However, the most alarming and also the saddest part of that incident was not hearing a member of the Party speak in such a derogatory way but that the other two black people who were present did not react when he made that comment, nor during our argument. After they told me, "You make sense but it's best to just stay quiet. It's not good to turn yourself into a target."

Chapter 19

Human Race? Ah . . . It Had to Be!
Yohamna Depestre Corcho

I find it difficult to talk about race. I wonder, is it is because I am afraid to fall inside of my own trap? It means revisiting feelings that I no longer have and revealing those I do. I believe that I judged the color of my skin more when I was in school. As a center of social integration, it paradoxically released questions that I could not answer and for which I have not received any answers to date. For example, that idea that blacks are white inside and that whites are black inside was an intriguing enigma that made my parents too uncomfortable to attempt to answer. Was it a way of seeing everyone as equal, meaning who we truly are is found on the inside, even when knowing that white signifies purity and black cruelty? Daddy, why am I a black girl; why did I have to be born like that? These were questions that I answered for myself later in life; not at school, which like I mentioned only aggravated my questions. I never saw any black people on television other than when a slave was shown or when a minor character without a name was included. In our schoolbooks, there were never any illustrations of blacks, nor any Afro-Cuban stories (*pataquín*),[1] not even a well-founded explanation for the origin of the races. The *Larousse* dictionary defines the word *Race* on page 672 as "origin, lineage. Constant variety of an animal species. Race of dogs. Crack, rift." If I can see through the image and symbol, I would say that the word *rift* is well placed to categorize the human race, especially because scientists clarify that to call man with the word *race* is vulgar. However, then why does the *Larousse* dictionary become so vulgar as to use the word under the term *man*, stating that human beings are defined by three races? The definition becomes more ignorant when it states that the first common trunk was white when it is known our mother Eve was born in Africa and it has been shown that black skin is the one that has changed the most. Skin (according to the *Larousse* dictionary): "Membrane covering the body of the people and animals. Waterproof, flexible, changeable and regenerative. Membrane that covers fruits." If this husk elevates or degrades me according to a scale in the eyes of others, then what are we, a mango or a grape? Measured by the level of sugar, dominated by a membrane as misleading as the one possessed by women between her legs that gives her the status of "ma'am or miss" and is nothing more than a parasitic veneer.

I returned to school once again, where I learned about only two black heroes. I lie! Three black heroes: Quintín Bandera, Jesús Menéndez, and Antonio Maceo. They spoke so little on the first two that I cannot tell you who they were. Hence I retract what I said, I know only one black hero. They said that Antonio Maceo was the "Bronze Titan" because he had countless wounds on his body, attributed to his fierceness facing brutality [in Cuba's wars for independence] while ignoring what Martí said about him: "Maceo's mind was as strong as his arms."

But I do not intend to speak on Maceo, or else I would become much too serious, and a black, as Josephine Baker said, must always be gracious. I also did not want to speak about the word [race], it is just that I do not know how to start this article. I have to explain how I did it. I went to see my friend Verónica to give me a topic; racism for me was like an invisible attachment that was locked from me for a long time. After reading the email from Achy asking me to write this article, I gave myself time to remember. I, as one of Alejo Carpentier's characters would say in *El reino de este mundo* [*Kingdom of this World*], have lived the cruelest racism, but as I understand it from the fact of one's own blood relations measuring you by the features of your face that they deem as more or less "refined" and who believe themselves entitled to the right to call you a female monkey.

I arrived at the bus stop and asked who was the last in line. The woman told me she was behind a man in a blue shirt. There were three men in blue shirts. "Him," the woman said indifferently, "The brown trousers, the briefcase."

"The *negro*, the black man," I said. The woman became startled and seemed put off. She corrected me, "The *mulatico*." "The *mulatico*? The *mulatico*," I repeated stepping onto the bus. I was not surprised. I used to be the same way. I swear that to this day I still do it like an unconscious habit. Phrases like, "Hey, *negro*! Look *negra*! *Negra*!" cause a reaction as if black is an insult. If we knew where the word *mulato* came from, we would find it even more shocking. Today, a symbol of beauty, sensuality, and of "advancement" in classifications in Cuba, *mulato* in yesteryear was a derogatory term. The term was invented by the Spanish slaver to categorize the *mestizo* born of a black woman (slave or free) and a Spaniard. The slave was the donkey and the Spaniard the good steed. *Mulato* is derived from the brute mule (or the donkey incapable of procreating without the horse).

But because we are not green, nor red, nor gray, why should the word *black* insult me? While the bus moved down the street and in seeing women passing by, it occurred to me that it would be a good argument to base my text on the great suffering of black women: her hair, her "*pasa*" [kinky hair]. With the slogan that woman must suffer to be beautiful, the hot combs, the chemicals, the burns on the scalp, the running from the rain so that your hair does not return to being what it was [before you straightened it]; all these things accost her. She has not stopped judging her hair, if not the name calling: *Cocotimba*![2] She insatiably seeks a shampoo for very rebellious hair, for "bad" hair. As if her hair could give her a cold, fever, or allergy. Verónica started laughing when I asked her that question. I smiled with her. I touched my dreadlocks as if by instinct. I had arrived at her apartment and we sat on some pillows on the floor. The gray and white striped cats purred between us. Is it perhaps that I am ungrateful of that popular saying that "the revolution made blacks into people"? Is it perhaps that my suffering, or our suffering, makes me say and believe that I am superior? Verónica was quiet; her eyes remained thoughtful. I looked toward the balcony. "I can no longer deal with this. I'll tell Achy to give me more time," I say to myself and remember the times I was about to start writing and went to sleep. Maybe the phrase I heard my dad say that "blacks are all lazy" is true. "Loafers? Bums while we built the Cathedral. And how about the cobblestones of Old Havana, who laid them?" My father did not know how to answer me, he did not even look at his *mulato* skin. How can I not speak about my racism today? "You are at another phase, simply at another," Verónica told me, and I caressed the gray and white streaks of her cat.

Where have my feelings gone? How is it that I do not remember my feelings? I can see the scenes but not how I felt. It is like having no place to complain. "And do you want to complain?" my conscience asks me. "No, no.... Yes." I move my head and look across the window. In that moment, I remembered the name of a feeling: impotent. This feeling would cause me to stay at home for hours, for days. At times, until I felt like screaming. But scream at who? Those who did not answer you with a phrase by Martí, the same one they told blacks who went to find work in the hotels and were told no: "Man is more than white, more than *mulato*, more than black, say that you are a man and already it is claiming all rights, all duties." Apparently, my neighbor never heard this phrase. She is a nurse dedicated to caring for patients, preferably white, and urges their daughters to do the same. On one occasion she was chatting with another neighbor who lives on the third floor and a woman who was passing by greeted them. The neighbor on the third floor greeted the woman back, while my neighbor was silent. The woman who was passing by addressed her and told her that she had also greeted her.

To that she replied, "It is because I am educated, and I am well aware how one must behave: when whites are speaking, blacks should stay silent."

"Is that woman crazy? In what century is she living?" I said. Verónica's cat escaped from my lap reacting to my abrupt gesture, reacting to my discomfort. "If I go today to a hotel," she told me, "they will not attend me well. They will help the one who has more money. It does not matter if the person is black, they will attend the foreigner the best, it does not matter if the foreigner is black. There is always a reason to exclude. Today, there is racism pertaining to nation."

"I want the fundamental law of our Republic to be the tribute of Cubans to the full dignity of man" was what I read on Encarta when I stumbled upon the Cuban Constitution. I do not know why it came to my mind that day, I also remembered that when I tried to copy it, Encarta placed a letterhead: Microsoft Corporation. All rights reserved.

NOTES

1. Editor's note: *Pataki* is the Yoruba word for the stories of the Orishas.
2. Editor's note: *Cocotimba* is pejorative term used in reference to a black woman with a short, male-looking, nappy haircut.

Chapter 20

A Room of Our Own for Black Cuban Women

Yesenia Selier Crespo

The vilified Afro-Cuban identity, which was bloodily restrained in the 1912 Massacre, the Escalera Massacre, and the Aponte Conspiracy, has come to light as part of the global scope of the African diaspora. Like a tender creature, it searches for horizons and mirrors to look for its reflection. For some of us, these histories can be framed alongside the Civil Rights Movement, the figure and movement of Malcolm X, and the tenet *Black Is Beautiful*.

Although postmodernism has centered othering, thus blowing up the essentialism of whole centuries of human thought, *lo negro* [blackness] continues to be mostly theorized by white intellectuals. In the process, they invent power and knowledge from the possibility of the imagined, a dynamic that expresses colonial realities, possibly postcolonialist, but that point to a real, numerical lack of intellectual production from blacks and our experiences of blackness.

Almost a century ago, Virginia Woolf in *A Room of One's Own*[1] reflected upon the necessary conditions for women to write a fiction novel. According to her, she needs "500 pounds a year and a room of one's own, where I can write without interruption." I wonder in the analysis that follows, despite the immense distances, geographies, histories, and temporalities that separate us, if we could locate one of the dilemmas found in our discursive absence, especially because her iconic essay illustrates excellently the dilemmas of the subaltern subject in articulating, creating, and re-creating their experiences. Woolf affirms the need to be one's own subject as a fundamental premise of the writer, a woman in this case, with an explicit denunciation of the mental construction imposed on women by patriarchal society.

Patriarchy, tabula rasa against which feminists of all ages have rebelled, has been a landscape, remote and, at minimum, inconsistent for black women. According to bell hooks, the symbolic constructions of black women were created to emphasize her condition as a body meant for sacrifice.[2] On this point, let us consider Cecilia Valdés, María la O, "the *mulata*" of the Cuban bufo theater, and all archetypes of black women; more than their qualities as disposable women, or of immorality,[3] more than anything, black women are sacrificial. Black women—statistically and not only stereotypically—will be located at any era in the deepest poverty, with less education, and with more children than other women. They will also most likely not have economic and emotional support by male providers. Additionally, black women, at any time, have been more easily used and sexually abandoned as easy targets of verbal and physical violence. Their feminine attributes have been degraded and their sorrows have been made less deserving of our sympathy.

The alienation of blacks and of blackness, and especially of black women, is a constant in the flux of the historical and the everyday in which fundamental and foundational notions are imposed and conveniently distanced from the thresholds of ethics that include black valuations on art and aesthetics. The (de)valuation of our art may worsen because of a lack of "a room of one's own." We barely register the notion of "high culture" denoted by the Western artistic canon to the appreciation of our art.

It is notable that the contested term *afrocubano* [Afro-Cuban] has been accepted by Cuban scholars for over fifty years to classify music of African descent. The definition by Fernando Ortiz creates an escape valve to digest the noisy and fearsome omnipresence of the drum and *clave* instrument in Cuban culture. We have our own space not only for the sacks of ebony stubbornly re-created from Africa but also autochthonous creations like the *rumba* and *conga*, and even the *son* and its subgenres, impossible without the alternations of their creators from both "high" and "low" spheres. The need to limit *lo negro* is extended as a curious trend throughout our history, found in jail, in the notion of "folklore," or in the National Rap Agency. These barriers give rise to a polemic in terms of Cubanness and blackness.

Black women, the eternal domestic in the popular imaginary, are allotted the incontestable terrain of aesthetics. Nappy-headed [*pasa*], thick lips [*bemba*], flat-nose [*ñata*], "*negra bonita*" [pretty black girl], and "*tremenda blanca se perdió*" [an incredible white woman that got ruined][4] are value judgments internalized at a common sense level in Cubans. Our identities are constructed on this backdrop. The concomitant feminine condition with the beautiful, and the centrality of appearance, is another. Although the subject of black aesthetics abounds in different cultural documents, rap lyrics, poetry, and other written works in Cuba after the decade of the 1990s, the aesthetics of black women continue to be a pivotal topic, unresolved, for most women of the diaspora, yet a topic that affects us most in everyday life.

Beyond the puddle of the sea surrounding the Island, another backdrop constitutes the aggressive, subtle, and colonizing subjective character of the postmodern and globalized state. The context of neoliberalism exaggerates the place and value of personal choice, rejects collective action, and places a major focus on personal success. They are the echoes of neoconservatism, reawakened and revitalized with Viagra and new blood, ready to bury every social gain of the 1960s, ready to certify the death of feminism and the introduction of its imposter, postfeminism.

The infamous postfeminism frames at least a series of attitudes of contemporary women. The rejection of feminism as a stigmatizing and androgenic doctrine that although it had gestured toward new degrees of freedom for women did not grasp women's happiness, while it extended the notion that equality is legally guaranteed in contemporary societies. Thus a return was orchestrated to a corporeal geography and to the normative pressures on the body: diminished sizes, improved with [plastic] surgeries, corrected with injections for an extreme standardization of beauty and sexiness. Skinny, retouched, sheered like sheep, postmodern women are professionally successful, sweet wives to not scare away the husband's desire, and selfless mothers empowered by consumption. *Sex and the City* represents the height of the ideal female consciousness in the postfeminist context.

In a context in which power equals one's capacity to consume, the tabula rasa for Afro-descendant women is abysmally far from that of white women. In the United States, research shows that the average wealth of a black woman between thirty-six and forty-nine years of age is five dollars, while that of a white woman is forty-five thousand, with wealth being defined as the difference between cumulative assets and debt. A country that transcended an intellectual discussion on the rights for blacks for more than two hundred years and had a successful civil rights movement in the decade of the 1960s is currently contemplating a regression of values conquered fifty years ago.

Black American women's "bad" hair has died, but to replace it they have adopted dead hair. The fabulous "extensions" and mythic "products" have become part of the discourse of black Cuban women for decades, admiring import products that contain close to 90 percent natural human hair. The clientele of women who get hair extensions keeps growing silently. Women who get them are primarily women who know about extensions, thus initiates "who enter by the back door so that no one may know," to the point that it has become practically normalized.

The stigmatizing of every feature of the physiognomy of black people was an obsession of modernity. More than a fashion trend, the "vice" of hair extensions redeploys the notion of good hair, which Chris Rock centralizes in the documentary *Good Hair* (2009). Women of all ages, classes, and educational levels confess to the camera without the slightest conflict that "straight smooth hair, relaxed, helps whites feel more at ease while we look more well-groomed." "Doing our hair" is part of what it means to be a black woman, actress Nia Long claims, "a black man should welcome it, accept it." Her affirmation implies that black women should do our hair because we do not have any and black men should accept the absurd expense that completely oppresses women. "We have reached the point where we comb our oppression and exploitation every morning. You conform to it or overcome it every day. How can you think clearly when you're wearing your exploitation all the time? There is a basic need for a movement that reconsiders the notion that we can't even control something so close to us as the hair on our own heads," Reverend Al Sharpton states while wearing the perm that he has used for more than twenty years.

African American men, facing structural and historical blocks to integration in American society, and because of endogamy, are the guinea pigs for women who have this vice. "The vice of hair extensions is an investment that costs more than the education of our children," Sharpton comments. Music executive Andre Harrell adds, "The price of supporting a woman is like New York's real estate market, it is sky-high. A visit to the beauty parlor can leave you bankrupt." If this is not enough, hair extensions impose bizarre limits on personal and intimate relationships between couples. Regarding recreational options: no beaches, no pools, a panic when it rains and the traumatizing *Do not touch* my hair in bed. "If you're with a woman with hair extensions, focus on her breasts," recommends Harrell, humorous and painfully.

The documentary presents other viewpoints less entranced by the demands of late capitalism imposed on women, breaking them with the economic and aesthetic aberration that strains their intimate relationships. Shelia Bridges, a black interior designer with alopecia, embraces her condition and differences at the deepest level while affirming that black women "use hair like currency . . . attaching our self-esteem to it. In actuality, beauty standards are completely unreal and out of reach for black women."

Regardless of the notoriety attached to phallologocentrism, according to Derrida,[5] the notion of humanity as foremost defined by brotherhood is a fundamentally phallocentric concept. Hegemony is, moreover, hiddenly white. Women, white and black, in every part of the world, have advanced greatly in terms of our education, economic, and social participation, with de jure and de facto gains, but there is a lot of work that needs to be done in terms of equality and respect in our lives as we live them day to day.

This chapter does not pretend to challenge our sisters with permed hair, but in considering the diversity and complexity of the subjectivity of black women, it became indispensable to critically address some of our realities. Our choices, even the most personal ones, have political consequences beyond the blare of the horn. Black women and men, with permed hair or not, whitened or not, do not alter the social consequences of the technology of classification of racism. However, as one of the interviewees asserts to Rock in *Good Hair*, "leaving my hair in the natural texture with which it grows out of my head is seen as a revolutionary act so I must have conviction in wearing it."

Black Cuban women at the periphery of consumerism, and from whatever position in the fabric of our social and educational continuum, also face a daily battle in front of a mirror. While we sing the national anthem "La bayamesa" and honor the national coat of arms that depicts an image of "la cubana," the Cuban woman as a beautiful *trigueña* [light colored woman] with long, straight hair under the Phrygian cap, black Cuban women need a place of our own. Ten percent of the population live in hot Havana where one-fifth of the national population is concentrated. They are mostly black people who continue to reside in the deteriorating *solares* [tenements]. I invite us all therefore to dream of a room of our own, to re-create it every morning in front of the mirror, to document our experiences in every way possible, and to argue against, like salmon going upstream, the negations that oppress our true beauty.

NOTES

1. Virginia Woolf, *Una habitación propia* (Barcelona: Seix Barral, 2005).
2. bell hooks, *Black Looks: Race and Representation* (Boston: South End Press, 1992). See the work "Gender and Raciality," on bell hooks, chapter 13, this volume.
3. Inés María Martiatu, *Bufo y nación: Interpelaciones desde el presente* (Havana: Editorial Letras Cubanas, 2008).
4. Editor's note: This phrase is used to refer to a beautiful woman whose only "defect" is her blackness as in "a waste of a hell of a white face on a black skin."
5. Jacques Derrida, *The Politics of Friendship* (New York: Verso Books, 1997).

BIBLIOGRAPHY

Adriaens, Fien. 2009. "Post Feminism in Popular Culture: A Potential for Critical Resistance?" November 9. http://www.politicsandculture.org/.
"Alpha Wives: The Trend and the Truth." 2010. *New York Times*, January 24. http://www.roomfordebate.blogs.nytimes.com.
bell hooks. 1990. "Postmodern Blackness." 1990. In *Postmodern Culture*, 1:1. Baltimore: Johns Hopkins University Press.
———. 1992. *Black Looks: Race and Representation*. Boston: South End Press.
———. 2004. "Understanding Patriarchy." In *The Will to Change: Men, Masculinity and Love*. New York: Atria Books.
Bennet, Jessica. 2010. "Feminismo or Bust." March 23. http://www.newsweek.com.
Bernard, Tinamarie. 2009. "Postfeminism Femme Fatales." July 2. http://www.community.feministing.com.

Derrida, Jacques. 1997. *The Politics of Friendship*. London: Verso Books.
Douglas, Susan J. 2002. "Manufacturing Postfeminism." May 13. http://www.alternet.org.
Dowd, Maureen. 2005. "What's a Modern Girl to Do?" *New York Times Magazine*, October 30.
Martiatu, Inés María. 2008. *Bufo y nación: Interpelaciones desde el presente*. Havana: Editorial Letras Cubanas.
Meizhu, Lui. 2009. "The Wealth Gap Gets Wider." *Washington Post*, March 23.
Moshenberg, Dan. 2008. "Protection: Women Bear the Brunt." November. http://www.womeninandbeyond.org.
Nedeau, Jen. 2008. "Is Feminism Dead? An Overview of PostFeminism." October 4. http://www.womensrights.change.org.
Piepmeier, Alison. 2006. "Postfeminism vs the Third Wave." March 17. http://www.electronicbookreview.com.
Roberts, Sam. 2010. "More Men Marrying Wealthier Women." *New York Times*, January 24.
Rock, Chris. 2009. *Good Hair*. HBO documentary. Los Angeles: Roadside Attractions.
Traywick, Catherine A. 2010. "How We're Doing: Women and Wealth." *Pittsburg Post Gazette*, March 15.
West, Cornell. 1994. *Race Matters*. New York: Vintage Press.
Woolf, Virginia. 2005. *Una habitación propia*. Seix Barral: Barcelona.

Part Three

CULTURAL PRACTICES

Chapter 21

Oriki for Elder Black Women of the Past

Georgina Herrera Cárdenas

Oriki for the Elder Black Women of the Past

*In the funerals
or in that hour in which dreams become the veil
that covers our eyes,
they were like fabulous open books
with golden pages.
Elder black women, beaks
of mysterious singing
birds
in song of what had reached
their ears in the past.
We were, without knowing, owners
of all occult knowledge
in the profundity of the earth.
But us, who today
should be like them, have been
know-it-alls.
We didn't know how to listen, and took
courses on philosophy.
We didn't believe.
We were born too close to another
century. We only
learned to question everything
and ultimately, find we don't have answers.
Today, in the kitchen, the patio,
anywhere, someone
I am sure, is waiting
for us to tell what we should have*

learned.
We remain silent.
Looking like sad
mute parrots.
We did not know how
to empower ourselves with the magic of
telling.
Simply
because our ears
were closed.
Remained stubbornly deaf
to the gift of listening.

Except for a few minor exceptions that remain basic and vague, there is no trace of black Cuban women in literature, which is a written record of a time, place, and mode of life or events, until the dawn of the twentieth century. This is easily explained. First, because of the slavery that they were submitted to, and later, in being the most excluded in society. Thus, this is how they were blocked from bringing forth, in the light of the world, the creative sensibility that resided in them. However, did they or did they not have talent? The response is a resounding yes because oral literature nurtured female and male writers, whether free or owned. Picaresque, science fiction, magical realism, *testimonio*, poetry, drama—it is all there. They wrote in every mode. Their literature was and remains unique. They did everything they could and more given their assigned roles. They gave birth and, like the saying goes, "took to the mountains," created rebellions, and then armed them. After gaining their freedom, they dedicated themselves to the storytelling of everything. Among the recognized roles is that of being an elder black woman reclaiming her place in the world.

White women, who were granted certain cuddles and privileges, immersed themselves in intimist, restricted, prudish, and modest literature. However, what options did black women have, enslaved because of their race and sex, and illiterate too? Nothing, but it was not because they were not sentient beings. Did they not have the imagination to also be creative?

Searching through Cuban literature from the dawn of the eighteenth century to today, there is close to nothing of black women's literature. I am referring to the written word. But not knowing how to read or write, without even thinking of these as a right, because I am speaking about human rights, in what way could these women build their knowledge? The black woman did not enjoy the luxuries of traveling to other continents. They could not become ecstatic at seeing a different landscape. Her memory recounted the voyage between Africa and America, guessing, crossing the ocean unable to decipher the noises nor smells because lamentations, lashes, and infernal plagues were all that penetrated her senses.

She did not participate in sumptuous festivities. Of these, she only knew threats and punishments if the crystal and cutlery did not shine like the sun. Praises whispered in the ear were intended only for white mistresses and white masters, astonishing and heightening their sensitivity. But where are all those stories that they used to tell, especially in the kitchen, or sitting in a chair or on a stool in the evenings, next to a cradle or a hammock, or perhaps in front of a simple poor pallet of straw?

Like Minerva, goddess of wisdom, and all the white muses, the sensibilities in the distant branches of the arts were developed solely around white women. What could be expected then of black women in the emergence of women's literature?

The Old and New Testament attest that everything occurred in the world through a miraculous creation by a unique male energy: God. Men bear witness to everything on why things are the way they are from the first woman to the first birth. No female saint, woman, or even the woman who felt the pangs of pain of the first birth are allowed an opinion. If women were denied their testimony since then even when they were white, because from a sexist and racial point of view Eve was white, how could black women testify when they were devalued as women? Black women were considered closer to a unique animal that had some human attributes like walking on two feet, not having a tail, etc. But I will resume my discussion more concretely. Black women's oral literature was brought from Africa in the memory of black women resisting the brutal crossing even as they birthed the master's children along with their own children. Their oral literature is vastly diverse and holds an unlimited richness.

When my grandfather died, the women of my family, now elders, worried about my mother and especially me because we were very close to him because of his storytelling that wove together truths and lies. Later, female neighbors, friends, and black women from all over town visited and began raising their voices, losing that respect that grandpa inspired, or better said imposed, because only him, an unacknowledged *machista* to the core, could own the spoken word. His "shut up, shut your mouth" would garner a silence that seemed to last forever. However, the silence stopped little by little and the women began to tell stories. Many of these were new stories, others the same ones that he used to tell, uplifting me as if I was suspended in the air. What happened, however, is that the stories of these elderly black women not only suspended me but transported me. Where? I don't know! But I came and went between what I heard, enjoying myself so much that even today my heart fills with that memory. After more than half a century, I ask myself questions to which I do not have the answers that I am trying to find here, with the help of those who are present.

My great aunt Sabina used to like to tell the story about her sister Victoria who would "*cimarroneaba*," rebel. It took several men to make her obey by attempting to distract her. This was not easy because with machete in hand, she would crouch with her legs open, keeping watch all around her. Also, the story of Oweni that was hunted like a leopard, unnecessarily bludgeoned and driven to Cuba in the hold of a slave ship, well under the other slaves so that he would remain still. He had just been purchased and taken to a sugarcane plantation when he "*cimarroneándose*," also rebelled. This heartbreaking testimony extolls an awareness that cannot be mistaken.

Ma' Leoncia would tell stories that were pure science fiction. She was thin, short, and slow because of her old age. She would tell about seeing the dead with electric bolts attached to them, walking alone from her house to the cemetery. And to prove she had witnessed this, she would become light-footed, animating her whole body walking back and forth, so that to this day, I'm still so deeply attached to the magic of her words and gestures that I think I see her. Besides, I still believe her.

Ma' Cocó, Juliana, or Ma' Luisa would tell the story of Good Friday when slaves were forced to work on the Montalvo plantation mill. They say an ox spoke three times prohibiting them to work, but they couldn't obey. This caused the mill, its workers, and the main house with the owners and their descendants to sink in the earth. When I retell about what I heard, who doesn't feel the tremendous roar and see the earth opening, swallowing everything for not respecting the day the son of God died for our salvation? Is this story something other than magical realism?

And what do we make of the theatrical dramaturgy of the young slave and mother Isabel? Although we all knew that story, it could be retold many times over because facts were added, ratified, and rectified, each time achieving more and more dramatic versions. Isabel was prohibited from breastfeeding her baby because her owner's baby was gluttonous, so he was the only one allowed to enjoy the sustenance of her prodigious breasts. But one day, Isabel sensed that her son was crying from hunger. He would always cry but she felt him that day, possibly in her blood. So she gave him the nourishment that belonged to him. She fed him the next day and the day after so that she stopped caring what might happen to her if she was found out. The law of probability allowed what ultimately happened. The white female master worried about her slave's absence and took her husband to see for himself how the dark lips of Isabel's son enjoyed suckling the nourishment that was meant for the pink lips of their white child. With his whip, the man separated the little boy's mouth from his mother's breast. There were three shaken bodies, but a single shudder. Isabel screamed like a mad woman and ran like crazy so that they were unable to catch her. With a child in each arm, she threw herself from a cliff a distance from the main house.

The story would end there with us feeling a strange tightening of the throat, all of us without saying a word, but pensive with many reflections. But wise Ma' Encarnación would be waiting for just the right moment with her sneaky smile, transporting herself to a hut of Congolese Benito and Matilde. They were a couple of African ethnicity, but he seemed to be somewhat slow because Matilde had to find other companionship when Benito would leave to work their *conocu*, small parcel of land. To let her lover know when the coast wasn't clear, Matilde would hang a bone at her window. One day, Benito drank too much *malafo* [cane alcohol], and Matilde forgot about the bone. So then what happened? Well, when the other man thought the husband was gone, he found himself with a locked door and the window without the usual bone. Whistles came and whistles went to which Benito, half startled, told his woman that there was someone there other than him. "Matilde, do you hear something like the sighs of a hurt anima?"[1] "Yes, Benito, but I'll pray for that poor animal. You'll see." Matilde walked over to the window where she'd hang the bone, projecting her voice toward the weeds where the lover waited. "Poor, suffering animal, in case of anything, my husband is at home, I forgot to hang the bone!" She saw her African Don Juan quickly hide among the trees. His passionate ardor had seemingly fallen to his feet given how fast he moved. Congo Benito sighed, alleviated, and Matilde was even more so, confident that she would never again forget the sign meant for her love entanglements. As the story shows, the naive and picaresque oral literature of the African *criolla* acquires a relevance that surely, in getting to know it, would have pleased the European cultivators [of this genre].

The detective story, a horror, or mystery tale were a part of this singular literature, preserved always on the lips and the memories of elder black women like this following tale.

There was a disobedient, inquisitive, and sleepless young woman who every night would come to the living room window. Her mother would remind her that past midnight, the dead wandered freely, but she would pay her no mind, until one day when a well-dressed man, very proper, with white impeccable teeth and holding a candle, got near her and asked her if she could hold the candle for him until the following day when he would surely pick it up. He seemed so proper, so well dressed, and with such good teeth that the young woman took the candle, which immediately turned into a human leg bone. This caused so much horror in the house, and scolding, and then the coming and going early in the morning of people who knew how to take care of these types of things. One of them recommended that the young woman look for a small child and wait with the child and the femur at the window at midnight for this supposedly proper gentleman, and that when the gentleman arrived, she would have to pinch the child until he cried. She did just that and when she returned the bone to the gentleman with the child crying, the femur turned into a candle once again. The man then very curiously told the sleep-deprived woman, "You were saved because the cry of the child is like the voice of God, but stay away from the window during the hours that are mine." Sure enough, his warning worked.

Returning to the subject of the literature of the past that was impossible for black women to write, let us consider that after all the years that have passed since the end of slavery, we have achieved many gains. We learned to read and write. We have gone to college and traveled the world. Better late than never, possibilities have been opened for us. We now have writers that are well established, and unfortunately others not so well known, but learning new names every day is part of our apparently eternal struggle, which comes and goes like "a wash of light."

NOTE

1. The original is phrased "¿Matilde, tu tá cuchá cosa así como suspiro de un ánima en pena?" which highlights the unique colloquial nature of the rural spoken language and is completely lost when translated into English.

Chapter 22

The Black Female Imaginary in Cuba

Aymée Rivera Pérez

Before the revolution, Cuba was "the most racist of the Hispanic Caribbean territories."[1] Miguel Barnet's narrative, which reflected on that era through the genre of *testimonio* [testimonial literature], confirms this claim. Acebal, a secondary character in Barnet's *testimonio Canción de Rachel* [Rachel's Song], is an actor like his friend Rachel and personifies the famous *"negrito"* of Cuban theater. He described his "costume" in this way: "A handkerchief at the waist, preferably red, another one around the neck, a sharp switchblade, little straw hat and white teeth like [the inside of] a coconut."[2] He explains in the novel, "Blacks to me, as a white man, are different. They move more like dolls than men of flesh and bone. . . . It was this essence that I tried to give to the public. The true spirit of the negro: frivolities and eccentricity. Blacks have never suffered as much as whites because they are very *guaracheros*, partyers, letting what could hurt them roll off their backs. There is no better proof of this than their song and dance."[3]

Until when will blackness in Cuba be a transcendent signifier whether as a negative absence or positive presence in literature and art? How does Henry Louis Gates Jr.'s claim that "blackness is produced in the text only through a complex process of signification"[4] apply to our literary production?

The creation of literature by black women writers in Cuba is a recent phenomenon contingent on the existence of a black female imaginary that synthesizes the re-creation of countless possible worlds—real or not—and that resignifies terms such as "black," *"mulato,"* and "of color" in the Caribbean and the socialist context of the island. The phenomenon makes Africa's footprint live on in literature as well. This article discusses the representation of Africa in the work of some Cuban artists: the black poets Nancy Morejón and Georgina Herrera, the filmmaker Gloria Rolando, and the *mulata* poet Excilia Saldaña.

THE "CUBAN STEW" OR THE INVISIBILITY OF BLACKS

Although the Cuban Constitution, amended in 1992, prohibits all types of discrimination on the grounds of race, skin color, sex, national origin, or religious beliefs, the juxtaposition of a politics of equality versus a politics of identity had already persisted for more than thirty years despite socialism. As Smith and Padula note about Lourdes Casal's 1976 research, "During the first years of the Revolution it was considered that women's equality was a lower priority than the elimination of racial differences and of classes. It seems that the same still applies."[5] However, according to Carlos Moore, in Cuba "la raza" [the race] is a nonsubject, an eloquent absence, a matter silenced by "negrophobic" policies applied in the name of cultural assimilation. Recent research on race relations in contemporary Cuban society corroborates the existence of negative valuations with respect to blacks by nonblack groups and by the black population itself.

The revolution tried to eradicate racism to the point of considering it an ideological problem. But its antiracist politics, based in socialist thought and far from a true identity politics, have not been effective. While these policies imposed integration, their results also led to the invisibility of black people and the persistence of racism, which pushed Cuba's government to revise its race policy in the 1980s.[6]

Moreover, the Department of Ethnology at the Center of Cuban Anthropology recently conducted a study on the perceptions of racial groups on the Island, determining that blacks see themselves homogeneously and that prejudices and negative racial stereotypes prevail. The researchers concluded that these negative valuations are determined, to a large extent, by the influence of the family and customs perpetuated, like belief in the Orishas, from one generation to another.

Guanche defines this phenomenon as familial endoculturation, which explains how "the adoption of behaviors [are] transmitted through examples, moral and labor values, inherited or acquired in historical conditions of poverty."[7] However, I believe that the causes of the persistence of racism in Cuba are partly linked to its history of literature.

In Lydia Cabrera's prologue to *Cuentos negros de Cuba* (1950–1961), Fernando Ortiz wrote, "this book is an important contribution to Cuban folkloric literature. What is Blanquinegra besides the negative attitudes that are adopted because of ignorance?"[8] Ortiz's words became the "official version" of the cultural identity of Cuba as a *mestizo* nation. This consensus continues to be assumed to this day primarily because he is considered "the father of Cuban anthropology" and also because the concept is extremely conciliatory.

This idea of *mestizaje* is also deeply rooted in bourgeois programs of Latin American national reconstruction since the first decades of the century. The "cosmic race" was founded on the visionary promise of the redeeming *mestizo* (as Mexican scholar José Vasconcelos argued in his essay "The Cosmic Race" in 1925). Especially since 1959, *mulatos* have come to represent the synthesis of cultural and national unity. Cuba is a bit of that: a version—though socialist—of the model of racial relations in Latin America whose essence is the ethnic mix and an unjustifiably paternalistic colorblindness that only leads to reinforcing the invisibility of black people. Literature has sustained this phenomenon, though inconsistently.

THE BLACK PROBLEM IN CUBAN LITERATURE

Since the *negrista*[9] movement in literature in the decade of the 1930s, Cuba has defined black and *mulato* poetry as work identified with Afro-Cuban culture (which can also be seen as Cuban) regardless of the skin color of the author. The *mulato* poet Nicolás Guillén has emphasized the fact that the period did not represent a confrontation between "black" and "white" poetry but the search for a national poetry.[10] Although race, class, and gender determine each other, for women, all these categories are concentrated in gender. Cuba remains a place of differences and tensions between identities derived from race, sex, and gender, although it is puzzling to admit it; these tensions become more evident in the poetry of the black and *mulata* women writers. Although having to adapt cultural theory to make it applicable to Cuban specificities has always been required, several theoretical suppositions are appropriate to carrying out an approach to this literature. Among them are African American and Caribbean womanism,[11] Latin American theories on *mulato* and *mestizo* nationalisms, and Marxist cultural theories.

The need to insist on European and American concepts of race for Cuban cultural analysis leads to the consideration of Fredric Jameson's proposition to "map the paradoxes and dilemmas of the dialectic of otherness"[12] in reference to Cuba, although he is referring to the Anglophone Caribbean. As it pertains to Cuba, Evelyn O'Callaghan considers the need to use an eclectic multiplicity of critical perspectives suggesting an "aesthetics of pluralism." In other words, the work is theoretically located within the *criollo* ethos that gives it life.

It should not be overlooked that in Cuba nonblack poets such as Minerva Salado (1944) also employ African themes and write what would be classified as Afro-Cuban poetry. In her long poem "Canto del ácana" (*Palabras en el Espejo*, 1987),[13] Minerva Salado adopts a black persona (possibly feminine) in three of the fourteen sections. The poem conjures the trafficking of slaves, mingling descriptions and invocations of the principal African deities. The poem also expresses an intensely lyrical love for Africa and solidarity with "my black brothers." The poet embodies a slave (or maybe a slave woman) who has arrived in Cuba and establishes an intimate relationship with the Island, referred to as the object of love and maternal protection. His or her body is the testimony of his or her reconstructed kinship relations, a family tree that extends and flows over the seas:

Canto del ácana III

Island, next to the serene recess of your mantle
I am going to love your mysteries with my hands
and my children will see the profound dawn of the light
as if it were honey.

But mine is another land with a tree that kindles me
across the foam and horror,
my skin is the slope of its branches
and the fruit of its home
my heart breaks like a shell
fragile in the yearning for its voice.[14]

The presence of Afro-Caribbean traditions and deities in the poetry of black Cuban women is one of the most interesting tendencies in postrevolutionary poetry. The most significant is the identification of all poets as women and as Cubans with Africa as a cultural, historical, and political construct that facilitates the trope of memory and its roots.

The bibliography representing the black movement in Cuba is abundant with the work of black, white, and *mulato* poets among whom was Nicolás Guillén. However, black female literary production was scarce before the revolution of 1959. Like in the rest of the Americas, it was the prerogative of *mulato* men to reflect on the racial conflict and its consequence through literature while black women were and remain a stereotype of rampant sexuality and emotional freedom.

The black feminine body gained a poetic form as native animals or Africans, fruits, vegetables, and musical instruments, at the fingertips to be touched or consumed. She was dehumanized or converted to merchandise in prerevolutionary consumer society. Sander L. Gilman in the nineteenth century claimed that "female genitalia came to define women. . . . The perception of the prostitute . . . became founded on the perception of black women. . . . Black women do not represent merely sexualized women but also women as a source of corruption and disease";[15] such was the perception of the male and white observer. Thus black female subjectivity could only be inscribed through the gaze of another. Some of the first *negrista* poems written in Cuba by Francisco Muñoz del Monte in 1854 and a famous poem by Guillén written in 1947 exemplify the perspective of a male observer. They illustrate what black and *mulata* Cuban women have to confront as objects of desire stereotyped by the arts:

Elastic snake, ravenous boa mulata grips her victim,
And her elastic hips crackle, she oppresses him, tightens, crushes, entangles,
Squeezes, and sucks and licks and bites in her fury and touches with an intense
  magnetism each leaf reveals a profound abyss of appetite, rage and passion.[16]

Madrigal

Your womb knows more than your head
and as much as your muscles.
That is the strong black gift
of your naked body.
Sign of the jungle that is yours
with your red beaded necklaces,
your curved gold bracelets,
and that dark caiman
swimming in the Zambezi of your eyes.[17]

Regrettably to this day, due to socioeconomic conditions and a misguided cultural policy, in some scenarios, Cuban black women are still shown from this simplistic and degrading stereotype.

THE FEMININE IMAGINARY FROM BLACKNESS AND *MULATEZ*: NANCY MOREJÓN, GEORGINA HERRERA, EXCILIA SALDAÑA, AND GLORIA ROLANDO

In 1970, eleven years after the triumph of the revolution, Ildefonso Pereda Valdes published a study on Afro-Cuban poetry. Only one woman is mentioned: Nancy Morejón. However, the first five years of 1970s were marked by two events: the celebration of the International Year of Women (1975) and Cuba's participation in the Angolan War (1975–1976). Cuba's relations with Africa were transformed to an unimaginable degree. These political events led to an increase in the awareness of Afro-Caribbean identity on the island and the official and active encouragement of perceived cultural and historical commonalities that could not fail to affect Afro-Cuban poetry.

Nancy Morejón, a black woman poet born in 1944, published over ten books of poems beginning in the 1960s. Her work is the most translated from her generation. I will examine two poems from her books *Baladas para un sueño* [Ballads for a Dream] (1989) and *Piedra pulida* [Polished Stone] (1986). She was a close collaborator of Guillén who wrote about her in 1972: "I believe her poetry is black like her skin. . . . For that same reason, she is also Cuban with her roots buried deeply, so it appears, to the other side of the planet. . . . I like her smile, her dark skin, her African hair."[18] Guillén was concerned with the construction and affirmation of a syncretic Cuban identity. His poetry defined blackness by way of Africa, which is a key trope in this public and political project along with the articulation of a more personal Afro-Cuban subjectivity, which exemplifies what Sylvia Molloy marks as "individual bios" regarding a "national ethos." Nancy Morejón did not privilege "the black" as an analytical tool. She suggests that it is impossible to produce an exclusively epidermal criticism of literature. In this way, her poetry continues the tradition of *mulato* poet Marcelino Arozarena (1912), whose book of poems *Canción negra sin color* [Black Song without Color], written in 1933 and 1966, invites a polychromatic reading.

Until 1990, Nancy Morejón had reservations with the term "Afro-Cuban" because she maintained the opinion that Afro-Cuban identity would be subsumed into a Cuban national identity, which cannot be understood without the black cultures of the America. She wrote the following:

> Cubans . . . we have given ourselves the task of creating a homogeneous nation through the very heterogeneity of the nation, created for the political purpose of the Cuban Revolution headed by Fidel Castro rather than because of any cultural or racial controversy. We are a mixture. We are not assimilated. We haven't acculturated to Spanish nor African customs . . . we produced ourselves as a *mestizo* people that has inherited and sustained both components without being African nor Spaniard but simply Cuban.[19]

Nancy Morejón's voice is feminine and from what can be inferred from her quote, she is carrier of the idea of the official *mestizo* intermixing that disappears black Cubans within the paternalistic heterogeneity of the "*ajiaco*" national stew. However, the poet accepts the womanist term, coined by Alice Walker, "it is very important in my literature the fact that I am a woman. It would be a stupidity to say that I am not, or that I think that women don't write in a unique mode, experience and position."[20] Nancy Morejón resolves in a "politically correct" way the tensions between sexual politics, the struggle of class and ethnicity, and inscribes Africa in her poetry, indelibly but ecstatic.

"Mujer Negra" [Black Woman], one of her most translated poems of post-revolutionary Cuba, exemplifies a narrative of freedom that centers women.

It is a first-person recollection of Cuba's collective resistance to the exploitation of slavery, colonization, and neocolonialism that culminates in the revolutionary apotheosis. The epic journey over time is narrated by a black female slave, who is the subject of the poem and of Cuba's history. A black anonymous woman becomes the symbol of the national independence of Cuba, giving voice to the collective consciousness.

As a worker, black person, and woman—in that order—black women epitomize the survival and rebellion of the dispossessed who thanks to their own efforts finally gain revolutionary triumph:

Perhaps I have forgotten the lost coast and my ancestral language.
They left me here and here I've lived.
And because I worked like an animal,
Here, I was reborn.
How many mandinga epics did I try to return to.[21]

The poem assumes a Marxist construction of the identity of the subject through productive activity: work ("I worked like an animal"), to rebel ("I rebelled," "I rose up," "I left for the mountains") transforming the mode of production of the slave that leads them into being, without forgetting their African origins ("How many mandinga epics did I try to return to"). The described process is the act of constructing a Cuban communist identity that entails a personal and collective awareness. Note the use of the first person plural:

Now I exist: only today do we own and create.
Nothing of ours is foreign.
Ours the land.
Ours the sea and sky.
Ours the magic and vision.
My equals, here I see you dance
Around the tree that we planted for Communism.
Its prodigal wood already resounds.[22]

Endowing the nation with the female gender in this poem could suggest an androcentric perspective, but in actuality, the poem reverses the usual sexual configuration of rape and domination by the metropolis of the feminized Third World. The exploited subject struggles and succeeds not in a utopian future or a mythic African past but in the Cuban reality of the present. The poem also projects an ascetical instead of erotic vision of the *mulata* as a representation of national cohesion. However, two contradictions emerge in the poem: it closes with a dialectic projected into the future, thus the story is absorbed by a myth, and specifically feminine experiences are scarce. By excluding female sexuality, only the (re)productive force of "giving birth" and the ancillary of "embroider" identify this narrative as that of a woman, hence the paradoxical significance and the gradual annulment of the title of the poem, "Black Woman."

"Mujer negra" can be compared to one of her prior poems, "Amo a mi amo" [I Love My Master] in which the feminine voice is much stronger. The narration spoken in first person also describes the gaining of social consciousness by an enslaved black woman domestic, but in this case, the sexual exploitation (colonial violence) is as significant as racial subjugation. An individualized white master who demands sexual satisfaction and domestic labor from the acquiescent woman who is part of his property represents the patriarchal and colonial hegemony. The despotic law of the father is disguised with an erotization of the masculinizing values of the mode of production that the master represents (violence, domination, control of the word):

I love my master,
I gather wood to light his daily fire.
. . .
I love his hands that deposited me on a bed of grass:
My master bites and subjugates.
. . .
I love his red mouth, refined
From where words emerge
That I have yet to grasp and decipher:
To him, my language is not his.[23]

Another poem from the same section is "Madre" [Mother]. There is a possible subtext in it: *In Search of Our Mother's Gardens* by Alice Walker. The poet focuses on the experiences of her mother, a poor woman in prerevolutionary Cuba, and speaks on the legacy of work and hope that she bestowed to her daughter:

My mother did not have a garden
but a rocky island
floating, under the sun,
on its delicate corals.
Her pupils did not reflect a clean switch of the branch
but many garottes
. . .
My mother had the song and handkerchief
to cradle the deep hope within me
so that she may raise her head high, an unheeded queen
And leave us her hands like precious stones.[24]

The intertexual inscription possibly alludes to the need to differentiate among the different experiences of black women and *mulatas* from the Caribbean and the United States, however, simultaneously, possibly as a response to Walker's book, the poem identifies itself with the possessive pronoun in its title, with womanism, and inscribes the experiences of black Cuban women onto the histories of other black women.

In the collection of poems *Baladas para un sueño* (1989), "Africa" no longer is assimilable as the heart of the construction of a collective and personal identity, rather it is a contemporaneous political reality; this move constitutes a rare exception regarding the treatment of the black continent, which appears in most poetic compositions as arrested in its slave past. The center here is on political solidarity, and the figurative value of "Africa" like a waning trope. Through various persons, the poet refers to the South African situation, she pronounces herself against apartheid and in favor of the National African Congress (CAN). The private feminine voice is silenced once more. "Baas" translated in the footnote as "Master" returns to the themes found in "I Love My Master" projecting them onto a contemporary South African landscape.

You are my master.
Lucky and hard blow of history
that made you my master.
You own all of the land
and I the sorrow.[25]

The verses "In the middle of the night / you pounce like a jealous animal / My sweat and my hands are yours" suggest possible sexual exploitation represented here through the workings of race and class oppression. The implications are obvious. Black men from Africa explain that white feminism is complicit with patriarchal colonialism, which propagates the hegemonic structures of power. These poems by Nancy Morejón indicate then a perception of a feminine, Cuban, black identity constructed on a narrative of African slave freedom, articulated through a Marxist frame, but no longer viewing Africa suspended in time and space as only a place where ancestors come from, a place of jungles and orishas.

Georgina Herrera (1936), who works as a writer for radio, deploys another way of confronting negritude from the site of poetry. Her first books of poems, *GH* (1962), was followed by *Gentes y cosas* (1974) [People and Things]. The poems analyzed here are taken from two later poetry collections: *Granos del sol y luna* (1978) [Grains of Sun and Moon], dedicated to her children, and *Grande es el tiempo* (1989) [Time Is Great]. Herrera's poetry holds a strong maternal tone. In this sense, it has a different emphasis from the poetry of Nancy Morejón. However, her poems in which "Africa" prominently appears

give her work a historical and international dimension and a politics that is
less obvious. "Canto de amor y respeto por Doña Ana de Souza" [Song of
Love and Respect for Doña Ana de Souza] is not an invocation to a Catholic
saint or to Mary herself as the first verse might suggest but to a historical
figure the queen Nzinga (or Yinga in the poem) of Angola (1582 [?] to 1663).
The queen defied the Portuguese and later when she converted to Catholicism
changed her name to Ana de Souza.

Ultimately, Saintly Lady
and queen of the banks of the river Kuanza
mother of beginnings and unity
...
At the very border of the scorched earth
free of Ngola you entered the world.
In the midst of the cries of war,
your cry was the first signal.[26]

The poem's character Nzinga is more mythic than historical in spite of the
references to dates, names, and geographical places. Historically, Nzinga
established her reign despite local resistance to women intervening into politics. However, later she allied herself with Dutch slave traffickers and came to
an agreement with the Portuguese, even allowing their slave caravans to cross
into her territory. Obviously, the poem privileges gender politics and not class
in the struggle against racial and colonial oppression. Ana de Souza / Madre
Yinga Mbandi, a dually named and dual-voiced character, is inscribed like a
singular syncretic figure of Amazonian qualities: African, Catholic, mother,
saint, a lady, warrior queen, and liberator. She fights a (masculine) god and
usurper king. She opposes the written word with the collective oral culture
and her feminine physical presence. Her figure suggests a personification of a
universal resistance that eludes the patronymic and patrilineal:

You, madam, Ana
with that Western name that you took
as a strategy, used
only in documents.
Mother Yinga Mbandi for your people.
Sometimes defeated but never a prisoner
always emerging
among men, without any weapons,
than those in your eyes
ignited like a furious flame
the desire to capture the enemy by
the tremendous sea from which he came.[27]

The contemporary analogies make Yinga a symbolic precedent of resistance of Afro-European women against white hegemony (masculine, foreign, exploitative). Yinga is in part a historical figure (though Angola barely recognizes her as such) and in part a projection of the poet's imaginary. However, through real historical characteristics that Yinga represents, the poet articulates her own subjectivity.

It is interesting that Herrera looks toward Africa and not Cuba to legitimate a syncretic feminist revolutionary legacy. Herrera's poetry steadily breaks the boundary between public and private life. A good example of this is "Respeto, presidente Agostinho" [Respect, President Agostinho] published in 1978. It is a tribute to the disappeared Angolan poet and president. From the poem's very first words, a global politics is linked to the subject's family, that is, the president (a present political reality) to the "grandfather" (memory and collective myth).

The grandfather's Manichaean vision of Africa and the West—the lost paradise versus hell—and his idealization of slaves as saints, kings, and queens contrasts with the king's presence in the text as a man of flesh and bone. A twist develops with the inscription of the president as the Messiah, as maker of miraculous who resuscitates the dead grandfather to reaffirm Africa as a reality and not a fantasy. However, in the poem, the "real" Africa is also an effect of a discursive practice and susceptible to mythic representation like the grandfather. Hence the president embodies the dead grandfather's desire, and the dichotomies that are established in the poem—men/gods, heaven/hell, war/peace—that belong to a rational order, dissolve through key oppositions—life/death and past/present—that lose their division.

An idealized past becomes incorporated in its modern myth. The poem's foundation is racial identity and political solidarity not gender differences. However, when we consider that the feminine voice of the first-person narrator, her compassionate and maternal attitude toward her ancestor, suggests a minor parody of master narratives.

In *Grande es el tiempo* [Time Is Great], a 1989 book of poems, Georgina Herrera returns to the history of women. "Fermina Lucumí"[28] is dedicated to a female slave whose syncretic and generic name (Lucumí is a name for Yoruba people in Cuba) saves her from patronymic anonymity. The date is significant because it refers to the slave rebellions of 1843, which marked the beginning of a terrible period of violence against slaves. An estimated five thousand were assassinated by use of torture in 1843 and 1844. More than one hundred were whipped to death during the sadly famous Conspiracy of the Ladder. However, the slave rebellions continued until slaves were integrated in the fight for independence beginning in 1868. In this poem, slave women once more occupy the position of subjects of a history of Cuba's fight for freedom. The poet focuses on the slave women's inner source of energy and sees their courage as a specifically feminine strategy associated with love (which generates cunning and rage) and above all memory that generates empowerment.

In "Africa"[29] the poet's emotional response is converted into a process of self-exploration and self-esteem. Her identity is centered on the condition of women that is gradually integrated in the object to which it is directed. The word "Africa" once again gains sacred connotations of adoration and (self-)respect. In the beginning of the poem, Africa adopts the figure of a familiar god, of a beloved being, of a child that awakens feelings of protection and unbreakable loyalty and who the poet coddles with maternal care. The subject and object are clearly differentiated until verse seven:

When I mention you
whenever someone speaks your name in my presence
it will be to praise you.
I protect you.
I remain close to you, like at the trunk
of the largest tree.[30]

From there, the poet is aware of the self-perpetuating relation between her and Africa; each is the product of the other. Purity and illumination are reinscribed in the black continent; however, the poet goes further than that: she is Africa. Her face is a self-reflecting mirror in which she can see her own reflection as Africa (the poet). Her body (her face) represents a feminine body subsumed in the political collective organism. She carries images and sounds "of Africa" like ritual objects. Africa constitutes her desires, her maternal and pleasurable feelings, and is the source of her spiritual life. In this way, the poem constructs Africa as a project of the self (black, feminine) and the identity of women (black, Cuban women) mediated by the imaginary of Africa:

I love those gods
With histories like these, like mine:
Coming and going
From war to love or from love to war.
You can close your eyes calmly in rest, recline
for a moment in peace.
I'll take care of you.[31]

These poems of Herrera express an Afro-centric perspective through paradigms relative to family and history, to maternal heritage and social formations whose center are women. The boundaries between personal, familiar, national, and Third World identities are constantly displaced. Autobiography is converted into a theoretical act—in keeping with Baker and Redmond—of "familiar identity" in the "black national design of empowerment."

Nancy Morejón and Georgina Herrera's poems celebrate and affirm a black, Cuban, feminine identity. Any potential conflict is projected to another time or another place. These poems inscribe the resistance against sexual, racial, and class exploitation from a clearly feminine, socialist, and multiethnic perspective. At the same time, both poets write themselves in a mythical-historical process that nurtures their own actual identities. They create worlds with the poetic power of the imagination.

In their explorations of histories, myths, and the interrelated politics between Cuba and Africa, and their identifications with each, Morejón tends to privilege a Marxist dialectic while Herrera links to the maternal. For both, Africa is a key trope for their utopian projections: it signifies the self-figuration of black, Cuban women. However, in my critical view, the poems lack a contemporary vision of Africa and contemporary African women who continue to be uprooted, subverting old galley slave rows in flimsy boats, now to arrive to Europe.

Excilia Saldaña, born in Havana in 1946, was the only daughter of a black middle-class family. She was raised in her grandparents' house with a submissive mother and an absent father. Her family did not sympathize with the revolution of 1959. She left her home at the beginning of the 1960s, after which she published several books of poems and short stories. Of all of Cuba's post-revolutionary writers, she was possibly the one who showed the most interest for Afro-Cuban culture. Her book *Kele Kele* (1987), which means "smooth, smooth" in Lucumí, is a collection of short stories told in prose that follows the model of *patakín* (Nigerian oral stories). The book also frequently references Afro-Cuban traditions, especially the ritual of Santeria in her stories and poems for children like *Cantos para un mayito y una paloma* [Songs for a Little Boy and Dove] published in 1979 and *La noche* [The Night] published in 1989, among others. What is unique to this poet is her perfect dominion of Castellan verse employed in the defense of African roots.

Though stripped of its sacred breath, the African world of which we are fortunately heirs is shown to us in all the immensity of its universality when Saldaña affirms in *Kele Kele*, "Ignoring them would mean ignoring us and not knowing them would mean not knowing us." Many children have learned the perfection of the Greek Olympics. They identify Aphrodite with love, but do they know that Ochun is also the goddess of fertility, beauty, and love? Saldaña describes her as, "Her voice was a song, her hair was long and silky, her skin clear and fine, with bedroom eyes. She smelled like spearmint, basil, lily flower, *mulata* salt and pepper, and lemon balm, sung to in a silver basin. An oil lamp, haughty sunflower, honeycomb, sweetened sugarcane, the dawn at her waist, a smile like a crystalline spring."

In the prologue of *Kele Kele*, Saldaña remembers, "By the Caribbean ocean, you can hear the African drums. The islands were populated by sweat and work and rebellion and heroism, love dance and songs. . . . The islands were populated by the Caribbean seas, giving birth to the children: whites, blacks, blacks and whites; whites, blacks, *mulatos*, by the Caribbean seas, by way of the route where the whites arrived."

A close analysis of the dramatic fifteen-page poem, titled "Monólogo de la esposa" [The Wife's Monologue], brings the reader closer to the *mulato* world, that is, to speak of Africa in "the voice" of Europe. The poem exemplifies what Paul Gilroy calls a "contact zone" between a local and a global culture. The poem gives voice to a plurality of discourses that cross cultural and gender frontiers using fundamentally intertextuality. Similarly, the poem reinterprets and incorporates other texts, especially canonical Western literature. According to Nikos Papastergiadis, in order to trace the map of "the force capable of interrupting hybridity and . . . to realize the innovating potential of a foreign text . . . we need to measure the extent to which the memory of a foreign code has been preserved and examine the resulting impact of the insertion of that foreign text."

"The Wife's Monologue," published in the cultural journal *Casa de las Américas*[32] and brought to the stage in Switzerland, was included in a prior book of poems titled *Mi nombre* [My Name]. The book consists of five sections and was published in Mexico, but the edition was destroyed because it contained several typographical errors. Another section in the book, "Antielegía familiar" ["A Family Anti-Elegy"], was published separately in Havana in 1991. She like other Cuban writers found it difficult to publish during Cuba's economic crisis following 1990, but this situation was symptomatic of the marginalization of writers because of the people who were leading the cultural political sphere in Cuba at that time. The destroyed book poetically recounted key moments in the history of her life. Like *My Name*, "The Wife's Monologue" is a psychological biography of confessions that inscribe in an ostensible way what some scholars call the double consciousness of Caribbean writers.

Catherine Davies in *A Place in the Sun: Women Writers in Twentieth Century Cuba* (1997) claims that this poem represents an internal game of self-presence constantly being proposed, which makes the poem an example of a hybrid text that shows, in the words of Homi Bhabha, "the traumatic ambivalence of a personal psychic history and the wider disjunction of a political existence." The poem illustrates the consciousness raising of a bride/wife and her revolt against the restrictive roles assigned to wives and daughters in a patriarchal society. It is a poem about the rebellion of black female subjectivity and the reinvention of a cultural space from a dissonant point of view.

Additionally, the girlfriend/daughter adopts the appearance of virgin Santeria priestess, vestal-woman of the house who maintains the sacred flame lit of the kitchen-temple. The kitchen-temple is a Cuban version of the Yoruba temple-house *illeocha*. In the Yoruba religion, worshipping of the orishas can occur at any home altar. Also, god-parenting relationships are extremely important in Santeria rituals, similar to the structure of the king of each local organization or *cabildo*. From the private place of home, the bride summons her powers and puts them to work. Through an invocation, she conjures images of the men in her life: lovers, husbands, her father. She does not understand why her hands are stained:

The curls of the night hang from the sky.
The long scented hairlocks of silence are scattered by the men
throughout the house.
I comb them.
Gently, I comb them:
I am the anonymous one smoothing down the waves of sleep.
I'm also a girl of the water
braiding and unbraiding the
mane of my memory.
. . .
The hands. The hands. The hands.
There isn't enough water to clean my hands,
to bleach the stigma of blood
—of my own blood—
Staining my hands forever.
. . .
The hands. The hands. The hands.
When will I see these hands clean?

This is I. The wife.
All the pain of the world came to ask for my hand:
"I'm not the Bride," I told it, "but the Wife.
Can you wash my hands?
Is there enough sorrow to cleanse my hands?"
. . .
The hands. The hands. The hands.
What detergent will remove the crust
of blood from my hands?[33]

She continually asks open-ended questions and refuses to remain in the thresholds. Her hands are covered in blood. But what was the crime and who is the culprit? The wife resolves the enigma with an old oxidized key, a syncretic key that she inherited from her ancestors. The key (that opens a racial and sexual identity) reveals a hybrid sexuality of the *mulata* repudiated because of a traumatic experience in her past: she was sexually abused by her father. Discovering the repressed trauma and responding to it allows the decentered subject to reconstruct her sexuality.

Contrary to what is expected, the texts incorporated into "The Wife's Monologue" are not African but belong to the literary canons of three powerful imperial cultures, Greek, Spanish, and British, and incorporate the Hispanic American literary tradition with some nods to "Sonatina" by the Nicaraguan poet Rubén Darío. There are numerous allusions in the poem to established Hispanic authors like Cervantes, García Lorca, José Martí, and Rubén Darío, popular song lyrics and tangos, and to Sapho and Oscar Wilde. But the most significant texts to the poem's palimpsest are the classical tragedies: Shakespeare's *Macbeth* and Esquilo's *La Orestiada*. Of special importance are the two female protagonists, Lady Macbeth and Clytemnestra. The poem abounds with signifying strategies that can be analyzed through a hypothetical lens, depending on the position being occupied and one's familiarity with other cultures and traditions.

What do Lady Macbeth and Clytemnestra have in common? What does she share with the Cuban "wife"? Catherine Davis responds, "The Wife's Monologue" tells the story of a crime that has stained the hands of the wife and that has produced in her feelings of guilt and need for atonement. On the poem's superficial level, the crime is the violation of the girl by the father, which underscore allusions to the work of García Lorca in which "blood" (weddings of blood) suggests dead kinships. The verse "I don't want to see her," which alludes to Lorca's "Lament for the Death of Ignacio Sánchez Mejías," refers in "The Wife's Monologue" simultaneously to the girl, shame, and blood. For that reason, the wife needs to "exorcize" from her memory her victimizing father. The woman/lady of the house is a victim (of masculine violence), the fault is exerted against herself, and her father is the victimizer.

Some features of the poem suggest a more complex subtext. In the first place, the wife is not cowardly. She is a powerful subject and full of desires with the capacity of agency, a witch-priestess who conjures supernatural forces to help her get rid of the paternal figure. Note the references to the Santeria ritual: *ebbó* (ceremony), *omiero* (sacred water or herb baths), *apetedbi* (the priest's helper). The intertextual and intercultural references to *Macbeth* by Shakespeare or *La Orestiada* by Esquilo escalate the poem's drama. These texts point to a second crime that is not explicit on the surface level of the poem. What Lady Macbeth and Clytemnestra have in common is that both of them kill the king, the father/king of the family/estate, the husband (for Clytemnestra) as a substitute for the father (for Lady Macbeth).

In both cases, the king is stabbed to death and his blood stains the hands of the women. Both are assaulted by nightmares caused by guilt, the "torture of the mind" according to Lady Macbeth. All these heterogeneous motives are embedded in changing temporal frames of the poem.

It is also significant that Clytemnestra kills her husband the king because he had killed Iphigenia, their daughter, as a sacrifice to the gods to promote the advance of their invading fleet. Clytemnestra affirms that "he sacrificed his own daughter like a victim." In "The Wife's Monologue," the crime is double: violation (it is equivalent to the killing) of the daughter, followed by parricide, or to be more precise of regicide. The effect of the crimes extends beyond the confines of the family. The poem is subversive in addressing two social taboos: incest and parricide. The political connotations of killing the king in a Cuban domestic context are suggestive but perhaps simplistic. This is because the target for atonement in the poem is not just the father figure but also all the social categories of men who unlike the king are explicitly associated with a domestic Cuban culture through the poem's localized vocabulary.

The wife, who refers to herself as the "tutelar goddess of the Avenue de los Dolores," invites the men to her house. They knock on her door. She dresses like a priestess and invites them to come in as she carpets "the house up to the bathtub" (like Clytemnestra who welcomed Agamemnon before stabbing him in the bathroom). The suitors give her (in the kitchen-temple) promised offerings that are clearly Cuban: papayas, plums, *caimito* star apples, shells, and gourd bowls. Apparently, the wife kills the men (or imagines that she does) and puts them to rest on a clothesline where they are hung "in the democracy of wires and the noose."

The men, sorted hierarchically by order of color, represent the various facets of masculinity in a multiethnic national context. The poem, then, is a feminist text, an accusation against patriarchy at home and state levels, in which a female subject is defended though she carries guilt.

The word "*hipsipilas*" communicates the tension in this love-hate relationship, which also denotes a postcolonial dimension. The wife's suitors pin "*hipsipilas*" on their clothes. The word is taken from "Sonatina," a famous poem by Rubén Darío, the founder of Latin American modernism. Darío's verse is "Oh, who was *hipsipila* that left the chrysalis." The neologism "hipsi-pila" suggests an insect in its chrysalis going from the state of larva to adulthood. In "Sonatina," the final perfect stage, the insect/princess liberates herself from the prison of the chrysalis/castle, an analysis that supports a feminist reading of the poem. The King of Scotland and the King of Argos not only represent patriarchy but also the white imperial king, if read between the lines in Saldañas's poem, is killed at the hands of a black, female, subaltern subject. Tentative intertextual connections are drawn between a feminist and postcolonial agenda. In the poem, the "black continent," Freudian, is finally rid of the colonial master, and the misogynist Western texts are flipped and retold through what Sara Sulieri calls the "feminine racial" voice.

Unlike Nancy Morejón and Georgina Herrera, Excilia Saldaña does not look to imaginary or real Africa for tropes of self-reconstruction. "The Wife's Monologue" constructs an imaginary domestic space able to reappropriate colonial paradigms and reinvent them to use them in favor of a feminist agenda, giving its voice an Afro-European character of African essence.

Sadly, the promotion of the work of our filmmakers in the audiovisual universe is not extensive although, after the legendary Sara Gómez, other female voices have expanded the creation of film and video as a means of expression. Their films shown from the perspective of the gaze of the other where gender is explicit as a form of manifestation of the self that could grasp the substance of history and humanity. Gloria Rolando has made a mark among these female filmmakers for her black roots.

Gloria Rolando is the director of three documentaries: *Oggún, Forever Present* (1991), on the mythic figure Lázaro Ross that interpreted the African chants; *My Footsteps in Baragua* (1996), on the presence of Anglophone immigrants in Cuba coming from the Caribbean; and *Eyes of the Rainbow* (1997), which interviews the African American activist Assata Shakur, dedicated to all women, white and black, that struggle to make a better world. In her fictional film *Roots of My Heart*, she uncovers the occurrences of 1912 through a personal history linked to the Independent Party of Color. It is a reflection, a search into the complexities of historical investigation about an unjustifiable act. For this filmmaker, research is an indispensable instrument of exploration for the creative process.

Gloria Rolando defines herself when she explains, "We didn't fall for the mechanism of sex and superficiality. For that reason, we must eat dirt but with pride." Perhaps she derived her purpose from her African ancestors, a nutritional substance of being and national identity. But it was in her fieldwork where she grew and continued to forge her vocation as a filmmaker. Later, because of technical and financial limitations, she became a video maker. She was assistant director and collaborator of notable documentary filmmakers such as Santiago Álvarez, Bernabé Hernández, Santiago Villafuerte, Rogelio París, and Enrique Colina, among others, and in fiction, Pastor Vega, Sergio Giral, and Manuel Herrera. She worked with Santiago Villafuerte in the making of *Tumba francesca* [French Tomb]. She took up the investigation and wrote the script through intense research on Haiti, the Haitian Revolution, and the presence of this immigrant group in the eastern part of Cuba.

The exhibition of her documentary *Oggún* in different universities in the United States gave her films exposure where she was received, not without contradictions, and was well respected. As a black woman and as an artist, she was concerned with the apprehensive of an African American platform, the knowledge of their specificities, and the awareness of their convergences and divergences with the natural life of the Afro-Caribbean and in particular Cuba. In New Jersey, she gained contacts in the whole decade of the 1990s, which she continued to develop and have allowed her to bring the voice of Cuba to Oregon, Florida, Washington, Boston, Atlanta, New Orleans, and New York.

Her documentary *Oggún* allowed her to travel to and get to know Jamaica and Barbados with its inclusion in television festivals like that of the 1993 festival in Barbados. There was an interchange of knowledge and information with local colleagues who noted that it was necessary to show "our own images of the Caribbean and not what is shown, the exotic, the coconut palm and the *mulata*; to discover and denounce the distortions of our true histories which are never told."

Her work on the Caribbean diaspora, a theme she had already been strongly exposed to when working on *Tumba francesa*, allowed her to come to know the social differences in the *batey*: the poorly constructed area where American, Latino and Cuban, and Antillean immigrant sugar cane workers lived on sugar plantations. She decided to tell the whole story of their emigration concentrated in a town of eastern Cuba. Gloria Rolando would launch herself to the exploration of universal essences to bring them into her discourse as video maker. She dedicated her work to George Lamming, Rex Nettleford, and Nicolás Guillén, three emblematic figures of the insular Caribbean from Barbados, Jamaica, and Cuba, respectively. The history of immigration began for her "from the eyes of the ancestors." The documentary reveals the processes of transculturation that leave the roots of African culture in the imprint of spirituality.

Rolando inhabits the world of the Caribbean explicitly in *Eyes of the Rainbow*, a film that reflects the struggle of today's women and re-creates the myth of Santeria from the universe of female warriors, from the figure of Oyá, the queen of Koso. "They know how to survive in this world . . . fighting, fighting." It is true, we are facing a very personal motivation for this fight. Rolando makes of her own artwork an alter ego. With Assata in *Eyes of the Rainbow* she manifests "the life of a female activist in this century. It is the testimony of a woman from the African diaspora where her family emerges from ancestral roots." A friendly relationship opens the dialogue and brings to light the powerful and concrete expression of some ideas, from a will to be of service to change the life of people and to be part of society in the United States.

"I began to feel that all those people were part of my history," she reflects. Two cultures, two peoples are translated in the documentary when she captures in film experiences and anxieties from the African American community. She comes to know through testimony the presence of the legendary

Malcolm X, Martin Luther King Jr., the Black Panthers, and the complex world of the civil rights struggle for blacks in the United States. The process itself contained changes and contradictions that she revealed passionately with rigor and professionalism. The film helped her to amplify her own perspective as a black woman in communion and dialogue with Caribbean, Cuban, and North American cultures. The heartbeat of her relatives, ancestors, and own imaginary lives in every one of her documentaries.

When I asked her to comment on her new project that is in production, *Historias de caimaneros y cubanos* [Histories of Caimaneros and Cubans], she stated that its antecedent is the documentary *My Footsteps on Baragua* (1995) that explores the theme of immigration from the Anglophone Caribbean to Cuba. If *My Footsteps on Baragua* was immersed in the world of a *central* [sugar cane plantation town] in the province of Ciego de Ávila and the history of those who came from several islands of the Caribbean to work on those cane plantations in Cuba, Roland explained, then the prequel documentary *Historias de caimaneros y cubanos* "is immersed in the world of the sea, inter-Caribbean relations."

CONCLUSIONS

Though race is considered a sociocultural construction and its concept is antiscientific from an anthropological point of view, in Cuba, people continue to be valued hierarchically by their skin color, the shape of their nose or lips, and type of hair. The terms "*negro*," "*mulato*," and "of color" are charged with social, economic, cultural, and very precise racialized historical connotations that influence and at times determine the position each individual occupies from a specific color in the socioeconomic structure of the country, individual, or collective self-esteem and in the concept of the other and their cultural creations. Black and *mulata* Cuban women continue to suffer to this day from prejudice in multiple forms. Despite considering the contribution of the revolution in establishing equality for women, it is useful to ask how cultural production has reconstructed the image of Afro-Cuban women. The intellectual and artistic contributions of Afro-Cuban women have not received attention in a society that supposedly exists without colors, a society utopianly "blind" regarding the races.

NOTES

1. Pedro Pérez Sarduy and J. Stubbs, *An Anthology of Cuban Writing on Race, Politics and Culture*, Latin America Bureau Center for Cuban Studies (New York: Ocean Press, 1991).

2. Miguel Barnet, *Canción de Rachel* (Havana: Instituto Cubano del Libro, 1969), 120. Editor's note: This book has been translated into English; see Barnet, *Rachel's Song* (New York: Curbstone, 1995).
3. Barnet, *Canción de Rachel*, 119.
4. Henry Louis Gates, *The Signifying Monkey: A Theory of Afro-American Literary Criticism* (New York: Oxford University Press, 1988).
5. Lois M. Smith and Alfred Padula, *Sex and Revolution: Women in Socialist Cuba* (London: Oxford University Press, 1995), 151.
6. See Sandra Morales Fundadora, *El negro y su representación social* (Havana: Editorial de Ciencias Sociales, 2001).
7. Ibid., 86.
8. *Blanquinegra*, which translates to black and white, is a folkloric literary genre. Fernando Ortiz, "Prologue," in *Cuentos negros de Cuba* [Black Tales of Cuba] (Havana: Nuevo Mundo, 1961).
9. Editor's note: Called the *negrista* movement in Cuba, in most US works this period of artistic and literary explosion about black themes in Cuba is called the Afrocubanismo movement.
10. Nancy Morejón, *Nación y mestizaje en Nicolás Guillén* (Havana: Ediciones Unión, 1982), 64.
11. Alice Walker coined this term to differentiate it from other feminist movements.
12. Fredric Jameson, *Postmodernism, Or the Cultural Logic of Late Capitalism* (Durham, NC: Duke University Press, 1989), 123.
13. Translates to "Song of the Acana Tree" in *Words in the Mirror*.
14. Minerva Salado, "Canto del ácana," in *Palabras en el espejo* (Havana: Unión de Escritores y Artistas de Cuba, 1987), p. 51.
15. Gilman Sander, *The Latin American Subaltern Studies Reader* (Durham, NC: Duke University Press, 2001), 235, 248, 250.
16. Jose Manuel Carbonell, "Francisco Muñoz del Monte (1809–1868)," in *La poesía lírica en Cuba* [Cuban Lyric Poetry], *Imprenta El Siglo XX* 2, Havana (1928): 72–74.
17. Nicolás Guillén, *Sóngoro Cosongo: Poemas mulatos* (Havana: Ucar Garcia, 1947).
18. Nicolás Guillén, *La rueda dentada* (Havana: Ediciones Unión, 1972).
19. "Entrevista a Nancy Morejón," *La Gaceta de Cuba* (October 5–November 1966): 2.
20. Elaine Savory Fido, "A Womanist Vision of the Caribbean: An Interview," in *Out of the Kumbla: Caribbean Women and Literature* (Trenton, NJ: Africa World Press, 1990), 265–69.
21. Ibid., 18–20.
22. Ibid.
23. Nancy Morejón, *Piedra pulida* (Havana: Editorial Letras Cubanas, 1986).
24. Ibid., 100–102.
25. Nancy Morejón, *Baladas para un sueño* (Havana: Unión de Escritores y Artistas de Cuba, 1989).

26. Georgina Herrera, *Granos del sol y luna* [Grains of the Sun and the Moon] (Havana: Unión de Escritores y Artistas de Cuba, 1978), 12.
27. Ibid., 13.
28. Georgina Herrera, *Grande es el tiempo* (Havana: Unión de Escritores y Artistas de Cuba, 1989), 48.
29. Ibid., 14–15.
30. Ibid., 48.
31. Ibid., 18.
32. Excilia Saldaña, "Monólogo de la esposa," *Casa de las Américas*, no. 152, Havana (1985): 86–100.
33. Ibid., 86–100.

BIBLIOGRAPHY

Barnet, Miguel. 1969. *Canción de Rachel*. Havana: Instituto Cubano del Libro.
Barquet, Jesús, and Norberto Codina. Editors. 2002. *Poesía Cubana del siglo XX*. Mexico.
Bhabha, Homi K. 2004. *The Location of Culture*. London: Routledge.
Davies, Catherine. 1997. *A Place in the Sun: Women Writers in Twentieth Century Cuba*. London: Zed Books, Ltd.
Fernández Retamar, Roberto. 2000. *La Poesía, reino autónomo*. Havana: Editorial Letras Cubanas.
Gates, Henry Louis. 1988. *The Signifying Monkey: A Theory of Afro-American Literary Criticism*. New York: Oxford University Press.
Griffith, Glyne A. 2001. Caribbean Cultural Identities. *Bucknell Review* 44, no. 2: 1–178.
Herrera, Georgina. 1978. *Granos del sol y luna*. Havana: Unión de Escritores y Artistas de Cuba, Havana.
Hulme, Peter, and Edward Kamau Brathwaite. 1998. *New Frontiers of Space, Bodies and Gender*. London: Routledge.
Jameson, Fredric. 1989. *Postmodernism, Or the Cultural Logic of Late Capitalism*. Durham, NC: Duke University Press.
Moore, Carlos, Tanya R. Saunders, and Shawn Moore, eds. 1995. *African Presence in the Americas*. Durham, NC: Duke University Press.
Morejón, Nancy. 1982. *Nación y mestizaje en Nicolás Guillén*. Havana: Ediciones Unión.
———. 1989. *Baladas para un sueño*. Havana: Unión de Escritores y Artistas de Cuba.
Pérez Sarduy, Pedro, and Jearn Stubbs. 1993. *An Anthology of Cuban Writing on Race, Politics and Culture*. New York: Ocean Press.
Rocasolano, Alberto, ed. 1985. "Poetisas cubanas." *Casa de las Américas*, no. 152. Cuba.
Saldaña, Excilia. 1985. "Monólogo de la esposa." *Casa de las Américas*, no. 152. Havana.

Sander, Gilman. 2001. *The Latin American Subaltern Studies Reader.* Durham, NC: Duke University Press.
Smith, Lois M., and Alfred Padula. 1995. *Sex and Revolution: Women in Socialist Cuba.* London: Oxford University Press.
Vitier, Cintio, ed. 1952. *Cincuenta años de poesía cubana (1902–1952).* Havana: Dirección de Cultura del Ministerio de Educación.
Zalamea, Jorge. 1965. *La poesía ignorada y olvidada.* Bogotá: La Nueva Prensa.

Chapter 23

Contradictory Binaries in Nancy Morejón's *Octubre Imprescindible* and *Cuaderno de Granada*

Lourdes Martínez Echazábal

Without a doubt, Nancy Morejón[1] is the most recognized postrevolutionary Cuban poet in Cuba's academic and literary world. Her first book *Mutismos* was published in 1962 when Morejón was barely eighteen years old. In *Mutismos*, anguish, desperation, and the alienation of the dislocated self are imperative characteristics treated and dispelled in all her works. Processes of displacement and intellectual and political maturity reach their maximum expression in *Octubre imprescindible* (1983) and *Cuaderno de Granada* (1984).[2]

This chapter does not explore the ideological evolution of the author or her poems, nor the parallelism of the internal revolution of the writer to Cuba's external revolution;[3] rather, the focus is to link the implicit presence of contradictory binaries and to unravel her "reason of being" in both books of poems.

Binaries, understood as significant pairings of opposite signs, are implicit in both texts and manifest repeatedly in individual poems and throughout the book. For example, the first section of *Octubre imprescindible*, which is divided into four parts, addresses the conflict between the bourgeois and proletarian home and life before and after the revolution, among several other examples. However, we will limit ourselves to the analysis of contradictions that emerge from a central symbol that predominates Morejón's poetry: the sea. It is enough to say that for the islanders, the sea always possesses a polyvalent and paradoxical aura, a sensation that Morejón textualizes as contradictory binaries that allows her to explore dialectically sociohistorical aspects of Cuban and Caribbean realities.

The sea in her poetry is a revolutionary and reactionary force, tempest and calm, alliance and enemy, source of life and death. The following poem "Octubre imprescindible" holds the same title as the book:

The leaves of the trees whirl in the gutters.
They rise up together from the ground as if bewitched,
yellow, red, even grey
and they huddle in front of me.

An indomitable drizzle falls on the city.

Hurricane and Cyclone nearing their snouts from the North.

The visit of the air in October cannot wait:
She kisses your feet like a little bird
> *Such a smooth heart*
> *of those that walk*
> *block to block*
> *yearning for their love*

Such solemn uprisings of October,
> *they are so logical.*

So much tenderness in the blowing of the magical bazooka
Blaring in a winter palace in Russia
against sad princesses,
against terrible czars,
and against the spirit that bats the eyelashes
of an ancient albatross.

All the waves rise up and rustle over the Malecón

Unprepared, Havanans run to their houses.

The automobiles are avoiding the blows of the sea.

The noise and vigor of the waves
paralyze our vision
with which we contemplate
things of the day-to-day.

To see a sail boat enter the bay,
stand over the stilts of the bay,
to awaken with you
in October, and the air

turning us, calming us,
like in that dawn that was so dreamed about.

A whirlwind of strange cries
appeared so monumental this afternoon.

The armies of the summer have disappeared
at the sound of a flute from a nearby coast,
at these hours,
when the twilight favors
wayfarers.
Tell me if it is possible
to shake the columns of foam
that the sea erects
when October arrives silently upon us
with its mortal air.

     Say it
What an indispensable October and its air of consent,
and its painful air,
and its air of absence and tempest,
and its air of assaults and uprisings of auroras,
and its air of distant tears,
and its vegetable air
that tousles our hair, urgent, with its diaspora,
like eternal dwellers of the Caribbean.

  The poem begins by noting the coming of hurricanes and cyclones, a familiar story for the people who live in the Caribbean: "Hurricane and Cyclone nearing their snouts from the North" is a common occurrence. However, in the context of the poem—a Cuban and Caribbean context—a double signification occurs: the inherent meteorological condition and the hypercodification of the historical political condition of the Caribbean, especially when we consider that "Hurricane and Cyclone" are used as proper names.
  The meteorological climatology (the season of cyclones and hurricanes in the Caribbean) is juxtaposed to another patrimony in October: the Russian Revolution of October, a historical uprising that serves as a bridge between the first and third lines. In the first verse, it is the leaves of the trees that "rise up" and "huddle" in an act of violence, an aggression against the city, an aggression also seen in "The automobiles are avoiding the blows of the sea." Associating the meaning of "snouts" and "blows" with "Hurricane and Cyclone" as proper names gives the sea an animalistic character, like the beast of "the North," conjuring José Martí. Therefore the tension between the

first and third lines is not only at a phonetic level—(leaves/waves)—but also at a metaphorical one.

The idea of uprising persists also in the fourth stanza through a subtle change of poetic meaning. The sea is no longer the violent aggressor, enemy of the people in the city, nor are uprisings abrupt and solemn. Now the sea joins the poet in creating a sign: the couple's enjoyment waking together in the dawn. A sailboat navigates on a calm sea as a symbol of tranquility and peace.

Morejón's use of multiple meanings gives the poetic referent unresolved tensions that are referred to in the sixth stanza when the poetic voice questions if it is possible to let down her guard, which would eliminate the tensions held by the "real referent":[4]

To *shake* the columns of foam
that the sea erects
when October *arrives silently upon us*
with its mortal air. (Emphasis added)

"Column" is a sign that contains multiple and contradictory meanings. The "columns of foam" refer to the waves, and as we have noted, the waves are a destructive force on the city. However, the columns are also what protects the city from the "snouts" and the "blows" of the sea-beast-aggressor in "October."

Positioning this poem in the contextual frame of Caribbean history, and in particular Cuba's postrevolutionary history, affirms that the tensions manifested in the poem as a result of their binary relation to the sea correspond to a concrete state of the country. Let us remember the numerous pirate invasions in the eighteenth and nineteenth centuries, the invasion and occupation by the British in the seventeenth century, but especially we must remember the Bay of Pigs invasion and the October [Missile] Crisis in the twentieth century. Only in light of these historical events can we understand the deeper significance of the poem.

For the insular Caribbean, the sea has always been connected with the enemy and reactionary and revolutionary forces. The fact that the sea was a vehicle of conquest and colonization, a bridge between Africa and the Caribbean Basin, emphasizes this point, however and paradoxically, the sea also brought the ghost that traveled across Europe.[5]

As proposed in the opening of this chapter, contradictory binaries occur inside of the poem as throughout the whole book of poems. In "Humus inmemorial" [Immemorial Humus], which serves as a concrete example, Morejón textualizes the sea like a vehicle of oppression during the crossing of the Atlantic. The sea in this case is not the sea of lovers or transients looking for its calm in the dawn. The sea is

The graying sea of the boat holds
spurting out
gagged blacks,
casting them
over the mist,
of any port.

Yet the sea differs in another poem titled "El camino de Guinea" [The Path to Guinea] found in the same collection. The sea reappears as an ally:

Now the ocean pours its waters over the first
Portuguese Royal Guard
who lean their swords back, drowned and defeated,
no more conquistador.

Finally, "La hora de la verdad" [The Hour of Truth] is a long poem that is part of the fourth and last part of the book. The sea is once again allied to blacks as a vehicle of liberation:

The chum stored his knife in the Bay of Matanzas.
Went sailing through the Atlantic Ocean,
until he reached the Gulf of Guinea, and there he sank
to sleep in his abode.

The tensions found in *Octubre imprescindible* are also present in *Cuaderno de Granada*. This fact is not a coincidence. Cuba and Grenada are Caribbean islands that underwent a socialist revolution, and the United States has considered both countries a threat to the Caribbean and Central America. Due to this historical consanguinity, the sea holds multiple meanings for Cubans and Grenadians. In *Cuaderno de Granada*, Morejón condensed this reality in a short poem titled "Historia" [History]:

I barely come from the siege,
I barely can cry,
the Obús short cannon arrives scheming
over the sea.

I barely come from the mountain
I can barely cry,
My fingers are the best weapon
facing the sea.

I barely come from the orchard
I barely can cry,

Grenada is barely born
by the sea.

The sea is a vehicle of aggression in the fourth line and an enemy in lines eight, eleven, and twelve. However, "Grenada is barely born / by the sea" implies an irony that points to two recent aspects of Grenadian history. First, the Grenada that wanted to control its own destiny, [Maurice] Bishop's Grenada, was born by the sea. However, the second Grenada had a short life, ill fated from the blows of the sea/aggressor. The sea therefore appears as a dialectical sign that unites death with life and creation.

With three stanzas, Morejón dexterously creates a poetics of the historical problems of the Caribbean, of which Cuba is a fortunate exception, while defining the job of the poet and the function of literary creation. The book's title, *Cuaderno de Granada*, connects with the seventh and eight lines, "My fingers are the best weapon / facing the sea." These two lines are a direct response to the poetic enunciation in line three, "the shell casing arrives scheming," and suggests a context of war. That line recreates a reality in which the poet, like the soldier, defends a cause. The pen is her weapon held between her *fingers* to cleverly produce a book of poems that becomes the best weapon of resistance against the enemy and the enemy's distortion and obliteration of history. *Cuaderno de Granada* becomes a witness to political and social genocide and is a product of anger and frustration. The interior need for a revolutionary praxis is fulfilled by a poetic creation that births the poem and ultimately the book of poems.

I chose this poem because of its concise form and meaningful content. Morejón gathers the history of revolutionary Grenada, the history of the Caribbean, and the history of nations navigating US interventions. The tensions in this and other poems discussed in this chapter are chapters of that history. Nancy Morejón, as a "revolutionary" poet, with the word's dual connotation, though the use of contradictory binaries related to the sea, has brought forth a dialectic[6] of the Caribbean and its multiple signification.

NOTES

1. Morejón was born in Havana in 1944. She is a poet, essayist, and researcher. Her poetic works include various books of poems such as *Richard trajo su flauta* (1967) and *Parajes de una época* (1979). She is the author of a chapter and the prologue to *Recopilación de textos sobre Nicolás Guillén* (1974) and of *Nación y mestizaje en Nicolás Guillén*, for which she received the Premio Nacional de Ensayo de la Unión de Escritores y Artistas de Cuba (UNEAC) [Cuban Union of Writers and Artists National Prize] in 1982. She is currently president of UNEAC.

2. Morejón, *Octubre imprescindible* (Havana: UNEAC, 1983); *Cuaderno de Granada* (Havana: Casa de las Américas, 1984).
3. Heather Rosario Sievert, "Nancy Morejón: Artist/Revolutionary," unedited paper presented at the Seventh Annual Symposium on Afro-Hispanic Literature, City University of New York, New York, 1982.
4. By "real referent" I am alluding to the situation in which Cuba lives, having to keep a continuous watch against [US] aggressions to Cuba's national security since 1960.
5. I am referring to the French Revolution, though I would also have to add the Industrial Revolution to it. I owe this idea to the book by Manuel Moreno Fraginals, *El ingenio* (Havana: Comisión Cubana de la UNESCO, 1964).
6. By dialectic, we mean the union of a dynamic of opposites. It is a union that is established in terms of an active identity that includes differences and contradictions. The dialectical relation, in being a dynamic relation that joins opposites, eliminates the alternative metaphysical it is either "this or that" proposed by traditional methods and more radical ones like dualism and reductionism. The method of dialectical analysis offers a more complete and complex vision of history.

BIBLIOGRAPHY

Barradas, Efraín. 1980. "La negritud hoy: nota sobre la poesía de Nancy Morejón." *Areito*, no. 24.
———. 1984. "Reseña de Octubre imprescindible." *Hispanoaméria*, no. 37.
Morejón, Nancy. 1983. *Octubre imprescindible*. Havana: UNEAC.
———. 1984. *Cuaderno de Granada*. Havana: Casa de las Américas.
Sievert, Heather Rosario. 1982. "Nancy Morejón: Artist/Revolutionary." Unpublished. New York: City University of New York.

Chapter 24

In Memory of Excilia

Coralia de las Mercedes Hernández Herrera

I had the opportunity to see Excilia Saldaña twice in my life. First in 1976 during the Student Scientific Conference, where she presented on linguistics and the relationship between *charada* lottery numbers with some words from the Afro-Cuban religion, how people expressed themselves, and how some leaders were named. That is how I know that the number one represents the horse, which connects to a moment in Afro-Cuban religions. It is said that when someone is "mounted," this means that she or he is riding a horse; it is the spirit that has possessed the person, and during this moment, it is believed that everything the person says during the trance is true. Her linguistic reflections explain and justify why after the triumph of the revolution the people began to call Fidel the horse.

The second time I saw her was in a postgraduate course on the Golden Age at the School of Arts and Literature. There I witnessed an unforgettable class on *La perla de la mora* [The Pearl of the Moor Woman] and poem number XLII of the *Versos sencillos* [Simple Verses]. I was very pleased with her analysis, how she developed and presented her claims, and her confidence, simplicity, and depth. Later I got to know her better through her work and also from my friendship with her son Mario Ernesto and her daughter-in-law.

The work of Excilia Saldaña, like that of other creators, shows its human dimension. From the pages of each one of her creations, the sensual woman emerges, in love with life and full of worries of the world that surrounds her. She was a professor of Spanish literature, a translator, essayist, and editor. Her work flourished in the literature of Cuba and earned several awards and distinctions that credited the value of her literary creation from very early: Honorable Mention in the prize Casa de las Américas (1967) for her book *Enrolló*;[1] UNEAC's Ismaelillo Prize (1979), and the prize Premio Rosa

Blanca in 1984 and in 1987; as well as the *La Edad de Oro* [Golden Age] award in 1989.

Researchers who have focused on her work (Davies, González Mandri, Vitier, López, Lemus, Morejón)[2] highlight the poet's feminism, evaluating it as a form of personal reaffirmation in carving out her own space. They also concur on the presence of Caribbean *mestizaje* [racial mixing] in her work.

Excilia Saldaña came from a middle-class family. From an early age, she expressed her political concerns and showed an aversion to the tyranny of Fulgencio Batista. She joined the revolution when it triumphed in 1959. Her acceptance of the new process caused great difficulties with her family relationships. During that time, the future poet, who was then a teenager, had to confront individual, family, and social conflicts.

A reading of her less-known works by the general public reveals the difficulties her poems tackle in the course of her life. The book of poems *Mi Nombre* (2003) collects poems with elements of references of the self, identity, feminism, and cultural formation. "The Wife's Monologue" is part of this collection. It is an anthological composition within its poetic creation, which uses everything that the universe offers to express emotion: nature with its flora, fauna, and minerals and religion and its multiple readings.

It is I: The Wife:
A wasteland under the thunder.
The fertile land, I know I am
But I harvest a yield of fears.

It is I: The Wife:
Shaped in Tempered steel.
I thought I would be a shield . . .
But yoked, I arrived at the muleteer

It is I: The Wife:
An open pit facing the sky.
I dreamed myself ruby red . . .
Others saw me as a piece of ebony.
. . .

It is me: The Wife:
Apetedbí del omiero.[3]
Feudal cloistered nun . . .
Penelope without Odysseus.[4]

The verses reflect strength of verb and character. The poem is mature poetically and intellectually. It contains an autobiographical element that recognizes its origin, frustrations, and pains. She reminisces about bitter experiences in her life; for example, in school she was mocked because she was a cross-eyed little *mulata* who would take refuge in the bathroom or in the park to weep. She also recounts the violation of her innocence by her gypsy father's incestual act. Expressively, the author manifests the pain of an adult subject that narrates the horrible passage mixed with the suffering of the girl who can barely defend herself and does not realize what happened until she faces the "puddle of shame" that she does not want to acknowledge. She claims in one of the verses, "Pain is never idle." This clear reflection on the suffering of many in life, especially of women, proposes that we must not be frightened but must move forward. She continues:

Brothers, there is no recipe, because it is only that I am in life:
I sing my moment in the great cosmic festival.
The flight of a bird in search of air
is the expression of my freedom;
the beast's submission
is the drawing of my power;
the vileness of the serpent
reaffirms my nobility.
In life I savor each phase in time
as I will in death take comfort in eternity.
I refuse to stay on the thresholds.[5]

She must complete domestic duties as part of her role as a woman and wife. Her hands execute daily all chores in the home, a role given to women since time immemorial. The poet had an African great-grandmother: "A beautiful black grandmother, sweet and good: who would pass her day riding on an elephant, daughter of a queen; who would teach her how to make *malarrabia*; from her she would learn how to split wood. The one who put Africa and every treasure of those lands in her blood."[6] In this short and simple portrait, the author underscores the physical and moral beauty of her ancestors. She highlights the social class her great-grandmother belonged to in her natal land and how she would spend her time riding one of the most emblematic animals of the African fauna. She also highlights her great-grandmother's industriousness and strength because she knew how to split wood and make *malarrabia* sweets. The great-granddaughter feels love and pride for this ancestor. This grandmother's granddaughter was closest to Excilia, they were constantly interacting. The author's grandmother, a "handkerchief of tears," is featured in *La Noche* [The Night], one of her most accomplished books: "eyes of smudge, voice of a glass bell. Grandmother in the ravines: jute petticoat, striped blouse, white apron. Grandmother on a stroll: shawl of Manila, jingling bracelets and coral earrings."[7] The granddaughter admires the grandmother's clothing and establishes the contrast between how she dresses to work in the house and to go out.

Both descriptions allude to the role that these women play in the home. The grandmother from Africa ignores her social class, prepared to serve as a good landlady or mother of family that here on the Island becomes an obligation to serve others. The other grandmother grew and developed her life with breadth in Cuba. However, although both grandmothers belonged to different generations, they shared an identifying trait: they were prepared to serve others inside and outside the home.

Her book *My Name* contains poems that compel a closer and deeper look at Excilia. In her poem "Okán Iya," dedicated to her mother and the earth, the poet states, "Flight, strength and sweetness are my motto,"[8] characteristics that are manifested in compositions such as "Non son Circe" and "Segundo descanso" [Second Rest]. The first poem uses the Homeric magician to highlight the mixture of cultures that converge in the poem from every point of view. Without being a priestess, she knows how to read the *dilogún* [oracle of the shells], the twenty-one avatars of Eleguá, and the crossroads. Without being the queen of the dead, she can get death to work for her. She is not a soloist in the chorus of the sirens, but she knows how to cast a spell with her song, aware of the value of her verses. She is a dreamer who enjoys her memories. She feels immense, sensual, deep, moving, beautiful, and mysterious as the sea. She is able to provoke passion in others.

"Segundo descanso" announces Égloga I of Garcilaso de la Vega's footprints. She does not cry tears of mourning but of joy, satisfaction, and happiness. When she wrote this poem, the writer was a mother who with deep expressiveness refers to her state of bliss contemplating her baby's rattle, bottle, diapers, and *tentempié* [toy]. In the poem, the lyrical subject looks at her body and stops with satisfaction at her uncovered nipple, her thick waist because of motherhood, and her womb. Her tears begin to flow along with her laughter. She feels her happiness is envied and that the earth and heaven are jealous of her. This is a beautiful poem about motherhood in which the mother as creator rests in realization that she has fulfilled her desire and affirms: "My harvest is mine and I care for it: with my breasts I feed it!"[9]

Excilia Saldaña also express a pedagogical edge to her work. She attaches great importance to history and literature, both constituting sources of values for the training of the public reader. As an illustrious pedagogue said her poetry deals with real occurrences and also with the imaginary. Saldaña in *Un Testigo de la historia*[10] (1979) [A Testimony of History] refers to the importance of an archive in making use of its stored documents. In *Flor para amar*[11] (1980) [Flower to Love], she conducts a small investigation that shows the apostle, José Martí's, beliefs on women. Her books *De la Isla del tesoro a la Isla de la Juventud*[12] (1979) [From Treasure Island to the Island of Youth] and *Bulgaria, el país de las rosas*[13] (1986) [Bulgaria, Country of Roses] address the history of these places, the most significant historical facts and important sites.

A significant aspect of her intellectual trajectory is that she opened a space to the Afro-Cuban culture through her literary work that represents Cuba's *mestizaje*. Her book *Kele Kele*[14] (1987) reaffirms this. In the prologue the author proclaims, "I arrived with the language of our African and Spanish ancestors. With Orisha and romantic rhythms. . . . Our Afro-Spanish and Hispanic-African folklore is both guitar and drum resolved in the Cuban son." Her words recognize the language of her ancestors, poetic forms, gods, beliefs, traditions, and musical instruments. She does not give greater attention to one element over another, rather both nourish, fortify, and grow Cuban culture.

Delving into cultural issues, Saldaña discovers the values and beauty of our mixed culture capable of renewing and humanizing its members, especially those who have been the most devalued by traditional literary discourse. Her books *Enlloró, Kele Kele, Soñando y viajando, Compay Tito, La noche*, and *Jícara de miel*[15] offer numerous examples of this. It is not that she was the first to analyze this problem within our literature, rather the author continues the works of Fernando Ortiz, Nicolás Guillén, Alejo Carpentier, Rogelio Martínez Furé, and Miguel Barnet. The work of the poet also contributes by creating space, deserved rightfully, for those who have been discriminated for years and who have not enjoyed the estimation of others, either because of their physical traits, economic position, or because their culture has been considered inferior.

Admirably, in *Kele Kele* the author rediscovers the beauty of our African ancestors and their culture, breaking with Eurocentric discourse. The different histories or *pataquíes* exalt the physical beauty of black men and women, whose appearance has been practically ignored in traditional literature. The author describes enthusiastically this type of individual and their way of acting. Thus in the *pataquín*[16] that refers to Obba, a couple dreams of becoming parents of a beautiful daughter:

> I want to have a daughter as black as these gems, as black and precious as this wood; that her eyes reflect like crystals, that her teeth glow like pearls—said the mother without wanting to leave her dream, and from the same dream her partner responded to her:
> What you want is what I want, my queen.
> And they continued dreaming of her during the long night, together, with their heads close together.
> That is how Obba came forth: from one dream, from one desire and from only one promise. That's how they waited for her. That's how she arrived on this young and inexperienced world. That is how the most beautiful girl in memory was born.[17]

The story about Obba not only highlights the physical beauty of the girl, it also praises her intelligence, her desire to know the secret stories and the world, her dexterity for cooking, and to attend to a house and husband. The *pataquíes* also refer to male characters like Chango. She highlights his physical beauty and general characteristics: "Red suit, wide and bare chest; With one hand he grabbed the white horse, with the other he yanks the mane. He was Isancio, Seven Rays, Changó of Oyó, Lubbeo. A man as beautiful as a black night, boastful, talkative, a partier. Lord of the Lightning. Owner of the Storm. King of Thunder." The poet describes these characters from the African world without prejudice, exalting their physical beauty and skin color.

Her books devoted to primary school teachers are *Compay Tito* and *Soñando y viajando*. They re-create the peasants' way of life. The poet takes a tour of the Cuban countryside, depicting how peasants lived and live in our fields. They are simple and beautiful books that highlight the beauty and the color of these places. Both books show their humanity and their general culture. They re-create their typical forms of speech, with idiomatic turns like "the song of a rooster"; ways to cultivate the land, build their houses, and celebrate their parties playing musical instruments like the guitar. With these books, the author manages to get children from an early age to come into contact and learn, through literature, about other fundamental matrices of our people.

Underneath each line in her books, the reader senses the teacher. This is noticeable in the way the books bring knowledge to the reader, found even in her more mature works such as *Mi nombre* and *En el vórtice del ciclón*.[18] For example, in *Lengua de trapo*, written for children, the poet provokes the enjoyment of learning that reflects on the meaning of the *jitanjáfora* technique in literature. Alfonso Reyes has studied this concept. Additionally, she writes examples of *jitanjáforas* in our poetry and suggests how we can create others for amusement.

As a pedagogue and writer, she offers her books *Cantos para un Mayito y una paloma, La noche*, and *Jícara de miel* to the Cuban nation with its customs and characteristic, depicting all its diversity. The poet continues the theme originally drawn in *Kele Kele* of our *mestizo* culture. Her books contain historical individuals who parade down her pen to enter and occupy a space in literature. In her works, Saldaña manifests and reaffirms popular wisdom, individual behaviors in different segments of society, and the ways in which people express their appreciation of reality and thoughts about life and religion. The poem "Como fue?"[19] serves as an example in *Cantos para un Mayito y una paloma*, which refers to the Cuban struggle for freedom. The poem references the *mambí* [independence soldier] machete and the blood shed on our soil, neither of which has race nor color. Our brothers shed their blood involved in our Wars of Independence because of their love of freedom, for the sovereignty of our country, and in believing that all Cubans are equal. For example, "Ovillejo por Maceo" emphasizes courage, tenderness, and honor as the primary personality traits of the son of Mariana [Grajales; Maceo's mother], while "Martí" refers to the apostle as a new pine, wings, dark gold, star mine, honeycomb, and as the "arrow of the white rose / turned into a flare."[20]

Besides bestowing these qualities on both heroes, by paying tribute to our glorious history, she proves that regardless of the color of the skin, these heroes were driven by an altruistic ideal representative of the multiracial masses that followed them, which is why they are part of the most glorious pages of our history.

La noche is the poet's most famous book. It reflects our people's beliefs and traditions. In it, we encounter Tata Cuñengue, a type of spirit, owner of the woods, never seen by anyone, yet people believe in him and his powers: he has knowledge of herbs and plants and can concoct remedies to cure social ills and illnesses of the body. For example, with a sage leaf placed on the forehead, tobacco smoke, and coffee grounds he can cure an illness that reverses everything, "the poor will become rich, the Ceiba will become the *jaguey*."[21]

This beautiful belief reflects the naivety of people who believe in this kind of entity that meets their need to believe in something that can make them change their status in life even if it has a mystical tone.

Saldaña includes another popular belief in this book of the *güije*, a character of peasant Cuban folklore. *La noche* depicts the *güije* as a fantastic, naughty, and funny creature that sometimes hides and appears suddenly. Sometimes quiet, at other times it creates mayhem. She presents it as a kind of elf that we should not be afraid of because we carry it inside. However, in *Jícara de miel*, this same character appears in the "Nanas of the güije" as a kind of restless peasant worker that "sharpens the machete," "has its *conuco* field," "smokes tobacco," "sows yam," "drinks *mofuco* firewater," "eats flour," is capable of frightening the mules, does not sleep, frightens, and could steal a child from his crib. The author in this nursery rhyme presents a great rhythm and catchy chorus of *"yen yen yen"* that makes the child sing, dance, or play. The story moves from the simple exposure of the characteristics of the *güije* in the beginning of the composition to drama in the middle of the poem that ends with a kind of fright and rejoicing of the child before the antics of this Cuban goblin.

Another aspect that Excilia Saldaña alludes to in her book *La noche* relates to our traditions of the carnival. In this popular festival, blacks, whites, and *mulatos* meet with music and dance. In the carnival everything mixes and is represented, including the sacred drums, Iyá, Okónkolo, Itótele, and the drums made of sheepskin, the bongo. The guitar entertains the festival. During the festivities the whip sleeps, hunger remains in the tenements, and pain in the cane fields. The tale contains characters that are representative of carnival with their costumes: masquerades, grotesque masks, groups of dancing men. In this multiethnic and multiracial party we find a black woman represented as the great queen, *mulatas* of course as a great attraction within the carnival, black men of the nation, a girl in a car with a serious and starched gentleman, the girl sweats like the drummer and all are diverted, singing and dancing, following the parade, singing popular songs.

Saldaña captured the image of the carnival as a kind of representative space where all the ethnicities that compose the country unite without distinction of any kind:

> Let's go with the conga, the carnival's arrived! White on white, white on black, black on white, black on black: Now, no. The Fatherland—Fatherland, a single man, the Fatherland—Fatherland a heart. Yes, sir. No longer the carriage, nor the sandal, the whip, or the slave quarters. Not anymore. You with me and me with you. Part of the same son. Yes, sir. Let's go with the conga, grandma, the carnival's arrived!
>
> *Get off the sidewalk,*
> *looks like you might fall,*
> *since I'm walking with my people*
> *cleaning up the world!*[22]

The writer creates a similar image of the carnival and the street conga as part of our traditions shown in "Nanas de zarambeque"[23] in *Jícara de miel*. Once again, she captures the image of everyone dancing the popular conga, *mulatas* parading, musical instruments, tricksters, all combined, creating an image of our people, on the outside and inside as a great mixture.

In *La noche*, the same as in *Jícara de miel*, the poet deals with human beings emphasizing their moral qualities and as in *Kele Kele*, she reiterates the fundamental matrices that make up our people. She turns to an aspect of our culture: the lullabies. On "Sorbo del recuerdo VIII"[24] she explains:

> The lullabies arrived from Spain and Africa. The nanny arrived chubby and Cuban. The drum arrived. The guitar arrived. Color is not important nor race. The black mouth sings a lullaby and the white mouth repeats it. The white mouth sings and sings, and its tune is faithfully echoed in the black throat.

Hence *mestizaje* is found in musical instruments and shown in the communication of love established between the wet nurse who sings and the child who repeats the song in response to the love of his nanny.

In *La noche*, Saldaña expresses a relationship of love for her two grandmothers. She also refers to heroic women such as Mariana Grajales, exalting her not only as the biological mother of her own blood children but also as a woman, mother, wife, and flower, positioning all Cubans as the children of her love. In "Paisaje con mujer angolana"[25] [Landscape with Angolan Woman], she describes an image depicted in an instant photo. The photo shows the head of an Angolan woman carrying her son on her back. This woman sees and upholds everything.

The writer's interest to include this group of people with their characteristics led her to represent in her work the worth and beauty of blacks and *mulatos*, as well as peasants, and the *mestizo* culture of Cuba in general. Little by little, the writer is teaching young generations—from childhood and youth—to appreciate our culture and to feel respect and admiration for it. When addressing the *mestizaje* of Cuban culture in her work, she recognizes or makes apparent the quantitative and qualitative contributions of the Yoruba ethnicity, and our African and Spanish ancestors found in songs, dances, musical instruments, religion, love of nature, botany knowledge, and food. In other words, her work shows how the process of transculturation is observed in all aspects of life in Cuba. Additionally, she highlights the oral tradition and the transmission of experiences and knowledge from one generation to another as contributions that shape our culture.

NOTES

1. Though she received honorable mention from such an important award, she never intended for this book of poems to be published that references *abakúa* secret sect ceremonies.

2. Flora González Mandri, "El interes de autodenominarse en la obra de Excilia Saldaña," in *Hermanas de la diaspora: Escritores afrohispanas* (Miami: Kingston Publishers); Cintio Vitier, "De este salterio," in *Mi Nombre* by Excilia Saldaña (Havana: Ediciones Unión, 2003); Virglio López Lemus, "*Epílogo*," in *Mi nombre* [My Name], by Excilia Saldaña (Havana: Ediciones Unión, 2003); Nancy Morejón, "Prologue," in *In the Vortex of the Cyclone, Selected Poems by Excilia Saldaña* (Gainesville: Florida University Press, 2002).

3. Medicinal spiritual water from the wife of Orula (orisha) and assistant of the Santero priest.

4. Saldaña, *Mi nombre*, 30.

5. Ibid., 14.

6. Excilia Saldaña, *Cantos para un Mayito y una paloma* (Havana: Editorial Gente Nueva, 1983), 58.

7. Ibid., p. 19.

8. Saldaña, *Mi Nombre*, 58.

9. Ibid., 58.

10. Excilia Saldaña, *Un testigo de la historia* (Havana: Editorial Gente Nueva, 1979).
11. Excilia Saldaña, *Flor para amar* (Havana: Editorial Gente Nueva, 1980).
12. Excilia Saldaña, *De la Isla del Tesoro a la Isla de la Juventud* (Havana: Editorial Gente Nueva, 1979).
13. Excilia Saldaña, *Bulgaria, el país de las rosas* (Havana: Editorial Gente Nueva, 1979).
14. Excilia Saldaña, *Kele Kele* (Havana: Editorial Gente Nueva, 1987).
15. *I Cry, Kele Kele, Dreaming and Traveling, Compay Tito, The Night*, and *Honey Gourd*.
16. There are several versions of these *pataquíes* or *pataquines* of this religion. Saldaña re-creates them and turns them into literary material for young readers.
17. Saldaña, *Kele Kele*, 55.
18. Excilia Saldaña, *In the Vortex of the Cyclone: Selected Poems by Excilia Saldaña* (Gainesville: Florida University Press, 2002).
19. How did it occur?
20. Ovillejo is an old form in Spanish poetry, thus the title translates to "Ovillejo for Maceo" in *La noche*, 31.
21. Both are types of trees with the *jaguey* being a fig tree. *La noche*, 31.
22. *La noche*, 99.
23. *Nanas* mean both lullaby and nanny, depending on context, and *zarambeque* is a type of boisterous dance.
24. Sip of Memory VIII. *Jícara de miel*, 141.
25. *La noche*, 103.

BIBLIOGRAPHY

Aguirre, Mirta. 1980. "La influencia de la mujer en Iberoamérica." In *Ayer de hoy*. Havana: Ediciones Unión.
Alfonso, Vitalina. 2002. *Ellas hablan de la Isla*. Havana: Ediciones Unión.
Araújo, Nara. 1989. "Apuntes sobre el significado y valor de la identidad cultural." *Unión*, October–November–December, no. 8. Havana.
Davies, Catherine. 1999. "Madre Africa y memoria cultural: Nancy Morejón, Georgina Herrera, Excilia Saldaña." *Revolución y Cultura* 41, nos. 2–3 (May–June). Havana.
Facio, Alda. 1992. *Cuando el género sueña, cambios trae*. Venezuela: Editorial La Escarcha Azul.
González Mandri, Flora. 2003. "El interés de autodenominarse en la obra de Excilia Saldaña." In *Hermanas de la diaspora: Escritores afrohispanas*. Miami: Kingston Publishers.
Lanza de Jesús, Afonso. 2001. *Vitoria: Equidad y participación social de la mujer mozambicana*. Ediciones Tricontinental, OSPAAAL.
Lescaille, Nidia, et al. *La cubana a traves de La noche de Excilia Saldaña*. Unpublished.

López Lemus, Virgilio. 1988. *Palabras del trasfondo*. Havana: Editorial Letras Cubanas.
———. 1999. *Doscientos años de poesía cubana*. Havana: Editora Abril.
———. 2003. *Epílogo a Mi nombre de Excilia Saldaña*. Havana: Ediciones Unión.
Montero, Susana. 2003. *La cara oculta de la identidad nacional*. Santiago de Cuba: Editorial Oriente.
Morejón, Nancy. 2002. "Prologue." In *In the Vortex of the Cyclone: Selected Poems by Excilia Saldaña*. Gainesville: Florida University Press.
Pedroso Torres, Francis, et al. 2006. *Tratamiento lingüistico de La noche de Excilia Saldaña*. Unpublished.
Randale, Ian. 2003. *Hermanas de la diaspora: Escritores afrohispanas*. Miami: Kingston Publishers.
Saldaña, Excilia. 1967. *Enlloró*. Unpublished.
———. 1969. *El refranero de la víbora*. Havana: Editorial Letras Cubanas.
———. 1979. *De la Isla del Tesoro a la Isla de la Juventud*. Havana: Editorial Gente Nueva.
———. 1979. *Un testigo de la historia*. Havana: Editorial Gente Nueva.
———. 1980. *Flor para amar*. Havana: Editorial Gente Nueva.
———. 1983. *Cantos para un Mayito y una paloma*. Havana: Editorial Gente Nueva.
———. 1986. *Bulgaria, el país de las rosas*. Havana: Editorial Gente Nueva.
———. 1987. *Kele Kele*. Havana: Editorial Gente Nueva.
———. 1987. *Soñando y viajando*. Havana: Editorial Gente Nueva.
———. 1998. *Lengua de trapo*. Havana: Editorial Gente Nueva.
———. 2000. *Jícara de miel*. Havana: Editorial Gente Nueva.
———. 2002. *La lechuza y el sijú*. Havana: Editorial Gente Nueva.
———. 2002. *La noche*. Havana: Editorial Gente Nueva.
———. 2002. *In the Vortex of the Cyclone: Selected Poems by Excilia Saldaña*. Gainesville: Florida University Press.
———. 2003. *Mi nombre*. Havana: Ediciones Unión.
Vittier, Cintio. 2003. "De este salterio." In *Mi nombre*. Havana: Ediciones Unión.
Vittier, Cintio, and D. Chericián. 1987. *Company Tito*. Havana: Editorial Gente Nueva.

Chapter 25

The Thick Skin of Teresa Cárdenas

Leandro Estupiñán Zaldívar

Teresa Cárdenas has been published in Korean and English though she writes in Spanish. Her Spanish is as clear and sweet as the stream where her African ancestors drank water to deal with the midday sun. She also has a voluptuous body and lucid eyes like those of a Nubian lover. However, there is something to her that is more striking than her translations, body, and keen gaze. She holds the power of transmutation. She can transform when she wants to what she wants: glass, steel, bark of the *abobad* [baobab tree], silence.

Teresa is black and writes about blacks: "I'll keep writing about blacks until I fade,"[1] she replied with a fine irony to a person who was attempting to mock her and her writing. At thirty-seven years of age, she knows plenty about the harshness in life because besides being a writer, she is also a social worker, "like the types from past," she warns. "I actually only practiced for three years, but it was during my studies when I grew closer to people. I'm more of a social worker through my books. My book, *Tatanene cimarrón* was the fruit of this experience. I suffered a lot at the Cárdenas nursing home. I was not prepared for what I experienced. Then, that book came out."

Teresa Cárdenas has won several awards among which some that stand out are the 2005 Casas de las Américas Prize for Children's and Youth Literature as well as the National Critics Prize in 2007 for *Perro viejo* [Old Dog]. Also worthy of mention are the Dan David Prize and Cuba's Premio Calendario for *Cartas al Cielo* [Letters to Heaven] in 1997, which also received the National Critics Prize.

Tatanene cimarrón received honorable mention in the UNEAC contest in 1998 and first mention in Casas de las Américas in 2002. *Cuentos de Macucupé* won the Edad de Oro award.

She visited our city during the most recent Feria del Libro, the book fair that gave her the opportunity to go back and forth among the children (and adults). She told anecdotes of her life as a writer since childhood when she wanted to find the type of literature that she writes today. "I had no model for comparison. I was a girl who lived in a tenement building, daughter of a single mother and drunken father. . . . My literary paradigm was Lil, a literary character with eyes the color of time, who had nothing to do with me. I did not have access to books with stories that looked like me. I couldn't find any [role] models."

And if that little girl had found literature like the one you write today?
"I would have been a lot happier. I would have felt more confident and secure. Life, reality would have been more in focus for me."

Would it have been shocking?
"I don't think so since I knew harsh realities. More shocking was when I read in a story, 'her blue eyes seemed lost, her amber-colored eyes, her red lips, the girl blushed.' That was like a riddle for me. What did blush mean? When I looked in the mirror, those words had nothing to do with me. It's as if those stories were using another language when speaking to me.

"Today, powerful work is being done. There are many writers breaking barriers, eliminating taboo subjects. Although my stories are not folkloric, because I don't write stories that have already been written. I do rewrite stories about Afro-Cuban mythology. With that, I constantly answer questions to myself that I had as a child."

Have you ever encountered racial intolerance?
"I remember an editor who told me once: 'I can't stand the Afro-Cuban.' From her point of view, the Afro-Cuban delays the development of literature. But, thanks to the saints, my career has not been affected [by those types of ideas] which would have blocked bringing joy and knowledge to children."

What type of temperament is necessary to write children's literature?
"I was asked once if there is a formula. I write for the whole world who wants to read my literature, and anything can be a source of inspiration. My own children inspire me. It is not an issue for me that I am a woman or mother. All of my books are dedicated to my children."

NOTE: Teresa Cárdenas played volleyball as a student. This surprised everyone. In the press conference where I met her, she said that she could have been another team member of the Morenas del Caribe. Laughter. Lidia Ester Ochoa, astute in telling jokes on the radio, corrected her, stating she would be instead a Morena of letters. And I thought I heard René Navarro, the sports newscaster, calling out, "Score!"

NOTE

1. She uses the verb *destiña*, which means to become discolored or faded, playing with the word to also imply aging or withering.

Chapter 26

El Negrito and the *Mulata* in the Vortex of Nationality

Inés María Martiatu Terry

The man with painted blackface enters the zenith of the light. The legs move following the touch of the timbale. The blows mark each of his steps. His movements are agile. He moves toward the center of the stage. He stops. Comes forward and accompanies the timbale again. You start to hear a rumble. It grows. The rumble fills the entire scope of the theater. It goes up from the windows, bounces in the balconies, reaches the first floor, second, third, the women's dressing room. You hear laughter. The face of the *negrito*[1] shines and the white area around his eyes stands out. It has been left unpainted with the burned cork. His hands are gloved also in black. The trousers, a little short, leave the ankles uncovered. His shirt is cinched at the waist. The slender body performs a pirouette, moves while the zenith follows. She arrives at the side of the stage. The *mulata* woman. The orchestra strongly announces her. Applause. The orchestra begins to play a guaracha. The *mulata* woman makes her broad saya skirt undulate. The manila shawl falls below her shoulders. Her face is also painted dark. A colorful scarf wraps her haughty head. She arrives flip-flopping, moving her waist and flexing her arms with the grace of a bully.

She dances to the rhythm of the music and laughter rises, exclamations and slaps of the public rejoicing delirious to her charm. She stops provocatively in front of the *negrito* who looks at her with sarcasm. The dialogue begins. Suddenly they startle each other. They side glance each other. The gestures are so exaggerated they become grotesque. They laugh. They notice the character that has appeared under the zenith. It is the *gallego*, the Galician. He wears black corduroy pants. On his head, a beret. On the face, huge mustaches. The Galician flirts with the *mulata*. She is coquettish with him. The Galician smiles, pleased. The *mulata* gestures at the *negrito*. They both mock the Galician. The respectable public laughs. They mock him too. The timbales burst into a shrill and rhythmic sound. The three characters vibrate like puppets, move, shudder with the total revelry. The voices of the *guaracheros* burst into the background of the stage: "Here has arrived Candela, / negrito of the tear and slash, / he flies with the knife, / and cuts with the blade." The public sings along to the *guaracha*, applauds. "Oh! Chinitica, what are we going to do? / If the good negrito / they want to burn." The *negrito, mulata*, and Galician exit dancing. The curtain falls. It closes. It opens again and the three come out to the proscenium: "The good negrito / they want to hurt."[2] The *negrito* and *mulata* continue dancing about: "the good negrito / they want to hurt." The Galician dances showing that he has two left feet while the *negrito* and the *mulata* sing, "the good negrito / they want to hurt."[3]

In the dressing room, in the light of the candles, the *negrito* removes his makeup. Gradually the white skin appears, pale by contrast with the color of the burned cork. The makeup slides greasily off the face that emerges beneath the black color. Dripping. A swab of oil and little by little the face becomes clear. It changes. The face transforms in front of the mirror.

The expression hardens, the countenance. On the street, the actor, the white man, must call a car. A black man drives one. The *negrito*, now a white man, dressed up with a jacket and tie, calls for the black driver with an authoritarian gesture that is almost offensive. The other one obeys. The car starts up. The *negrito*, now white, has taken possession of his new role.

This scene represented the *negrito* of the bufo,[4] the *negrito* of the common vernacular, and the *negrito* of the circus. The *negrito* with a painted face or not emerges as a contradictory expression of nationality that remains incomplete. He is still present, emphasizing his character of subalternity in theater, cabaret, media, radio, and television. However, to find this *negrito* for the first time we would have to go back to Spanish theater of the Golden Age in Spain. The presence of black Africans in the Iberian Peninsula is as old as its history. Its territory had been subjected for centuries to Africa from the North African Empire of Carthage to the Islamic vandals. From the Carthaginian armies of Anibal and Amilcar Barca, passing through the Roman legions, especially the Third Augusta Legion, the Arab-Moorish conquest to the Holy Wars of Almoravids and Almohads. Chief Koubba Yussef Ibn Tashfin's famous "Black Guard" came from the Sudanese savannas. To the sound of their huge drums, they destroyed the Christian armies and then remained in the south of Spain.

In the year 711 North Africa invaded the Iberian Peninsula. In a few years they conquered all the peninsular territory, except the mountainous areas of the Cantabria and the Pyrenees. The invaders (mostly Berber, although led by Arabs) brought a large number of blacks among their troops. This means that centuries before the beginning of the colonization in the Americas, nuclei of populations of blacks already existed in Spain, especially in the whole region of the south. They organized themselves in a similar way to how they did in Cuba by means of *cabildos* of nations. In 1393, a hospital for the black population was founded in Seville, and a few years later, laws and ordinances were established regulating the social life of blacks in that city.[5]

Don Fernando Ortiz quotes the Sevillian historian Bermejo, writing, "Navigation from the ports of Andalusia that took place to the coasts of Africa at the end of the fourteenth century and at the beginning of the fifteenth in search of black slaves to traffic them as it was done at the time in this city, attracted so many men of this class to her that eventually their numbers grew."[6]

Slaves constituted a very large group in Seville. According to a census carried out by ecclesiastical officials in 1565, there were an estimated 6,327 slaves, which gives an approximate proportion of one slave per fourteen inhabitants (7 percent of the population). Perhaps there were many more because it is probable that Islamic and unbaptized blacks were not included. Unbaptized blacks were few, but Turks and Berbers, who did not want to leave their religion, were a large number. A large majority of them were black, to which it is necessary to add a growing quantity of free blacks and *mulatos*. Hence it is not farfetched to say that blacks and *mulatos* constituted about 10 percent of the Sevillian population. At the end of the fifteenth and early sixteenth centuries, black slaves became familiar figures in the city. They were so numerous in Seville that a contemporary said that its inhabitants "resembled chess pieces: as many blacks as whites." From that reference, Seville was often compared to a "chessboard."

Hence we find black slaves, *mulatos*, whites, and slaves of mixed coloration walking through the streets, squares, markets, fountains, ports, and other central places like the Gradas, where they were auctioned. The Arenal or the Altozano added a colorful exoticness to the Seville population.[7] "In Valladolid during the court's stay there were so many black slaves that a traveler claimed that you couldn't take a step without stumbling on one of them."[8]

Some came to hold titles of nobility according to the chronicler Ortiz de Zúñiga, by means of a *real cédula*, royal decree, given in Dueñas on November 8, 1475, through which the Catholic Kings named their porter Juan de Valladolid count. He became known as "Count Negro." His name was immortalized with the Conde Negro street that still exists today behind the confraternity's chapel of the *negritos*.[9]

Moreover, many blacks were servants and maids and often used in the main houses in all of Andalusia. A bride's dowry could not be even considered without the inclusion of a black maiden for her personal service.[10]

It is necessary to emphasize moreover their presence in the arts and letters. The slave Juan de Pareja is a great example. His master, the painter Diego de Velásquez, immortalized him on his canvases. There was also the anonymous author of *El Lazarillo de Tormes* [The Guide of de Tormes], whose character, a stable boy, refers to his black stepfather. He is forced to distance himself from his mother who is fleeing from the law and his little black brother.

BLACKS IN THE THEATER OF THE GOLDEN AGE

Although the *Bufos Habaneros* [Bufos of Havana] premiered on May 31, 1868, their antecedents are found much earlier in the Iberian Peninsula, in Seville. Don Fernando Ortiz came to define that city as "overflowing" with blacks and where black men and women were put on stage as characters in the Spanish Golden Age of comedy. Later, on the Island, the brilliant Francisco Covarrubias introduced to theater the *negrito* character, among others, that has come to characterize our country with great public success. Bartolome Crespo Borbón, with the pseudonym of Creto Gangá, created works featuring blacks as they would later appear in bufo theater.

To understand this evolution, it is necessary to go back in time. In Seville, the first theatrical manifestations in which blacks participated were religious. The celebration of the Corpus Christi included black women who danced dressed in luxurious costumes, paid by the *cabildo*[11] itself. They embodied characters like the little devils, the *tarasca* monster, and the *cabezudos* or giant-headed figures, representing disorder and sin redeemable by the sacrament. At least twenty-one dance groups have been documented in Seville from the mid-sixteenth to the mid-seventeenth century with the revealing names of "the Negros," "the Negros of Guinea," "the Cachumba of the Negros,"[12] "The Black Kings," and "The Battle of Guinea." This last group was composed of "eight men and four women, and a tambourine and a guitar, four with paderetes[13] and rattles, others with ataballillos, and four with rattles and flags."[14] Additionally, they formed confraternities integrated by blacks and *mulatos* who paraded through the streets of Seville during Easter as the Brotherhood of Negros of Triana, the Mulatos of San Ildefonso, Our Lady of Los Angeles, and Los Negritos, established by the foundation of Archbishop Mena. To this day, one of the confraternities remains: Brotherhood of the Negritos.[15]

Black characters were already present in comedies, tragedies, morality plays, or *zarzuelas*, and performing arts in which blacks and *mulatos* were treated as a theme, but in which they also acted as musicians, dancers, soloists, and singers. They often played leading roles in the works by top authors such as Lope de Rueda, Manuel Coello Rebello, Quevedo, Lope de Vega, Alonso de Castillo Solórzano, Atento Feliciano de Silva, Jayme de Guete, and Jerónimo de Cuéllar, among others.

María de Córdova y de la Vega, better known as Amarilis, was one of the most celebrated comedians of that era, praised by Quevedo and Lope de Vega. She was *mulata*.[16]

In Cuba, the comic *negrito*, talkative with an exaggerated but trivial speech, came to be represented in bufo and popular theater until the twenty-first century. Black women almost always played roles of slaves, for example, Eulalia in the comedy *Eufemia*, and Guiomar in *Los engañados* [The Fooled], both of which were written by Lope de Rueda.[17]

> Lope de Rueda, for the first time (1544–1560) took to the Spanish stage real characters of his time . . . multitude of lower rank nobility, rascal students, party maids, braggart soldiers, scoundrel peasants, money sucking innkeepers, manly tarts, uncouth maidens, stubborn carriers, hardened prisoners, marshals and mischievous musketeers, screaming beggars, and I cannot forget them, black slave women.[18]

We can cite the work *El valiente negro en Flandes* [The Valiant Black of Flanders] by Andrés de Claramonte, contemporary of Lope de Vega. The protagonist of this curious comedy, in spite of his color, manages to become captain of the Tercio infantry. Simón Aguado debuted in 1602 *Entremés de los negros* with a blond main character, master of a brigade of negroes.

One of the elements used to represent the identity of blacks in this type of theater was speech. By this I mean a way of speaking that among us we call *bozal* [a creole Spanish ascribed to enslaved Africans and their descendants], versus its variant, *catedrática* [professor, or scholarly speech]. With this observation I want to add that Cuban bufo characters did not create this type of speech because it was very well established in Spanish theater of the time.

A paradigmatic example of this is the short act titled *El negrito hablador, y sin color anda la niña* [The Talkative Negrito and the Girl without Color] by Luis Quiñones de Benavente (1664). Blacks who were depicted represent an archetype extended also in North America, embodied by a singer and dancer who expresses himself in a deformed Spanish. His speech sounds familiar to us because those same lexical distortions were assumed by blacks of the twentieth century and unfortunately of the twenty-first: my h'art ickles me, / playin' gital. Oh, how it sounds! / don't know what the de'il it has / this mode of instulment: /As I have an affiction / and ev'y alm takes me, / here muzzled I hea's me, / although the day awakens.

The comic elements in the play are not only attributed to the nature of his speech but also the protagonist of *El negrito hablador*, who cannot stop talking despite the attempts by the other characters in the play to stop his endless chatter. I can't no mo'; as Christ lives! / and heaven witness!; I wish / with shoes planted on both sides[19] / my lips and tongue could be sewn shut. / Might silence me, but I thinks / the mo' they sew them / then I'd find a way to talk with my eyes, / my hands, ears, / with my feet, my knees, / and with my muscles, with my legs, / with my back and then / with the other eye that I still have.

Language as an element of exclusion emerges in this era from the alterity, difference, and subalternity of blacks. It became a way of conceiving a racial or ethnic identity through uttered speech that would later be transferred to the Cuban bufo.[20] This posture that deauthorized black subjects was transferred to the apotheosis of scholarly blacks, as it is referred to today.

What mechanisms of masking or social disqualification lie behind this act? A series of works were written and represented that mocked the level that many members of the middle class "of color" had achieved through free labor, study, and their betterment as a social group. Representing an exaggerated scholarly discourse was meant to mock them. The exaggeration was intended to imply that they should stay in their place as subalterns that the classist and racist society had assigned them.

Returning to the Golden Age shows that the black element is found not only in texts or characters but also on stage and in the histrionics of actors. The great Lope de Rueda not only distinguished himself as a playwright but was also recognized as a popular and acclaimed actor by the public. He would embody different characters, of which blacks and especially black women stand out. According to Fernando Ortiz, "Speaking of Lope de Rueda, one of his critics claimed that he was more of an actor than an author. His works were comedic. He would create black women in such a great way, it is said, and other similar characters, that these became vital to his work."[21]

To achieve greatness, he had to resort not only to masking his face with black paint but also to cross-dressing to characterize a black woman.

As already mentioned, these comedies represented blacks as subordinate characters: servants, gossipers, intriguing maidens, and friendly black dancers with a characteristic form of speaking almost identical to the talk of Cuban bufo. The black masking is present in our bufos and in the minstrels of North America. We already have many coincidences between the Spanish Golden Age of comedy and Cuban bufos.

This roadmap is intended to chart the process through which the black subject, as a racialized subject, is being configured from their representation in the theater of the Golden Age as a subaltern entity, always gazed upon artistically from the hegemonic discourse of whiteness. Such strategies of subordination, as we will see later, were transferred and appropriated by the emerging theatrical scene of Cuban society of the mid-nineteenth century. Hence their dramaturgical and representational mechanisms constitute a clear expression of the permanent conflict between the different groups in that society.

By means of immigration to Cuba, and particularly to Havana, the so-called *negros curros* [blacks of Seville] influence significantly the plot of the city. We must emphasize here the importance of the language they introduced in the public space of Havana. Popular speech has been discussed extensively since the end of the twentieth century and the beginning of the twenty-first. Various opinions have been expressed and several polemics have been raised on this point including in the press. Blacks have been blamed for introducing certain words and linguistic turns still rejected to this day. Almost all social groups, especially young people, have assimilated these dialectal turns, which were not seen before, though many consider the integration of popular speech alarming and as accidents from the hegemonic linguistic norm.

A rigorous examination of this phenomenon of speech would take us irrevocably to Spain, and Seville in particular for Cuba and Havana. Blacks of Seville so well studied by Fernando Ortiz, together with other groups from Andalusia and Seville, brought specific types of speech modalities. They settled in and left their marks in different neighborhoods especially in outlying areas such as el Manglar, Carraguao, and Los Sitios o Jesús María. Ortiz points out peculiarities of the pronunciation of Castilian as said in Seville, which includes certain morphological characteristics such as the interchange of the letters r and l and its dissimilation from i.[22]

When we review the brief relationship that Ortiz makes in his book of speech introduced by blacks of Seville, taking from Sevillian jargon, we find that a considerable number of these terms were kept in use among us for a long time. Some remain to date in the traditions of the people. A few examples demonstrate this assertion: apencarse: "humillarse ante los pencazos," "azotes"; apolismar, "magullar a una persona a golpes"; butuba, "comida"; cabuya, "cuerda"; fajar, "reñir"; jalarse, "embriagarse"; jelengue, "reyerta"; zafarse, "escaparse"; and vilongo, "hechizo."[23]

However, some scholars have emphasized other possible influences such as those of Parisian bufos, the Madrilenian bufos, or the minstrels of the United States. Three companies of this last type were presented in this city between the years 1860 and 1865: Campbell's in 1860, Christie's in 1862, and Webb's in 1865. It is symptomatic that despite the relative success of these companies none were able to fully capture the enthusiasm of Havana's public. Although the situations were similar by the circumstances of slavery, according to Rine Leal the comic character of the black personage was an idiosyncratic factor that separated the public from Havana of the minstrels of the United States. Regardless, so-called Havana minstrels had a short time on stage when they debuted in 1862.[24]

The success of the Madrilenian bufos motivated the group Tanda de Guaracheros from the street Cuarteles to dedicate themselves to their journey in theater.

There is no doubt the history of the bufo theater in Cuba includes the theater of the Spanish Golden Age. Alongside the first steps of Covarrubias or Creto Gangá whose works would later be present in Cuba is the *negrito* that would be crystallized in the bufo that remains today. Fernando Ortiz and the work of other researchers provide some interesting elements in the debate on the origins of Cuban bufo theater, which, to a large extent, has been reduced or simplified.

BLACK THEMES IN TWENTY-FIRST-CENTURY CUBAN THEATER

The founding years of Cuban theater are located throughout the nineteenth century. Rine Leal in his whole work establishes the random trajectory of the presence and black themes in Cuban theater. The fear of blacks, negrophobia, and the contradictory interests of the Cuban-born slave-owning class characterize this period whose issues were written and represented in the theater. A romanticism appeared whose main cultists aspired to a Spanish Cuba ruled by the children of Spain. However, as Leal points out, the bloody Conspiracy of the Escalera buried their hopes. Leal states regarding the class in power: "His works are no more than the expression of a class that is debating between colonial oppression and the fear of a slave revolt that might destroy his riches."[25]

As to the Cuban comedy that emerged in the 1830s, it reflects the struggle between a Cuban aristocracy and Spanish traders that coincides chronologically with Romanticism. There is a *costumbrista*[26] tone in this Cuban comedy. It is in this context that black characters appear on stage.

"It is a shy, hesitant entry, which has more to do with the exoticism or the local color than with criticizing slavery, a critique that did not exist on stage until the war of independence. . . . Blacks are turned into a decorative figure, not dramatic. . . . And we get to see to what extremes this negrophobia was taken to the Bufa stage three decades later."[27]

If blacks were excluded in the works of the Cuban romance, then they were made to appear even if timidly in comedy. Blacks are also excluded from melodrama. Black themes were also excluded for the same reasons, which was to evade the thorny issue of slavery.[28]

THE GREAT THEATERS

The colony excelled in constructing theaters because it corresponded to the economic power of the dominant classes. The public space of the theater was par excellence where the stratification of the colonial country was shown in its structure. The construction and disposition of the spectators were well differentiated in the place that each occupied in colonial society. The comedians, singers, and the spectacle were foregrounded through the dominant and authoritarian position. The powerful social class squandered luxuries in the silver boxes, while people of color and poor whites gathered at the floors farthest from the stage.

Many theaters were built, true coliseums in some cases. In Havana and other cities, they possessed conditions and comforts equal to those of the most important European capitals. The best known of them, the Tacón theater, became called the Cathedral of the Opera, but it included others such as El Sauto de Matanzas, Caridad of Santa Clara, and Terry of Cienfuegos, to cite only three in the interior cities. Havana became an important place for the companies of Zarzuela, opera and dramatic and comic theater that would pass through here for its economic potential, as a privileged place from a geographical point of view, and because it possessed an amateur and avid audience for these forms of entertainment.

We must not forget the high level of Cuban musicians who could integrate orchestras capable of accompanying the most diverse spectacles, a detail always highlighted by the companies that acted in this city. From Havana they headed to North America or South America and to the mainland after having tried their shows on the Island. The public in Havana was composed of the most notable and rich classes, senior officers of the army, and foreigners on vacation or business trips, but also of employees, middle-class people, and Spaniards mostly working in commerce, and bureaucratic posts and services of the already populous and rich city.

The higher-ranking families used the theater as a stage to flaunt their wealth while enjoying the fun. It became a place of social encounter where the best clothes, jewels, and hairstyles were displayed. Blacks, servants, and maids were an element that denoted the luxury with which the most important families lived. They dressed them with livery and elegant suits appropriate to the rank of the family that possessed them as slaves and who accompanied the families in public and served them. However, when we look at theater with a broader vision as Don Fernando Ortiz wrote, we must account for a black presence in Cuban theater manifested in an alternative way to the context of commercial and conventional theater.

THE SACRED THEATER OF BLACKS

We know that Spain established on the Island Catholic festivities like the ceremony and procession of the *Corpus Christi*. These neighborhood precessions later incorporated the profane elements that also manifested during the celebrations in the metropolis. Of course, blacks who participated contributed their ways of doing things and expressing themselves. In the sixteenth century, the presence of nonreligious elements including some taken from African religions provoked protests by the colonial authorities.

We will see that these included the sacred theater of blacks. Among the most important were the *cabildos*. These institutions played a fundamental role in preserving the customs and traditions of transplanted slaves from Africa to Cuba and in integrating them into the life of the colony. Since the fourteenth century they had settled in the south of Spain in Andalusia: "from Seville came the cabildos and black brotherhoods to the Indies, reproducing them in the metropolitan organization where there was a great nucleus of Africans," wrote the sage Don Fernando Ortiz. They enrolled under the patronage of a Catholic saint and celebrated their religious or secular feasts in the manner of their land in Africa. In these *cabildos*, celebrations and ceremonies were held in which the members acted and, in some cases, represented scenes and dances parodying those of kings and queens, but with the music of drums from their own land. These representations, as well as other rituals of African origin, are eminently theatrical.

The Afro-Cuban feast of the Day of Kings reached great relevance in the expression of Africanity. It is one of the first and most complete theatrical manifestations known in the colony in which the protagonists were slaves. Fernando Ortiz left a very vivid description of those celebrations, the single day in which the *cabildos* of blacks of the nation and their descendants deployed what we would call a great happening. A whole city converted into an inconceivable scenic space only comparable to carnival celebrations in some European cities. These feasts of the Day of Kings constitute one of the antecedents of the carnival in the Caribbean.

As Ortiz proposes, the ceremonies of the different religions of African origin practiced in Cuba can be considered theatrical. Among them are those of Santería, Palomonte, and the secret society Abakúa.

"In the sacred precincts where different religions of African origin are conserved and disseminated, syncretism with Catholicism represents a ritual theatre, invisible to neophytes, where the mythological, based on a rich tradition of oral literature, has its expression in ritual, in scenery."[29]

Additionally, the theater of "relaciones" [relations] linked to carnivals of Santiago de Cuba, in which mostly black and *mulato* actors participated, and a few poor whites, is another example of black theater disconnected from the mechanisms of commercial bufo theater in which an element of self-loathing clearly appeared. Denigration was also expressed in the reception and complacency of the public.

BUFO THEATER AND NATIONALITY

It is in bufo theater where the black character takes real prominence on the Cuban stage of the nineteenth century, although always represented by white actors in blackface. The *negrito, mulata,* and Galician offered a complacent image of Cuban people in a peculiar theater in which they mocked themselves. They ridiculed and mocked the *negro bozal* for the way he spoke (newcomer, not fluent in the language), the professor (trying to imitate the "high" classes), and the lumpen. The superficial and exploited *mulata sandunguera* was added along with the brute Galician, always mocking the *negrito* and *mulata.* Guarachas, rumbas, and other autochthonous musical genres added spice. When these characters from the courtyard broke into the theater scene, they achieved the accession and enthusiasm of the public who until that time was accustomed to the repertoire of Spanish *zarzuelas* but began to identify with the expressions of an incipient nationality. But was it only that?

That first season of 1868 was very short. The anti-Spanish manifestations of the artists and the public sympathizing with the war of independence that had just begun that year made colonial authorities take harsh reprisals. It aroused the famous events of the Villanueva Theater on January 22, 1869.[30] However, under the black makeup of white actors, the *negrito, mulata,* and Galician were undoubtedly talented actors who managed to give life to the archetypes with proven theatrical effectiveness. Their interpretation has always been maintained in the variations of those characters. From the point of view of symbolic representation, we must point out that the phenomenon of the bufo concealed multiple connotations that are not confined to class only. The definition of a problematic nationality is just one of them. Important ideologues have emphasized the "fear of blacks" and the nonacceptance of Africans and their descendants as Cubans. Francisco de Arango and Parreño, along with José Antonio Saco, always dreamed of whitening the Island. Saco's well-known phrases, "Whiten, whiten, and then be respected" and "Once Cuba is white, it will then allow it to start being Cuban," were meant to exclude blacks from any possible national project. However, at this time, it has also become evident that the black element differentiated Cuba and had become the most important factor in the national identity. This was present in music and other manifestations. "Cuba already knows that it is mulata," Nicolás Guillén would claim later. However, it does not want to be *mulata*; it wants to be white. A great frustration and underestimation are designed into these characters. Cuban whites project on the *negrito* and *mulata* what they think of themselves. He paints his face to be able to scream this from the stage. Let us not forget that these characters were not black but were whites in blackface. A symbolism that does not escape us is part of this play. To reaffirm this assertion, we must bear in mind that bufo represents Cuban and foreign characters. The only Cuban characters, though insulted, are the *mulata* and *negrito.* The Catalan, Chinese, and later Galician characters are foreigners.

It is not really possible to claim these archetypal characters as an identity factor, especially because they were also masked under makeup. The *negrito* is not a black man and the *mulata* is not a mulata. They are white actors performing these archetypes as stereotypes that may not fully conform to the reality of those characters. They are the *negrito* and the *mulata* proposed by the theater. They are not a real black man and *mulata*. Why should we accept these supplanted characters as a representation of national identity? The incipient recognition of this truth, though not entirely conscious, is fraught with painful and violent contradictions. It carries a tremendous ambivalence. The white *criollo*, or Cuban-born Spanish whites, recognized that one of the most important factors that identify *lo cubano* [Cubanness] came from the African influence regarding various aspects of Cubans' material and spiritual life. He has no choice but to join them. He has no one else and no other option. Although masked and denigrated, these characters capture the characteristics of being Cuban, curiously established at a founding moment of the nation with the beginning of the struggles for independence. They become protagonists of a narrative not of inclusion but of exclusion, the negation of one of the roots that constitute Cuba. Affirming the hegemony of one of them leads to the devaluation of the ethnic or racial identity of the "other" black or *mestizo*.

All this makes us question the hidden sediments on which our concept of nationality has been built, a concept of nationality and identity that are born and weighed down by one of the most painful consequences of racism. For the imaginary and the memory of the nation, the image of the black subject has transcended time always associated with negative characteristics. However, the Cuban duality is indissoluble. Despite the differences between whites and blacks in social practice and of a prevailing ideology of racial hegemony, black and white Cubans continue to clash with the irresponsibility, vagrancy, deceit, trap, lack of seriousness, and disrespect toward themselves and others.[31] They find no other form of identification to confront the colonial hegemonic discourse imposed upon them.

This self-disqualification remained not only for the Spanish but would also lay the foundation for the recognition of subalternity. In other words, we see how this devaluation operates through the hidden spaces of consciousness. It is an ambivalence of impulse, a schizophrenia that characterizes it and explains, in part, the difficult interracial relations that remain present in different ways between us. The very fact of masking by playing blacks and *mulatos* through makeup and in creating a theater to present them confirms all this.[32]

With this dramatic paradox, we could say that the independence project is opposed to the national project, which thus arises with the original sin of racism, a stain very difficult to erase. This example of the bufo would lead us to no ingenuous positions about raciality and identity. As the sociological writer Rafael Hernández wrote,

> A historical perspective on racial inequality reveals it as part of a social order and as a culturally complex and changing construction, reflected in representations and images. However, some criticism that tries only to deny or replace those images produce insufficient results. . . . To surpass the ontological somewhat banal, making us creatures of an ineffable national identity, supposedly homogeneous . . .[33]
>
> Africans freed whites of almost every productive activity and condemned them to leisure, immorality and vice. Whites condemned the slave to exhausting and destructive work. Dehumanized, both clashed with heartbreaking, relentless violence: The class struggle was a race struggle.[34]

Additionally, as Fernando Ortiz comments, "One dominated the other because of the historical evolutionary progress of their positions and techniques, additionally, they nailed the other within a conception of 'bad life.' The religion of the dominated was ridiculous and diabolical; their language was 'a noise, not a voice'; their art, laughable; morality, abominable; family disconnected; their customs without entitlement; their ideas, absurd; their work, brutal; their economy, ineffective. . . . It was all denial and evil! Blacks were meant to be dehumanized."[35]

However, who are in fact these blacks, *mulatas*, and *mulatos* against whom the bufo theater deployed these rhetorical mechanisms of exclusion, retreat, and masking?

THE OTHER SIDE OF THE COIN: THE *NEGRITO*, NO; EL NEGRO

The characteristics of the *negrito* and *mulata* in a carnivalesque environment and leisure contrast with the reality of the black slaves in the plantations, the fundamental line on which the colony's economy rested.

The drama of the horrors in history in which blacks faced as protagonists on plantations contrast with the distorted archetypical representations of them on stage. From the cellars of slave ships in inconceivable and inhumane conditions in which they were transported, from the barracks in which they were sold and on plantations, these enslaved men and women performed different heroic acts of resistance and rebellion against the system that oppressed them. Conspiracies, uprisings, insurrections, and marooning were heroic solutions that most often cost them their life.

THE OTHER SIDE OF THE COIN: THE *MULATA*, NO; *MULATAS*

It is known that *mulatas* and *mulatos* appear as a product of crossbreeding between black and white individuals. More frequently between black women and white men. Due to the situation of slavery and subalternity of black women, *mestizaje* in Cuba, the Caribbean, and even in Spain, which was "overflowing with blacks" as Fernando Ortiz affirms, was historically carried out by means of the participation, tacit or not, of black women and *mestizas*. Rape from the hold of slave ships, in the barracks, plantations and main houses, statutory rape, prostitution, and in some cases economic coercion were frequently the origin of this *mestizaje*, admixing.

One of the most illustrative examples of the injuring racist discourse is the expression that the best inventions of Galician men were the *porrón* drink, espadrilles, and *mulatas*. We could not find a more rude and offensive statement. "The absolute and pejorative of the affirmation suggests that like Eve who was created from a man's rib, mulatas seem to have been born from the sternum of the Galician, without a black mother or Cuban roots and without an identity shown for centuries and consolidated to this day."[36]

However, the word's origin is even more offensive. *Mulatos* are compared to mules: children of a mare and donkey. A friend of mine commented with a sense of humor, "the donkey must have been the Galician that was such a brute that he wanted to make his children mules." The name *mulata* and *mulato* emerged from a derogatory expression that compared blacks to animals.

Mulatas became protagonists of abolitionist novels. Examples like *El Negro Francisco* by Anselmo Suárez and Romero, despite its limitations, depict her as a tragic character. The paradigm of these novels without a doubt is Cirilo Villaverde's novel *Cecilia Valdés o La Loma del Angel* [or the Hill of the Angel].

She became the femme fatale who has no place in the society because of her biraciality. Black women sometimes play secondary roles as an old woman or a witch in these novels. The *mulata* in trying to move up the social ladder, attempts to whiten herself, and becomes a tragic character without an alternative to her aspirations. She becomes ensnared in a triangle with a powerful white man or with the "master" who only wants to have fun and the rich white lady whom he must marry. In another variant that is no less tragic, a black or *mulato* man loves her but is despised by the *mulata* who prefers white men. Add to this tragic plot her self-denial in wanting to unsuccessfully "pass for white." This is what I call the "Cecilia syndrome." This is not meant to deny the success of the novelist Cirilo Villaverde in creating that character and reproducing many facets of life in Havana during that era.

However, Cecilia—like the *mulata* of the bufo—became an archetype that was reproduced in María La O, Rosa La China, María Belén Chacón, Amalia Batista, and in a number of other possible *mulatas*. Yet were they all *mulatas*? Were they all Cecilias? Did all *mulatas* of that era share Cecilia's aspirations?

The *mulata* as a distorted archetypal representation is found later and originates in guaracha music. That genre of popular Cuban music emphasizes real and popular elements. She is described as *chancletera* [wears flip-flops or sandals], quarreling, sensual, partier, prostitute and threatening to morality, family, and good manners. She is always ready to mock and exploit the Galician alongside the other character of the *criollo* picaresque, the *negrito*.

The image of black and *mulata* women has been associated with an unbridled sexuality or sexual freedom. It is known that initiation into sex and sexual relief of appetites of the white man, even in the manor houses, were fulfilled by de facto relationships with black and *mulata* slaves. A means of obtaining freedom by the domestic slaves was to become a concubine with their masters, and many freed black and *mulata* women practiced prostitution in the urban center sometimes obliged and rented by their own masters.

This very condition that makes the *mulata* a coveted sexual object places her on some other planet. She cannot be the wife of white or black men. She is thus associated with pleasure and the role allocated to her is as a dear and intimate friend or prostitute. Some of them were corrupted in such a way that they would claim to prefer to be the girlfriend of a rich white person than the wife of a poor black or *mulato* man.

In this context, *mulata* women emerged for the popular imaginary in the lyrics of the Guaracha as it joins the bufo. This account of the personality of the *mulata* became generalized as the American black feminist bell hooks theorized:[37] "black presence in early North American society allowed whites to sexualize their world by projecting onto black bodies a narrative of sexualization disassociated from whiteness. . . . It is the black female body that is forced to serve as an icon of sexuality in general."[38]

As we have already pointed out, the *mulata* archetype of the bufo theater was interpreted by white actresses in blackface. This element clearly shows the deliberate impersonation of the identity of *mulata* women expressed in their theatrical characterization. In a self-interested abusive generalization, we are supposed to believe that the generalization is a true *mulata*. Were all *mulatas* like the one in bufo theater? This vulgar archetype that pandered to the public came to permeate the sensibility and image of black and *mulata* women. The archetype was later reproduced by some *mulatas* who represented themselves in that way. An example of this is the actress Candita Quintana, the most popular *mulata* of popular theater in the twentieth century, though she may not have been *mulata*. After the triumph of the revolution, she masterfully interpreted the leading role in *El premio flaco* [The Thin

Prize] by Héctor Quintero. She played a remarkable dramatic role that moved her away from the *mulata* archetype. It was a great success; even the director of the group Berliner Ensemble and wife of Bertold Brecht, Helene Wiegler, compared it to the best interpretations of Madre Coraje.[39]

The acceptance and persistence of these schemes that distort and mask demonstrate how the falsity of these models does not prevent them from being accepted in the imaginary of the people that persist to the present day. Hence the importance of deconstructing them and offering a theoretical alternative to restore black and *mulata* women's true identities.

The lyrics of these guarachas, the works of the bufo, and even the arts of figures as relevant as Victor Patricio de Landaluze re-created images that make us easily believe the lives of blacks, *mulatos*, and *mulatas* in the colony: always wearing jewelry and gaudy suits, always loitering in street corners, falling in love, or, even more, performing soft domestic chores with a duster in hand. *Mulatas* like blacks suffered the disadvantages of slavery when it was their legal status. *Mestizaje* did not save them.

As we have seen, the ugly face of slavery and racist exploitation clearly personify the characters in bufo theater.

THE OTHER SIDE OF THE COIN: MIDDLE-CLASS PEOPLE OF COLOR

The existence of a small bourgeoisie of free blacks and *mulatos* with education, some of them with money, businesses, professions, and as slavers or in the military, caused fear of the rise of that social class that could result as natural leaders of a slave revolution like the one that happened in Haiti. Arango and Parreño were right to refer to this class, noting that "they are all black. . . . They have the same grievances and the same motive for being upset with us."[40]

Undoubtedly, since the eighteenth century this middle class of *pardos* and *morenos* had reached a certain economic, technical, and cultural level and a social representation. A little later, in 1844, the Spanish government's Conspiracy of the Ladder brutally attacked that social class in an attempt to make it disappear. The process served to terrorize slaves, eventually eliminate the middle layers of free blacks and *mulatos*, and intimidate white intellectuals. The measures of terror were brutal, but blacks always bore the worst of it.[41]

Many slaves were taken out of the mills, tortured, and killed. More than three hundred blacks and *mulatos* were taken to the scaffold and more than seven hundred were exiled. Others were deprived of the authorization to exercise trades and professions for which they were entitled, and all were stripped of their property. "I consider it very important, for the future of this country, the decline of this caste," stated Governor O'Donnell.[42] It is clear that one of the main objectives of the repression was to eliminate the emerging class of blacks and *mulatos*.[43]

In *Contribución a la historia de la gente sin historia*,[44] the researcher Pedro Deschamps Chapeaux introduced the study of the economic and social connotations that the emerging middle class of color had in the nineteenth century. Deschamps obtained almost all of his information from the confiscation of files on the Conspiracy of the Ladder. The files noted the economic level reached by this social group, the relationships that were established in it, and its insertion as a specific class in the colony although strictly segregated from the rest of the society divided into unassailable strata by customs and laws. They proved themselves in the so-called Battalions of Pardos and Morenos that offered them the opportunity to occupy military positions and in which they were very well received, as well as in the brotherhoods of the Catholic Church. Through the process of assimilation, they acquired ways and customs of their own, according to their social and professional performance.

Many mastered trades, crafts, and professions, engaged in business, the arts, teaching, or services. They were dentists, musicians, masters of great works, pier foremen, funeral workers, tailors, phlebotomists, teachers, school midwives, and other trades. Of the dossiers on the Conspiracy of the Ladder, it can be inferred that the so-called *pardos* and *morenos* and their families came to possess small but solid businesses and capital that allowed them to lead a comfortable life and to educate their children. Some studied abroad where they were allowed, especially the United States and Europe.

In his book, Deschamps discusses the following cases: Félix Barbosa in funerary; José de la Encarnación Muñoz, phlebotomist; Rosalía Portuando, midwife; Juana Pastor, free *parda*, poet, and teacher; Francisco Uribe, the popular fashion tailor; José Agustín Ceballos, foreman of the docks; Claudio Brindisi, director of the Concha de Oro, famed orchestra, and father of the famous violinist Claudio Brindisi de Salas; and many others.

A perspective that is contrary to this social group's reality of existence, roles, and history has branded them as imitators of how the white hegemonic class conducted itself. This is a prejudicial opinion that racializes certain behaviors and customs according to professional and social norms as a legitimate and private property of whites. Naming blacks and *mulatos* imitators promotes the idea that they should remain in their place.

The mockery and derision of the bufo theater included the characters of the *catedráticos*, lettered blacks and academic types, because it aimed to ridicule their image among blacks, *mestizos*, and within society. The very existence of that class and its activity constituted a danger and a challenge to the ideology of white supremacy. It was a way of excluding the groups "of color" from all instances of power, reinforcing the idea that all power and authority belonged exclusively to the dominant white class.

For blacks and *mulatos*: derision and mockery. Who are the blacks with letters? Undoubtedly, those belonging to the aforementioned social establishment. Hence the characterization in bufo theater of black professors. Their emergence and persistence symbolize the strength of this class.

It is interesting to highlight here that it was not only the omnipresent subject of the fear of blacks, nor the ghost of the example of the revolution of Haiti that the Spanish colonialists feared with respect to that class. It is clear that they managed to amass capital, albeit limited, and to develop as an emergent class with an economy outside of the structure that depended on the sugar industry and the relations of slave production. Many of them possessed domestic slaves or dedicated themselves to work on trades owned by their masters. However, they were not inserted into that economy in such a way that their growth depended on slave relations, as it happened with the owners who dominated the sugar industry. This fact could certainly reinforce the abolitionist ideas so feared by the sugar barons. Some incipient capitalist relations were brewing within the black lettered society.

Pedro Deschamps Chapeaux offers the other side of the coin in his aforementioned book. When we analyze the research sources this valuable historian relied upon to leave us documents and a testimony of an important social class, we come to understand the paradoxes of history and his research.

The researcher accessed the information and inventories of the facts listed in the documents that refer to the unfortunate event of the Conspiracy of the Ladder. Perhaps without this nefarious event, the information would not have been gathered in such an organic way, which shows us a fairly complete picture of the economic situation of this social group. The researcher produced documents of seizure of goods of the indicted. These files served to fill what would have been an empty historiography, a difficult achievement with isolated investigations.

This economy developed in a relatively independent way in the field of services, arts, and letters; for this reason, the government and sociologists of the time were greatly concerned.

THE OTHER SIDE OF THE COIN: BLACK AND *MULATA* WOMEN IN TWENTIETH-CENTURY SOCIETY

Since the early days of the slave regime in Cuba, the rest of the Caribbean, and black Americas, along with the slaves who revolted, fled to the mountain, became *cimarrones*, and established communities, black women were always present like the famous Mother Melchora, who was the head of a runaway community in the Sierras of Pinar del Río. The heroine and martyr Fermina Lucumí is well known for leading the triumvirate uprisings that cost her life. She was shot and executed in 1844.

It is not necessary to insist here on the number of black and *mulata* women who stand out in the wars of independence as nurses, aides, and even combatants. Many of them led a life of forced labor on the sugarcane plantations and as domestic slaves where they were also brutally exploited. In the urban areas, they worked as ironers, cooks, maids, and nannies and in the best of cases street vendors. They fulfilled the most disparate trades sometimes to acquire their own freedom or of their children.

Many were able to better themselves. The cases of black and *mestiza* women who owned their own business within the colony, most of the time without male assistance, are interesting cases. The historian María Cristina Hierrezuelo shows another aspect of the other side of the coin to which we refer.[45] In one of two essays that compose this book, the author refers to the economic resources attained by women on their own or with company: "The protocol notary of the time collected innumerable operations of purchase and sale by women 'of color' of slaves, houses, roofing, docks, small plots of land, lowlands for tobacco and haciendas which constitute a sample of what this population owned in the dynamic economy of the territory."[46]

Her research draws attention to the fact that the majority of them remained single. Therefore it is not possible to attribute their accomplishments in business to the help of men or benefits acquired through marriage. But the most relevant detail, in my opinion, is that many were born in Africa. They were brought up as slaves and it is astonishing that they achieved their freedom and then inserted themselves in the economic life of the colony with so many disadvantages because of their status as women and blacks, besides foreign, ex-slaves, and unfamiliar with the language, customs, and laws of the country. Some Africanists would explain that the women came from merchant towns in which women played a part in the market economy. However, were they prepared for business even in such different legal and economic conditions?

In his research, the historian Pedro Deschamps Chapeaux offers enough elements to enrich this image, which we tried to reconstruct offering a redefinition, a rereading of black women and *mulatas* in the colony, so distorted in different media especially in bufo theater that has been among others the most effective and persistent means to distort the image of black and *mulata* women.

In Deschamps's book mentioned earlier, we can collaborate that "numerous neighborhood schools in primary education were attended by women of color, of which the free *parda* poet Juana Pastor excelled."[47] The racial proportion was inclined to favor women of color as doulas and midwives: "The Guide of Foreigners corresponding to the year 1839, records eleven midwives, of which six are of color, among them Rosalía Portuondo, María del Carmen Alfonso and María Vicente Carmona, who have more than five years of service."[48] In addition, in the field of arts and letters we can cite black and *mulata* poets like Juana Pastor and Cristina Ayala. In music, the outstanding Catalina Berroa[49] was the first female composer born in Cuba. She was an instrumentalist and a Trinity professor who composed religious music. She trained her nephew, the famous Lico Jiménez.[50]

As this work shows, there is a clear distinction between "la mulata"—as the archetype of bufo theater—and *mulatas* as true protagonists of labor, struggles, and efforts in colonial society. The *mulata* and *negrito* of bufo as biased archetypes were deployed as a justification to disqualify and exclude blacks, *mulatos*, and *mulatas*, and people "of color" in general, as an integral part of the nationality that emerged in the second half of the nineteenth century.

NOTES

1. *Negrito* is a diminutive of negro, meaning black man. It was also a stock stereotypical character in Cuban bufo theater.
2. The term in the song is *degraciar*, which means to disgrace, demean, but also to cause great physical injury.
3. Guaracha *El negro bueno* by Francisco Valdés Ramírez. First presented June 17, 1868, reaching mass popularity. The character of the *negrito* Candela emerged then (cited by Rine Leal in *La selva oscura. De los bufos a la colonia* [The Dark Jungle: From the Bufo to the Colony] [Havana: Editorial Arte y Literatura, 1982], 17–18).
4. A comedic character that can be grotesque, vulgar, and buffoonish.
5. Alfonzo Pozo Ruiz, "Página personal sobre los esclavos en Sevilla del siglo XVI," University of Seville, http://www.personal.us.es/alporu/histsevilla/esclavos_sevilla.htm.
6. Fernando Ortiz, *Los negros curros* (Havana: Editorial de Ciencias Sociales, 1986), 156.
7. Ruiz, "Página personal sobre los esclavos en Sevilla del siglo XVI."
8. Ortiz, *Los negros curros*, 156.
9. Ruiz, "Página personal sobre los esclavos en Sevilla del siglo XVI."
10. Ibid.
11. An ethnic association or chapter of blacks.
12. *Cachumba* was a type of dance.
13. An instrument that is similar to a tambourine. *Atabalillos* are a type of drum.
14. Ruiz, "Página personal sobre los esclavos en Sevilla del siglo XVI."
15. Ibid.
16. Ortiz, *Los negros curros*, 162.
17. Ibid., 160.

18. Ibid.
19. "Con sapatilla á dos caboz."
20. Take note that these characters appear in the Golden Age of Spanish theater more than three hundred years prior to the bufos from Havana.
21. Ortiz, *Los negros curros*, 163.
22. Ibid., 66.
23. Ibid., 216–20. These translate to: apencarse, the idea of being humbled by one's sins; azotes, to beat or hit hard; apolismar, to cower or to bruise someone by beating them; butuba, food; cabuya, a rope or cord; fajar, argue; jalarse, to get drunk; jelengue, brawl; zafarse, to free oneself; and bilongo/vilongo, the evil eye or a spell.
24. Rine Leal, *La selva oscura*, 415–16.
25. Rine Leal, "Para leer a nuestros clásicos del XIX," "prologue" in *Teatro del siglo XIX* (Havana: Editorial Letras Cubanas, 1996), 10.
26. Costumbrism.
27. Rine Leal, "Para leer a nuestros clásicos del XIX," 14.
28. Ibid., 17.
29. Inés María Martiatu Terry, "Los bailes y el teatro de los negros en el folclore de Cuba, la obra orticiana en el teatro contemporáneo" [The Dances and Theatre of Blacks in the Folklore of Cuba, Ortizian Work in Contemporary Theater], *América Negra*, no. 11, Pontificia Universidad Javeriana, Bogota (1996): 83–92. Also published in *Rito y representación. Los sistemas mágicos religiosos en la cultura cubana contemporánea* (Madrid: Editorial Iberoamericana, Vervuert, 2003), 153–66.
30. Leal, *La selva oscura*, 63–67.
31. Jorge Mañach, *Indagación del choteo*, digital and third edition (Havan: Editorial del Libro Cubano, Colección Clásicos del Pensamiento Cubano siglo XX, 1995).
32. The character Chivichana from the television program *Jura de decier la verdad?* [Do You Vow to Tell the Truth?] is a notable example. The show has resuscitated this character, which for over seventy years since its creation has lowered the self esteem of Cubans. However, what is more disturbing is the character's popularity and the public's identification with it.
33. Rafael Hernández, "1913. Notas sobre raza y desigualidad," *Catauro, Revista Cubana de Antropología* 4, no. 6, Havana (July–December 2002): 99.
34. Enrique Sosa, *La economia en la novela cubana del siglo XIX* (Havana: Editorial Letras Cubanas, 1978).
35. Fernando Ortiz, "Mas cerca de la poesía mulata, escorzos para un estudio," *Revista Bimestre Cubana*, no. 3, Havana (May–June 1939): 439.
36. Onelia Chaveco Chaveco, "Propuesta de una mirada incluyente y no sexista. Las mulatas, un invento profanado?" [Proposing an Inclusive and Nonsexist Gaze: *Mulata* Women, a Profane Invention?], Ponencia en el VII Encuentro Iberoamericano Genero y Comunicación, Havana, May 27 and 29, 2008. Sent by way of Servicio de Noticias de la Mujer de Latinoamérica y el Caribe [SEMILACI, News Services for Latin American and Caribbean Women].
37. See note 5, on bell hooks, in chapter 13, this volume.
38. bell hooks, "Selling Hot Pussy: Representations of Black Female Sexuality in the Cultural Marketplace," *Criterios*, no. 34, Havana (2003): 31.

39. Inés María Martiatu, "La negra y la mulata en el teatro cubano, sus avatares" [Black and *Mulata* Women in Cuban Theater, Her Avatars] (unpublished).

40. Francisco de Arango y Parreño, "Discurso sobre la agricultura de La Habana y medios de fomentarla," in Hortencia Pichardo, *Documentos para la Historia de Cuba* (Havana: Editorial de Ciencias Sociales, 1971).

41. Eduardo Torres-Cuevas and Oscar Loyola Vega, *Historia de Cuba 1492–1898. Formulacion y liberación de la nación* (Havana: Editorial Pueblo y Educación, 2001), 187.

42. Ibid., 188.

43. The prominence achieved by the members of that middle class in the nineteenth and twentieth centuries, despite its disadvantages, is evident in the arts, letters, politics, and culture in general. Figures like Antonio Maceo, Claudio Brindis de Sala or the poet Plácido in the nineteenth century, Nicolás Guillén, Salvador García Agüero, the architect Gustavo Urrutia, and many more in the twentieth century are examples of this.

44. Pedro Descamps Chapeaux and Juan Pérez de la Riva, *Contribuciones a la historia de la gente sin historia* (Havana: Editorial de Ciencias Sociales, 1974).

45. María Cristina Hierrezuelo, *Las olvidadas hijas de Eva* (Santiago de Cuba: Ediciones Santiago, 2006).

46. Hierrezuelo, "Women 'of Color' in Santiaguera Colonial Society," in *Las olvidadas hijas de Eva*, 12.

47. Deschamps Chapeaux and Juan Pérez de la Riva, *Contribuciones a la historia de la gente sin historia*, 8.

48. Ibid., 9.

49. María Catalina Prudencia de Berrora Ojeda (1849–1911) (cited by Alicia Valdés Cantero in *Con música, texto y presencia de mujer. Diccionario de mujeres notables en la música cubana* [Havana: Ediciones Unión, 2005], 94–95).

50. José Manuel Jiménez [Lico]: (Trinidad, 1851–Hamburg, 1917). Pianist and composer. Member of a family of outstanding *mulato* musicians. He studied piano in Germany and France and played concerts with great success in the capitals throughout Europe. He settled in Hamburg where he died.

BIBLIOGRAPHY

Arango y Parreño, Francisco de. 1971. "Discurso sobre la agricultura de La Habana y medios de fomentarla." In *Documentos para la Historia de Cuba* by Hortencia Pichardo. Havana: Editorial de Ciencias Sociales.

Chaveco Chaveco, Onelia. 2008. *Propuesta de una mirada incluyente y no sexista. Las mulatas, un invento profanado?* Havana: Ponencia en el VII Encuentro Iberoamericano Genero y Comunicación, May 27 and 29.

Descamps Chapeaux, Pedro, and Juan Pérez de la Riva. 1974. *Contribuciones a la historia de la gente sin historia.* Havana: Editorial de Ciencias Sociales.

Hernández, Rafael. 2002. "1913. Notas sobre raza y desigualidad." *Catauro, Revista Cubana de Antropología*, 4, no. 6 (July–December). Havana.

Hierrezuelo, María Cristina. 2006. *Las olvidadas hijas de Eva*. Santiago de Cuba: Ediciones Santiago.
hooks, bell. 2003. "Selling Hot Pussy: Representations of Black Female Sexuality in the Cultural Marketplace." *Criterios*, no. 34. Havana.
Leal, Rine. 1982. *La selva oscura. De los bufos a la colonia*. Havana: Editorial Arte y Literatura.
———. 1996. "Para leer a nuestros clásicos del XIX." In "Prologue" in *Teatro del siglo XIX*. Havana: Editorial Letras Cubanas.
Mañach, Jorge. 1995. *Indagación del choteo*. Digital and third edition. Havana: Editorial del Libro Cubano, Colección Clásicos del Pensamiento Cubano siglo XX.
Martiatu Terry, Inés María. 1996. "Los bailes y el teatro de los negros en el folclore de Cuba, la obra orticiana en el teatro contemporáneo." *América Negra*, no. 11. Javeriana, Bogota: Pontificia Universidad.
———. 2003. "Los bailes y el teatro de los negros en el folclore de Cuba, la obra orticiana en el teatro contemporáneo." In *Rito y representación. Los sistemas mágicos religiosos en la cultura cubana contemporánea*. Madrid: Editorial Iberoamericana.
Ortiz, Fernando. 1939. "Mas cerca de la poesía mulata, escorzos para un estudio." *Revista Bimestre Cubana*, no. 3 (May–June). Havana.
———. 1986. *Los negros curros*. Havana: Editorial de Ciencias Sociales.
Sosa, Enrique. 1978. *La economia en la novela cubana del siglo XIX*. Havana: Editorial Letras Cubanas.
Pozo Ruiz, Alfonso. "Página personal sobre los esclavos en Sevilla del siglo XVI." University of Seville. http:personal.us.es/alporu/histsevilla/esclavos_sevilla.htm.
Torres-Cuevas, Eduardo, and Oscar Loyola Vega. 2001. *Historia de Cuba 1492–1898. Formulación y liberacion de la nación*. Havana: Editorial Pueblo y Educación.
Valdes Cantero, Alicia. 2005. *Con musica, texto y presencia de mujer. Diccionario de mujeres notables en la música cubana*. Havana: Ediciones Unión.

Chapter 27

Popular Theater and Collective Resistance

Fátima de la Caridad Patterson

Grupo Macubá was founded May 1992 at the twelfth Festival of the Caribbean, in part inspired by the accumulation of visual information during our struggle in organizing the festival throughout the years and as part of our heritage of the Cabildo Santiago Theater. This group was paradigmatic in the theatrical framework of our country, although not sufficiently quoted or recognized. What has holding on to this aspect of popular culture cost us? How much have we lost or gained according to the angle we take?

Many things would have to be said, many accounts to make. All our efforts have been directed to themes not always recognized or validated as fundamental elements in the processes of formation or breakdown of our social network, marginality, women, and death. Why create a character out of death? It is something that is always present. Death is something that cohabitates with daily life, with marginalization, and that stalks women as a vulnerable element or as the most vulnerable in the list that we have cited.

Sixteen years ago, when we decided to take this path, we knew we were going to have to deal with many things, among them the temptations of banality, the misunderstanding by elites and nonelites, and our own falls and confusion. However, we knew that there was something or someone that would mark our way, the route toward clear communication without any taboos, to tell us if we were in the right, if we were trying to make a lie credible, or whether we were truly trying to discover the truth, what would be our truth or theirs. Our and their truths would become so mixed that these no longer would be their truth or ours solely but a shared truth, the one we were searching for without having to identify ourselves. What we didn't know was that we shared the same truth that hurt both of us the same way because we were, or are, the same.

Beginning the work with this group of people to immerse ourselves in the framework provided by traditional popular cultures was a challenge. To start with, we had to choose not to lose ourselves in the fabric of the group and then to decide on the which, how, why, and for what—because forms and expressive modes would become interchanged substantially—in establishing the foundation of the group. We had to reach an agreement on which themes to prioritize and to aim for in clarifying our ideas in doing the work of deep observation. This work needed to be done during the whole process prior to the founding of the Festival of the Caribbean, which at that time was named the Festival of Performing Arts of Caribbean Origin. We began to draw relations among essential elements:

Popular religion.
Marginality.
Women's roles in these frameworks.
The roles of blacks, *mestizos*, and whites.
Conditions of life.
Cultural tastes and preferences.
The relation of life and death.
Spaces of representation.
The actor.
The public.

Religiousness, in intermixing in a diverse way its rites and traditions of conga, Yoruba, spiritism, and what we had been able to observe in *Vodú*, gave us a way to delve into the analysis of expressive forms. The trance and semi-vigil became tools; all the dances gave us a foundation for body movements that led us to locate ourselves in a common gesture expressed in our geographical region with a deep sense of identity. We journeyed toward our subconscious to make it conscious.

Women became a thematic priority by the fact that the majority of the group was women and by the circumstances in which women have been mired throughout history. We thus would privilege this woman who had not been made visible by her "social relevance," the invisible woman that was black, *mestiza*, or white.

We found ourselves as protagonists of this phenomenon, generally as it related to blacks and the history of slavery, uprooting, and its consequences in what it unleashed in the relationships with others, especially whites, and in the aspirations of *mestizos*.

CONDITIONS OF LIFE

What significance did death have for those people or what significance did death have in life if its terms were subverted or not? This is when the theme of death became a priority for the group.

Everything was becoming clearer, but there was an important decision that remained to be answered: What would be our space? Would it be the street like when we did *teatro de relaciones* [street theater], or the conventional theater room, as when we began to think differently on the same theme of street theater? We had to decide and so decided upon symbiosis, an alternative space that we sometimes tried to turn into theater and also took it to the street that offered us an audience that would later accompany us to the theater or not, but who provided us with live communication that helped us to continue to identify issues and causes.

The actor became part of a framework that drew from their deepest knowledge of popular cultural traditions, which included ways of expression (dances, songs, and religious practices). Contrary to thought, actors held expressive possibilities. The knowledge that they had about their culture was at times surprising. They began to create codes as a group that allowed us quick and clear communication among us and with the majority of the public to whom we directed ourselves. In the beginning, some actors were questioned and taken for granted as equals to other actors.

Our first work of what would be the embryo of the Macubá group was the text "Repique por Mafifa o la Última campanera" [Ringing for Mafifa or the Last Bell Ringer] based on the life of Gladys Linares, bell ringer of the Conga de los Hoyos. This last group was emblematic of our city, a drum group that was all male, except during the time that Gladys belonged to it. The second attempt at serious communication was with "N'fumbis loas y orichas," a mixture of Antillean poetry, songs, and dances combined with tales, riddles, puns, etc., that have given us our popular imaginary. The communication was immediate, and the proposal was received with euphoria when it premiered at the Festival of the Caribbean in 1992. Our shows became more and more complex but still faithful to tradition. Amplifying our process of inquiry and rescue gave us better tools to work.

To concretize in images the slave voyages that arrived at our shores, a character that would be in one way or another recurrent in our works, the union of the Hispanic elements, the processes of struggle, became a long journey that took us more than ten years.

In all this framework, we were able to reach important moments that addressed our initial objectives, which above all began to be noted from 2003, with the staging of scenes like from "Ayé N'fumbi o" [World of the

Dead]; this piece is about women in the environment of Santiago de Cuba, the Santiaguera quarters, and its relationship with signs and symbols taken from the mixture of spiritism and Santeria. *El espiritista* dealt with the history on the exclusion of humans because of their sexual preference and religious beliefs and showed us a philosophy of survival; *Mamarrachos* showcased the history of the foundation of the city and its transformations until today with the inclusion of current folk dances and contemporary choreographic designs; *Restos en la noche* as a version of *La noche de los asesinos*. Except for the last piece, all of the above are original ideas of the directors of the shows.

At this moment, Macubá counts on two artistic directors, a playwright, and the assistance of researchers, sociologists, investigators, and specialists who link us to our community because we have the active participation of the informants that are part of our public. When I decided to call this work "popular theater" or "group resistance," I wanted to be able to share in an intimate way the tour of a group of *locos* [crazies] that through their connection with traditional popular culture and a close relationship with the Festival of the Caribbean has allowed it to resist the onslaughts that this part of the heritage of the people has been submitted to. It has been able to resist and survive. Because we are part of popular theater, and because we are a living expression of the people that generate it and make it what it is, we have the responsibility to give our people a vision that reflects on our problems, on our way of living and our way of dying, so that together we can find solutions or alternatives of group resistance, because it is also in resistance that gives life. Aché.

Chapter 28

Catalina Berroa, the Audacious Trinidadian

First Female Composer of "Cultured" Music in the Nineteenth Century

Isabel González Sauto

Lydia Cabrera recounts that a very old friend warned her on the eve before she left for Trinidad, Cuba, around 1877, that she should be careful drinking the water of Táyaba in the company of women if she wanted to return to her town. This story implies a dual spell: from the water of the river, but also by the women. Trinidadian women were notorious for their beauty; however more likely the legend refers to their power of seduction. Their confidence and highly attractive personalities were taken to the extreme by the implication that they were able to cast a "spell."

One of those personalities was Catalina Berroa, born in 1844. She has been considered according to the *Dictionary of Notable Women in Cuban Music* "the first female composer born in Cuba and the founder of the musical movement in [the town of] Trinidad."[1] We do not know if she was beautiful; however, she appeared to have a strong temperament, determination, and an obvious artistic sensitivity.

She was endowed and prepared for an exceptional destiny as an independent woman, with the mentality of being a provider who did not depend on marriage to give meaning to her life. She learned how to perfectly play the mandolin, violin, clarinet, and flute. She played the organ for two churches and led the choir of the Santísima Trinidad Church.

Catalina Berroa's life developed in an extremely complex context in which different social strata coexisted in the midst of the colonial and slaver regime. One of them was the so-called middle class "of color." They were educated free blacks and *mulatos* with money, businesses, and professions that since the eighteenth century had reached a certain economic, technical, and cultural level and social representation.

Catalina Berroa belonged to this class. This class played a prominent role in music and from which great figures emerged such as Claudio Brindis, director of the Concha de Oro, famed orchestra leader and father of the famous violinist Claudio Brindis de Salas. Whole families devoted themselves to the musical art, including the Jiménez family related to Berroa. Hence, given the exemplary music education that this Trinidadian acquired, it is not strange that she would excel brilliantly as a composer, instrumentalist, and professor.

Middle- and upper-class white families viewed art and letters as attributes to highlight femininity and not as a profession for women. However, there were always some exceptions like the most famous Cuban writer, Gertrudis Gómez de Avellaneda.

Black and *mulata* women, on the contrary, saw performative arts as a profession or a way of life; such was the case with Berroa. Evidently her family trained her so that she could stand up for herself in life, to maintain a simple and tranquil appearance in Trinidad. From the time of her birth to the end of the war in 1868, Trinidad flourished as a cradle of great fortunes basically created from sugarcane plantations.

Named at birth María Catalina Prudencia Román de Berroa Ojeda, there is no doubt that prudence did not ruin her audacity because it did not limit her to the church, which was considered the natural environment for women of this time. She definitely fulfilled her ambition, and with great prestige significantly exceeded it. She was so bold as to play violin in the Brunet Theatre for several years and in the Orchestra Dávila that interpreted more than one of her compositions. It is here that this black woman, Catalina Berroa, surpassed anything common. As a multi-instrumentalist, she did not withhold her talents, something that for women was simply amazing in music or any other medium.

Of course, she composed religious works for the masses and celebrations, but most remarkable were her songs for voice and guitar that she would so well interpret: *La trinitaria* in 1867, *Canción a Belisa y La Josefa* in 1902, *Condenado, El talismán, La conciencia, La súplica, Rosa gentil*, all registered in the National Museum of Music, according to the aforementioned researcher and musicologist. Her two *guarachas* and three waltzes with very Cuban titles are well known: *De La Habana al Cerro, La cena del gato, El negro Miguel, Cecilia y las flores*.

As I already stated, we do not know anything about her appearance, and this has meaning. An older sister of hers, it is unknown if she was the only one, married a famous Trinidadian violinist, José Julián Jiménez (Trinidad, 1823–Havana, 1898), father of the cellist Nicasio and the renowned pianist José Manuel (Lico) Jiménez (Trinidad, 1851–Hamburg, Germany 1917) who was born when Catalina was seven years old. Lico, her nephew, accompanied the German celloist Karl Werner for fifteen years. Werner was visiting Trinidad during his Cuban sojourn—mainly in Havana—when he "discovered the genius and decided the fate of our countryman,"[2] according to Guillermo M. Tomás.

The astonished German proposed decisively to send him to Europe in 1867, which was made possible by the patronage of the powerful Justo Germán Cantero and Monserrate de Lara and also because of Juan Guillermo Béquer and Smith. Smith was an American who Hispanicized his patronym Béquer to Baker. Well, guess who taught the child Lico to play the piano? Of course, it was his aunt Catalina, his mother's sister. She definitely taught many others as well because that profession enabled a livelihood that could offer her independence. However, no other reason was needed to teach someone as talented as Lico.

I imagine Catalina in her twenties, walking early morning on the cobbled streets composed of smooth flat river stones, crossing the square to meet her commitments in Saint Francis of Assisi or the Parroquial Mayor Church. After lunch and a nap, she would give her classes to students who saw in music a way of life possible for *pardos* and *morenos* of that era prior to the first *carga al machete* [Charge of the Machete]. After evening mass, orchestra rehearsals, and some dreamy evenings, it would be performance time. This was a well-coordinated routine at the time. Catalina must have had fun, frank laughter, and natural conversation. She chose to be active and avoid a long wait for a husband or children. This greatly talented woman greeted everyone in her Trinidadian bustle. She was well known and would reach such acclaim that she presided in her forties in the Philharmonic section of the *Sociedad La Luz* in 1891. The society offered instruction and promoted the "overcoming" of people "of color" but using white societies as a model.

She was undoubtedly a character, almost an institution in Trinidad, which would protect her from disparages motivated by her race and sex, disadvantages that she was trained to overcome. However, all her effort and mastery did not earn her a patronage as it happened with her brother-in-law and later with her nephew. She could not stand for this. Did not Cantero, Borrel, Béquer, and others believe she deserved it? Was she a timid woman, lacking personality? Why was her work and ability discarded? The response is very simple: she probably was not a beautiful woman, a capital sin that still ensnares women today. It is not just that she was black and female, worse, it was by chance that she did not have physical beauty, because surely she was not lacking in grace. Was she a patriotic Cuban woman, tall, short, thin, thick, flat, busty? How did she style her unruly hair? What size were her feet? Some might think that these are trivial factors, but it has never been so for women. Additionally, although patterns of beauty are varied, everyone reacts to the canon. I am confident that she developed her talent to make herself notable for her creativity and musicality.

In 1844 when Catalina was born, Trinidad was one of the wealthiest centers on the island. Pianos would have arrived by the port of Casilda and all the other musical instruments were essential for the comfort of the great families, for their evening concerts or soirées in their palaces that still stand today. She was around four years of age when the Mine Conspiracy of the Cuban Rose or of Trinidad failed, led by Narciso López. At the age of seven, José Isidoro de Armenteros and two companions of martyrdom and glory were shot at Mano del Negro. Then when she was twenty-four came the war of '68, which ruined Trinidad, a zone where Pedro Iznaga and Borrell owned five mills, thirteen hundred slaves, and a thousand yoked oxen.

One year before the beginning of the Ten Years' War, Catalina's nephews Lico and Nicasio landed in Europe. They arrived in Hamburg with Werner's letter of introduction. The city would be hospitable to the brothers Jiménez Berroa. Providentially, they found the wise and paternal direction of the famous Armbrust.

In Hamburg, they cultivated their talent and completed a training with the tools that Catalina Berroa had already given them in developing their musical intelligence. Later, when they culminated their musical studies, their father joined them. They created a famous trio of chamber music called Trio de los Negros, with which they attained great fame, first in Germany and later in Paris. After having passed through the Hamburg Conservatory and only six months after their arrival, they won first prize in the Conservatory of Paris awarded by a jury made up of Charles Gounod, Jules Massenet, and Camille Saint Saëns. Such fame in Paris preceded their performance in Cuba, which was extraordinarily celebrated and welcomed. Ignacio Cervantes said of Lico, "He's a first-class pianist." Carpentier said that as a composer, "He was the first Cuban musician to tackle the lied. The best of his production is in his *Valse Caprice, Solitude, Elegía, Murmullo del céfiro.*" However, dilettantes that opposed Lico Jiménez began making detracting and absurd comparisons between him and Espadero, which according to Guillermo Tomás would be like comparing Mendelssohn to Schumann. He said:

> If Espadero attained among us a greater aura of glory, it was made possible by the environment of those times and because of his social and economic independence and the extreme way he isolated himself. Had he started his artistic career following that sad and disappointing "pact of the Zanjón" poor and desolate, carrying on his face the distinctive seal of belonging to a race made object of the most foolish and cruel provisions, he undeniably would have had worse luck than Jiménez. But Jiménez was able to return to Europe where "the habit does not make the monk."[3]

For Guillermo Tomás:

> Jiménez only remembered what after his successes made his spirit stronger. The worst passions, most clumsy appetites, envy, slander, hypocrisy, all the low bases of a sick consciousness, carried their mud to the soul of this great artist: sometimes in suspecting the success of foreigners, others by instinct of conservation with vested interests—reputations built on sand—many by ignorance and by arrogance (although this is a corollary of the first), more so because of the poor scruples of race, and, almost always by the frivolous indifference of those who respond more to aristocratic pruritus than to deep spiritual and aesthetic yearnings. And when the admirable artist sank into misery, alone with his genius, without influential friends, amid the indifference of his countrymen, seeking in artificial procedures to sooth the immense pain of his heart, he was ridiculed with the gesture, applying to him, as if it was a minor molestation, the epithets most degrading to his race and his habits.
>
> For those of us who witnessed the inferred grievances to the greatest of our artists, for whom we saw pain prematurely traverse that beautiful forehead, which had already been weathered by fame, for those of us who knew how to admire his inexhaustible love for the ungrateful homeland and the stoic resignation that in the midst of his abandonment, I remembered the painful verse: "I will weep, but I will love my weeping and my sorrow" for those of us who loved and accompanied him in the eternal sad hours as in the merry hours of his bitter sojourn from Cuba, the arrival of the year of 1890 was certainly a blessing from heaven—oh shame!—José Manuel Jiménez was returned to Europe."
>
> There in old Germany, he renewed his brilliant accomplishments, he reconquered it rather, because it was like his life started anew, in which he triumphed socially and artistically like a giant.
>
> There in old Germany, he formed his home, saw his children born. There, he conceived his richest hopes, nourished his spirit and strengthened his culture. But at all times, in the hours of glory, the long vigils of winter and in the moments of family tenderness, he always remembered Cuba, "without aversion, without resentment."[4]

Even with his fame and endorsements, and though he served as director of the Conservatory of Hamburg to the end of his life, Lico suffered in Cuba. What would have happened if Catalina Berroa would have dared to leave the boundaries of Trinidad? It might have destroyed her. She opted for a provincial routine, which she defeated with the brilliance of her compositions. Trinidad came to respect her. When she died in 1911, she could not have foreseen the fortuitousness of the full circle of her life because she did not get to witness her great-niece, Manuela Jiménez, perform in the National Theater (today García Lorca Hall of the Great Theater of Havana). A native of Hamburg and daughter of Lico Jiménez the musician, pianist, and organist, she performed on January 22, 1933. She interpreted César Franck's *Symphonic*

Variations for Piano And Orchestra, accompanied by the Philharmonic Orchestra of Havana directed by Amadeo Roldán, and whose encore was the vals capricho *Homage to Milanese* by Lico Jiménez. A victory fulfilled by the daughter of her best disciple.

Lico would have felt proud to see his daughter succeed in Havana. This was also Catalina Berroa's triumph, the audacious Trinidadian that by composing music laughed at her disadvantages as a woman, as a black woman, and for not being a great beauty, a triple leap taken from her talent toward life.

NOTES

1. Alicia Valdés Cantero, *Diccionario de mujeres notables en la música cubana* (Havana: Ediciones Unión, 2005).
2. Guillermo M. Tomás, *Musicalia*, Havana, January–February 1929, no. 5, 157.
3. Ibid.
4. Ibid.

BIBLIOGRAPHY

De Varona, Esteban A. 1946. *Trinidad de Cuba*. Havana: Alfa.
Giro, Radames. 2009. *Diccionario enciclopédico de la música en Cuba*. Second edition. Havana: Editorial Letras Cubanas.
Montejo Arrechea, Carmen. 2004. *Sociedades negras en Cuba 1878–1960*. Havana: Editorial de Ciencias Sociales.
Tomás, Guillermo M. 1929. *Musicalia*. January–February, no. 5. Havana.
———. 1929. *Musicalia*. March–April, no. 6. Havana.
Valdés Cantero, Alicia. 2005. *Diccionario de mujeres notables en la música cubana*. Havana: Ediciones Unión.

Chapter 29

The Marathon Exists for Both Men and Women

Edelvis López Zaldívar

From her artistic stature, Maestra María Elena Mendiola is impressive and moving on stage. The years of experience and great sensibility always accompany her on the podium. Her *mestizaje* has never prevented her from being active either in life or in her profession, which she does not define through race and gender, real issues for society and mass media: "I have always accomplished my work recognizing myself as a musician and conductor. To think otherwise seems like an extreme archaism."

Few artists can undertake so many different and complementary roles and all satisfactorily: orchestra director, musical pedagogue, cultural promoter, and musical critic. She is also in charge of management positions at the National Center of Concert Music and the Higher Institute of Art. Maestra Mendiola's exquisite and rigorous selection of her repertoire is evident throughout all of her performances. She interprets these according to the type of musical format she is presenting and the characteristics that are integral to each piece.

"Each and every time that I create a program for a concert I put a lot of thought into it because in a live concert, as much as on a disc, balance is very important, the contrasts and the diversity of styles included, although within that diversity, you have to look for a sense of harmony.

"I consider it very important to offer the public a diverse program that is at the same time coherent and that will keep them interested in what we are playing in the concert hall from start to finish. When a program has not been chosen well, there is an element that I have observed in the public's reaction that is an unmistakable: people start to fidget in their seats, look to change their position on more than one occasion, or begin to look around and observe the rest of the attendants or even worse, they look up at the ceiling: these are sure signs of tedium which must be avoided at all costs."

She has been the titular director of the Soloists of Havana since 2009. Additionally, she saw the birth of this group:

"Soloists of Havana is an endearing name for me to which I am closely linked from its very emergence, when I did not even remotely think that I would become its titular director. I attained this position, first of all, because of the artistic, and professional confidence that Maestro Iván Valiente has always had in me. As founder and CEO, he has invited me often to lead the collective and has let me have a say from the beginning. Also, because since its birth, it has had members who are dear to me. Some of them because their professional roles have progressed to undoubtedly superior positions such as concertino-founder, the violinist Reynier Guerrero. Others have moved on because they have left us forever, or rather, because a sad blow has taken them away from us. The violinist Niuris Naranjo was another one of the orchestra's brilliant concertinos. She died in a tragic car accident. There are many others that are today in various parts of the world measuring their strengths in the professional field and drawing from their years of experience as Soloists.

"Either way, the different cohorts that have gone through demonstrate without a doubt, and I dare to affirm an opinion shared by the musical community in Cuba (and among them the dilettante too), is that the Soloist's performances from start to finish, execute the musical pieces with a level of tuning that transcends what is correct, a successful differentiation of styles and an interpretative delivery of high caliber, if I can say without blushing. Of which, I do not deny that I have been very proud, I repeat, from the beginning."

Specialists like composer, professor, performer, and music critic Juan Piñera in an article published by CMBF National Musical Radio, where he has other professional roles such as a writer and director of programming of radio, affirmed that La Mendiola mastered her performances: "María Elena Mendiola's principal task was indispensable. She articulated organically the discursive elements of the piano and directed in a very organized and disciplined way the body of the orchestra." He was referring expressively to Ernest Bloch's *Concerto Grosso for Piano Obligato and String Orchestra*, which had as an invited pianist Javier Rodríguez, who accompanied Soloists of Havana.

Every performance is like that, showing rigor, talent, and mastery, apart from the culture that it conveys in the montages of scores by the National Symphony Orchestra of Cuba and the Chamber Orchestra of Havana, which has over three years of impressive performances.

ALWAYS A PEDAGOGUE

In a recent interview by CMBF National Musical Radio, the Maestra commented:

"Teaching is a gift I was born with. Today I have become more accustomed to seeing how my students boast of having been my students, something I found strange in the beginning. The thing is that each class I give, I teach it as if I was going to die the next day and I try to leave students as well prepared as possible. I am very, very demanding, and I have the reputation of being 'hard,' but my students adapt very quickly to the quality of my teaching, come to understand why and, in the end, always end up thanking me. Teaching is something I enjoy very much, and I am pleased to see that they enjoy it too."

There are several outstanding names among her students, who are today professionals leading different symphonic groups on the island, the new generation of conductors are, in the vast majority, women.

"Actually, the percentage of women conductors in the Greater Antilles is a phenomenon worthy of study by sociologists. Zenaida Romeu and I, who sealed the orchestral direction in Cuba as pioneers in the era of women at the podium, began an avalanche that to today has not ended.

"Every year, when the admissions season arrives at the art institute, Superior de Arte, Maestro Guido López-Gavilán, looks through the applicant files which he soon closes disappointed, saying: 'Not a single male in all of these, how terrible.' Today, it no longer surprises us that we are the overwhelming majority. What is a fact, however, is that women who opt for this career must have among her qualities, a gift of natural leadership, a strong character, no timidity, and also have the quality of being well organized and disciplined with her time. I also believe that an orchestra director is, additionally, an actor who should be able to portray any character, masculine or feminine, with the capacity to be both a gladiator and a damsel."

As general coordinator of the Program for the Development of Symphonic Music in Cuba, how does this work relate to all your other occupations?

"The time that I dedicate to the Program for Symphonic Development.... Really, is not separate from my daily agenda. However, I need more than twenty-four hours, especially since all the directors that are part of the program (the majority of whom are very young), and the professionals who are in the final years of their career as orchestra directors in the Instituto Superior de Arte, do not ask me permission, but simply invade me daily, either with telephone consultations of more than one hour or appearing in my house so that I can advise them on steps the repertoire should undertake, to solving daily challenges dealing with the musicians' praxis (that is, understanding them as workers: human beings), to helping them solve issues with the authorities of their territories, to how to successfully resolve the assembly of a piece or a very difficult work of performance. . . . But it is something I do with pleasure, because I see this work as an extension of my soul as a teacher."

ART AND VIRTUE

The Maestra committedly brings respect and love to a musical career that she developed with courage and tenacity to achieve high goals such as the spectacle of the 1812 Overture *by Piotr Ilyich Tchaikovsky, which was a successful event:*

"The live performance of Tchaikovsky's *1812 Overture* and *Tres Pequeños Poemas* by Amadeo Roldán in the Plaza de la Revolución Calixto García, with the Symphonic Orchestra of Holguin, alongside its provincial band and the staff of the Eastern Army, including the army's gunners and canons with actual detonations in the final part of the work, was a wonderful experience that I will always remember as an important and very beautiful moment of my career.

"I remember that I made many objections to the director general of the orchestra, violist Harold Ricardo, when he called me with their proposal, wanting to stage the *1812 Overture* in the gala opening of the XXV Concert Day that is celebrated every year in that city.

"Picture it! In an open-air plaza! And where is the microphone? And what are we going to do about the orchestra that has missing members? And where are we going to practice? But none of that stopped the Holguin people. They found substitute musicians (and some of the best on the Island), so that the orchestra grew to eighty-five musicians.

"Cultural workers and not just orchestra musicians in the province worked together to stage the event. They invited media, television, the press, and even held fireworks which became the climax to that memorable moment. It is a pity that not all of the territories of the country show that level of dedication and love for culture in that same way.

"Among the emotional moments that I remember of my career in particular is Gala *Quiéreme Mucho*[1] that I presented together with Omara Portuondo and the National Symphony Orchestra of Cuba in the Sala Avellaneda of the National Theatre of Cuba in 1998, on the 14th of February, the day of love. It was a beautiful project, but it had a great risk: Omara was afraid of singing live with the symphony, and on my behalf, I could not afford to make any mistakes, which fortunately did not happen.

"Also, another show with the National Symphony Orchestra of Cuba, with a theme that corresponded to its title 'Love and Cinema,' which brought together classics such as *Prelude* of *Tristan and Isolde* by Richard Wagner, *Romeo and Juliet* by Piotr Ilyich Tchaikovsky, its American musical version of the same work by Shakespeare, *West Side Story* by Leonard Bernstein, and *Cinema Paradiso* by Ennio Morricone. The show did not feature a soloist nor did it include any important national musical figure with the power to draw a large audience. I will never forget that around eleven in the morning the head of the scene who is also my friend, Alejandro Banegas, came to the dressing room to tell me: 'Maestra: You have to wait a little longer, because there is a long line at the box office and most of the public is still entering.' And I answered him: 'You must be joking, I'm sure there's no one there.' To which he replied, 'So there's no one there? Go see for yourself at the side of the stage and see if there's no one there.'

"Another performance that I will never forget was recently on my national tour of 2009 with Soloists of Havana on the last performance of the tour in the city of Las Tunas. It had rained a lot that afternoon and I thought that that plaza would not pay much attention to concert music and therefore would be poorly attended. I was so surprised when I got on stage to see a crowded audience that applauded for us deliriously.

"That is why I share an expression of the always great Master of violin, Bulgarian Radosvet Boyadjiev who lived many years in Cuba: You have to be prepared and play with equal rigor in Carnegie Hall as in the Pico Turquino."

CUBAN CLASSICS OF THE NINETEENTH CENTURY

Among her greatest joys are her first CD and DVD *Clásicos cubanos del siglo XIX*, which won awards in the Concert Music and Making Off categories at the XIII International Fair Cubadisco 2009. Producciones Colibrí of the Cuban Institute of Music decided to take a bet on the invaluable, extraordinary material in recording the discography of the nation about a period of formation of Cuban identity.

"I have had the satisfaction of producing records by the National Symphony Orchestra of Cuba directed by Maestros Leo Brouwer and Ivan del Prado. It was precisely all this experience that allowed me to produce my own album as Orchestra director: *Clásicos cubanos del siglo XIX* with my orchestra, Soloists of Havana, for which I received two awards from Cubadisco 2009."

Moreover, her vast career as a musical producer for more than twenty years with the firm EGREM has brought her other laurels, some of which are unique such as *The Guitarist Oeuvres of Leo Brouwer*, a collection in eight volumes, which won Cubadisco's Grand Prize in 2001; *A todo Piano*, winner in the compilation category section; and *Cuban Classics Volume II and III*, winner in the symphonic music category of Cubadisco edition 2003.

The list of awards grew with *Líricos cubanas, volumen I y II* that won the Special Prize in Cubadisco 2004 and *Álbum de oro, Jorge Luis Prats*, which in the soloist concert category, 2005 edition.

Regarding areas of specialization, she responded:

"Musical production is a summation of various factors, all of which are important. The producer of an album is the equivalent of a film director, only that album producers don't yell 'Cut!' but instead tell the sound engineer, 'Stop.' But to say that, the producer needs to know why what was being recorded does not work, either because it was out of tune, or the instruments did not all enter simultaneously, noise was heard, or there was a musician that was not keeping time. It is a job that demands a great level of auditory alertness which is why it is so fatiguing. And that is just one aspect of the job. A preliminary part is the selection of the repertoire, choosing which musician to invite, which chorus to use, which engineers to work with, choosing the right orchestra members (such as in the case of recording a singer), and assigning the right pieces to each according to their individual strengths, within the theme or themes that must be orchestrated. Then, there is the editing phase, mixing and mastering, in which the producer must have a sound judgment to know which part of the project must be left to the engineer. Ultimately, it is a very complex job though it is as interesting as it is exhausting.

TWO PROFILES OF AN ARTIST

"I have developed two profiles within musical production: the production of archives, a task I undertook since 1999 when I started to work on the anthology *La obra guitarrísta de Leo Brouwer* which gave me the surprise (and satisfaction) of winning the Cubadisco Grand Prize in 2001. It was an extremely complex project because in this collection, I brought together not all, but a good part of the work by guitarist Brouwer who that year was given the Manuel de Falla Award in Spain for the body of his work, which paradoxically had never been recorded in his country. His works were very heterogeneous recordings, some with four decades of difference in their recording date, some mono, others stereo, some live, others studio, in short, getting a cohesive sound as much as possible from those recordings was a strenuous task.

"Thus, this is how the Parnassus Collection of EGREM was born which now consists of more than thirty CDs. I was awarded several prizes or nominations for subsequent works in that collection from other editions of

Cubadisco. Just now, I am completing another anthology (the fifth in my series), which is called *Obras maestras de los Clásicos Cubanos* in six volumes that bring together the most significant creations by Cuban composers of the twentieth century in different genres: music for solo instruments, chamber music, choral music, vocal and mood, and symphonic music which encompass the last two volumes of the anthology.

"And the other aspect that I have deployed is to produce new studio recordings and curiously in genres as diverse as jazz (Roberto Fonseca), instrumental music (Quinteto Diapasón and Alejandro Valdés, guitarist), vocals, and of course concert music."

CULTURAL PROMOTER

Within the current musical panorama in Cuba, she also stands out as a tireless promoter of festivals as an artistic director. For several years, many lovers of good music have chosen the Guitar Festival Americana Arias (Biennial), a renewed and beautiful project that she proposed and organized in each edition from the repertoire, the instrumentalists, and the event program.

Two events at the national level, the Chamber Music Festival and the Symphonic Orchestra Forum, have counted on her ability and ingenuity. First, they have depended on her as an interpreter and producer, and second, as the technical director during their four conventions (2004 to 2007).

María Elena Mendiola chose to contribute to the greater knowledge of concert music on national television and thus to increase the genre's audience through the television show *¿Puedo pasar?* The show runs for forty-two minutes and has six episodes. From writing the script to hosting, the show brings us closer to renowned figures at the national and international level, revealing their artistic value, especially between music and cinema. The show is seasoned with timely anecdotes and audiovisual materials of high quality with excellent images.

Meanwhile, she has also continued to write for specialized publications like *Clave, Salsa Cubana, Tropicana Internacional,* and *Pulso Latino.* Additionally, she shares her skill as musical critic in numerous Discography Notes. These texts accompany the discs and complement the music, the jewel, that each disc contains. *Canciones inéditas* (Latin Grammy Award, 2002) by Chucho Valdés and *Cancionero cubano* which won her the Cubadisco prize 2006 in the category of Discography Notes are two examples of the recognition of her work in this area.

The media speaks a lot on race and gender, propelling society into controversy at all levels. Turning to the initial question, she said, "It is true that this career entails certain physical challenges, however these are not related to force specifically, but to resistance. And if we analyze the issue of resistance, we should stop and consider that the race in the marathon exists equally for men and women."

NOTE

1. Song title that translates to *Love Me Very Much.*

Chapter 30

Making One's Dreams Come True Is Not the Same as Dreaming

María Elena Mendiola

Her dreams were pillars on which she built her life. Her dreams did not remain fantasies but became the columns to her own Parthenon.

Tania León (Havana, 1943) is a composer, pianist, orchestra director, professor, and Cuban cultural ambassador in the United States, her adopted country for the last four decades. She is a black woman endowed with great talent. Her belief in her own talent has sustained her faith in her work and her decisive dedication to her life's work with absolute commitment. Her path has been great, encouraged by her own unstoppable steps.

She began her musical training in Cuba at the Peyrellade Conservatory and the National Conservatory. Additionally, she also took business administration, which helped her to get her first job in the United States in 1967 though she did not speak English. She arrived in the United States with almost nothing beside her huge goals. Shortly after her arrival, she moved to New York, where she found shelter in a tiny apartment occupied by several musicians.

Early on she received indispensable assistance. An organization dedicated to helping immigrant professionals, after an initial interview, advised her to apply to the New York College of Music, where she immediately obtained a scholarship, beginning a career that has not stopped since. After only one semester of studies, the institution itself sent her to New York University, where in addition to revalidating her knowledge of piano, theory, and solfège, she added composition and conduction. She then furthered her training at the prestigious Julliard School of Music and at the Tanglewood festivals in Berkshire, Massachusetts.

A glimpse of her impressive catalogue of work, concerts offered on five continents, courses and lectures given around the world in the most prestigious universities and music studies centers, and her membership in advisory boards in important musical institutions and festivals in several countries have made Taina León renowned and recognized in the most demanding international music circuits. It is also very important that her name is connected not only to Cuba but also the United States, a country that has a long musical history with huge names such as Gershwin, Copland, Bernstein, Paul Robeson, Barbara Hendrix, and Jessye Norman, among many others.

Her start in music links to dance when she substituted as a pianist for her sick college classmate in the ballet classes at the Harlem School of the Arts. This led to her first job as a musician in 1968, but it also introduced her to dancer and choreographer Arthur Mitchell, who founded the Dance Theater of Harlem. She moved very quickly from being the company's class pianist to musical director and composer of many of its ballets.

Her talent and restless industriousness led her to become the company's ballet composer and then chief conductor of orchestra in its international tours. Her career took off in the early '70s. In 1993, the head director of the Philharmonic of New York, Kurt Masur, asked her to become an artistic advisor to the famous symphonic group. Her dossier is full of similar milestones.

The diversity of genres and forms in her work attest to her encompassing creative vision. Her themes indicate a concern for improving communication and the affective climate among people. "If you want to achieve a better society, you need to support and encourage young people to help them express their dreams. Dreams are the same in Spanish, English, French, German, Mandarin or in any indigenous dialect in any part of the globe."

The wide dissemination of her music around the world has not prevented her from being a manager and cofounder of events like *Sonidos de las Américas*. Each year, the festival is dedicated to a Latin America country, and in 2000, it was dedicated to Cuba. That year's festival included a large number of resident composers from both inside and outside the Island, including Juan Piñera, Alfredo Diez Nieto, Guido López-Gavilán, Keyla Orozco, Ileana Pérez, and Aurelio de la Vega. With that same desire to bring music to the people as a spiritual good intended to unite them, she cofounded with composers Julio Eastman and Rasul Talib Hakim the concert series Conciertos de la Comunidad [Community Concert Series] with the Brooklyn Philharmonic Symphony Orchestra, playing thousands of concerts in the urban communities of New York. The series earned them an award from then mayor of New York Edward I. Koch.

Among her many and most important collaborations is the opera *Scourge of the Hyacinths* (1994), a radio play written by Nigerian Wole Soyinka, winner of the Nobel Prize for Literature. The new Music Biennale in Munich commissioned the work that won the BMW Award as best new opera. Since then, the play has been staged twenty-four times in France, Austria, Mexico, and Switzerland, where this work was presented at the Grand Theater in Geneva for the ceremony celebrating the fiftieth anniversary of the United

Nations Declaration of Human Rights. The famous soprano Dawn Upshaw recorded the play's aria "Oh, Yemayá" in her album.

Manmade barriers on the basis of economic position, race, social class, and ethnicity have no place in the imaginary of Tania León: "It is something like an illusion of power: I can do more than you, I have more than you, I am more important than you, and on and on until the appreciation that some beings have of themselves is in constant doubt. They live in a constant fear of not being accepted, fearful of not following the rules that others impose on them. That happens wherever we are, whether it is from person to person, from society to society, or group to group."

Her ideas on this are reflected in her work *Drummin* (1997), composed for percussion and orchestra, commissioned by the Miami Light Project and the New World Symphony Orchestra. Premiered under her conduction, the work bridges African American and indigenous, Japanese, Brazilian, and Korean cultures.

The outstanding quality of her work has earned her many awards and merits, among which include in 1991 the music award of the American Academy of Arts and Letters. In 1998, she received the New York Governor's Lifetime Achievement Award and was granted the Fromm Residency of the American Academy in Rome. In 2007, she obtained the Guggenheim Fellowship, awarded by the Solomon Guggenheim Foundation. She has also been a visiting professor at Harvard, Yale, and Ithaca College in New York, teaching graduate courses at Hamburg Musikschule in Germany. In 2008, she became resident composer and conductor at the Central Conservatory of Beijing. During her tenure, the National Symphony Orchestra of China interpreted her work *Horizons* (1999, for orchestra), performed at the opening concert for the Beijing International Congress of Women in Music.

She has stepped onto the podium of the most prestigious world symphony ensembles, among which she especially recalls the occasion when she directed the Orchestra of Beethovenhalle in Bonn, Germany. She has also considered of great significance the premier of *Kabiosile* (1988), for piano and orchestra, and *Desde* (2001), for orchestra, commissioned with the support of Serge Koussevitsky Music Foundation and premiering at New York's Carnegie Hall.

A constant itinerary on five continents as ambassador of the arts on behalf of her adopted country, professor, adviser, cultural promoter, composer of opera, ballet, and cinema, Tania León has erected a gigantic monument to her work that not only refers to her catalogue as a composer but also the different profiles of music she developed with outstanding results in all of them. Today, her name is an important one as it resounds in world of music, reached from the only patrimony with which she counted when she decided to enter music. She relied on her talent and a confidence in herself that she would be able to attain a place in a highly competitive world where many surrender before even attempting to engage in combat.

After her initial stage as a composer, since the decade of the '80s, she became receptive to her patrimonial inheritance as much as to the most avant-garde tendencies, incorporating all the "magma" that a city like New York provides an Afro-Latina composer. She finally held similar advantages with respect to her Anglo-Saxon colleagues. The rich components in her rich mixture placed the composer in a position to express herself not only according to a trend but of intermingling, juxtaposing, alternating not one voice but many simultaneously.

Browsing the composer's vast catalogue, also reflective on its diverse formats, and by listening to the works that have reached us in Cuba, we can observe that her Cuban roots passed through a fine filter. Her work for guitar, *Bailarín* of 1998, *Satiné* for piano for four hands of 1992, *A la par* of 1986 for piano and percussion, and *Batey* of 1989, composed in collaboration with the Dominican pianist and composer Michel Camilo, for vocal ensemble and percussion demonstrate this. These two last works in particular reveal a Cuban composer in her most regal authenticity, in which she does away with that mentality of "Cubans on the Island" and "Cubans in exile." Though the barrier exists as such, it is artificially enclosed.

Additionally, her work *A la par* (1986) interweaves a rhythmic timbre, very well accomplished and mounted in the first section where the counterpoint of motives between the piano and percussion show an explicitly Afro-Cuban face. The central interlude's slow, suggestive, and excellent use of the timbre of the vibraphone alludes to African ancestry and thus is not simply metaphorical. The last section is a rumba blurred by the piano that alludes to its academic patrimony but also (and why not?) to its European roots: French and Spanish. The several voices in *Batey* show a very fortunate symbiosis between the forms of primitive polyphony (*Organum*, *Dicantus*: by intervals of fifths and fourths) juxtaposed with Yoruba ritual songs, many of which run by fourths established in Afro-Cuban culture. While works that are so different to these are noted in the vanguard of the late twentieth century in works as dissimilar as *Arenas d'un tiempo* (1992) for piano trio, clarinet, and cello, creating sound variations by the three instruments used at the same time. The combinations become carriers of motifs that are juxtaposed, first in proportion of two against one and, then, each against the others, as in *Ritual* (1987) for piano. This last piece achieves a slow and suggestive introduction in which the sounds are isolated first in sequential intervals where ninths prevail, followed by augmented fourths and major sevenths always preceded by a serious note and pedal. The author unites these sequences, abbreviating them in duration until they become an *ostinato* loaded with a strong rhythm.

A work that in our judgment constitutes an opus of maturity is *Horizons* (1999) for orchestra. It is evident here that the composer has been able to take advantage of the sound options offered by each section of the orchestra, as well as in its entirety. It is based precisely on that: with a beginning led by the wood instruments with very little density and short participations of each instrument, possibly resembling the sounds of nature, which also enters later in waves of *tutti* of great density that exploit the overwhelming possibilities of the orchestra as a mass of sound, which then shifts afterward to the transparencies of the strings. The clarinet is a great protagonist in this piece, while the timpani and the piano are in charge of other motifs or sections (as in the case of the timpani) as a counterpoint to the rest of the orchestra. Play and contrast of variable sound densities possibly, and in line with the title, describe the outline of the horizon in the course of twenty-four hours of the day and as the visual perspective is transformed with the changing intensity of the light.

Tania León is currently a composer with her own unique voice, who chooses at will her media of sound. More significantly, she presents a coherent discourse of avant-garde exempt from dilettantism, making her evocative works easy for the listener to follow in their world full of exuberance and vigor.

Chapter 31

The Contributions of Sara Gómez

Sandra Álvarez Ramírez

Mi aporte (1972) is a documentary by filmmaker Sara Gómez Yera (Havana, 1942–1974) that incisively addresses the contradictions that emerged between the social incorporation of women in the Cuban Revolution versus the obstacles that women were made to face daily limiting their effective participation. Beyond the good intentions of the announcement of inclusion to this population sector, the contradiction was dealt with at an individual level in the search for solutions. More than ten years after the triumph of the revolution, social conditions remained that put in question the achievement of the "new woman"[1] as a result of her participation in salaried jobs and her work in a society under construction.

The film's use of the hymn of the Federación de Mujeres Cubanas (FMC, Federation of Cuban Women) immediately returns us to the ideals of women that motivated and drove the revolution: "Cuban women, forward, forward, the love of work is most important," the song lyrics dialogue with the different elements addressed in the documentary. Then the voice of Consuelito Vidal comes forward as the narrator of the new role assumed by Cuban women in accessing jobs that traditionally were filled by men, which was considered a gain of the revolutionary process. The place: a sugarcane factory where women contribute to the harvest, the main economy of the country at that time.

The reason for the title of the film becomes apparent from the start. Posters are shown inviting women's participation in citrus production, the sugar industry, as sanitary brigadiers, etc. The camera pans all the posters, arriving at the name of the documentary, illustrated with a sack of sugar with the words "my contribution." At this moment the camera stops and closes in as if trying to personalize such a contribution. The following image contains the phrase "around 10 million combatants," which is an explicit reference to the harvest of 1970. At this moment we arrive at the reason for the title of the documentary: Sara Gómez conceived it as her contribution to the harvest of greater political transcendence in the national history following the triumph of the revolution, which explains why she chose the sugar industry specifically and the location of central Camilo Cienfuegos, once named Hersey, in the Havana town of Santa Cruz del Norte.

The film consists of three key moments. An initial one consists of interviews of several women who work in a sugar mill and a man, their boss. The second part happens while Sara Gómez, Gladys Egües, Lucía Corona, and Mirta Valladares are having a conversation on the same topic, only that these women are not laborers in the strict meaning of the term. They are professionals or university students. The third and final segment shows how tobacco workers value, during a post-film "cinema debate," the information recorded during the first two sections of the documentary, a technique that Sara Gómez reused in *De cierta manera* (1974).

To understand the contextual framing of *Mi aporte*, it is necessary to remember that on August 23, 1960, the FMC was founded with the aim of reaching the female unit that guaranteed the participation of women in the construction of the new society. Therefore the female theme of "the revolution inside another revolution," as it used to be called, was placed in a singular way on the social agenda. Women were considered a priority sector. Fidel Castro would come to explain it in the following way:

> Women within society have interests that are common to all members of society; But they have interests that are their own as women. Especially when it comes to creating a different society, of organizing a better world for all human beings, women have large interests in that effort, because, among other things, women constitute a sector that is discriminated against in the capitalist world in which we lived. In the world that we are building, we need to end all traces of discrimination against women.[2]

To ensure women's access to paid work and inclusion in public life in general, social institutions and training spaces were created that would supposedly allow them to join the revolutionary process: children's childcare centers, boarding and semi-residential schools, cutting and sewing courses, and chauffeuring were some of them. However, reality was different from what had been anticipated. Many contradictions appeared between the individual goals of women and what society expected of them, some of which are shown in *Mi aporte*.

However, the revolutionary process opened doors for women, those in their homes entered public life to work in paid employment, etc. Conversely, the inverse was not the same for men because they were not encouraged to participate in the domestic world, which the documentary makes evident.

In this sense, the only man who participates in *Mi aporte* is the boss, who assumes a critical position against women and their roles as workers. Almost mindlessly, he speaks on a series of incidents that happened in his factory as he tries to testify on women's inefficiency, inadequacy, and even opportunism. The behavior of this boss, who does not differ much from a capitalist pattern, exposes the excessive demands placed on women's workload.

During the first segment of the film, each of the women interviewed exposes the particular reasons that prevent them from working. Hence the film presents a mass of subjective and objective situations, such as those that preclude their real work participation despite the need to receive a salary. The obstacles are multiple and of varying complexity: the husband doesn't want her to work, she has no one to take care of her daughter, she has to do the domestic chores, pregnancy, a son is sick. They all point to certain measures never taken by the revolution to resolve these issues.

However, the incorporation of women into the new society is shown in *Mi aporte* as their desire to collaborate in the revolution beyond their own interests and earnings, which is reminiscent of something that Luisa Campuzano expressed about the work of women during the Campaña de Alfabetización [Literacy Campaign] and the imprint left on their gender identity: "This [the incorporation into society] was assumed by women as a concession rather than as a conquest, as a contribution to the Revolution and not of her own emancipation, and did not imply at all the development of a gender consciousness."

Women put at the fore their contribution to the process, which far from visualizing primarily the impact of individual access to paid work certainly would not allow them to carry out a personalized analysis of this question. Similarly, in the absence of the necessary social conditions, this personalization is only expressed when women are in peril, translated in "it is not worth going to work if it will cost me more."[3]

At the moment in which Gómez needs to reinforce the reasons why women do not participate in paid work, she decides to use a children's song as musical support: "A girl went to play but she could not because she had to do the wash and dry." These lyrics are sung by boys and girls who appear in the documentary and it is a scene that takes place in at a children's center. Another scene follows this one that shows women in charge, in this same institution, preparing and serving food. We assume that at this moment, Gómez is turning the viewer's attention to how the new institution reproduced, and therefore legitimated, the traditional roles played by women, which is quite contradictory and evidently a double discourse inside Cuban society.

The second segment of the documentary contends with the subject of motherhood, which focuses on three positions that are usually assumed when discussing how pregnancy influences the return of women to the home and therefore legitimating the traditional role played by women.

Mirta is a professional woman who denounces the conflict she has lived through since she decided to be socially active out of her personal desire (not only for economic reasons but also for personal causes) and in constructing a family. She has trouble working because of her need to find childcare for her sick son, which also reveals the exceeding demands placed on women. Mirta is living in an extremely conflictive situation. She feels trapped and guilty of not being able to be a good mother or a good worker. She exposes the absence of men inside the home and their lack of commitment in the domestic world. Men continued to be on the sidelines inside the house, which puts extra demands on women, who continue to perform their function as "mother-wives."

Lucía, a researcher, prioritizes her professional needs, declaring that she has given up the goal of establishing a home and having children but instead finding professional fulfillment. This same woman recounts the quickness that is expected in socially changing the traditional feminine role at a mental level and in the individual lives of people. She recognizes that the solution cannot be a labor of education only and entails, rather, a very long process that demands an excessive amount of patience that will bear fruit in future generations; however, she wants social change here and now in the life she is living.

Gómez is once again a character in the documentary, hence taking a chance on the rupture of passivity, preferring to take a more aggressive position. She does not want to make concessions but relies on confrontation to actively demand cooperation from men. It is worth noting that during the filming of this work, Gómez was pregnant with her third child; perhaps this informs why she questions the topic so strongly. She declared, "At least I will not give up." Agnès Varda in the interview found in the documentary *¿Donde esta Sara Gómez?* (2005) spoke with her on this subject as she would reiterate that she intended to have it all.[4] She would not give up her professional life or her realization as a mother. She would accomplish this.[5]

Gladys, however, made different arguments that seem less personalized and were more sociological, even philosophical, on this matter. She is the one who introduces the discussion of the value of education and the role of the family. Similarly, she questions whether the traditional family is relevant to a country in revolution and speaks of "family disintegration." Moreover, she assumes a close role as interviewer or provocateur of the debate—of course because she comes from a school of journalism—and although her position is the least experiential, she gives the discussion a futuristic nuance, placing the solution to such problems at the hands of education. However, her assessment of motherhood, focused on the alleged frustration of women who have no descendants and therefore do not fulfill their social function, refers us to the thesis of cultural feminism on the essence of women, such as the supreme role (presumably enviable) of women who must be able to bear children, rejection of the masculine, and all that makes reference to the reduction of the differences between men and women. Similarly, Gladys raises a fundamental conflict when she states:

> It is all a big circle, and it is a difficult and vicious circle. Right now the situation is that you have to work with all those limitations: that you have to queue, with the problem of the child centers, with the problem of the child, with the problem of having to attend to your husband, means women end up working almost twenty hours a day which is what happens to women who work. At the same time, you have to contribute to that material base, so that you do not have to continue living with that mop in hand, so society may advance. It is a contradiction, but I think it is a contradiction that I understand is falling apart as it's being resolved.

However, the most impactful claim that Gladys brings to light, with such lucidness that thirty years later still is surprising, is the fact that for women to be able to participate actively in society, she has to leave another woman to take her place, whether it is her mother, the mother-in-law, or any other woman. The important thing about this revelation is that today, in countries that have specific laws that guarantee women's rights, they have realized that professional women, academics, researchers, etc., could reproduce gender inequity as long as they leave another woman in their homes doing the domestic chores. Of course, the debate is strong and complex because with the increase in the rate of female unemployment and the feminization of poverty and migration, it is unknown what would happen if all these feminist or gender-conscious university women decided to stop employing other women, who are generally unable to access the labor market for being low skilled, immigrants, or belonging to the most disadvantaged social classes.

However, the attention to the reproduction of machismo by Cuban women is another success of this documentary, this time in the voice of Lucía, who openly points to women's roles in educating their sons and daughters to totally replicate sexist beliefs and behaviors. She synthesizes the point in a shrewd way: "Cuban men permeate with the machismo that his mother fed him with the bottle.... The great perpetuators of machismo are women as the great recreators of the myth of women's limitations and of what is masculine and what is feminine in what women should do to be considered women."

Perhaps we are not entirely in agreement, but for us the important thing to note here is that this woman anticipates the consequences of patriarchy, distinguishing the reproductive role of women and the role of men in sustaining that myth created supposedly by women. Today, we recognize the exact role that both men and women play in the maintenance of the subordination of women over the centuries. Moreover, our familiarity with this does not stop making it complex analytically and in need of complex approaches.

Lucía also goes a little further when she highlights the different kinds of women attending to their training or the jobs they occupy and how their interests change according to their class condition. It is not the same to be a woman who stays in the house, for women who also do creative work, and do not work in factories, and who may feel immune to machismo and the problems of other women. This intellectual woman, who is bound to be detached from the problems of ordinary women, is not the "new woman" who needs the revolution. Lucía issues a judgment of high value for socialist feminism: women workers are not the same as intellectuals (substituting bourgeois); their lives make their worldviews different.

Lucía also speaks in terms of "the woman who belongs to the masculine world" in reference to women intellectuals and those who do creative work, a very interesting argument because this is the only time gender is assigned to creative work. In this instance women travel through the "masculine world." Ultimately, the argument equates masculinity with creativity and femininity with reproduction. Similarly, Lucía alludes to one of the premises of this research: creative work that has been historically legitimized has regularly been masculine.

During the post-film debate, tobacco workers express dissimilar opinions on the topic in question, whose central ideas come into conflict when approached by intellectual women. The first ones feel very capable of assuming various duties in their working days: in the house (with their sons and daughters, husband, etc.), in voluntary and productive work, and in salaried work as such. They also defend maternity unanimously and emphasize how suffering is linked to the female function, which is not an impediment to achieving happiness.

In this way, the film resumes what Lucía said about the difference in perspective of women according to their social origin. Ultimately, they, the university women and these other women, tobacco workers, perform obviously differentiated analyses. This is a reminder of the fact that in Cuba before the triumph of the revolution, when feminists were demanding women's access to public places and paid work, black and poor women were already in those spaces, working in the streets, many times earning miserable wages to feed their sons and daughters.

It becomes necessary then to address the supposed reasons why the documentary was not exhibited. In my view, the motives may have been related to the contested nature of the documentary that makes evident that gains for women can also be experienced as disadvantages. *Mi aporte* shows how the revolution had not been able, after ten years, to find effective solutions. Such was the case of paid labor, which became a barrier when it becomes a new demand for women, without disappearing the previous demands and without doing the intense work that propitiates the participation of men in the family and at home, so that women could enter social life. Moreover, the conflict around motherhood in relation to personal fulfillment and the realization of personal projects is a critical issue still being discussed today.

Additionally, the documentary can also be linked to the impossibility of proving the commitment of the revolution to the fathers and husbands of those women and girls. Luisa Campuzano synthesizes it very well with the term "revolutionary pact." The complaint made by some women about the double standards of men who were called revolutionaries or communists might be another reason that influenced why the film was not shown commercially.

Mi aporte is a documentary that brings up questions, contradictions, and conflicts rather than satisfactory solutions, results, or flattering praise. Sara Gómez attempts to reveal what lies behind the facade of the face of happy women integrated into the workforce without disadvantage or demerit. Rather, what is shown is the reality for everyday women, those who have sons and daughters, attend to husbands, and leave for work at five in the morning.

In the end, one is left with the feeling that there are no complete answers for such a complex subject that is also embedded with many other issues. It had never been the intention of Sara Gómez to present a perfect answer. Her contribution becomes part of the many other contributions made by diverse women that are at the same time so similar and different from each other.

NOTES

1. Let us remember that according to Alexandra Kollontai for the "new woman" to be constituted, the destruction of capitalism and arrival of a socialist society was necessary. However, it also required the self-awareness of women of her subordination and of a change in the social roles of men and women, as well as of the participation of both in the family and the care of their sons and daughters.

2. Fidel Castro Ruz, "Discurso en el I Congreso Nacional de la FMC" [speech in the first national congress of the FMC], Havana, October 1, 1962, in *Mujer y Revolución* [Women and Revolution] (Havana: Editorial de la Mujer, 2006), 87.

3. Luisa Campuzano, *Las muchachas de La Habana no tienen temor de Dios. Escritoras cubanas* [Havana Women Do Not Fear God: Cuban Women Writers] (S. SVIII–XXI) (Havana: Ediciones Unión, 2004), 140.
4. Alexandra Müller, "Entrevista a Agnès Varda," in *¿Dónde esta Sara Gómez?* Anka Films, 2005.
5. During the filming of *Salut les Cubains!* [Hello Cubans] in 1963, two years before her eldest daughter Iddia Veitía Gómez was born.

BIBLIOGRAPHY

Campuzano, Luisa. 2004. *Las muchachas de La Habana no tienen temor de Dios. Escritoras cubanas* (S. SVIII–XXI). Havana: Ediciones Unión.
Castro Ruz, Fidel. 2006. "Discurso en el I Congreso Nacional de la FMC." Havana, October 1, 1962. In *Mujer y Revolución*. Havana: Editorial de la Mujer.
Miguel Álvarez, Ana De. 2001. "Presente y futuro de la Teoría femenina. Movimiento feminista y redefinición de la realidad." In *Feminismo es y será, ponencias, mesas redondas y exposiciones*. Asamblea de mujeres de Cordoba, Servicio de publicación de la Universidad de Cordoba.
Müller, Alexandra. 2005. "Entrevista a Agnès Varda." In *¿Dónde esta Sara Gómez?* Anka Films.

Chapter 32

Belkis Ayón Manso, Between Heterogeneous Sensibilities

Lázara Menéndez Vásquez

Belkis Ayón Manso (1967–1999) lived thirty-two Gregorian calendar years, however for other systems of ancestral belief, she lives on. Like for Guayasamín, we can leave a candle on for her because she will always return.

Tu y la Sikán is the beginning of a long journey through the history of art from a position of subversion of the traditional ways as the greats always do. *La Cena* and *La Consagración* visit Byzantine iconography. The *Paño de la Verónica* represents a walk through the great themes of the history of art that "others" have written with capital letters and that our artists upset with joyful imperturbability, Belkis Ayón among them. Multiple layers of meaning are manifested as we travel from the periphery to the different centers that her work proposes. She was able to create new compositional models in admirable mastery of the trade. She learned immersed in the atmosphere of the workshop, seemingly without being discriminated against.

All her figures look forward to the outside world in a penetrating, insistent, and even defiant way, a vibrant way for Belkis Ayón to distance herself from the stereotype with which traditional iconography has depicted the image of women. She did not live like Elizabeth Vigée-Lebrun and Adélaïde Labille-Guiard through the debate that was unleashed in the eighteenth century on whether the art of women was comparable to that of men when they were able to enter the French Academy. Nor did she employ the traditional manifestation of the self-portrait and autobiography focused on the materialization of the inner world as with Frida Kahlo. Ayón's art moved the borders of the public and private, problematizing the value of the hegemonic and subaltern when referring to questions of ritual, developed without having been an eyewitness.

FIRST THRESHOLD

Katia, her eldest sister, a doctor by profession, and who concerns herself with conserving and favoring the knowledge and promotion of the family collection of Belkis's work, tells me: "My father is a retired captain of the Ministry of the Interior and my mother is a housewife. They are of humble backgrounds. Our childhood was very happy with the support of both our parents who today remain together. The family relationship with the grandparents, uncles, cousins, was always very good with a lot of communication. We have a large family. Belkis's relationship with me was very special. We got along very well. I'm the older sister, and although we studied different professions, she the artist and I doctor, we understood one another very well and I admired the worked that she did, enjoyed it a lot. I could not be very close in her moments of creation because I was in the midst of my career as a doctor, which occupied most of my time, but I was aware of everything she was doing and supported her in everything I could within my reach.

"Belkis began to approach the visual arts from a very young age through a circle of students that existed in the Library Máximo Gómez, directed by the teacher Zenaida Díaz, who thought that Belkis had magnificent skills for the arts. Both the teacher and my parents supported her in all the events she participated in since childhood."[1]

She became a great engraver as a girl. She studied in the Elementary School of Plastic Arts October 20 in Havana (1979–1982), completed the engraving specialization at the Provincial School of Plastic Arts San Alejandro (1982–1986), and graduated from the Higher Institute of Art in 1991. She employed lithography, chalcography, and collagraphy techniques through which she was extraordinarily productive approximately between 1986 and 1998.

Talent, creativity, and a splendid and wide smile were currencies that accompanied her throughout her life, attested to by her intense professional activity and the documentation associated with her work. She shared her creative work by teaching lectures, workshops, and engraving courses in different national and international institutions. Between 1993 and 1998, she occupied the engraving chair of the San Alejandro School and the Superior Institute of Art. Her work found spaces in multiple artistic and cultural institutions and obtained important prizes and distinctions such as the First Prize Biennial of Fine Arts Academies, Maastricht, Holland, Netherlands in 1993; Prize from Provincial Center of Plastic Arts and Design of Havana, also in 1993; Prize XII Biennial of Printmaking Latin American and Caribbean, San Juan, Puerto Rico, 1997; and artist in residence/lecturer/instructor in Philadelphia in 1999. Beginning in 1991 she was a member of the UNEAC and a member of the Experimental Workshop of Graphics; in 1998 she was the vice president of the Association of Plastic Artists of UNEAC. The Council of State awarded her in 1996 the Distinction for the National Culture.

She was a young woman of her time. A look at her resume reveals that early in her career, when she was nineteen years of age, she chose the myth of Sikán as one of the thematic elements of her work in accordance with the logics that dominated the decade of the '80s. Critiques that focused on art production at that time coincide in pointing out that one of the privileged lines in the artistic creation of those years, on the anthropological side, was the importance granted to the mythical. Osvaldo Sánchez elaborates in "Syncretism, Postmodernism and Culture of Resistance" that "the importance of the mythical, the cosmogonic, the ritual in the Cuban art of the Eighties can derive from an urgency to establish spiritual archetypes, and to possess models of greater coherence between the ethos and ethnos of social life."[2] In the field of iconographic appropriation, the same critic indicates that it was a strategy highly favored by several artists of the time, especially as a resource that allows the exploration of the "metonymic exuberance of the popular imagination."[3]

Belkis Ayón's production employs a critical lens. Eugenio Valdés accounts for the provocative nature that enters the appropriation of the myth of Sikán by a woman: "Her work does away with the hackneyed versions of expository characterization. The artistry penetrates the nature of the myth as a reflective matter, and manages to create new exploratory and speculative angles, especially because her discourse is marked regally by a sexual consciousness that is almost contestatory."[4] Sometimes the engraver makes the myth run through issues legitimized by the pictorial discourse of the history of art to stress individual subjectivity and allude to the absence of limits that divide "high" and "low" culture.

As we have already pointed out, the story of Sikán is the axis around which the function of Abakuá societies are ideologically articulated in Cuba and one of the nodes around which Belkis Ayón, from the knowledge provided by the academy, builds a world of transcultural relations. *Adoración al güiro* (1986), *¡¡¡Ekue será mio!!!* (1986), *Nasako vigila día y noche* (1986), *Ndíseme I y II* (1986), *Syncretism I and II* (1986), among others, were some of the works created for the defense of her thesis in San Alejandro. The titles evidence her affiliation to a very complex and problematic traditional practice in the Cuban context.

A culture's tradition is monotonous and invariable only on the surface. To assume a tradition is to become aware of it, and the feeling of belonging that develops motivates us to become cocreators of it because when we feel part of a tradition, we can critically reactivate it. Only then is it subverted and rewritten. Belkis Ayón was aware of this: "I create images for the most varied stories of the myth, motivated by its lessons on human questioning, on the struggle for conservation and survival, on symbolic and meaningful coincidences with other distant cultures in space and time."[5] As Helga Montalbán explained, "It draws from the most hermetic memory of our culture and also shows us the paths of rebellion and justice."[6]

Experts in cultural anthropology, sociology, and ethnography do not need to legitimize Belkis Ayón's work for it to have recognition at the national and international level. Little credit is given to the work's reach when it is reduced to the question of Abakuá or when we declare that a few brushstrokes representing the knowledge of the universe in the myth of Sikán are sufficient for the viewer to understand the work's meaning. It would be worth asking if the painting the *Annunciation* by Antonia Eiriz motivates the same sense of dense perception when we know that the religious subject matter has been profusely and deeply treated by artists at different times. We resort to our knowledge and not to our religious faith to explore the substitution of one of the protagonists of the biblical account, the impact that the news provokes and the transgression that it consecrates.

SECOND THRESHOLD

It is not new for social sciences and the humanities to consider that cultures define cultural matrices. These tend to vary depending on the temporo-spatial logics and the thresholds or cultural horizons that condition their actions. Boundaries can be used to challenge an accepted cultural canon. Thought and language are noninnocent channels of the reproduction of knowledge and in the context of Cuban culture are impregnated with public and private prejudices, overlapping or uncovering the cosmogonies of African origin. To highlight its density constitutes a cognitive exercise of distancing, exclusions, and cultural hierarchies from the Eurocentric.

It is not a question of settling into a monolithic conception of identity or of purporting fundamentalist postures about African cultures and their imprint on Cuban culture. The old "civilizing" thought of a colonial nature that has historically tried to distance African religiosity of any cultural practice for reasons of criminality, primitiveness, atavistic irrationality, insistent presence of banal orientation, or folklorism is expelled from the world that the artist created. Belkis Ayón has a clear awareness that "this has been a mistreated theme by the population because of ignorance and notoriety created by some of its members and also by those who do not know its roots,"[7] insufficient for the elaboration of sophisticated, layered work.

The body, rhythm, and positions of Belkian characters do not pretend to represent the quotidian Abakuá man. Hence, with great force, and drawing from the elaboration of her thesis, the artist insisted throughout her career that the creation of her characters is not linked to realistic mimesis. Carpentier's claims on the text-image relationship applies to her work. Pierre Mabille illustrates the text-image relationship when he comments on the difficulty he encountered as a European lecturer to describe his first night in the Americas to his son as he was missing references for "how to describe a yagruma [tree], or the trunk of a Ceiba?" In Carpentier's words:

> Speak to me of the railway station of Manaus, of Ameca-Ameca, of Quetzaltenango. I bet you that you will need four pages of tight prose to situate it, to paint its public, environment, its frame. There are no models of comparison for her: Nothing has been painted nor described. She is an absolute virgin and therefore she is unknown.[8]

The visual universe of the Abakuá occurs in a similar way, in the context of the pictorial tradition, the Abakuá has no visual antecedents. Belkis Ayón's figures are moved by a timeless scenario, for them there are no railway stations or special references. The figures are "marked bodies"[9] tattooed by yesterday with an unknown past, immobilized in the absence of time that is part of mythic time.

The selection of a cultural practice in the field of artistic production does not necessarily imply an affiliation as an exercise of faith, whether it is religious or of sharing a spiritual commitment between Belkis Ayón with Abakuá societies. Anyone who is informed about the events of these groups on the Island knows that the myth of the Sikán is part of a practice that excludes women—from certain speeches it is classified as phallocentric and homophobic—because the axis of its cosmovision is located in the center of male sociology. Belkis Ayón was conscious of this.

Art is not just about the past due to the sense of its own presence to the past. Moreover, the myth of Sikán in Belkis Ayón's work is a pretext. The choice of action in fact becomes something extraordinary because it suspended what is customary in the field of artistic creation. If for Heidegger the common means the forgetting of origins and implies the "forgetfulness of being," then it should be supposed that when the artist is placed in the framework of the unaccustomed, her work made it possible to erect a world. What the artist accomplishes does not respond only to an exercise of style but to a need to be. She selects thematic axes, not exclusive of religion, philosophy, and literature, as these relate to existence, the transcendent, sacrilegious, the sacred, eternal, and the existential in frank articulation with the artistic tradition itself.

The entry to the topic of Abakuá societies and especially on the myth of Sikán by Belkis Ayón was, from the beginning, an acutely penetrating and transgressive critical response to key interests of the time. Therefore it is not difficult to realize that the artist assumes a different viewpoint from those who have marked the norms in which ancient customs and conceptions of a patriarchal nature have settled. Belkis Ayón chooses for her work the story in which Sikán declares the desire to become the owner of the sacred drum that will restore the voice of Tanze. *¡¡¡Ekwe será mio!!!* (1986 collagraph) explains her renunciation to accept the myth of Sikán as representative of female submission[10] to thus reject the most widespread interpretations of Sikán's story.

Pieces such as *La Consagración* (1991), *Nlloro* (1991), *La Cena* (1993), *La Sentencia* (1993), and *Vamos* (1993) allow us to compare the strong attachment of the artist to the poetics derived from the myth of Sikán and the rituals of initiation, purification, renewal, and death found in its literature, especially in books published by Lydia Cabrera and Enrique Sosa. Various versions of Sikán's story have been told by enlightened initiates who know that a lot of information is supposedly maintained and kept secret through games involving paths of memory, stories that nonetheless could be rewritten.[11] The narrative versions describe markings like those that appear in *Sincretismo I* (1986 lithograph).

THIRD THRESHOLD

In her painting *¡Ven!* Belkis Ayón places a figure on a shore and diagonally to a fish identified in the artist's visual discourse as Tanze. We might be interested to know who calls whom; we could ask, does Sikán capture Tanze? Or does Tanze choose Sikán? In the legitimized narrative version by the Abakuá brotherhoods, after Sikán fills his jar in the river and goes back to his house, Tanze bellows from inside the flask and frightens Sikán. Belkis Ayón's work alters the mythical event and modifies the relations of power. The representation of the power of Abasi (expression of the mystery, the numen, of the sacred) is not within the reach of the members of the Abakuá confraternities; in the ritual field, only Iyamba (the highest authority in the Abakuá games or powers) has direct contact with Ekue, the sacred drum, representative of the power of Tanze. In another piece, some hands are projected on a surface. The title of the piece is *No te vayas* [Do Not Leave] (1986). It is fitting to ask who is making this request.[12]

It is necessary to penetrate Belkis Ayón's process of revision of the myth. When the artist appropriates the part of the narrative in which Sikán dies, she is preserving that space of struggle. Sikán comes to signify an expression of life, a possibility of realization, a desire for survival, and most importantly a loophole for the redistribution of power. Sikán is a woman and acts in a double condition in the Abakuá universe. First, she is in the center of that cosmovision, around which turns the discovery of Tanze. Second, she is a treasure delivered as a sacrifice by the community, offered in order to restore the balance of life. Her skin is supposed to restitute the voice of Tanze. The event of the sacrifice of Sikán does not repair Tanze's voice. We do not know what would have happened if her skin had recovered the bellow of the fish, and how that would have shaped how women are treated as representatives of sacred power. In the universe that revolves around the brotherhoods Abakuá, this is not the preferred version. Once women's communication with the sacred was severed, they were excluded from the ritual.

With her creation of *La Cena* (1988 collagraph), Belkis Ayón explicitly inserts a deep transcultural relationship to weave with gold threads two traditions that follow different paths: the sacrifice of Sikán and the sacrifice of Christ. They both represent systems of restrictive thoughts that are not exempt from contradictions.

What is the race and religion of repression? In *La familia* (1991 collagraph) and *Sálvanos Abasi*, the name of the numen Abakuá is inscribed on the crucifix that hangs on the neck of the figures, whereupon Abasi is located in the place of Jesus Christ. *Dormida* (1995) depicts a dove that could well be the Holy Spirit. Sikán is represented in the distance as that of Eve, Mary, Mary Magdalena, and the Veronicas in the iconographic tradition associated to Christianity, recognized in the history of European art—and this includes even the black Eve of which Ramón Gómez de la Serna speaks.[13] The Abakuá do not exclude with respect to the practice of other religions. Acceptance of religious plurality is a norm, unlike Christianity, which assumes to be the one and only true religion that could offer salvation. However, the Abakuá cosmovision shares with Christianity the primacy of the masculine, hierarchical, and androcentric experience.

What *model* of civilization does this cultural weaving suggest? As soon as we unweave the iconographic manipulation that the artist performs, we realize the following: first, the intellectualization of the ñáñigo rite has been derived essentially from the academy; second, the flourishing of the iconographic tradition from which it emerged; and third, the conception of Cuban culture as a result of the transculturation of different cultural registers favors the tension between conceptual fixed nodules in the alternation of the nuclei such as sacrifice/benefit, justice/punishment, prestige/disrepute, prohibition/transgression, and inclusion/exclusion.

The expression of cultism and a sophisticated visual lexical rhetoric become palpable in four works in which the artist uses *My Vernicle* as part of the title, accompanied by a fragment of *vallenato* [the Columbian folk music]. *Vernicle* does not seem to be a term of habitual use in theology and less in everyday life. The term coincides in theological studies and history of religion that *vernicle* is a derivative, a kind of corruption of *vero*, which means truth in Latin, and *icon*, which means image in Greek. The title's other meaning signifies fragments of *vallenatos*, very popular in Colombia in the decade of the '90s and especially those of Carlos Vives. The artist explains:

> *My Vernicle or La honda herida* was the beginning of a series that has the characteristic of combining a fixed title *My Vernicle* in combination with another title.
>
> It is the first work that I made very recently that uses two interesting titles in one, playing a little with two levels of reading with the meaning of *Paño de Verónica* emphasizing the idolized image that is longed for, a presence always present unites with this line that connects to a whale that uses the same formal and expressive resources that I have expressed so far in my work that I will explain later. The title also connects to a fleeting and exciting moment of my life. I constantly make direct and more stylized allusions of the Colombian vueltero hat and so, this single element becomes face, mask, handkerchief, background.[14]

The theme in *Paño de Verónica* is not a preferred topic in the European artistic tradition when compared to *The Last Supper*, *The Annunciation*, *The Adoration of the Kings*, *The Crucifixion*, or *The Descending of the Cross*.[15] The transmutation of the handkerchief in Ayón's version does not contain the memory that Merleau-Ponty analyzes as part of intersubjective exchanges that does not annul difference but converts it rather as a necessity in ensuring that the relationship I-other, which must be conceived as complementary functions that cannot be sustained separately, and that according to this point of view, masculinity implies femininity.

The Abakuá practice from the perspective of the artist is as an other, and she only assumes the part that she identifies with (Sikán). The recognition of the other as a subject is not only a theoretical question but also an important motive for the transformation potential that it implies because it defines our being in the world. The handkerchief or veil that becomes "face, mask, handkerchief, background" is also another presence "always present." The body does not act in isolation but always in commitment to the world that is part of a symbolic foundation that respects individual reality, social relations, and cultural diversity.

The artistic praxis of the decade of the '80s appealed not only to the object but to the gesture, to action, to dialogue, and to conceptual recovery by some artists of a renewed vision of syncretism and transculturation that opened the doors to a constant intersubjective appeal. From the place of belonging, we can open ourselves to other cultures, to the complementariness of differences and the exchange of viewpoints. Difference is necessary for relations.

FINAL

The engravings by Belkis Ayón are extraordinary because of the layers of meaning that can be permanently accessed. The work is obligatorily consulted on the grounds of contemporary Cuban art. It courageously appropriates and validates the myth that refers to Sikán, penetrating the closed zones of cultural memory, while tackling in a complex way a problematic and controversial world. It appeals to sociocultural practices that institute and subvert canons. It emphasizes the capacity of reactualization of the accumulated cultural capital and allows viewers to feel the tension between the latent and the manifest.

The myth of Sikán, connected with the oral tradition, has found a space in writing as a socioritual micro-practice in the context of contemporary culture in Cuba. Its cultists are carriers and specialists who dedicate themselves, from different disciplines, to studying its manifestations integrated into traditional popular culture. Unlike the historical artistic avant-gardes that tended to cut ties with literature since the visual arts needed to become independent of the written letter, Belkis Ayón reclaimed the connection with oral stories. The narrative turn allows her to approach the self tentatively and indirectly. The construction of the self emerges between the subjugation to logical thinking and the pleasure of seduction in the depth reserved in the image. Thus it precludes the argument that the visual code is intended for the illiterate and the alphabet for lawyers. This argument is widely used as a semiotic foundation to sustain differences in class and race. This perspective anchored in the scope of the difference between natural signs (images) and conventional signs (words) in the style of Ernst H. Gombrich has a history that goes back to Plato's *Cratylus* that "cements the oppositions between literacy and a code for the illiterates, while the assimilation between image and the 'natural sign' makes this the sign of the masses, of the racial other, and links it to idolatry and fetishism."[16]

The emotional resonance does not occur because it promotes individual identification with the characters, rather, the distance between the images and the receiver calls for a process of deep intellectualization of the events and the cosmovision created by the artist, which produces the strong emotion provoked by her works. It causes, in the words of Martín Hopenhayn, the "opening of the subject to the flow of becoming as the flow of one's own subjectivity."[17]

NOTES

1. Personal communication, Havana, June 5, 2010. Editor's note: We are grateful to the Belkis Ayón Estate for the art work on the cover of this book.

2. Osvaldo Sánchez, "Sincretismo, postmodernismo y cultura de resistencia," in *Antología de textos críticos: el Nuevo Arte cubano*, edited by Magali Espinosa and

Kevin Power (Havana: Perceval Press, 2006), 55. This text was originally published in the Catalog Kuba Ok. Städtische (Dusseldorf: Kunsthalle, 1990).

3. Ibid., 55.

4. Eugenio Valdés Figueroa, *Belkis Ayón: la revelación de un secreto* (Havana, 1991).

5. Belkis Ayón, the artist's own words provided in the program catalogue, II Salón de Arte Cubano Contemporáneo, Centro de Desarrollo de las Artes Visuales, Havana, 1998, 30.

6. Program from the personal exhibition of the work of Belkis Ayón, *El desafío de la permanencia*, Galería Pedro Esquerré, CPAV, Matanzas, June 2006.

7. Belkis Ayón, manuscript was made available by Katia Ayón.

8. Alejo Carpentier, "Novelas de América," in *Información*, Havana, June 3, 1944; "El Pinar de Ancón," in *Información*, Havana, June 7, 1944.

9. See the text by Yolanda Wood, *Belkis Ayón. La resurrección de los cuerpos marcados* [The Resurrection of Marked Bodies], Siempres vuelvo: Exposición homenaje VII Bienal de La Habana, Galería Habana, 2000.

10. Enrique Sosa, *Los ñáñigos*, EFOR version of the sacrifice of Sikán (Havana: Editorial Letras Cubanas, 1984), 192–206.

11. See the Sikán myth version that appears in *Tato Quiñones: Ecorie Abakuá* (Havana: Ediciones Unión, 1994), 25–31.

12. The title alludes to the recuperation of the disturbed relations of domination by Sikán's unintended discovery. (See version EFOR, by Sosa, previously cited, 193).

13. Ramón Gómez de la Serna, "Negrismo," in *Negrismo, negritud, negrólogos. Algunos textos de literatura y crítica*, VII Encuentro de Estio 2005, Coordination: Maria Bolanos, accessed August 20, 2006, www.extensionycultura.vva.es.

14. From the artist's documents. Access facilitated by Katia Ayón (Havana, 2006).

15. Examples of this theme: *Master of Saint Veronica* 1400–1420 in Colonia. *Saint Veronica with the Sudarium* [oil on wood], Monaco, Alte Pinakotheke, cm 78 x 48; Mandyllon Russia, S. XVII. Via Crucis Venetian School. S. XVIII; *Padua Cathedral Sixth Station, Veronica Wipes the Face of Christ*; George Rouault (1871–1958), *The Sacred Shroud*, 1933 oil on canvas, Paris, National Museum of Modern Art, cm 91 x 65.

16. Carlos Rincón, "Texto e imagen más allá de la comparación. Presentación," in *Revista de Crítica Literaria Latinoamericana*, Lima-Hanover, 2nd semester, 2002, year XXVIII, no. 56, pp. 7–17.

17. Martin Hopenhayn, "Transculturalidad y diferencia (el lugar preciso es un lugar movedizo)" [Transculturation and Difference], *Cinta de Moebio*, Faculty of the Social Sciences. University of Chile, March 2000, no. 7, https://www.moebio.uchile.cl/07/hopenhayn.html.

BIBLIOGRAPHY

Ayón, Belkis. 1998. Palabras de la artista. In *Catalog of II Salón de Arte Cubano Contemporáneo*. Havana: Centro de Desarrollo de las Artes Visuales.

Carpentier, Alejo. 1944. "Novelas de América." In *Información*, June 3. Havana.
———. 1944. "El Pinar de Ancón." In *Información*, June 7. Havana.
Gómez de la Serna, Ramón. 2005. "Negrismo." In *Negrismo, negritud, negrólogos. Algunos textos de literatura y critica*. VII Encuentro de Estio.
Hopenhayn, Martín. 2000. "Transculturalidad y diferencia (el lugar preciso es un lugar movedizo)." In *Cinta de Moebio* 7: 2–5. Santiago de Chile. https://www.moebio.uchile.cl/07/hopenhayn.html.
Program from the personal exhibition of the work of Belkis Ayón. 2006. *El desafío de la permanencia*. June. Matanzas: Galería Pedro Esquerré, CPAV.
Rincón, Carlos. 2002. "Texto e imagen más allá de la comparación. Presentación." In *Revista de Crítica Literaria Latinoamericana*, no. 56. 2nd semester, XXVIII. Lima-Hanover.
Sánchez, Osvaldo. 2006. "Sincretismo, postmodernismo y cultura de resistencia." In *Antología de textos críticos: el Nuevo Arte cubano*, edited by Magali Espinosa and Kevin Power. Havana: Perceval Press.
Sosa, Enrique. 1984. *Los ñáñigos*. Havana: EFOR version, Editorial Letras Cubanas.
Wood, Yolanda. 2000. *Belkis Ayón: La resurrección de los cuerpos marcados*. At the conference Siempre vuelvo: Exposición homenaje VII Bienal. Havana: Galería Habana.

Chapter 33

Black Women in Sports

Irene Esther Ruiz Narváez

INTRODUCTION

Cuba is one of the countries in Latin America and the Caribbean with a major sports tradition. Since the revolution of 1959, sports have relied on state support, which has allowed the development of multiple sports disciplines. However, in these fifty years, there has been a lack of studies of the history of sports and other disciplines of the social sciences.

Sports scholarship has barely been realized until recently in limited studies that explore behaviors of sexism, machismo, and discrimination linked to the inherent complexities of ethnicity, gender, and sports. Most sports research, although important, is only concerned with highlighting the record of achievement at both the individual and collective level.

Historically, sports in Cuba were practiced by "the white *criolla* bourgeoisie that saw in sports activity a cultured and civilized example of modernity and good taste and an effective pastime for the hygiene and health of the sensible and well-educated youth who wanted to develop its cultural strengths in proportion to the intellectual ones."[1] Women's participation was initially limited to "'madrinas' [godmothers] and as spectators.... Black and *mestiza* women showed their love for the sport through their press, the magazine, *Minerva*."[2]

Sports since antiquity has been mainly considered a male activity, such as in the ancient Olympic Games held in the cities of the Roman and Greek empires. Archaeological research shows that in many of the cultures of Egypt, Mesopotamia, China, and India (500–1500 BCE), some women participated in games and other physical activities. However, the physical activities of women in sub-Saharan Africa during that period are not recorded in the reviewed literature.[3]

The nineteenth century saw the birth of modern sports on an international scale with the resurgence of the Olympic Games of antiquity. On April 6, 1896, due to the efforts of Baron Pierre de Coubertain, the first modern Olympic Games were held. Athens was the seat of this meeting but without female participation. Women were excluded. Coubertain, as a man of his time and class, referred to the presence of women in sports in extremely discriminatory terms: "The inferiority of [women's] intelligence is too obvious to discuss. . . . Women's craniums are more similar because of their volume to gorillas than to the most developed craniums of men."[4] Hence they were denied the right to compete in public. It was not until 1912, in the fifth Olympic Games held in Stockholm, Sweden, that fifty-seven women paraded for the first time with equal sports rights alongside 2,447 men. None of those women were black or *mestiza*.

However, Cuba was making its own advancements. In 1929, Cuba held the Third Carnival of Feminine Athletics though Cuba was already being affected by the start of the economic crisis that would scourge the world, deepening misery, unemployment, and political contradictions. Four young black women members belonging to the Union Fraternal Club,[5] an association with a long history, connected to the Central Directory of the Societies of Color of the Island of Cuba, raced in the 400 and 800 meters, which were held at the University of Havana on April 8 and 9 of that year. This is the oldest information on female participation of Cuban black female athletes, according to the investigations of the sports historian Carlos Reig.[6]

The Amateur Sports Organization of Cuba (ODAC)[7] was established in 1930, in opposition to the race and class discrimination of the Amateur Athletic Union of Cuba (UAAC), which was founded in 1922 and part of the Athletic Union of the United States. For the first time, black and white poor athletes had an institution that provided them with a space for sports and the opportunity to participate in free competitions. However, a new obstacle emerged for people "of color": almost all the clubs that integrated the ODAC did not have adequate facilities for their training activities and competitions due to the economic difficulties inherent to their class status. In 1938, according to the data of sport historian Carlos Reig, the clubs that integrated the ODAC were Atenas, Unión Fraternal, Progreso, Antilla, Magnetic, Jóvenes del Vals, Deportivo La Fe, and Artístico Cultural.

Suárez Rocabruna, president of ODAC and member of the Cuban Olympic Committee, declared in *Dario de la Marina*: "The circumstances of having enrolled in our bosom a large majority of the athletes of limited economic condition, who are in considerable proportion those athletes of more or less dark skin, does not mean that the ODAC is an organization created for a particular class, but rather to give the sport a real popular orientation and to do away with discriminatory actions."[8]

The first sports to be incorporated in the ODAC were track and field, baseball, cycling, and boxing. Likewise, in 1934 the Athletic Association of Cuban Women "initiated the realization, annually, of athletic competitions that contribute to the impulse of this sport (track and field). The Amateurs Athletic Union of Cuba, the Athletic Organization of Cuban Sports, the University of Havana and other institutions have joined this effort"[9] of including competitions in which black women were allowed to participate.

At the close of the twentieth century, black female athletes began to represent Cuba at international events. Great athletes such as Regla Carcasés, Marina Herrera, Esperanza Makenzi, Nereida Bataille, Elsa Villa Fuerte, Alejandrina Herrera, Mercedes Herrera, Noemi Díaz, Berta Díaz, Nereyda Borges, Belkys Rodríguez, Carmen Valdés, Cristy del Pino, Berta Fernández, Vilma Santos, Haydée Claver, Hilda Harvey, Lidia Hernández, Alejandra Coffigny, Julia Padrón, Caridad Agüero, Luisa Polledo, Verónica Torralba, Amelia Puig, and Isidra Rodríguez emerged since 1946, among others.[10] Many of them are pioneers of Cuban athletics, participating in Central American and Caribbean games and in competitions organized by American clubs and colleges[11] that selected the best athletes from other countries for sporting events in the United States. They were all in track and field.

Before 1959 there were important athletic competitions organized by the National Athletic Federation of Secondary Inter-Institutional Teaching (Federacion Atlética Nacional Inter-Institutos de Segunda Enseñanza, FANAI) and the National Athletic Federation of Secondary Schools (Federació Atlética Nacional de Escuelas Secundarias, FANESA). Both federations were governed by state entities of the General Sports Direction (Dirección General de Deportes, DGD) and the Ministry of Education.

BLACK WOMAN AND SPORTS IN CUBA

For the majority of black and especially poor women, it was not easy for them to get to perform in some of the sports disciplines. These women were also blocked from participating in sports that traditionally and until a few years ago were considered elite. The testimony of Haydée Claver Larrinaga, the first black woman basketball player on a Cuban team and the first female national record holder in the long jump, is an example of this:

"I was born on October 14, 1929, here in what is now the municipality Diez de Octubre. I am the youngest of three sisters of a very poor family. My mom, who was single and alone with us, had to work outside of the home to provide for us. When she would leave for work, she would leave us locked in the room of the tenement where we lived, because she had no one to take care of us. Her situation caused her one day to try to commit suicide by throwing herself and us into a river, which did not happen because of our cries that shocked her out of her despair, and she realized the insanity of it all. We couldn't go to school because we did not have the conditions for that. After I was eight years old, I started attending school and what I learned in school, I came home to teach my sisters. At the age of twelve, I started working as a domestic. I would take home the food that they gave me and what I had leftover to help both my family and some other children of the solar [tenement] who were as poor as we were, but whose father or mother did not have work.

"We never had toys. I received my first gift when I was fifteen from the Roberto Fernández Retamar family, when I worked in their home. It was a lipstick and face powder. I have held on to the empty cases. Though I was a domestic worker, during my free time, I studied shorthand and typing, and I took several piano classes which I paid for on my own with my scarce resources.

"I would attend Club Antilles [Las Águilas, The Eagles] ping pong games. I liked it. When the professor Gerardo Arago saw my physical condition, he selected me for the integrated basketball team of men and women for that club. I stood out because of my speed and my accurate shots at the hoop. Also, my speed allowed me to participate in the competitions of track and field, relay races and long jump. By that time, I was twenty years old.

"But it sounds easy to say. I worked as a domestic in the morning, so I wasn't able to train until the afternoon. I would practice on the grounds of the park Jose Martí, in Vedado, and at night I would practice basketball at the Asturian Center located in Cerro. On many occasions I had to go to those places on foot because I did not have money to pay for the bus fare. But all that effort, sacrifice, and dedication was not in vain. I was able to reach the top and represent Cuba in different international competitions in both sports.

"After the triumph of the Revolution, my life in sports continued. I competed inside and outside the country. In 1986, I retired, and continue in spite of my eighty-one years to participate in marathons and competitions organized by the Committee of Veteran Athletics. I feel sorry for athletes who are interested in sports in order to get out of the country. These athletes have what we didn't have then. I think we have to put more love, dedication, effort and resistance when we face difficulties. I wish I was younger so I could do more for sports and Cuba."[12]

It is undeniable that since the triumph of the revolution, blacks have advanced greatly in the field of sports, extremely relevant to women, who are the focus of this chapter. But it is necessary to recognize that for them to be able to reach prominent positions requires a level of delivery and sacrifice much higher than in that of men if we take into account, besides the rigor of training and competitions, what achievement implies for women athletes' private and spiritual life, given the macho patterns our society has yet to surpass. All of which allows us a better and greater appreciation of Claver's contributions in this important sector of our society.

Regardless of the measures taken by the revolutionary government in the first few years, which had among other objectives to enable the participation of black and *mestizo* people in activities that were held in former private clubs, racism and discrimination persisted in the minds of its members for a long time. The following anecdote exemplifies this:

"In the year 1959, I studied high school at the Víbora Institute where I had stood out as a fencer. I am thankful that my coach, called the Captain, who was also a professor at the private school Edison Institute, selected me because of my results to participate in the provincial competitions of that sport where I went from the junior to senior category, which was necessary to someday reach the National category. The meet was scheduled in the Sports Casino, today's Social Center Cristino Naranjo.

"I still remember my father's words when he accompanied me to the entrance of that majestic building: 'My little girl, I never imagined that you would be able to enter this place as an athlete, this club has always been for white and wealthy people ... the only time I was able to get near this neighborhood was as a bricklayer.'

"The looks I got from the club members and visitors were of astonishment and racist contempt. Walking through those large halls seemed endless. When I finally got to the place of the competition, I found out that it had been suspended. No explanation was given. There was no one in the designated place for the sporting meet. The next day, a fencer from the Edison Institute told me that the athletes and their coaches had withdrawn when they heard that a black woman would be participating. I was fourteen years old, but since then, I knew that discrimination did not disappear with laws only, even those that seemed to be in our favor."[13]

Regardless of this, black and *mestiza* female athletes have continued to break down historic barriers by entering sports traditionally performed by white women such as swimming, fencing, table tennis, rowing, basketball, artistic and rhythmic gymnastics, and archery are among the most significant. Entering these fields is fundamental in achieving goals established by the International Olympics Committee.[14] These female athletes are present quantitatively and qualitatively in the most important competitions of the globe with outstanding results. Every event or modality of the sporting universe counts today with a greater number of athletes, including black Cuban women. The best example of these are the Olympic Games.

Hence black Cuban women have shown themselves to be protagonists in sports, illustrated especially by their prominence in the Olympic Games and what that means because these competitions represent the best expression of the height that an athlete can reach that includes greater recognition at the world level.

Table 33.1 Participation of Cuba in the Olympic Games

	City	Year	Men	Women	Total	Black/mestiza women	White women
01	Melbourne	1956	15	1	16	1	0
02	Rome	1960	9	3	12	1	2
03	Tokyo	1964	25	2	27	1	1
04	Mexico	1968	109	16	125	9	7
05	Munich	1972	112	27	139	25	2
06	Montreal	1976	139	25	164	22	3
07	Moscow	1980	181	33	214	31	2
08	Barcelona	1992	134	54	188	49	5
09	Atlanta	1996	111	56	167	55	1
10	Sidney	2000	151	87	238	70	17
11	Athens	2004	96	55	151	46	9
12	Beijing	2008	103	55	158	53	2
	Total		1,185	414	1,599	363	51

Observations:

1. There are differences in the figures of the sources consulted for tables 33.1 and 33.2 for athletes participating in Olympic Games and sports. It does not affect the objectives of the analysis for this work.
2. The classification of the athletes by the color of their skin was made by the author of this work in consultation with the Commissions of Sports of the National Institute of Sport, Physical Education and Recreation (Comisiones de Deportes del Instituto Nacional de Deporte, Educacíon Física y Recreación, INDER) when necessary.

As shown in table 33.1, before 1959, Cuba included a woman athlete for the first time in the Olympic Games of Melbourne. She was Berta Díaz, in track and field, who was also part of the Cuban delegation in the Olympic Games in Rome in 1960.

Just five years after the triumph of the Cuban Revolution, the figure of Miguelina Cobián Echevarría burst into the Tokyo Games of 1964. She obtained fifth place in the Olympic Games as Miguelina attained the nickname the Eastern Gazelle. This athlete was the most outstanding female figure in the decade of the 1960s in Cuba, selected time and again as one of the best in all of Latin America. She demonstrated to the world at that time that the slogan the Rights of Sport for the People was and continues to be a reality.

A few years later, another young black woman from Guantanamo, only nineteen years old, Silvia Chivás obtained two bronze medals in the race of 100 meters and the relay 4 x 100 meters in Munich in 1972.

From the Olympic Games held in Moscow in 1980 until the last games in 2008 in Beijing, Cuban women athletes have obtained 46 medals: Track and

Table 33.2 Women's participation in the Olympic Games by sport and race

Sport	01	02	03	04	05	06	07	08	09	10	11	12	Black/mestiza	White
Track and Field	1	1	1	7	10	8	3	17	21	15	20	26	130	5
Basketball							12	12	12	12			48	6
Cycling									1	2	1	3	2	9
Diving			1			5	1							6
Fencing				2		5	5		3	4	2	2	20	
Gymnastics				7							1		2	6
Judo								7	7	7	7	7	35	
Synchronized swimming								2						2
Swimming										2	1	3	1	3
Basque pelota									2					2
Rowing											2	3	5	
Softball										15			12	3
Taekwondo										2	1	1	4	3
Table tennis								2		2	2		1	7
Shooting								2		2	1	1		2
Archery										2	1		1	
Volleyball					12	12	12	12	12	12	12	12	96	
Beach volleyball										2	2	4	8	
Yachting										1				1
Total													365	49

Black Women in Sports

Field 15, Judo 22, Volleyball 4, Taekwondo 1, Cycling 1, and Shooting 1. These medals rise to 96 medals hanging on the chests of our athletes if we consider that 48 correspond to the 12 players of the volleyball team, who have won in four Olympics games, and the 8 members of the track team in the two relay races of 4 x 100 meters held in Mexico and Munich. Of all of the female athletes within this short timeline only 2 are white.

It is significant for the analysis of the achievements of Cuban women in the Olympics Games in consideration of their race how fencing, which together with track and field were the first sports to compete with a team of white fencers at a world level: Mireya Rodríguez, Margarita Rodríguez, and Milady Tack Fang. Inclusion has increased after twelve games, which now includes a total of nine white women athletes and twenty black women and *mestiza* athletes. If we consider that fencing has always been at the national and global level an elitist sport because of the costly resources it requires, the increase of black women participants in Cuba constitutes an important developmental index, although the development is not reflected with Olympic medals.

Cuban women's track and field has participated in twelve Olympic Games with 130 athletes since 1956 who have obtained 15 medals. Volleyball has won 4 medals, 3 gold and 1 bronze in eight Olympic Games, as shown in table 33.3.

These successes transcend national pride. Cuba is currently the country that holds the most Olympic medals from Latin America and the Caribbean. In Beijing 2008, according to data compiled by the journalist Oscar Sánchez in the newspaper *Granma*, we obtained 24 medals, 9 corresponding to the women (7 for black and *mestiza* women, 2 whites). We have won more medals than Brazil (15 medals) and Jamaica (11 medals).[15]

The king sport, track and field, deserves special attention for the outstanding result of its athletes and for its history in Cuban sport. The javelin thrower María Caridad Colón was the pioneer in the field. She played in the Olympic Games in Moscow in 1980 to become the first Latin American woman athlete to win a gold medal and establish Olympic records in that sport.

This triumph debunked a thesis launched by an Anglo-Saxon sports specialist who claimed that javelin was not designed for nonwhite athletes.

Cuban javelin thrower Osleidys Menéndez, disc throwers Maritza Martén and Yarelis Barrios, Yumisleidi Cumbá in shot put, and Yipsi Moreno in hammer throw have all won Olympic medals. Moreno reached second place in the qualifiers for the Diamond League.[16]

Ana Fidelia Quirot also deserves special attention. She is among the best in the world. She won two world championships in 1995 and 1997 and won the Olympic [Silver] Medal in 1996. Countless medals, distinctions, and trophies are treasured by this simple and spectacular woman. Currently, she is in fourth place among the fastest women in the world. But her greatest

Table 33.3 Medals won by female Cuban athletes in the Olympic Games

Name/Team/Event	Games	Year	Sport	Medal
María Caridad Colón	Moscow	1980	Track and Field	Gold
Maritza Martén	Barcelona	1992	Track and Field	Gold
Odalis Revé	Barcelona	1992	Judo	Gold
Team	Barcelona	1992	Volleyball	Gold
Driulis González	Atlanta	1996	Judo	Gold
Team	Atlanta	1996	Volleyball	Gold
Legna Verdecia	Sydney	2000	Judo	Gold
Sibelis Veranes	Sydney	2000	Judo	Gold
Team	Sydney	2000	Volleyball	Gold
Yumileidi Cumbá	Athens	2004	Judo	Gold
Osleidys Menéndez	Athens	2004	Track and Field	Gold
Relay 4 x 100 m	Mexico	1968	Track and Field	Silver
Estela Rodríguez	Barcelona	1992	Judo	Silver
Ana Fidelia Quirot	Atlanta	1996	Track and Field	Silver
Estela Rodríguez	Atlanta	1996	Judo	Silver
Daima Beltrán	Sydney	2000	Judo	Silver
Driulis González	Sydney	2000	Judo	Silver
Urbia Menéndez	Sydney	2000	Taekwondo	Silver
Yipsi Moreno	Athens	2004	Track and Field	Silver
Daima Beltrán	Athens	2004	Judo	Silver
Yanelis Labrada	Athens	2004	Taekwondo	Silver
Yanet Bermoy	Beijing	2008	Judo	Silver
Anaisis Hernández	Beijing	2008	Judo	Silver
Yalennis Castillo	Beijing	2008	Judo	Silver
Yoanka González	Beijing	2008	Cycling	Silver
Yarelis Barrios	Beijing	2008	Track and Field	Silver
Yipsi Moreno	Beijing	2008	Track and Field	Silver
Silvia Chivas	Munich	1972	Track and Field	Bronze
Relay 4 x 100 m	Munich	1972	Track and Field	Bronze
Yoamnet Quintero	Barcelona	1992	Track and Field	Bronze
Ana Fidelia Quirot	Barcelona	1992	Track and Field	Bronze
Amarilis Savón	Barcelona	1992	Judo	Bronze
Driulis González	Barcelona	1992	Judo	Bronze
Amarilis Savón	Atlanta	1996	Judo	Bronze
Legna Verdecia	Atlanta	1996	Judo	Bronze
Diadenis Luna	Atlanta	1996	Judo	Bronze
Osleidys Menéndez	Sydney	2000	Track and Field	Bronze
Yunaika Crawford	Athens	2004	Track and Field	Bronze
Amarilis Savón	Athens	2004	Judo	Bronze
Yurisleydis Lupetey	Athens	2004	Judo	Bronze
Driulis González	Athens	2004	Judo	Bronze
Yurisel Laborde	Athens	2000	Judo	Bronze
Team	Athens	2000	Volleyball	Bronze
Idalis Ortíz	Beijing	2008	Judo	Bronze
Eglis Cruz	Beijing	2008	Shooting	Bronze
Dianeylls Montejo	Beijing	2008	Taekwondo	Bronze

Note: Volleyball Team 1992. Tania Ortiz, Lily Izquierdo, Regla Bell, Mercedes Calderón, Marlenis Costa, Idamnis Gato, Regla Torres, Ana Ibis Fernández, Mireya Luis, Raisa Ofarrill, Magalys Carvajal, and Norka Latamblet.
Volleyball Team 1996. Yumilka Ruiz, Lily Izquierdo, Regla Bell, Marlenis Costa, Idamnis Gato, Regla Torres, Ana Ibis Fernández, Mireya Luis, Raisa Ofarrill, Magalys Carvajal, Mirka Francia, and Taimaris Agüero.
Volleyball Team 2000. Yumilka Ruiz, Lily Izquierdo, Regla Bell, Marlenis Costa, Idamnis Gato, Regla Torres, Ana Ibis Fernández, Mireya Luis, Zoila Barros, Martha Sánchez, Mirka Francia, and Taimaris Agüero.
Volleyball Team 2004. Yumilka Ruiz, Martha Sánchez, Ana Ibis Fernández, Anniara Muñoz, Maibilis Martínez, Rosir Calderón, Zoila Barros, Dulce María Tellez, Nancy Carrillo, Daimí Ramírez, Liana Mesa, and Yaima Ortiz.
Relay 4 x 100 meters. Track. Mexico 1968. Miguelina Cobián, Marlene Elejalde (deceased), Violeta Quesada, and Fulgencio Romay.
Relay 4 x 100 meters. Track. Munich 1972. Marlene Elejalde, Fulgencia Romay, Carmen Laura Valdés, and Sylvia Chivás.

achievement, above all her merits, was to continue her successful sports career after a regrettable accident that distanced her from the track for a long period. The author Ana Segar in her book *Ana Fidelia Quirot, en el carril de la vida* [In the Lane of Life] describes her as "the only Phoenix of the universe that has lived on the track."

Another index of the strong female presence in our sports is the Hall of Fame, created in the year 2003 by the Confederation of the Central American and Caribbean Athletics to honor the best athletes in the region. Of the thirty Cubans exalted in this sport, ten correspond to Cuban women, eleven of whom are considered outstanding in the whole region. They are Silvia Chivás, María Caridad Colón, Ana Fidelia Quirot, Miguelina Cobián, Marlene Elejalde, Violeta Quesada, Fulgencia Romay, Carmen Laura Valdés, Martiza Martén, and Silvia Costa.

At the XII Athletics World Championships held in Berlin in 2009, the triple jumper Yargelis Savigne reached the universal title in her specialty and was selected the best Latin American athlete. Her compatriot, Mabel Gay, won the silver medal. That same year at the Youth World Cup in Edmonton, Canada, Savigne was selected the undisputed leader of the Diamond League.

The outstanding social attention given to Cuban sport is reflected in the results achieved by the disabled athlete Suslaidys Girat, record holder. She attained her status as world champion in the flat 100 meters with gold and silver medals in the long jump in the XXI Deaflympics.

At the 2011 IPC Athletics World Championships held in New Zealand in January, the distinguished Yunidis Castillo from Santiago de Cuba was awarded three gold medals. She took two new records in the specialties of 100 meters (12, 20) and 200 meters (24, 86). In addition, she obtained first place in the 400 meters, category T-46 for athletes with a single amputation below or above the elbow.

At only nineteen years old, Yunidis formalized her status as an absolute champion by surpassing her performance in the Paralympic Games held in Beijing in 2008 as a bichampion at 100 meter and 200 meter. Her youth, strength, and decision to continue will lead to future and greater triumphs.

CARIBBEAN *MORENAS* AND MUCH MORE

Since the Olympic Games from Moscow to Beijing, seventeen Olympic players have added to the successes in volleyball. Among the spectacular Morenas del Caribe is Regla Torres, selected the best athlete of the twentieth century.

Thanks to their extraordinary effort in their rigorous daily training, these athletes have cast honor and glory to our country through real world championships in fencing, cycling, and taekwondo. Some of these athletes are Zuleydis Ortiz, World Fencing Champion; Lisandra Guerra, Yumari González, and Dalila Rodríguez, World Champions in cycling; and Dainelis Montejo and Yaimara del Rosario, World Champions in taekwondo. Adding to this constellation of athletes are the stars Oleiny Linares, the new Champion of Chess in Cuba. She is a young black woman from Santiago de Cuba who also holds the title of International Master.

The successes achieved at the Olympic level are multiplied when other international competitions are considered. The World Championships and World Leagues, as well as the meetings organized by the different sports federations, are increasing the glories attained by black women in Cuban sports.

For the first time the inaugural Youth Olympic Games were held in Singapore, Malaysia, in August 2010. Cuba stood at the head of the American continent between 205 countries, where 3,600 athletes participated between fourteen and eighteen years old.

Overcoming difficult obstacles to attend this Olympic event, our young people had to compete in various qualifying events on the continent. Of the fifteen medals attained, three were won by women. Leydy Laura Moya won gold in modern pentathlon, Lismania Muñoz won silver in the javelin throw, and Yuleimi Abreu won bronze in taekwondo.

This first experience of our young athletes is a good starting point for the upcoming Olympic Games in London 2012.

These data show only indexes in reference for this analysis. They do not include the competitive levels prior to the pre-Olympics, leagues, and world events, including those that are regional. The greatness and importance of sport in Cuba is another index whose figures are truly spectacular for black women and girls participating in physical and sporting activities.

WHAT DO WE NEED?

In spite of all the contribution of black women to Cuban sports, there is no equivalence as to their participation in the levels of maximum decision making as directed by INDER. We have only four commissioners, though thirty-six sports are practiced. We have no provincial director and no National Directorate of Cuban Sport. Moreover, we must train our athletes to make them culturally and politically prepared. Women are trained in the strict discipline of the sport, prepared psychologically to overcome any obstacle and to assume new responsibilities. Their experiences as athletes should be taken advantage of by granting them greater participation in those spaces where important decisions related to this activity are made.

In recent years, the Cuban Olympic Committee (COC) has had among its members important greats in sports. The first woman was the stellar runner of 400 and 800 meters Autrelia Pentón Conde. Currently these greats include María Caridad Colón, Cecilia Juara, Daima Beltrán, Legna Verdecia, and Yumilka Ruiz. This last outstanding athlete, captain of the volleyball team, has been a representative of the Olympic International Committee (COI). She is also a member of the Commission of Athletes, the International Solidarity Olympic Committee, and the Pan-American Sports Organization (ODEPA) of the International Olympic Committee. Additionally, she was also selected as an exemplary athlete, as a model to be followed by the young generations, given for the first time to a Cuban woman. Mireya Luis is also a greatly distinguished volleyball athlete and captain of her team. She was a member of ODEPA and the Athletes Commission of COI.

The initial work in this chapter does not aim to exhaust the issue of the successful presence of black women in Cuban sport but to contribute to a greater knowledge of them and to sports in popular culture. I have aimed to show the role that black women and *mestiza* athletes have played, explored from a different angle. These athletes should be known for their struggle to reach the space that they had set as their goal that now belongs to them because of their passion, courage, effort, dedication, and love, which in turn has filled Cuba with sports glory.

NOTES

1. Cited from Carlos E. Reig, "Para una historia de los deportes en Cuba (1800–1899)," *Temas*, no. 49 (January–March 2007): 31.

2. María del Carmen Barcia, *Capas populares y modernidad en Cuba (1878–1930)* (Havana: Fernando Ortiz Foundation, 2005), 163.

3. Susan J. Bandy, "De la Antigüedad al siglo XIX," *Olímpica* 26, no. 31, Ecuador (February–March 2000): 18.

4. Yves-Pierre Boulongne, "Pierre de Coubertain y el deporte femenino," *Olímpica* 34, Ecuador (February–March 2000): 23–26.

5. See Carlos Reig Romero, "Las primeras competencias de atletismo femenino en Cuba," *Olímpica*, nos. 1–2, Ecuador (January–April 1998): 43; del Carmen Barcia, *Capas populares y modernidad en Cuba (1878–1930)*, 130–31.

6. Fraternal Union, the association was founded at the end of 1885. It was created as a Society of Instruction and Recreation for people of color. It was one of thirty-eight associations that integrated the Feminine Section of the Federation of Cuban Societies from the province of Havana.

7. ODAC, Organización Deportiva Atlética de Cuba [Sports Organization of Cuban Athletics] was created by the private sector meant for school, social, and professional sports that organized competitions in junior and senior categories.

8. Newspaper, *Diario de la Marina* [Marina Daily], Havana, June 11, 1942, p. 15.

9. Reig Romero, "Las primeras competencias de atletismo femenino en Cuba," 44.

10. This information was obtained from three of the athletes who participated in the competitions.
11. See the *Comité Olímpico Cubano Las Memorias de los Juegos Deportivos Centroamericanos y del Caríbe* corresponding to the years 1946, 1950, and 1954.
12. Fragment of an interview of Haydée Claver conducted in her home.
13. Personal testimony.
14. Women would not be integrated into sports and reach an equal level of participation at 50 percent until the twenty-first century.
15. Oscar Sánchez, "Latinamérica y el Caribe en Beijing–2008," *Granma*, September 19, 2008, p. 14.
16. Testimony of the specialist Lázaro Betancourt Mella.

BIBLIOGRAPHY

Arbona Lorenzo, Humberto V., and Josefa M. Aguirre García. 2001. "Algunas características del movimiento de cultura física en Cuba anterior a 1959." Year 6, March. http://www.afdportes.com.
Bandy, Susan J. 2000. "De la Antigüedad al siglo XIX." *Olímpica* 26, no. 31 (February–March). Ecuador.
Barcia Zerqueira, María del Carmen. 2000. *Una sociedad en crisis: La Habana a finales del siglo XIX*. Havana: Editorial de Ciencias Sociales.
———. 2005. *Capas populares y modernidad en Cuba (1878–1930)*. Havana: Fernando Ortiz Foundation.
Boulongne, Yves-Pierre. 1997. "Pierre de Coubertain, sus raíces y el Congreso del Havre, 1897." *Olímpica*, October–November. Ecuador.
Boulongne, Yves-Pierre. 2000. "Pierre de Coubertain y el deporte femenino." *Olímpica*, February–March. Ecuador.
Confederación Centroamericana y del Caribe de Atletismo. 2007. *Salón de Fama (2005–2006)*. Santo Domingo, Dominican Republic; Puerto Rico: Editora Buho.
Congreso Olímpico Internacional (XIII). 2009. *Contribuciones*. Copenhagan.
Entine, Jon. "Raza y Deporte." www.pponline.co.uk.
FEMPRESS. 2005. *Mujeres Negras*, special issue. Chile.
Forbes, Irene, Ana Maria Luján, and Juan Velásquez. 2001. *Olímpicos Cubanos famosos y desconocidos*. Havana: Editorial Científico-Técnica.
Juegos Deportivos Centroamericanos y del Caribe. 1926–1959. Memorias del Comité Olímpico Internacional.
Kidane, Fékrou. 1995. "Las mujeres en el Movimiento Olímpico." *Olímpica*, February–March. Ecuador.
Montejo, Carmen. 2004. *Sociedades Negras en Cuba* (1878–1960). Havana: Centro de Investigación y Desarrollo de la Cultura Cubana Juan Marinello.
Reig Romero, Carlos E. 1998. "Las primeras competencias de atletismo femenino en Cuba." *Olímpica*, nos. 1–2 (January–April). Ecuador.

———. 2007. "Para una historia de los deportes en Cuba (1800–1999)." *Temas*, no. 49 (January–March).
Ruiz, Irene Esther. "El pensamiento feminista y el deporte en Cuba." Unpublished.
———. 2007. "Derechos cívicos de la mujer en el deporte." Conferencia en III Seminario sobre la Mujer en el Comité Olímpico Dominicano, November.
Sánchez, Oscar. 2004. "Nuestra Mujer, Vanguardia Olímpica de Latinamérica." *Granma*, June 11.
———. 2008. "Latinamérica y el Caribe en Beijing 2008." *Granma*, September 19.
Tamburnini, Claudio M. 2002. "El retorno de las Amazonas." Article from the Department of Practical Philosophy. Switzerland: University of Gutenberg.
Temas. 2007. "Deporte: Terreno Cultural." *Temas*, no. 49 (January–March). Havana.

Chapter 34

A Lexical Semantical Analysis on the Discourse of Women in Cuban Rap

Yanelys Abreu Babi and Anette Jiménez Marata

Hip-hop emerged at the start of the 1970s in the marginalized neighborhoods of the South Bronx. From its beginning, hip-hop fused rhythms with an account of the happenings of daily life of the neighborhood. It is composed of four elements that make up and support its ideology, rap, breakdance, DJ, and graffiti, which makes it thus a movement. For our study, we will focus only on rap because it is the form that uses spoken language.

Rap arrived in our country in the late '70s and early '80s from the United States. In the beginning, rap in Cuba resulted in a mimetic reproduction of the American model. Over the course of time, "cubanization" occurred as rap was adapted through themes that addressed our reality in Cuba.

From a formal point of view, rap is characterized by a very dynamic musical genre that, in addition to communicating ideas, tries to make the spectator dance. It does not seek an order, nor a linearity in its structure, and places the listener as the central figure as the recipient of an elaborated message. A symbol of protest, the rapper tries to transform the surrounding reality by using a discourse of certitude that is almost authoritarian.

Rap is defined as spoken word poetry. According to Rodolfo Rensoli, "It is a powerful lyric that speaks of life on the streets. It is a street aesthetic that shows poetry in different ways. It uses words that are commonly used, as it also disguises these—the same function as in written poetry—it is also very effective."[1]

The creative universe of Cuban rap is divided, in my judgment, into five critical thematic zones that are fundamental:

- The female figure
- The social
- Race and the search for identity among the races of African origins in Cuba

- Self-referencing of the movement and the exaltation of the self
- The commercial

These five thematic nuclei represent two ways of assuming or interpreting reality. The first four are included in what has been called underground hip-hop or "subterranean" that tries to validate those elements that in some way are in the periphery: to critique, to propose solutions to social problems of the times, and to assert rap as a form of expression. The last thematic area registers in what can be considered "commercial" hip-hop that aims to promote rap music as a form of diversion, to incite dance, and that alludes to *Cubanía* [Cubanity/Cubanness], landscapes, etc. This rap is designed for the market, which deemphasizes social problems. This chapter is only concerned with rap that focuses on women.

Since ancient times, women have served as inspiration in all forms of art. Women have also played a vital role in Cuban music, especially in popular music. Within the genre, the female figure is not an exception, and rather different aspects or topics on women that touch on subject matter concerned with maternity, sensuality of the female body, self-esteem, gender relations, violence, and prostitution are addressed.

According to Lagarde:

> Sexuality is a historically determined cultural complex consisting of social relations, social and political institutions, as well as in conceptions of the world that define the basic identity of subjects. In particular, sexuality is constituted by ways of acting, of behaving, of thinking, and of feeling, as well as by intellectual, affective and vital capacities associated with sex. Sexuality consists also of the roles, functions and economic and social activities assigned based on gender to social groups and individuals, at work, in eroticism, in art, in politics, and in all human experiences; It also consists of the access and possession of specific knowledge, languages, know-how and beliefs; It implies rank, prestige and positions in relation to power.[2]

As the author points out, sexuality transcends the limits of the biological body and comprises a much broader social and cultural environment. Therefore because it is not determined solely by the biological factor and by anatomical-physiological characteristics, it can be altered, modified, and subverted and with it the set of values and cultural representations that are attributed to it.

When we talk about female sexuality, invariably the psychosocial factors associated with motherhood emerge as one of the most strongly linked roles to women from a social and cultural point of view. The binomial woman-mother affects all the vital spheres of women. Moreover, it organizes her life independently of any condition. The traditional performance of it is so strong that many of the professions and labor considered "typically" feminine (and that actually covers most of the female workforce) are thus valued because they represent a continuation of the functions associated with motherhood, for example, teaching, the care of children, care of the sick and the elderly, etc.

Artistically, the topic is often addressed as an idealization of the mother figure associated with the effort that is necessary in raising children. Rap maintains this vision, although it also shows a peculiarity in presenting abandoned mothers who are trying to rise above the slums of society. They are mistreated and undervalued by their partners and have to make a life on their own, with few economic resources, and struggling with some social conventions that become obstacles to their progress. These women play a double role in raising children. They are both mother and father to them:

Mother, fact is time has become your enemy.
Caring for your child like a wild feline
just to watch him play, run, grow.
Unquestionably without any money,
what more can you do?
Always looking out for options
with no solutions.[3]

Together I have lived with my mother in this hard-hitting and fucked-upped life.
In the '80s, my father abandoned us
90 miles from where we live.[4]

There are no intellectual mothers, no perfect homes, only abandonment and lack of understanding. These are broken homes marked by a destiny that can only be reversed through a personal struggle. There are allusions to social change in rap that refer to the Cuban Revolution with regard to women's rights and the need for women to internalize this change to fight against the remnants of discrimination that still prevail in our society despite the government's efforts to eradicate them:

Woman, respect yourself,
maintain your pride before society.[5]

Out with the thorn of oppression.
I make this dream come true; with unity
It's possible today, so pay attention.[6]

The high indexes of violence against women are a constant in today's society. Although women are victims of abuse outside the home, that includes mistreatment, rape, and harassment, the family sphere is often a place of cumulative injuries that are equal or greater. In this sense, the domestic environment often conditions more subtle forms of violence (but that are not less damaging).

Rap's discourse often refers to the issue of domestic violence. This may be as a result of patriarchal society, in which the home becomes a marginal environment that serves as the stage for conditions or addictions that transform human behavior, such as alcoholism:

Minute by minute,
Beaten by the brute,
macho absolute.[7]

The one you thought would give his life for you
Ended up being like one of the machos at the corner
Those that associate love with drinking.[8]

Don't run from me, let me see.
Ah! I know,
That guy hit you yet again.
When did it happen? Yesterday?[9]

Latin American society, traditionally *machista*, limits (through the values, norms, beliefs, and myths that it legitimizes) the rights of women over her own body and her own sexuality. Women constitute an especially vulnerable group, in great measure because of social stereotypes that define or identify them as passive, complacent, bound, and subordinate to the decisions made by men, who must organize, regulate, and evaluate (according to his demands and expectations) everything related to the sphere of love and sex between couples.

For the artists, and musicians in particular, the sensuality of the female body has been a source of inspiration. In rap, this topic emerges as a way to emphasize the virtues of the variations of the female form and the sensations they provoke in the opposite sex. The feminine walk, which has been so praised traditionally, is readdressed but not with the double entendre heard in the Cuban musical genres of the *son* or the *guaracha* but in a more direct way and, in some cases, aggressively. The sensuality of the *mulata* woman is exalted, capable of seizing the senses of any man. This is in reference to the myth that has been created around the sexuality of Cuban women with a supposed insatiable sexual appetite. Women are also praised in rap for their talents in dance whose movements arouse virile sexual desire:

You have a seductive way of moving in front of me.
Baby, you make me vibrate.[10]

*Cuban woman, you intoxicate me with your temperament
And your disposition too, at all times.*[11]

*To me, you are a flower
whose lips release honey
I would like to get drunk with the sweetness of your skin
imagining a thousand ways to love you all at once.*[12]

On this topic, the basic theme is carnal love, sexual pleasure, and therefore the ephemeral. Women are merely a means of achieving pleasure and only their superficial qualities are exalted, regardless of their feelings or virtues.

Within the creative universe of rap exists another important issue: prostitution in which exercising sex for money becomes a necessity, a forced end. Prostitution is presented as the result of poor distribution of social goods. If there is a culprit, it is society; women are only victims who try to prevent their lives from taking that route. However, it becomes more important to be able to feed your children than morals and prejudices. Being a prostitute becomes a livelihood when the father of the child abandons them or when scarcity in the house is pressing:

They call her a whore.

*Society does not refute her,
prostitutes roll around for money
and all of a sudden, you're in line, scratching for any job.*[13]

*Desperate
but the competition's tight,
though you go a thousand times and nothing,
you sleep listening to the sound of doors they close
on your face.*

Then society throws you the hook and you take the bait.[14]

The sex market adopts the most varied forms. Not only is a prostitute the one who goes to the street offering her body for a price, but prostitutes are also women who are in a relationship because of material advantages and not because of love:

*Last night, I was meditating alone.
What's up with Lola?!
The living room's missing grandmother's gramophone,
   the piano, 2 picture frames and*

even a bouquet of poppies,
I ran up to my room and found my jewelry missing and
I saw a note.[15]

A defense of the prostitute is made, giving the reasons why a woman would become one though society marginalizes and judges her for it. The lyrics show the sacrifice it takes for a woman to have sex without love, forced by circumstances and how that can lead to her alienation as a human being. Behind the figure of the prostitute stands a human being with feelings and needs, not just a machine of pleasure:

She's a wind-up body that's agitated transmitting
an inner fire she does not feel.
Teeth bite into her breasts,
the time to shout has arrived and pretend mad passion.[16]

Imagine that everything turns against you, woman;
there's no money.
You don't have enough for anything with the little you have,
you just don't have any.
You're so low as usual,
but this time's more than usual.
Your head is cracking for solutions.[17]

The lexicon used in these compositions is in the popular or vulgar registers as a result of the environment in which the texts are built and the reality they reflect. The repetition of some words like "woman," "*negra*" [black woman], "abandoned," and "macho" are keys to the intention of the message that the authors want to transmit.

As shown, there are two large oppositional semantic fields in the texts: women and men. The treatment of women is marked by negative and positive themes in two areas, whereas the first are those that are associated with abuse, prostitution, and abandonment, and the second constitute an invitation to emancipation, liberation, and rupture from the macho model.

However, the field of men is defined by purely negative themes as a result of the dominant role that they have always had in society, excluding women. Often this translates into the dichotomies of abuser/molested, seductive/seduced, buyer/merchandise in which women are always secondary, placed in the background.

There is also a semantic opposition between presence and absence in relation to the topic of motherhood. The mother is always next to the child, responsible for her upbringing, while the father has left the home for one reason or another. This binomial antagonism reflects one of the constructions by the aforementioned patriarchal society, which places all the responsibility of educating the children on the shoulders of women.

According to Díaz,[18] among the norms that define female sexuality are:

- To be an adult and heterosexual.
- Always be linked to love (in contrast to the rules governing male sexuality).
- To be fulfilled for the purpose of procreation.
- To be inferior to male masculinity.
- To have great ignorance about the body itself that then reinforces the feeling of modesty.

Rap discourse is predominantly constructed from the space of masculinity. In this sense, femininity is defined by what Díaz explained. Only when women develop their own rap discourse is there an attempt to subvert the masculinist canons:

And if I don't give birth,
I'm still a woman.
And if I don't smile,
I'm still a woman.
If I don't cook,
I'm still a woman.[19]

The economic and social situation of ethnic groups in the world has a direct impact on their limited social representation and the marginalization that they have traditionally suffered. Often these ethnic groups occupy the bottom strata of the social pyramid, which translates into unequal opportunities to access resources; their participation is reduced in the decision making in solving their own problems. They are stigmatized by society for their cultural practices and worldviews.

Afro-descendent women belong to the nondominant ethnic group and are therefore condemned to social silence. As long as their rights are not recognized, their realities are ignored and undervalued; however, even when their rights are recognized, it is only through formal discourse and not from a social practice.

Women in rap lyrics suffer from double discrimination, first for being women and second for being black. There is an attempt to highlight her figure and values as a human being:

Negra [black woman], your voice teaches.
Negra, princess owner.
Negra, she's a beauty.

Negra, woman that dreams.
Negra, eternal purity.
Negra, my mother.[20]

In concluding this brief treatment of the female figure in rap, we can arrive at the following conclusions:

- Although rap tries to break with the social stereotypes of women, it does not achieve it completely. The masculine voice that enunciates the discourse, although it tries to advocate for emancipation, continues to see women as mere instruments of pleasure or reinforces the traditional role of the mother. Only when the discourse is constructed by the female voice are the traditional codes, canons, and meanings subverted.
- Work on the semantic fields analyzes the opposition between the rights of women and men and the various cultural meanings attributed to them in today's society.
- A biased vision on women is offered. Lyrics underscore motherhood, prostitution, or the sensuality of the female body as independent aspects, forgetting that all these issues simultaneously affect women as social beings.
- A phenomenon as complex as prostitution suffers, in the texts that assume prostitution as a thematic reference, from an integral valuation. However, although this may seem like a deficiency, it has an intentionality: to not heighten the feeling of social repudiation that prostitutes have historically received. By treating them as "other," women who sell their bodies cease to be blamed and become victims: individual blame is set aside to make way for human contact and for sensitivity to this social issue.
- Rap discourse also becomes an ideal place to denounce violence and violence against women both in the social and family spheres. The texts I analyzed defend the rights of women to confront and subvert the patriarchal regime that marginalizes them to secondary, subordinate, and dependent positions.
- The compositions that make up the sample of this research constitute a claim in favor of female self-esteem. To love oneself represents a right and a vital need for every woman. Virtues are found in white or black skins, and in more or less curly hair. Our value is not found in the judgment that others have of us. Our value lives within us and it depends on each one of us.

NOTES

1. María del Puerto, "Altas expectativas," *La Jiribilla* (digital).
2. Marcela Lagarde, *La sexualidad* (digital document), 5.

3. "Madre," interpreted by Orichas. CD. *A lo Cubano*.
4. Ibid.
5. "Rejas dentro el corazón," interpreted by Anónimo Consejo, featuring Las Krudas.
6. Ibid.
7. Ibid.
8. Ibid.
9. "Pretextos," interpreted by Obsesión. CD. *Grandes cortoletrajes*.
10. "Mística," interpreted by Orichas. CD. *A lo Cubano*.
11. "Mujer cubana," interpreted by 100%.
12. Ibid.
13. "La llaman puta," interpreted by Obsesión. CD. La Fábrik.
14. Ibid.
15. "Lola (Uchi-cuchi)," interpreted by Obsesión.
16. "La llaman puta," interpreted by Obsesión. CD. La Fábrik.
17. Ibid.
18. Elena Díaz, professor of the FLACSO-Cuba program, *Antropología de género: salud* [Anthropology of Gender: Health], PowerPoint, slide 19.
19. "Rejas dentro el corazón," interpreted by Anónimo Consejo featuring Las Krudas.
20. Ibid.

BIBLIOGRAPHY

Alvarado Ramos, Juan A. 1996. "Relaciones raciales en Cuba. Notas de investigación." *Temas*, no. 7 (July–September). Havana.

Álvarez Reyes, Sady, and Tania Oyarzo-Hinojosa. 2004. "La historia del rap." *Movimiento* 2:1. Havana.

Cordero, Tatiana. 2004. "Una mirada sociopsicológica al rap en cuba." *La Jiribilla*, no. 172. Havana.

Del Puerto, María. 2001. "Altas expectativas." *La Jiribilla*, Havana.

Del Río, Joel. 2002. "Atlas expectativas." *La Jiribilla*, Havana.

Escalante, Ana Cecilia. *Perspectiva social de género*. Digital document.

Herrera Santi, Patricia. 2000. "Rol de género y funcionamiento familiar." *Revista Cubana Medicina General Integral*.

Lagarde, Marcela. *La sexualidad*. Digital document.

Index

ablation (excision of the clitoris), 35n22
Adriaens, Fien, 185
Africana Abakuá, 175, 299–304
African Americans, xviii, xxv, 183–84, 197, 212–13, 285,
African American spirituals, 135
African diaspora, xxxiv, 153, 181–82, 213
African deities, 92, 95, 198, 105, 109n19, 198. *See also* Orishas
African National Congress (ANC), 203
Africans, *passim*, but see especially: 20–21, 25, 27–29, 33, 39, 144, 242, 250–51, 253; essence, 212; in the Iberian Peninsula, 242; nonacceptance of, 251; testimonies of, 27; transcending nuclear family framework, 25, 33; women, v, xi
Afrocubana(s), *passim*, but see especially: xi, xiii, xiv, xv–xvi, xviii, xix, xxi–xxvii, xxxi, xxxviii; stereotypes of, 127–37
Agüero, Caridad, 311
Aguirre, Mirta, 236
Alba, Marinieves, xx
Albear, Timotea "Latuán," 94
Alfonso, María del Carmen, 260
Alfonso, Vitalina, 236
Alma, Karina, 334

Almeida Junco, Yulexis, xxxvii, 125n12, 337
"Alpha Wives," 185
Alvarado Ramos, Juan A., 331
Alvarez, Belén, xxxvi, 19, 21–29, 31, 33–34, 255
Álvarez Reyes, Sady, and Tania Oyarzo-Hinojosa, 331
Alvarez, Sonia, xxii, xxviin18
American literary tradition, 210
Amorós, Celia, 125
ancestors, the, xxiv, 21, 28, 105, 107, 108n9, 135, 203, 205, 210, 212–14, 229, 231, 235, 239
Angarica, Valentin, 110
Angola, Juan, 44, 55n13
Angolan War, 199
Arango y Parreño, Francisco de, 8, 251, 256, 252n40
Araújo, Nara, 236
Arbona Lorenzo, Humberto V., 321
Archivo de la Iglesia de Santa Lucía, 56
Archivo Histórico Oficina del Conservador de Santiago Cuba (AHOCSC), 54, 55n25, 56
Argüelles Medros, Aníbal, 108n2
Argüelles Medros, Aníbal and Illeana Hodges, 110
Argyriadis, Kali, 124n8, 125

athletes and athletic institutions, 310–21; XII Athletics World Championships in Berlin (2009), 318; XXI Deaflympics, 318; Amateur Athletic Union of Cuba (UAAC), 310; Amateur Sports Organization of Cuba (ODAC), 310–11, 320; Athletic Association of Cuban Women, 311; Autrelia Pentón Conde, 320; Committee of Veteran Athletics, 312; Confederation of the Central American and Caribbean Athletics, 318; Cuban Olympic Committee (COC), 319; Danielis Montejo and Yaimara del Rosario, World Champions in Taekwondo, 319; General Sports Direction (DGD), 311; IPC Athletics World Championships in New Zealand (2011), 318; International Solidarity Olympic Committee, 320; National Athletic Federation of Secondary Inter-Institutional Teaching (FANAI), 311; Lisandra Guerra, Yumari González, and Dalila Rodríguez, World Champions in cycling, 319; Lismania Muñoz, silver medalist in javelin throwing, 316; medals won in the Olympic Games, 317; National Athletic Federation of Secondary Schools, 311; National Directorate of Cuban Sports, 319; Oleiny Linares, Chess in Cuba, 319; Olympic Games in Rome in (1960), 314–17; Olympic Games in Stockholm (1912), 310; Olympic International Committee (COI), 320; Pan-American Sports Organization (ODEPA), 320; Third Carnival of Feminine Athletics, 310; volleyball team, 317; Yargelis Savigne, triple jumper and leader of the Diamond League, 318; Youth Olympic Games in Singapore and Malaysia (2010), 319; Youth World Cup in Edmonton, Canada, 318; Yuleimi Abrewu, bronze medalist in Taekwondo; Zuleydis Ortiz, World Fencing Champion, 319

Austria, 284

Ayala, Cristina, 63, 66

Ayón, Belkis, xxxix, 297, 299–305, 306n4–8, 306n14, 307

Bacardí Moreau, Emilio, 55n28, 56

Bandera, Quintín, 77, 178

baptisms and baptism certificate, 12, 25, 47, 68

Baquero, Gastón, 169n21, 171

Barbados, 213

Barcia Zequeira, María del Carmen, Barnet, Miguel, xxxv, xxxvii, xlin11, 33n1, 34n3–4, 36, 71, 137, 320n2, 320n5

Barquet, Jesus, and Norberto Codina, xxvin16, 216

Barradas, Efraín, 225

Barrios, Leyda Oquendo, 133

Bataille, Nereida, 311

Batista, Fulgencio, 173

Batista dictatorship, 175

Bazán, Emilia Pardo, 67

Beckles, Hilary, 16n1, 17

Beijing, 314, 316–18

Beijing International Congress of Women in Music, 285

Belkys, Rodríguez, 311

Bell, Eusebio, 43

bell hooks, 115, 124n5, 159n21, 162, 164–65, 168n7, 168n9, 172, 181, 185n2, 255, 261n37–38, 263

Bell, Clemente, 43

Bell, Eusegio, 43

Bell, Henry, 41

Bell Irady family, 41

Bell, Paulina, 43, 53

Bell, Pedro Alcántara, 43

Bell, Regla, 317

Bell, Victorina, 41–43, 46, 53

belly, the, 151, 156–57

Benin, 92, 103
Bennet, Jessica, 34n3, 185
Benson, Devyn Spence, xxvn2, xxvn4, xxvin15, xxx, xxi, 333
Béquer, Juan Guillermo, 271
Berliner Ensemble, 256
Bernard, Tinamarie, 185
Bernabeau, Casimiro, 62
Bernstein, Leonard, 284
Betancourt Estrada, Victor, 101, 103, 108n3, 108n5, 110n30, 119, 125n11, 149, 165, 321
Bhabha, Homi K., 208, 216
Biblioteca Provincial Elvira Cape (BPEC), 55n26, 56
black brotherhoods, 60, 250
blackface, xxi, 241, 251, 255
black men/males, xxx, xxxiv, 2, 8, 13, 34, 39, 43, 48, 115–16, 121–22, 141, 147–49, 154, 161, 178, 184, 214, 234, 244, 252, 255, 312, 314; aesthetic and sexual representations of, 115; allowed, under special circumstances, to purchase the "Title of Whiteness" or "Letter of Whiteness," 170n29; demonization of, 170n27; feminine depiction of, 115; masculinity of, 15; *negrito* (diminutive), xxxviii, 142, 195, 241–44, 251–53, 255, 260, 260n1, 260n3; stereotypes of, 115
Black Panthers, the, 214
black women/females, *passim*, but see especially: xiii, xvii, xvii–viii, xix–xxv, xxxiii–xl, 1–2, 7–9, 11, 14, 15–16, 19–20, 22–25, 33–35, 39–54, 61–70, 81–82, 85–87, 114–22, 127–35, 142–48, 151–58, 161–68, 176–79, 181–85, 189–94, 195–214, 229–34, 241–46, 253–59, 266, 269–71, 294, 303, 309–20, 328–30; Angolan, 235; aesthetic and sexual representations of, 115; as sensual and sexual, 129; body, 255; Eve, 303; girl(s), xxiv, 9, 12, 50, 51–52, 55, 65, 82, 86, 129, 130, 140,
162–63, 169–70, 177, 182, 209, 229, 231–32, 234–35, 255, 313, 319; *negra*, xxiv–xxv, 328–29, 341; *la Negrita* (little black woman), 136n6
Blanco, Pedro, 62
Bolivar Arostegü, 110
Bolivar, Natalia, 108n3
Bonafacio, José, 52
Bosmeniel, Félix Tanco, 7, 16n2, 71n13
Boulongne, Ives Pierre, 30n4, 321
Bourdieu, Pierre, 125
Borbón, Crespo (pseudonym Creto Gangá), 244
Borges, Nereyda, 311
Bosa, Mercedes, 41, 43, 53
bourgeoisie, the, 59, 132, 197, 219, 294; black, 40, 42, 44–45, 50, 52–53, 256
Boza, María Gregoria, 43
Brancato, Sabrina, 114, 124n3, 125
Brazil, xxii, xxxiv, 285, 316
Brecht, Bertold, 256
brides, 27, 29–32, 34n16, 36, 68, 208–9, 243
Brooklyn Philharmonic Symphony Orchestra, 284
Bueno, Salvador, 169n11
bufo theater, xxi, xxvi, 182, 185–86, 242–60

cabildos, xxxv, 60–61, 92–94, 209, 243–44, 250, 265
Cabrera, Lydia, 94, 108n4, 110n30, 196, 269, 302
Caldwell, Kia Lilly, xxii, xviin18–19
Campuzano, Luisa, 291, 295, 296n3
Cantero, Susana, 94
Carasés, Regla, 311
Carbonell, Jose Manuel, 215n16
Carbonell, Walterio, 55n28, 56, 159n11
Cárdenas, Herrera, xxx, 60
Cárdenas, María Josefa, 92, 338
Caribbean, the, *passim*, but see especially: xxii, 7, 15, 128, 133, 195, 197–99, 212–14, 219, 224, 228, 25, 254, 258, 298, 309,

311; Anglophone, 197, 214; Confederation of the Central American and Caribbean Athletics, 318; diaspora, 213; Festival of the Caribbean (aka Festival of Performing Arts of Caribbean Origin), 266–68;
Caribbean Philosophical Association, xiv
Carmona, María Vicente Carmona, 260
Carmona, Paula Oquendo de, 69
Carlos V, Emperor, 17n16
Carneiro, Sueli, xxxiv
carnivals, 134, 233–34, 250
Carpentier, Alejo, 178, 231, 272, 301–2, 306n8
Carneiro, Sueli, xxii, xxxiv, xln5, 125
Carvajal, María Teresa, 43
Castañeda Fuertes, Digna, xxxvi, 33n1, 335
Castillo Solórzano, Alonso de, 244
Castro Kustner, Rocio, 125n13
Castro Ruz, Fidel, xvii, 118, 143, 173, 200, 290, 295n2
Carthage, 242
Catholic Church, 46, 257
Catholicism, 46, 204, 250
Centro Islámico, 110
Cervantes, Miguel de, 210
Cervantes, Ignacio, 272
Céspedes, África, 63
Céspedes, Carlos Manuel de, 174
Changó, Oní, 93
Chavarria, Daniel, 133, 137
Chaveco Chaveco, Onelia, xxx, xxxviii
childcare, 124n7
China, 309. *See also* Beijing
Christianity, 303
Cisneros, Cardinal, 17n16
Cleofa, María, 63
Clytemnestra, 210–11
Cocotimba, 180n2
Coffigny, Alejandra, 311
Colombia, xxii, 304
colonialism, *passim*, but see especially: xxiv, 140–41, 201, 203

Confederación Centroamericana y del Caribe de Atletismo, 318, 321
Congreso Olímpico Internacional, 321
consciousness, 124, 129, 156, 162, 208, 291; black feminist, xxiii; collective, 201; critical, 155; female, 183; of gender and race, xxxvii, 165; historical, 147; national, 141; popular, 148; sexual, 299; sick, 273; social, 61, 77; unconsciousness, 128, 134; white, xxxviii
Consul General of England in Cuba, 13
Copland, Aaron, 284
Coraje, Madre, 256
Cordero, Tatiana, 331, 320n4
Corona, Lucía, 290
Coubertain, Baron Pierre de, 310, 321
criollo and *criollos,* xxiv, 8, 56n33, 61, 92, 108, 140, 169, 197, 255; black, 61; white, 132, 152
Criollo, Juan, 10, 47
Cuba, *passim*, but see especially: as misleadingly female, 200–2; as a *mestizo* nation, 196, 200, 232, 235; embargo of, xviii; growing *mestizaje* in, 144; historiography of, xxiii, 7, 19, 20, 24, 40, 60, 155, 258; negrophobic policies in the name of cultural assimilation, 196; past as "most racist of the Hispanic Caribbean," 195
Cuban Communist Party, 100, 173, 175–76, 201
Cuban National Film Institute, xxi
Cuban Revolution (Revolution for National Liberation in 1959), *passim*, but see especially: xxi, xxxviii, 86, 116–17, 119, 122, 143, 148, 174–79, 195–214, 223–24, 227, 289–95, 309, 312–25; racial "burden" and realities of, 175–76, 313

Dance Theater of Harlem, 284
Darío, Rubén, 210–11

daughters, xxxv, 10–12, 19, 26–27, 33–40, 42–4, 48, 52, 61, 82 105, 130, 133, 154, 179, 208, 293–95
Day of Kings (feast of), 60, 250
Davies, Catherine, 208, 216, 228, 236
death, 205, 210–11, 220, 224, 229–30, 265–67, 302
Diez Nieto, Alfredo, 284
Del Fuente, Alejandro, xiv, xxvn5, 19, 26, 34, 124n9
De Lahaye, Rosa Maria, and Ruben Zardoya Lauredo, 109n10, 110
Delisle, Charles, 42
Del Puerto, María, 331
Derrida, Jacques, 184, 185n5, 186
Depestre, Leonardo Catony, 144n1
Depestre, Yohamna, xxxviii, 338
Deschamps Chapeaux, Pedro, 16, 17n9, 36, 39, 54n13, 56, 70n1, 71, 257–59, 262n47
De Souza Hernandez, Adria, 110
De Varona, Esteban A., 274
Diapasó, Quinteto, 281
Díaz, Berta, 311, 314
Divina Caridad (Divine Charity), 68
divination, 103, 105–7, 108n9
divorce, 31–32, 36n23
Donrbarch, Maria, 110
Douglas, Susan J., 186
Dowd, Maureen, 186
Dryer, Richard, 169n13, 171
Duharte Jiménez, Rafael, 39, 45, 47, 55n14, 56
Dulce María Loynaz Cultural Center, xxiii

Eastman, Julio, 284
Ecuador, xxii
education, xxv, xxxv, 48–53, 64, 66–67, 69–70, 85–86, 117–20, 123, 292–3; higher, 89; Ministry of, 311; mis-, 13, 143; music, 270; physical, 314; primary, 259; racist, 166; religious, 94; societies and centers, 61, 85; universalization of, 123

Egües, Gladys, 290
Egypt, 309
Elbein Dos Santos, Juana, 110
Elementary School of Plastic Arts, 298
Elvina, E.T., 68
Encarnación Muñoz, José de la, 257
England, 16
Entine, Jon, 321
Escalante, Ana Cecilia, 331
Escribanía Gobierno, 34n5, 34n8
Espina, Rodrigo, and Pablo Rodriguez, 125n15, 136n8, 137
Estenoz, Evaristo, 175
Estrada, Victor Betancourt, 101, 108, 109n12, 110n23
Experimental Workshop of Graphics, 298

families, 17, 19–22, 25–33, 34n4, 35n16, 35n19–22, 54, 61, 66–68, 94, 117, 119–20, 122, 122, 133–37; dismembering/separation of, 9–11, 16; endoculturation, 196; higher-ranking, 249; mixed, 131; *Oshoshi* (patron of family unity), 107; religious, 100–3; slaver families who considered themselves revolutionaries, 134; sphere as a place of cumulative injuries, 326; stereotypes of black men in, 115; traditional, 292; white, 129, 270; whitening of, 168n10
Fanon, Frantz, xxiv, xxxi, 121, 125n13
fathers, 24, 29 31, 68, 103, 117, 295; abusive, 210, 229; absent, 103, 117, 207, 327–28; *Bàbálawo* (Babalawo, "father who possesses secrets"), 91–92, 94–95, 97, 101–5, 108n1, 109n21, 110n22, 110n30; *Babalochas* (roughly, "father of the saints [or defending deities or divine warriors]"), 91; drunken father, 240; father figure, 211; fatherland, 77, 82, 89, 234; founding fathers, 53; godfather, 52, 108n8; grandfathers,

52, 191, 205, 191, 205; despotic law
of the father, 202; mother as father,
325; proud, 313; selfish fathers,
81; spiritual, 63; stepfather, 244;
unemployed, 312
Federación de Mujeres Cubanas (FMC),
117
feminism, *passim*, but see especially:
xxvii, xxiv, xxxiv, xxxv, 128, 154,
181, 183, 211–12, 128, 212, 215n11,
255, 293; black, xiii, xvii–xviii, xx–
xxv, xxvii n21, xxxiii–xxxv, xxxix,
xln8, 128, 132–33, 137n11, 255;
cultural, 293; intersectional, xviii;
post-, 183; pseudo-, 81; socialist,
294; syncretic, 205; theoretical, 132;
white, 203
femininity, 102, 121, 137n9, 161–62,
168n8, 170n27, 270, 294, 304, 329
FEMPRESS, 321
Foucault, Michel 114, 124n2, 125
Facio, Alda, 109, 110, 236
Feraudy Espino, Heriberto, 30, 34n12,
36
Fernández, Ana Ibis, 317
Fernández, Berta, 311
Fernández, Don Fermin, 24
Fernández, Filhio, 108n7, 111
Fernández Retamar, Roberto, 312
Fondo Gobierno Superior Civil,
National Archive of Cuba (ANC),
17n13–14, 17n19–26, 18
Fonseca, Roberto, 281
Font, América, 63
Forbes, Irene, Ana Maria Luján, Fowler,
Victor, 321
France, 16, 47, 64, 212–13, 262n50, 284
Frank, César, 273
freedom, *passim*, but see especially:
v, 11, 21, 203, 205, 229, 232;
conditional, 150; emotional, 198;
degrees of, 183; hair, 146; love of,
233; precarious, 41; sexual, 255
Fuentes, Guerra Jesús, 37
Fuentes, Ileana, 137
Fuerte, Elsa Villa, 311

Galicians, 139, 241–42, 251, 254, 256
Garcia Agüero, Salvador, 262n43
García Albuquerque, Manuel, 62
García, Dona Loreto, 11
García, Guadalupe, xiv
García Lorca, Federico, 140, 210
García Lorca Hall of the Great Theater
of Havana, 273
García Rodriguez, Gloria, 37
Gates, Henry Louis, 195, 215n4, 216
gender, *passim*, but see especially: xviii,
xix, xxii, xxiii, xxiv, xxv, xxxiii–
xxxvii, 1, 23, 61, 91–102, 131, 144,
158, 174, 197, 201–8, 212, 275, 281,
291, 294, 309, 324; collective, 92;
-consciousness, 293; construction of,
114, 130; -based labor, 48; gendered
racism, 63; in the study of families
and sociability, 19; roles, 97; race-,
334; sex-, 165; subsumption of the
feminine in Spanish, 108n1
Geneva, 284
Germany, xv, 64, 262n50, 270, 272–73,
285
Gershwin, George and Ira, 284
Gertrudis, María Cruzata, 43
Ginsberg, Elaine K., 171n33, 171n36,
172
Giro, Radames, 274, 340
Gómez, Fermina, 93
Gómez García, Raúl, 337
Gómez, Loreto, 27
Gómez de la Serna, Ramón, 303,
306n13, 307
Gómez, Sara, xxi, xxviin5, xxxix, 158,
212, 289–95, 296n4, 340
González, Evarista, 21
González, Lucrecia, 63
González Mandri, Flora, 228, 235n2,
236
González, Natividad, 66
Goodman, Walter, 48, 51, 55n21, 56n32
Gordon, Jane Anna, xxxi
Gordon, Lewis R., xxxi
Grenada, 223, 224
Griffith, Glyne A., 216

grooms, 29–30, 32, 35n16
Guanche, Jesús, 36n24, 37, 196
güije, 233
Guillén, Nicolás, xxx, 141, 144, 159n15, 169n17, 197–200, 213, 215n10, 215n17–18, 216, 224n1, 231, 251
Guitar Festival Arias, 281

hair, xvii, xxii, xxxviii, 121, 129–30, 136n3, 145–58, 162, 167–68, 200, 207, 209, 214, 221, 249, 330; dreadlocks, 158; extensions, 183–5; nappy / "kinky," xxv, 136n5, 179, 180n2, 183, 271; "rebellious," 179; salons, 156; straight, xxiv, 161, 163–65, 169, 183, 185; straightening, 153, 156, 159n20, 162–63, 168, 169; woman untying her hair as a sexual rite, 161–2; white hair as "good," 136n4, 162, 165, 170n24;
Haiti, 174, 212, 256, 258
Haitian Revolution, 212
Haitians, 46
Haitian Revolution, 212, 256
Hamburg, 262n50, 270, 272–73, 285
Havana, xiii, xv–xxvii, xl, 8, 11–15, 20–28, 45, 60, 62–64, 68, 70, 75, 93, 140, 151, 185, 208, 246–49, 254, 290; The Great Theater of, 273; Philharmonic Orchestra of, 274; Soloist of, 276–77
Hazard, Samuel, 56n33
Hendrix, Barbara, 284
Hernández, Rafael, 170n21, 172, 253, 261n33
Herrera, Alejandrina, 311
Herrera, Georgina, xiii, xx, xxiv–vi, xxxviii, xln1, 195, 199, 203, 205, 207, 212, 215n26, 216n28
Herrera, Josefa "Pepa," 94
Herrera, Marina, 311
Herrera, Mercedes, 311
Herrera, Panchita, 93
Herrera Santi, Patricia, 331
heterosexuals, xxxv, 116, 147, 329

Hevia Lanier, Oilda, xxvi, xli, 33n1, 37, 70n2, 71, 335
Hierrezuelo, María Cristina, xxxvi, 37, 55n30, 56, 259, 262n45–6, 263, 335
hip-hop, xvii, xxxvii, xxxix, 132, 134, 154–55, 158–59, 323–24
Hispanic American literary tradition, 210
homophobia, 301
homosexuals, 116
Hopenhayn, Martín, 305, 306n17, 307
Hulme, Peter, and Edward Kamau Brathwaite, 216
Humames, Concepción, 68
Humoristic Seminar *Plante*, 144
hurricanes, 221–22

Ifá, 30, 92, 94, 96–97, 101–8
Independent Party of Color, 175
India, 309
Indo-Afro-Hispano-America, 128
Inés, Hilario, 10
Inquisition, the, 140
Instituto Cubano de Geodesia y Cartografía, 36–7
International Year of Women (1975), 199
Iphigenia, 211
Ishi-hum, 30
Italy, 64

jabá, xxiv, 163, 171
Jackson, Janet, 131
Jackson, Michael, 131
Jamaica, 213, 316
Jameson, Fredric, 197, 215n12, 216
jazz, 281
Jiménez, Lico, 260, 262n50, 272–74
Jiménez, José Manuel, 262
Juegos Deportivos Centroamericanos y del Caribe, 321

Kidane, Fekrou, 321
kidnapping freed blacks, 12–14

King Jr., Martin Luther, 214
Koch, Mayor Ed, 284

labor, 8, 13, 27, 39, 44, 48, 51, 53, 82, 115–18, 120, 124n7, 143, 196, 246, 260, 295; domestic, 202; feminized occupations, 117, 325; forced, 259; market, 293; masculinized occupations, 117
Lachatanere, Romulo, 111
Lady Macbeth, 210–11
La Bella Unión Habanera (the Beautiful Havana Union), 68
La Gaceta de Cuba, xi, 125
La Gaceta de la Habana, 14
Lagarde, Marcela, 111, 126, 324, 330, 331
Lagardere, Blanco de, 61
Lao-Montes, Augustín, xiv, xxii, xln4
Lamar, Aurora, 94
Landaluze, Victor Patricio de, 256
Lanza de Jesús, Afonso, 236
Laurence, Plassy, 12–15
Latin America, *passim*, but see especially: xvii, xx, xxiv, 137, 141, 153, 284, 298, 309, 314, 316, 326
Latin American Modernism, 211
Latin Americans, *passim*, but see especially: 197, 213–14, 318
Law of Civil Procedure, 26–27, 34n7
Law of the Press, 61
Leal, Rine, 247–48, 248, 260n3, 261n24, 263
Lescaille, Nidia, 236
León, Tania, xxxix, 283–85, 287
lesbians, 137
Long, Nia, 184
López-Gavilán, Maestro Guido, 227, 284
López Lemus, Virgilio, 228, 236
López, Magia, 156, 159n23
López, Narciso, 272
López, Ramona, 51
López, Yusimí Rodríguez, xxxviii, 338

Maceo, Antonio, 1, 178, 262n43
machismo, 91, 134, 293–94, 309
Madonna (the pop singer), 164
Magistrate of the Republic of General Machado, 77
Makenzi, Esperanza, 311
manumission, 10, 17n15, 20, 39, 43, 52, 54, 174, 190
Ma Monserrate González, 93
Mañach, Jorge, 261n31, 263
Mandiga people, 32
maroonage, 128
Marrero, Levi, 19, 34n2, 37
marriage, xxxvii, 10, 22, 24, 27, 41, 43, 47, 122, 142, 150, 158, 161, 259, 269; African marriage, 33; arranged, 29–33; brides, 34n16; children of, 36n23; civil, 68; ecclesiastical/religious, 68; interracial, 122 129; legal, 67; white sheet of blood, 35n16
Martí, José, xvii, 34n1, 27, 44, 51, 69, 76n1, 79, 137n11, 159n22, 178, 210, 221, 230, 262, 336
Martiatu Terry, Inés Maria, xiii, xvii, xviii, xix, xxi, xxii–iv, xxvin15–16, xxviin28, xin2, xln7, 137n11, 147, 158, 159n7, 159n10, 160, 185n3, 186, 261n29, 263, 339
Martínez Fuentes, Antonio, 125n14, 126
Martínez Furé, Rogelio, xlin13, 147, 159n5, 159n9, 160, 231
Martínez Heredia, Fernando, 126
Marxism, 119, 197, 201, 203, 207
Marx, Karl, 147
Masur, Kurt, 284
Mary (Jesus' mother), 204, 303
Mary Magdalena, 303
masculinity, xxxiv, 115, 124n4, 211, 294, 304, 329
Medina, Catalina (aka K. Lanita and Catana), 63
Meizhu, Lui, 186
Mendiola, Maestra María Elena, 275
Menéndez, Jesús, 178

Index

Mercedes (aka Ogún Toya and Mercedes la Balogún), 94
Mercedes, María, xxviin20
Mercedes Hernández Herrera, Coralia de las, xxxviii
Mesopotamia, 309
mestizos, xxvin16, xxxviii, 60–64, 66, 68–9, 116, 134, 136, 136n8, 144, 178, 252, 257, 266; as black outside stereotypes, 134–35; as *Blanquinegra*, 196, 215n8; as part of bourgeois programs of national reconstruction, 197; concern for education, 66; devaluing black women's hair, 154, 157; impact of abolition on in the public spheres, 60; in bourgeois programs of Latin American national reconstruction, 197; *mestizaje*, xxiv, xxxviii, 39, 140, 197, 254; mobilization and economic power of, 60; nationalism, 197; on prostitution, 129; whitening project, 130–32
Mestre, Jesús, 111
Mexico, 208, 284, 316
Miami Light Project, 285
Miguel Álvarez, Ana De, xxvin13, 296
Mitchell, Arthur, 284
Modestin, Yvette, xx
Moncado, Dominga, 1
Montejo Arrechea, Carmen, 274
Montero, Susana, 3n2, 237
Moore, Carlos, 196
Moore, Carlos, Tanya R. Saunders, and Shawn Moore, 216
Morales, Calixta, 94
Morales de Gualaba, Concepción, 69
Morales Dominguez, Esteban, 119, 124n10, 126
Morales Fundadora, Sandra, 215n6
Morejón, Nancy, xxxviii, 137, 158, 195, 199–200, 203, 207, 212, 215–16, 219, 221–25, 228, 235n2, 236–37
Moreno Fraginals, Manuel, 147, 159n6, 160, 225n5

morena, xxiv, xxv, 21, 27, 240
Morena Vega, Marta, xx, xxvi
Morrissey, Marietta, 16n1, 17
Moscovici, Serge, 126
Moshenberg, Dan, 186
Mother Melhcora, 258–59
mothers, xxi, xxv, xxxv, 1, 10–13, 19, 24, 32, 34–35, 41–43, 52–54, 61, 67, 82, 86, 92, 95, 100–3, 105, 139, 143, 191–93, 202, 230–31, 271, 298, 312, 325, 327–28, 330; absent, 103, 207; as nature, 135, 228; Eve, 177; faithful, 131; godmothers, 52, 92, 100, 10, 108, 309; grandmothers, xxi, 52, 95, 108n8, 309, 130, 159, 162–65, 170–71, 230, 234–35; 244, 254, 327; great-grandmothers, 95, 229; *Iyalochas* (roughly, "mother of the saints [or defender deities]"), 91, 95, 99, 100, 102, 109; motherhood, 35, 230, 292–93, 295, 324–25, 328, 330; mother-in-laws, 35, 293; mother-wives, 292; negligent, 129; of beginnings and unity, 204; selfless, 183; single, 41, 67, 108, 120, 192, 234, 240; submissive, 207; working, 124; *Yémojá* (Yemaya), 107
mulatas, xvii–xix, xxiii, xxiv–xxv, xxx–xxxi, xxxiv, xxxviii, 1, 19–20, 48, 52, 139–44, 161–71, 197, 203, 207, 210, 213–14, 244, 251–262, 270; access to education, 50; as "beautiful" or aesthetic and sexual preference, 56n33, 63–64, 140–44, 170, 199, 234, 241–42, 255, 326; as concubines of white men, 20, 133; as lustful, 147, 255, 326; as property-owning women, 40; as protagonists of abolitionist novels, 254; as representation of national cohesion and image, 201, 251; as specifically the offspring of white men and black women, 64; as tragic character, 254; black *mulata*, 255; "Cecilia syndrome," 254–5; *Cecilia Valdés*

o La Loma del Angel (the novel and character of plays), 162–63, 171n31; *clara* ("clear"), xxv; in bufo theater, 182, 251, 255–60; instead of "mulatta," xxxi; *La Mulata* (Diego Velasquez's painting), 139–40; *la mulatica* (little *mulata*), 136n6, 162, 229; *mulatísima* (*mulata* who presumes herself "superior"), 136n7; passing, xxxviii, 19, 25, 70, 94, 131, 161, 163, 165–67, 169–71, 179, 242, 284, 318; pejorative origin of the term, 64. *See also* the novel *Cecilia Valdés.*
mulatez, 144, 199
mulatos, xix, xxvi, xxxix, 8, 139–40, 147, 166, 169n16, 178–79, 195, 197–8, 200, 208, 233, 235, 241; actors, 250, 252–57; affluent, 269–70; as a softening of the word "black," 139; connotations of, 214; creation/definition of, 254; in Seville, 243–44; mockery of, 258, 260
Müller, Alexandra, 296n4

Ña Belén González, 93
Ña Inés Flores, 94
Ña Margarita Armenteros, 93
Ña Matilde Zayas, 93
Ña Rosalía, 93
National Archive of Cuba (ANC), 17, 34n5
National Symphony Orchestra of China, 285
nature, 77, 95, 106–7, 113, 228, 287; as mother, 135; biological, 98, 103; love, 235
Nedeau, Jen, 186
negritude, xviii, xxxiii–iv, 115, 141, 203
The Netherlands, 298
Nevis, 12–15
New Spain, 140
New World Symphony Orchestra, 284–85
Nigeria, 92, 102–3, 207, 284

Nobel Prize for Literature, 284
Norman, Jessye, 284
North Africa, 242
Núñez, Antonia, 50–51

odu, the, 96
Oña, Arabella, xxxvii, 89
O. Pala, Achola and Madina Ly, 35, 37
Orishas, 91, 93–4, 98, 103–9, 111, 131, 180, 196, 203, 209, 231, 235
Orozco, Keyla, 284
Ortíz, Fernando, 16n3–4, 16n6, 17n8, 17n10, 17n15, 17n16, 17n17, 113, 124n1, 126
Oviedo, Arabia, 93

Padrón, Julia, 311
Padrón, Marcos, 10
Pataki, 180n1
Palacios, Antonia, 41, 43–44
Pan-Americanism, 153
parda, xxiv, 12, 40, 50, 52, 166, 257, 259
pasa, xxiv–xxvi, 121, 124, 136, 145–46, 158, 164, 179, 182, 281
passing, xxxviii, 19, 25, 70, 94, 161, 163, 165–67, 169–72, 179, 242
Pastrana, Luis, 27
patriarchy, 114, 117, 181, 185, 211, 294, 302
Pedroso Torres, Francis, 237
Perez Alvarez, Maria Magdalena, 126
Pérez, Ileana, 284
Pérez Sarduy, Pedro, and Jean Stubbs, 214, 216
Perrera Díaz, Aisnara, and María de los Àngeles Meriño, 37
phallogocentrism and phallocentrisms, 184, 301
Philharmonic of New York, 284
Piepmeier, Alison, 186
Piñera, Juan, 284
Pino, Cristy del, 311
Pirón, Hipólito, 47

Plaza de la Revolución Calixto García, 278
Polledo, Luisa, 311
Portugal Filho, Fernández, 111
Portuondo, María Feliciana, 51
poverty, *passim*, but see especially: 49, 81, 82, 134, 136–37, 182
Pozo, María Agustina del, 43, 53, 83n1
Pozo Gato, Catalina, xxxvii, 83n1
Pozo Ruiz, Alfonso, 260n5, 263
prostitution, 327
Provincial Center of Plastic Arts and Design of Havana, 298
psychology, 239, 137
Puerto Rico, 13–14, 34, 49–50, 298
Puig, Amelia, 311
Pushkin, Alejandro, 69

Queen of the Cabildo, 94
Queen of England, 14–15
Queen Nzinga/Yinga, 204–5
Queen Oyá of Koso, 213
Queen of the dead, 230
Quintana, Candita, 255
Quintero, Hector, 256

race, *passim*, but see especially: xix, xxxvi–ix, 1, 19, 25–26, 123, 144, 177–8, 203, 303, 334; antagonisms of, 166; as also a system of ideas, values, and social representations, 119; as intrinsically insignificant geographical/physical differences among people, 169n13; biraciality, 161–67, 168n1, 169n16, 254; concepts of, 113–20, 197; configures a social hierarchy, 122, 129; constructivity of, 167, 214; Cuban expressions of, xxiv, 252–53; "cosmic," 197; deconstruction of, 132; embedded in the field of interpersonal relations and economic institutions, 122; fallaciousness of, 167; has been predominantly anti-black, 121; lived experience of, xxv, 178; pertaining to nation, 180; race-sex-gender, 130, 132–33, 334; "real," 171n31; so-called sexual superpotency of black race, 142; struggle, 253; survival of in Cuban society, 176, 196, 313. *See also mestizaje; mulata; mulato;* racism
racism, xi, xviii, xix, xxiii, xxv, xxvii, xxxiv, xxxvii, xxxix, 78n1, 116, 129, 132, 139–40, 159n18, 167, 179, 184; gendered, 3; presumption of blacks and *mestizos* as imitators of whites, 257; predominantly anti-black in Cuba, 121; versus prejudice, 130; within the Liberation Army, 174;
Ramos, Arthur, 111
Ramos, María Nicolasa, 51
Ramos, Pastora, 63
Randale, Ian, 237
rape, 201, 254, 326
Rebello, Manuel Coello, 244
Reig Romero, Carlos, 320, 321
Reyita, sencillamente: Testimonio de una negra cubana nonagenarium, xx, 33n1, 166, 168n10
Reyes, Alfonso, 232
Rincón, Carlos, 306n36, 307
Roberts, Neil, xiii
Roberts, Sam, 186
Robaina, Tomás Fernández, xi, 76n1, 78n1
Robeson, Paul, 284
Rocasolano, Alberto, 216
Rock, Chris, 183, 186
Rodríguez, Isidra, 311
Rodríguez, Rosa, 93
Rolando, Gloria, 212
Roldán, Amadeo, 278
Romero, Anselmo Suárez, 7, 16n2, 17n8, 254, 320n9, 321
Royal Decree and Full Instruction of the Indies on the Education, Treatment and Occupation of the Slaves, 17n17

Rubiera Castillo, Daisy, xvii, xxvi, xxvii, xxxvii, 2, 33, 37, 111, 168n10, 337
Rueda, Lope de, 244
Ruiz-Labrit, Victoria, 137n11
Ruiz Narváez, Irene Esther, xiii, xxxix, 137, 143, 260, 321, 341
Russian Revolution, 221

Saco, José Antonio, 251
sacrifices, 94, 102–3, 105, 107–8, 182, 211, 303; chicken and other birds, 35, 108n8, 109n19
Sagarra, Antonia, 43
Saint Francis of Assisi, 271
Saint Norbert, 107
Saint Saëns, 272
saints, 94, 99, 106, 107, 191, 204–5, 240, 250
Saíz, Ramón, 8
Saldaña, Excilia, 195, 199, 207–8, 211–12, 216, 227–8, 230–37
San Alejandro School and the Superior Institute of Art, 298
Sánchez, Martha, 317
Sánchez, Oscar, 307, 316, 321n15, 322
Sánchez, Osvaldo, 299, 305, 307
Sander, Gilman, 198, 215n15, 216
Santiago (city of) de Cuba, xv, xvii, xx, 39–42, 44–51, 53, 54n13, 60, 92, 94, 107, 111, 136n8, 250, 268, 318–19
Santos Souza, Nuesa, 137n12
Saunders, Tanya, xiv
Seville, 243–47, 250
sex, 1–2, 7–8, 25, 35n22, 49, 53, 63, 97, 130, 162, 164; -gender, 165; market, 327; roles, xxxiv, 96, 118; stereotypes, 2; tourism, xix; without love, 328
sexiness, 183
sexism, xix, 91, 99, 109n17, 115, 118, 123, 140, 159n18, 191, 293, 309
sexual exploitation, 166, 203, 207
sexuality, xxxiv, 116, 122, 140–42, 198, 202, 210, 255, 324, 326, 329
sexual orientation, xviii–ix, 174

sexual pleasure, 327
sexual politics, 165, 200
sexual preference, 146, 268
sexual preparation, 29
sexual promiscuity, xxxiii, 116, 147
sexual reproduction, 7–8
sexual rights, 31
sexual-romantic conquest, 164
Sievert, Heather Rosario, 225n3
Santeria or Regla de Ocha, xvii, xxxvii, 91, 93, 95, 100–1, 108n3, 133, 207, 209, 213, 250, 268
Santísima Trinidad, 47
Simpson, Mark, 124n4
slaves, enslavement, and slavery, *passim*, but see especially: xxiv, xxxiv–xxxvi, 7–28, 32, 34n2, 39, 41–46, 52–54, 62–68, 89, 92, 96, 140, 148, 151–53, 166, 167, 169n11, 192, 249–50, 253; abolition of, xxxiv, 53, 60, 71n18; barracks, 157, 253–54; distorted the sexual life of the enslaved, 147; domestic, 42, 95, 255, 258–59; drivers, 62, 242; families, 11, 16, 27–28, 137n11; former, xvii, 41–44, 52, 64, 66, 259; hunters, 152; idealization, 205; in the Liberation Army, 174; of silence, 73; part of patrimony of colonizers, 148; punishments, violence against, and abuses of, 8, 32, 147, 205, 234, 256; purchase and sale of, 40, 192, 259; regulation of, 10, 17n17, 95; revolts, 53, 60, 128, 190, 192, 201, 205, 248, 258; runaway, xx, 17n18, 258; slavers, 42, 45, 54, 134, 153, 256; traders and trafficking, xxv, 27, 33, 65, 71n30, 130, 133, 152, 198, 204, 243; treated as a type of livestock, 43–44, 147–48; women, 7–16, 16, 92, 95, 128, 147–48. See *also* abolition
Smith, Lois M., and Alfred Padula, 196, 196, 215n5, 217, 271
Sociedades Bíblicas Unidas, 111
sons, 36n23, 67, 293–94

Sosa, Enrique, 261n34, 263, 302, 306n10, 307
Soto, Jorge, 7
Sotolongo, Tibursia, 93
South Africa, 203
South Bronx, 323
Soviet Union, xviii
Soyinka, Wole, 284
Spain, 34n7, 59, 62, 65, 148, 234, 242, 247, 249–50, 254, 258
Spanish Bank of Havana, 21
Spanish government's Conspiracy of the Ladder, 256
spirituality, xxxix, 105, 213
Stolcke, Verena, Oscar Loyola Vega, 37
Storini, María Ángela, 63–64, 66
Suárez y Romero, Anselmo, 7, 16n2, 17, 310

Talib Hakim, Rasul, 284
Tamburnini Claudio M., 322
Tanco Armero, Nicolàs, 71n13
Tanco Bosmeniel, Félix, 17
Taylor, Paul C., 168n7
Tchaikovsky, Ilyich, 279
Toledo Benedit, Josefina, 34, 37
Tomás, Guillermo M., 272–73, 274n2
Tomás of the Apa nation, 42
Torralba, Verónica, 311
Torres-Cuevas, Eduardo, and Oscar Traywick, Catherine A., 262n41, 263
Towa, Maria, 94
Transatlantic Slave Trade, xxiv, 7, 16, 26, 116
Tratado de Ifá, 92
Trigueña, xxiv, 47, 185
Trinidad, 62, 94, 269–73

United Nations Declaration of Human Rights, 285
United States (USA), xviii–xv, xln8, 64, 69, 155, 166, 203, 212–14, 223, 257, 283–84, 311, 323, 334; Athletic Union of, 310; average wealth of black and white women in, 183; fear of Cuba becoming another black Republic, 174; minstrels of, 247; the "one drop rule" in, 171n29; University of Havana, 310–11

Valdés, Alejandro, 281
Valdés Cantero, Alicia, 262n49, 263, 274n1
Valdés, Carmen, 311, 318
Valdés Garriz, Yrminio, 108, 111, 162
Valdés, Pereda, 199
Valero, Don Jose, 24
Valverde, Úrsula Coimbra de, 63
Vega, Aurelio de la, 284
Vega, Maria de Cadova y de la, 244
Velásquez, Diego, 139–40
Verger, Pierre, 111
Valladolid, Juan de, 243
Vidal, Consuelito, 289
Villaverde, Cirilo, 7, 16n2, 17, 140, 162, 165, 167, 254
violence, xxxiii, xxxix, 128–89, 147, 148, 174, 182, 202, 205, 221, 253, 324–26, 330; domestic, 210, 326
Vitier, Cintio, 217, 228, 235n2
Vives, Carlos, 304
voice, xiv, xx, xxvi, xxxix, 30, 63, 73–74, 75, 79–80, 147, 153, 155, 159, 169n10, 171n38, 191, 193–94, 198, 200, 204, 229, 242, 253, 270, 286–87, 289, 293, 302–3; active, 147; female, xx; feminine, 202–5; "feminine racial," 212; historical, xxxiv; masculine, 330; of Africa in Europe, 208; of Cuba to Oregon, Florida, Washington, Boston, Atlanta, New Orleans, and New York, 213; pedagogical, 329; poetic, 222
voodu/voodoo, 46

Wagner, Richard, 279
Walker, Alice, 200, 202–3, 215n11
Walker, Madam C.J., 199n17
warriors, 108n8, 204, 213
wars, 66, 89, 143, 174–75, 178, 199, 204, 224, 232, 242, 248, 251, 259,

270, 272; historical erasure of black veterans, 174–75; Spanish-Cuban (U.S. intervention 1898 intervention in), 174; Ten Years' War (1868–1878), 64

Werner, Karl, 271

West, Cornel, 186

white master, 202

white men, *passim*, but see especially: xxxv, 8, 24, 63–64, 147, 154, 161, 254–57, 163, 166–67; as desirable, 133–34, 141–44, 165–68, 169n10, 169n20; exploring sexual fantasies with women of African descent, xix; "washing the womb," 169n20

white supremacy, 153, 165, 168n6, 170n28, 257

white women, xxxiv, 2, 44, 47–50, 115, 117, 121, 130, 144, 146, 170n22, 183, 190–91, 316; feminists, xln8, 203

Wiegler, Helene, 256

womanism, 197, 200, 203

Wood, Yolanda, 306n9, 307

Woolf, Virginia, 181, 185n1, 186

X, Malcolm, 181, 214

Yargelis Savigne, 318

Yemiló, Ofún, 103, 111

Yoruba, xvii, 29, 30, 31–36, 92, 96–97, 100–2, 106, 108, 110–11, 135, 180n1, 205, 209, 266, 286

Zalamea, Jorge, 217

Zaldívar, Edelvis López, xxxix, 340

Zayas, Etelvina (pseudonym E.T. Elvina), 68

Zinn, Howard, 174

About the Editor and Translator

Dr. Devyn Spence Benson is an associate professor of Africana and Latin American Studies and the chair of the Department of Africana Studies at Davidson College. Benson received her PhD from the University of North Carolina–Chapel Hill in the field of Latin American history, where her research focused on racial politics during the first three years of the Cuban revolution. She has taught at the University of North Carolina–Chapel Hill, Williams College, Louisiana State University, and now Davidson College. She is the author of published articles and reviews in the *Hispanic American Historical Review, Journal of Transnational American Studies, Cuban Studies, World Policy Journal,* and *PALARA: Publication of the Afro-Latin / American Research Association.* Benson's work has been supported by the Doris G. Quinn, Foreign Language and Area Studies, and Gaius Charles Bolin dissertation fellowships. Benson was recently awarded a National Endowment for the Humanities faculty fellowship for a new project, *Black Consciousness in Cuba: The Untold Revolution (1968–1978).* She has also held residencies at the Schomburg Center for Research in Black Culture in Harlem and the WEB DuBois Institute for African and African American Research at the Hutchins Center at Harvard University. Benson's first book, *Antiracism in Cuba: The Unfinished Revolution* (University of North Carolina Press, 2016), was based on over eighteen months of field research in Cuba, where she has traveled annually since 2003. In her spare time, Benson likes to read, play tennis, and cheer on her UNC Tarheels! Follow her on Twitter @bensondevyn.

Dr. Karina Alma (formerly Oliva Alvarado) was born in El Salvador and grew up in the LA regions of Westlake and Pico Union. She earned a BA in English and a PhD in ethnic studies at UC Berkeley with a focus on US

Central American literature. She was a UC President's Postdoctoral Fellow in the English Department at the University of California Los Angeles and is an assistant professor in the Chicana/o Studies Department at UCLA. She critiques systems of race-class-gender that intersect un/documented people and migrations in context to neoliberalism and settler neocolonialism, in particular as anti–Central American. Her interdisciplinary work continues to examine intercultural and transcultural texts, memories, and identities, especially in Latina/o/x communities, that include internal practices of domination and racial-gender hierarchies. Her classes on US Central Americans focus on cultural memory, cultural production, race-gender constructs, and narratives in both Central America and its US diasporas. She is currently completing a manuscript on antiblackness in El Salvador and how antiblack racism is replicated and challenged by Salvadoran communities in the United States. She coedited the anthology *U.S. Central Americans: Reconstructing Memories, Struggles and Communities of Resistance* (Arizona University Press, Spring 2017). Some of her publications include "Cultural Memory and Making by U.S. Central Americans," *Latino Studies* 15, no. 4 (Winter 2017), and "A Gynealogy of Cigua Resistance: La Ciguanaba, Prudencia Ayala and Leticia Hernández-Linares in Conversation," in *U.S. Central Americans: Reconstructing Memories, Struggles and Communities of Resistance* by Alvarado et al.

About the Authors

Digna Castañeda Fuertes (Pinar del Río, 1936). PhD in historical sciences, senior professor of Caribbean history and senior advisor for graduate studies in history, University of Havana, Cuba. Executive member of the Cuban section of the Association of Historians of Latin America and the Caribbean, her publications include *Between Race and Empire: African-Americans and Cubans Before the Cuban Revolution* (Temple University Press, 1998).

Oilda Hevia Lanier (Havana, 1970). Historian. Bachelor's degree in history with a master's degree in historical sciences. Researcher and professor of the Casa de Altos Estudios Don Fernando Ortiz at the University of Havana. She has published *El Directorio Central de las Sociedades de la Raza de Color* [Central Directory of Societies of People of Color], among other publications.

María Cristina Hierrezuelo (Mella, Santiago de Cuba, 1946). Historian. Bachelor's degree in history, senior professor of history at the University of Oriente. She is president of the Honorary Chair Doctor Francisco Prat Puig and member of la Union Nacional de Historiadores de Cuba [National Union of Cuban Historians, UNIHC]. She has published *Las olvidadas hijas de Eva* [Eve's Forgotten Daughters].

María del Carmen Barcia Zequeira (Havana, 1939). Historian. PhD in historical sciences and professor at the University of Havana. Academic with Honors from the Cuban Academy of Sciences, recipient of the National Prize in History and the National Prize in Historical Sciences. She has published, among others, *Capas populares y modernidad en Cuba* (1878–1930) [The Working Classes and Modernity in Cuba], *La otra familia* [The Other

Family], and *Los ilustres apellidos: negros en la Cuba colonial* [Illustrious Last Names: Blacks in Colonial Cuba].

Úrsula Coimbra de Valverde (Cienfuegos, birthdate unknown [1800s]). Professor of English, French, and piano. One of the editors of the journal *Minerva* (1888). Defending women's rights for black women and *mestizas* characterizes her journalism. She was also a collaborator in the newspaper *El Nuevo Criollo* [The New Criollo].

Carmen Piedra (Birthplace unknown, birthdate unknown [1800s]). Her journalism is a combative but little publicized example of the presence of women in the Partido Independiente de Color (Independent Party of Color).

Consuelo Serra (Havana, 1884). Professor and journalist. Daughter of the patriot, journalist, and activist for racial equality Rafael Serra Montalvo, who was the friend and collaborator of José Martí. When she returned from exile in the United States, she founded a private school and taught as an English professor at the Escuela Normal de Maestros de La Habana [Havana Normal School for Teachers]. She collaborated with several presses of the time and published *Para mis alumnas de la escuela Normal de Maestras* [For My Students of the Normal School for Teachers].

Inocencía Silveira (Birthplace unknown, birthdate unknown [1800s]). Teacher. She collaborated in newspaper articles about the limited opportunities for education and betterment for the black masses. Her works in the column Ideales de una Raza [The Ideals of a Race] are an example of her work.

Gerardo del Valle (Maracaibo, Venezuela, 1898). Journalist. He worked with several presses writing on racial themes, for example in the *Diario de la Marina* [The Marina Daily] in the section Ideales de una Raza [The Ideals of a Race].

Catalina Pozo Gato (Birthplace unknown, birthdate unknown [late 1800s/ early 1900s]). Journalist. She collaborated with newspapers of the time on the defense of black women. She wrote "La negra cubana y la cultura" [The Cuban Black Woman and Culture] in response to the article "La negra cubana" written by Gerardo del Valle. She actively participated in politics and ran for different positions in traditional bourgeois political parties.

Arabella Oña Gómez (birthplace unknown, birthdate unknown [early 1900s]). She always used journalism to defend the rights of the black population. Her work appeared in diverse publications, especially in *Adelante* [Move Forward], a journal of the left.

Daisy Rubiera Castillo (Santiago de Cuba, 1939). Bachelor's degree in history. Her research deals with topics on Afro-Cubans, gender, race, and religion. Among her most important publications is *Reyita, sencillamente* [Simply Reyita], finalist for the prize of Casa de Las Américas in 1997. Her work includes *Golpeando la memoria* [Striking Memory], *Desafío al silencio* [Defying Silence], and *Aires de la memoria* [Airs of Memory]. She has received among others, [the plaque] La Placa José María Heredia, la Medalla [medal] Raúl Gómez García, and la Distinción [distinction] Madre Melchora in 2010.

Yulexis Almeida Junco (Havana, 1977). Professor and researcher. Bachelor's degree in sociology and a master's degree in gender studies. She is an assistant professor in the Department of Sociology at the University of Havana, senior professor of research methodology, and a member of women's studies. She was awarded América Latina y el Caribe del Programa de Becas CLASCO-ASDI, a fellowship for researchers from Latin America and the Caribbean. She has published, among others, "Genero y racialidad: Un studio de representaciones sociales" [Gender and Race: A Study of Social Representations] in *Memorias del VII Taller Internacional "Mujeres en el siglo XXI"* [Memories of the Seventh International Workshop "Women in the Twenty-First Century"] held in Cuba in 2009.

María Ileana Faguaga Iglesias (Havana, 1963). Historian and anthropologist. Bachelor's degree in history. She holds a master's degree in sociocultural anthropology and postgraduate studies in social ethnology and anthropology. She has participated in various national and international events and has published works such as "Qué es el macroecumenismo en Cuba? Diálogo intercultural y diálogo interreligioso" [What Is Macro-Ecumenism in Cuba? Intercultural Dialogue and Interreligious Dialogue].

Onelia Chaveco Chaveco (Cienfuegos, 1961). Journalist and writer with a degree in journalism. Director of Corresponsalía de la Agencia Informativa Nacional [AIN, Correspondent of the National Information Agency] in Cienfuegos. She is the author of the book *Tania la guerillera: clandestina en Cienfuegos* [Tania the Guerillera: Clandestine Woman in Cienfuegos].

Carmen González Chacón (Havana, 1963). Poet, journalist, and promoter. She directs the project Alzar la voz (Raise the Voice) for female rappers, which received the Premio Memoria [Memory Prize] for merit from the Center Pablo de la Torriente Brau. She is a specialist at the International Poetry Festival Office and has published a book of poems *Una muchacha es siempre privilegio* [A Young Woman Is Always a Privilege].

Sandra del Valle Casals (Havana, 1983). Researcher with a degree in journalism from the University of Havana. She holds a master's degree in African studies from the University of Mexico. She works on questions of cultural politics, film, gender, and race. "Pasar por blanca" [Passing for White] was published in the compilation *Desafíos feministas en América Latina: la perspectiva de las jóvenes* [Feminist Defiance in Latin America: Young Women's Perspectives].

Yusimí Rodríguez López (Havana, 1976). Author and translator with a bachelor's degree in education specializing in English. She is a graduate of Onelio Jorge Cardoso Center. Her journalism includes digital media. Her work appears in anthologies dealing with topics on race.

Yohamna Depestre Corcho (Havana, 1970). Author and journalist. She was a member of Taller de Narrativa Onelio Jorge Cardoso, narrative workshop. She founded the group Grupo Omni Zona Franca and has performed and recorded with them. She received the award Premio Pinos Nuevos for her book of stories *D-21*. She is a journalist with *Cubaliteraria*.

Yesenia Selier Crespo (Havana, 1975). Actor, dancer, and researcher on the African diaspora. She holds a bachelor's degree in psychology from the University of Havana and a master's degree in Latin American Studies from New York University. She received the fellowship CLASCO for researchers in the social sciences. Among other works, she has published "Music: Since 1959: Why Has Cuban Hip Hop Received So Much Foreign Attention?"

Georgina Herrera Cárdenas (Jovellanos, Matanzas, 1936). Poet and director. In the 1960s, she worked with writers and poets in the independent press Ediciones El Puente [Bridge Editions]. She was awarded the National Culture Distinction and the medal Medalla Alejo Carpentier. Her most recent book of poems is *Gatos y Liebres* [Cats and Hares].

Aymée Rivera Pérez (Pinar del Río, 1958). Professor and researcher. Bachelor's degree in education. Master's degree in didactics in Spanish and literature. She is a literature professor at the university Rafael María de Mendive y Hermanos Saíz de Pinar del Río. She is working on her doctoral degree at the University de Alcalá de Henares; her thesis is titled *Mujer personaje e identidad: Catarsis narrativa de las Negras escritoras del Caribe hispánico* [Female Character and Identity: Catharsis Narratives of Black Women Writers from the Hispanic Caribbean].

Lourdes Martínez Echazábal (Havana, 1952). Professor and researcher. She obtained her doctorate in studies in literatures and cultures of the Caribbean and Latin America in the twentieth century. She teaches at the University of California, Santa Cruz. Among other publications is "Descolonizando el mito del negro" [Decolonizing the Myths on Black People] about *Adire y el tiempo roto* [Adire and Torn Time] by Manuel Granados.

Coralia de las Mercedes Hernández Herrera (Havana, 1953). Bachelor's degree in Spanish literature. She teaches at the Instituto Técnico Militar José Martí in Havana. She holds a master's degree in Latin American and Caribbean literature and has published in national and international journals. She received the Distinción Rafael María de Mendive on Cuban Education. She has won national prizes for her essays and stories and internationally in the genre of testimony.

Leandro Estupiñán Zaldívar (Holguín, 1977). Journalist and author. He holds a bachelor's degree in journalism from the University of Havana. He was awarded the prize for journalism Cultural Rubén Martínez Villena. His book *El invitado* [The Guest] received the prize from the city of Holguín, Premio de la Ciudad de Holguín, in narrative. He works at the center for books and literature, Centro del Libro y la Literatura de Holguín.

Inés María Martiatu Terry (Havana, 1942). Cultural critic, essayist, and author. Bachelor's degree in history with advanced studies in music, ethnology, and theater. She has presented in conferences in Venezuela, the United States, and Columbia. She is an advisor of Estudios Africanistas Angeliers León at the Instituto Superior del Arte. She is also a member of Consejo de Expertos del Consejo Nacional de Artes Escenicas del Ministerio de Cultura [Council of Experts of the National Council of Performing Arts of the Ministry of Culture]. She received the prize on theatrical critique, Premio de Crítica Teatral, from the journal *Tablas* on female-themed stories, organized by the University of Mexico and Casa de las Américas. She was also awarded the fellowships Razón de Ser [Reason for Being] from the Fundación Alejo Carpentier, and Creación Literaria [Creative Literature] from the writers' association, Asociación de Escritors, from UNEAC. She received the distinction for her contribution to the national culture, Distinción por la Cultura Nacional and made Professor Emeritus of UNEAC. Her work has been published in special editions and anthologies in more than ten countries. She has published fourteen books, among them *Bufo y Nación: Interpelaciones desde el presente (ensayos)* [Bufo and Nation: Interpellating Questions from the Present (Essays)], *Over the Waves and Other Stories*, and *Re-Pasar El Puente*, a theater anthology published about Ediciones El Puente.

Fátima de la Caridad Patterson (Santiago de Cuba, 1951). Actor, playwright, and director. She directs the group Grupo Macubá. She was awarded the Distinción por la Cultura Nacional [Distinction for National Culture] granted by the Ministry of Culture and State Council and also the prize Premio Iberoamericano de Mujeres Creadoras [COMUNARTE Iberian-American Prize for Women Creators].

Isabel González Sauto (Santa Clara, 1949). Philologist, publisher, and researcher. She is executive secretary at the academy of language, Academia Cubana de la Lengua. She edited *Diccionario Enciclopédico de la Música en Cuba* [Encyclopedic Dictionary of Cuban Music] published by Radamés Giro.

Edelvis López Zaldívar (Havana, 1964). Journalist. Holds a bachelor's degree in journalism. She is director of programming and editor at CMBF Radio Musical Nacional. She received the medal Medalla Félix Elmuza from the Unión de Periodistas de Cuba [Journalist Union of Cuba], and Medella Aniversario 50 [Medal Fiftieth Anniversary] from the Orquesta Sinfónica Nacional de Cuba [Cuban National Symphonic Orchestra].

María Elena Mendiola (Havana, 1944). Orchestra leader, professor, music producer, promoter, and critic. She has produced, among others, the series Master Cuban Classical Works. She is senior director of the chamber orchestra Solistas de La Habana [Havana Soloists].

Sandra Álvarez Ramírez (Havana, 1973). Investigative journalist and blogger. She holds a bachelor's degree in psychology from the University of Havana and a master's degree in gender studies, with her thesis *De cierta manera feminista de filmar, sobre obra de Sara Gómez* [A Certain Feminist Way of Filming, On the Work of Sara Gómez]. She publishes in digital mediums and in her blog. She is a web editor and journalist in Cubaliteraria y Webmaster at the Centro Nacional de Educación Sexual, CENSEX [National Sex Education Center].

Lázara Menéndez Vásquez (Havana, 1946). Art historian and professor. She holds a bachelor's degree in art history and a doctorate in arts and sciences. She is senior professor of arts and letters at the University of Havana. She has published, among others, *Estudios afrocubanos: Selección de*

Lecturas [Afro-Cuban Studies: Selected Writings] and *Rodar el coco: Procesos de cambio en la santería* [Encircling the Coconut: Processes of Change in Santería].

Irene Esther Ruiz Narváez (Havana, 1944). Communication specialist focusing on gender. Bachelor's degree in political science. She received a certificate in Gender and Communication from the Cátedra de la Mujer [Women's Studies Program] at the University of Havana. She published *Mujer negra y deporte: Una nueva mirada en el 50 Aniversario del INDER* [Black Women and Sports: A New Look on the Fiftieth Anniversary of INDER].

Yanelys Abreu Babi (Havana, 1983). Researcher and professor. Bachelor's degree in Hispanic philology and a master's in Hispanic Studies. She works as a researcher at the Literary and Linguistic Institute, Instituto de Literatura y Lingüística José Antonio Portuondo Valdor, and as an adjunct professor at the University of Havana. Among other works, she has published "Pa'rriba los pelos. Sobre el discurso racial en el rap Cubano" [Goosebumps: On the Discourse of Race in Cuban Rap].

Anette Jiménez Marata (Holguín, 1983). Researcher and professor. Bachelor's degree in philology and a master's degree in social development. She works as a researcher at the Juan Marinello Cuban Institute for Cultural Research, Instituto Cubano de Investigación Cultural Juan Marinello, and as an adjunct professor at the University of Havana. She has published "Qué leen los niños hoy? Notas para una cartografía del consumo de literatura en la infancia cubana" [What Do Children Read Today? Notes for a Cartography of Literature Consumption in Cuban Infancy], among other publications.